Don't Shoot That Boy!

Abraham Lincoln and Military Justice

Thomas P. Lowry, M.D.

Savas Publishing Company

Don't Shoot That Boy! Abraham Lincoln and Military Justice
by Thomas P. Lowry

Copyright © 1999
Thomas P. Lowry

Includes bibliographic references and index

Printing Number
10 9 8 7 6 5 4 3 2 1
(First Hardcover Edition)

ISBN 1-882810-38-4

99-071105

Savas Publishing Company ⚙
202 First Street SE, Suite 103A
Mason City, IA 50401

(515) 421-7135 (editorial offices)
(800) 732-3669 (distribution)

This book is printed on 50-lb. acid-free paper. It meets or exceeds the guidelines for permanence and durability of the Committee on Production Guidelines for Book Longevity of the Council on Library Resources

For Beverly

Friend, Partner, Sweetheart

President Abraham Lincoln

TABLE OF CONTENTS

Foreword   i

Introduction   v

Chapter 1: What We Know About Lincoln   1

Chapter 2: The Court-Martial Path   9

Chapter 3: Generals, Colonels, Majors & Captains   23

Chapter 4: Lieutenants, Chaplains & Surgeons   55

Chapter 5: Desertion: 1861-1862   85

Chapter 6: Desertion, January - March, 1863   95

Chapter 7: Desertion, April 1863 - April 1865   115

Chapter 8: Mutiny & Violence to Officers   143

Chapter 9: Murderers   169

Chapter 10: Confederate Recruiters, Spies & Soldiers   183

Chapter 11: Missouri Spies & Bushwhackers   203

Chapter 12: A Potpourri of Military Commissions   213

Chapter 13: Thieves and Robbers   225

Chapter 14: More Sleeping Sentinels   235

Chapter 15: Rapists and Miscellaneous Miscreants   245

Chapter 16: The Statistics of Compassion   257

Chapter 17: Lincoln at the Millennium   265

continued. . .

Table of Contents (continued)

Notes   279

Bibliography   295

Index   297

Photos & illustrations

Private William Scott   vii

Judge Advocate General Joseph Holt   8

Holt Signature   13

John G. Nicolay, John M. Hay, and Abraham Lincoln   15

Nicolay Handwriting   16

Hay Handwriting   17

Brigadier General James G. Spears   24

Brigadier General Michael Corcoran   25

Brigadier General Joseph W. Revere   26

Colonel Frederick G. D'Utassy   27

Lieutenant Colonel Frederick F. Cavada   31

Major Andrew Washburn   33

Captain Charles H. Roys   34

Captain John Wilbur   42

Captain John H. Behan   44

Captain Edward G. Hoffman   59

George W. New, M.D.   81

continued. . .

Photos & illustrations (continued)

Court-Martial Sketch   171

Major General John A. Schofield   187

April 14, 1865—Lincoln's Final Pardons,   217, 218

Tables

Table One   52

Table Two   83

Table Three   94

Table Four   113

Table Five   142

Table Six   167

Table Seven   181

Table Eight   202

Table Nine   202

Table Ten   211

Table Eleven   224

Table Twelve   234

Table Thirteen   244

Table Fourteen   255

Table Fifteen   256

Table Sixteen   259

Table Seventeen   260

Graphs

Graph One: Union Army Court-Martials For Desertion   84

Graph Two: 1863 Desertions   114

Foreword

Historians who prefer history written from "the bottom up" might profitably emulate Dr. Thomas Lowry, who for many years has waded through previously unexamined court-martial records in the National Archives. In bundles of documents lie the forgotten stories of Civil War misfits, soldiers who ran afoul of military justice and paid dearly for their transgressions, sometimes with their lives.

President Abraham Lincoln's mercy is legendary. Beneath the soaring language of his Second Inaugural Address, "With malice toward none, with charity for all," lay his celebrated compassion. Yet the army depended upon discipline. If legend has substance in this case, and Lincoln actually pardoned all offenders, then how could the Union army survive the whims and derelictions of its enlisted men? Lowry has discovered that Lincoln reviewed individual cases in a judicious manner, tempering the wrath of irate officers with wisdom acquired as a prairie lawyer.

During his presidential years, Lincoln established rare rapport with the men who fought the war, not by routinely forgiving offenses but by judging each case on its merits. Lowry demolishes a celebrated legend of Lincoln's pardon of a sleeping sentry, embellished with heroics and personal concern, yet demonstrates that Lincoln did care about the ordinary soldier caught in painful circumstances.

During the Civil War, at least 80,000 cases were tried before courts-martial, meaning that perhaps one of each twenty-five soldiers was charged with serious offenses. Not all such cases reached Lincoln, who reviewed only those appealed or involving the death penalty. Within those limitations, an enormous number reached the White House, where Lincoln spent agonized hours reviewing the cases and dealing with advocates of the accused. On one day in July 1863, two weeks after Robert E. Lee retreated from Gettysburg, Lincoln spent six hours reviewing cases; on another day, in April 1864, he reviewed seventy-two cases.

In that avalanche of cases, not a single officer was condemned to death. Instead, the offenders were enlisted men, or so the standard phrase ran. By other standards, including those of Lincoln, many of the condemned were boys, teenagers caught in a circumstantial web few understood before committing serious offenses. Judge Advocate General Joseph Holt normally briefed cases before Lincoln reviewed them. While stricter in his interpretations of law, Holt also showed a degree of compassionate good sense. Simply concurring in Holt's recommendations enhanced Lincoln's reputation for leniency. Yet Lincoln would go beyond those recommendations in his search for forgiveness and mercy. "I don't believe it will make a man any better to shoot him," Lincoln observed, "while if we keep him alive, we may at least get some work out of him." Lincoln defined "work" as continued service in the Union army. Lincoln practiced this policy especially in cases of desertion and cowardice, bringing back into the ranks youngsters who had learned such painful and terrifying lessons that they could be relied upon for faithful service during the war—or until killed in battle.

For many officers a court-martial verdict of guilty requiring dismissal from the army served as adequate punishment. Such officers, forever disgraced, had little hope of resuming their civilian roles. Punishments for officers appeared to be more lenient that those for enlisted men partly because officers were more likely to have political connections that brought prominent men to the White House as their advocates. Lincoln more easily found loopholes for the drunken and cowardly than for the disloyal. He approved the sentence of dismissal of a brigadier general from Kentucky who had railed against emancipation. "I say God damn the government, let her go to hell." Believing that it was "the policy of the government to prolong the war to free the slaves," the general had threatened to change sides. Another officer, who had characterized Lincoln as "a loafer and a traitor" earned Lincoln's approval of a sentence of dismissal that gave that miscreant his own opportunity to become notorious as loafer and traitor. One of the few common soldiers shot for desertion stated that he had taken "an oath that as soon as the war was for the abolition of slavery, I would take no further part." Lincoln's uniform policy was to avoid executing deserters, but he made an exception of those who joined the enemy. He proved an understanding and forgiving judge of human frailty but not of disloyalty. Although Lincoln appeared to be tougher on officers than on enlisted men, this was a matter of slight degree.

Common soldiers who deserted in wartime were liable to the death penalty. During the Civil War, total Union army desertions exceeded 250,000. Not all reported desertions involved criminality. Some soldiers responded to bad news from home by rushing there without considering or understanding the consequences. Others drifted away from service when they found camp life between battles burdensome, boring, and unprofitable. Each desertion seemed to have its own story, and there were far too many cases for Lincoln to deal with each adequately. In March 1863, following a great winter of discontent and discouragement, Lincoln issued a proclamation providing amnesty to any deserter who returned to the ranks within three weeks. In February 1864, Lincoln ordered a uniform policy of imprisonment for all deserters sentenced to death, something that spared him the necessity of examining each case in a timely fashion to spare some poor soldier from execution before a presidential decision reached camp.

Lowry gives us insight into Lincoln by providing an analysis of the cases he judged so carefully and conscientiously. At the same time he illuminates the character of Civil War soldiers by showing them in moments of weakness, drunkenness, and misbehavior ranging from trivial to detestable. Often that great conflict is remembered in terms of battles and leaders, of heroism and sacrifice. That perception is not without its truth. Yet in the cases that Lowry has so carefully studied are hundreds of human stories that bring us closer to the reality of the experience of boys who became men under stress. Here, indeed, is social history rich in material for understanding human beings who fought—or refused to fight—for the preservation of the nation.

John Y. Simon
Southern Illinois University Carbondale

Introduction

"They shall not shoot this boy!" More than the oft-heard words, "Four-score and seven years ago," more than the ringing phrases— "With malice toward none, with charity for all"— of the Second Inaugural Address, those six words of reprieve, of mercy, of the chance for redemption, define Abraham Lincoln as the President of Compassion. And of all the stories of all the men saved from the firing squad or the hangman's noose, none is more gripping than that of a young Vermont private, William Scott.

He was a farm boy, a member of Company K, Third Vermont Infantry, for only a few weeks, when he and two comrades were posted as sentinels on the evening of August 31, 1861, near the strategic Chain Bridge, which connected Virginia and Washington D.C. They were to share the night duty, with at least one awake at all times. At 3:00 in the morning, it was Scott who was to be the vigilant one, but the Officer of the Guard found him curled up, sound asleep. A court-martial three days later sentenced him "to be shot to death." (The entire phrase was necessary; inaccurate marksmanship sometimes only wounded the condemned man, who crawled about, clawing at his wounds, and had to be shot repeatedly until he was, in actual fact, truly dead.)[1]

The sentence was approved by Major General George B. McClellan, and execution date was set for six days hence. Scott's sister, who was living in Indiana, heard the dreadful news and, in spite of the hazards and delays of public transportation in 1861, arrived in Washington D.C. the afternoon before the scheduled execution. She made her first plea for mercy to General McClellan, but he refused her. She then rushed on to the White House, where she gained admittance and pleaded with the President, who listened in grave silence. The hour was growing late, the clock creeping toward Private Scott's appointment with death. At last, Lincoln scratched a few words on a small piece of paper: "Will Gen. Spinner please see and hear this young lady. A. Lincoln."[2]

Just as the President finished his note, General Spinner himself entered the room. The note was discarded as unnecessary (but carefully preserved by John S. White, a well-known educator and confidant of one of Lincoln's secretaries) and Lincoln spoke directly to General Spinner, who agreed to the pardon and departed to stop the wheels of deadly justice.

The press of affairs drove the Scott case from Lincoln's mind until late that night. Suddenly recalling the young girl's plea and fearful that his instructions might not have been followed, tormented with the vision of the first rays of dawn glinting on a dozen rifle barrels, the President called for his carriage and urged the driver onward. "It's a matter of life and death!" The horses responded to the whip and as they drew up to the guard tent where Scott lay in chains, their flanks were foamed in sweat.

The President ducked his great height under the entrance of the tent. Lincoln stood up and laid his long hands on the young man's shoulders. Their eyes met; Lincoln's were heavy with fatigue and the growing burden of the war; Scott's were alight with terror and hope. "My boy, you are not to be shot. I am going to trust you and send you back to your regiment. But my bill for this service is a heavy one and only William Scott can pay it. If from this day William Scott does his duty so well that if I was there when he came to die, William Scott can look into my face and say that he has kept his promise, and that he has done his duty as a soldier, then I will consider my bill as paid, and paid in full." Scott was so overcome that he was unable to speak, but his eyes spoke for him. The chains were struck away, he returned to his comrades and the next morning told them, "I wanted to tell him how hard I would try, but no words came and it had to go all unsaid. May God forgive me if I ever forget my promise or his kind words to me."

Eight months passed and at Lee's Mill on the Peninsula, east of Richmond, the Third Vermont dashed itself against the Rebel earthworks and was beaten back in bloody repulse. Scott, who had been foremost in the charge, was wounded in a dozen places, but still could speak. His comrades dragged him back to the Surgeon's station and gathered about to hear his failing words.

Barely able to whisper, he gasped, "You know what you can tell them at home, that I tried to do the right thing." His head fell back and he was

The "Sleeping Sentinel," Private William Scott of the 3rd Vermont Infantry. The poem about him suggests a barely pubescent youth; his photograph, complete with whiskers, suggests otherwise. From *Abraham Lincoln, the Merciful President*, by Allen C. Clark.

silent. Then a light suffused his face and he spoke again. "If any of you ever have the chance, I wish you would tell President Lincoln that I have never forgotten his kind words to me, that I have tried to be a good soldier and true to the Flag. I would have paid my full debt to him had I lived. I think of his kind face and thank him again." Scott crossed his hands upon his breast; a faint smile crossed his face. "Good-bye, boys, good-bye." And then he was gone.[3]

The newspapers took up the story of the sleeping sentinel, redeemed by his own blood. Francis de Haes Janvier, who had set "The Stars and Stripes" to music, and had sung at Lincoln's first Inaugural, wrote a long narrative poem, telling the whole story. A few months later, James Edward Murdoch, a teacher of elocution, declaimed Janvier's "Sleeping Sentinel" in the Chamber of the Senate, with the President, the Vice President, the First Lady and "the beauty and fashion of Washington" in attendance. From there, Murdoch set off on a two-month tour of the major halls of the north and "few listened to the end with dry eyes." The following year, the entire poem emerged as a book and it was a rare Union family who did not know of William Scott and his compassionate president.

As the decades passed, and Lincoln's memory became increasingly sanctified, the Sleeping Sentinel story grew *pari passu*. By the end of the century, the legend included Lincoln's pardon in the dead boy's pocket; by 1910, the pardon was wrapped around a carte de visite of the President, and the fatal bullet which pierced both pardon and image stained them with Scott's life blood.

There rests the story of the sleeping sentinel, revived every generation after, as a tale of perfect point and counterpoint in the balance between human failing and human redemption. It is a good story, but could it be too good to be true?

The sleeping sentinel perfectly illustrates the perils in trying to learn the real story of Civil War presidential pardon and reprieve. The actual handwritten records of these events, still preserved in the National Archives, have been carefully examined by the author. There really was a Private William Scott who slept at the Chain Bridge. Upon hearing his death sentence, most of the regimental officers addressed a petition to Brigadier General William F. ("Baldy") Smith, asking for mercy, and also sent a committee across the river to Washington, D.C., where they met with a fellow Vermonter, L.E. Crittenden, Register of the Treasury, who walked the group to the White House, a block away, where Lincoln agreed to delay the execution.[4]

Meanwhile, General Smith had read and endorsed the petition, which was carried to McClellan. While he was considering the request for mercy, Lincoln paid him a visit and expressed his wish that McClellan commute the sentence of death, if he could see fit to do so.

The next morning, the shooting was suspended and the men of the Third Vermont, instead of witnessing an execution, were presented with an instructive lecture, in which General Order Number Eight, issued by McClellan, was read. This document told them of the President's wish for mercy, the General's decision to grant it and the warning that future offenders should remember that sleeping on sentry duty was a crime "to which all nations affix the penalty of death."

What about the frantic sister from Indiana, and the note to "General Spinner?" No such sister has ever been identified, and there was no General Spinner on active duty during the Civil War. Francis E. Spinner was Treasurer of the United States in 1861, and had been a general in the New York militia, but he had no military jurisdiction over Scott and there is no record of Spinner having any hand in Scott's life or death. Further, this Spinner note, which actually does exist, was dated thirteen days after the scheduled execution. John S. White, the man who allegedly rescued the discarded note from a White House wastebasket, was a 16-year-old schoolboy in Boston in 1861.

Lincoln's wild nighttime carriage ride and the foam-flecked horses seemed to be equally the product of journalistic imagination and poetic license. The final chapter of the story, Scott's dying words, are also fiction. Scott's military records all agree that he died of "gunshot wound to the chest," an injury that makes breathing, much less long speeches, unlikely. Further, the regimental surgeon noted that Scott was unconscious when brought to the hospital tent.

It can be argued that all this quibbling is mere nit picking, that the story and its uplifting moral serve a higher purpose, that the poetry of the tale of William Scott transcends mere fact, and illuminates the greater issues of life, death, and the meaning of human affairs. There is merit to such an interpretation of Civil War stories and events, merit in the concept that they are instructional tales, like the morality plays of the Middle Ages, a human bridge across the chasm of doubt and melancholy, in brief, a path to a higher truth. That may be true, but it is not history.

Scott's escape from a firing squad and his subsequent death in battle are sufficient unto themselves, and entitle him to his claim upon our history and our nation's memory and gratitude, far more than any poet's soaring imagination.

In a further turn of the wheel of fate, Scott may find his real place in history by serving to illuminate the conflict and interplay between myth and reality, and be one more reason that he did not die in vain.

Lincoln's reprieves and pardons of condemned men are reality, not just legend, and from them many lessons can be learned, and to the extent that the "real" Lincoln can ever be fathomed, can tell us much of that remarkable and complex man.As if to further such understanding, a previously untapped resource, a collection of over 500 Lincoln decisions on courts-martial, decisions not previously described or catalogued, has come to light and forms the basis of this narrative.

But first it is necessary to examine the scope of what is already known about Lincoln, to describe how that information was found and organized, and to justify how anything about Abraham Lincoln could possibly be "new."

Acknowledgments

Once again, it is a pleasure to acknowledge the irreplaceable part of Beverly Lowry in my life and in this research. Not only does she read and interpret the old records faster than I can, but her speed, skill, and accuracy with the computer are things of wonder. These virtues, coupled with years of deep companionship, make words of thanks inadequate.

A Civil War book which has not had the input of the National Archives' legendary Michael P. Musick is open to grave doubt. This book would not exist if it were not for his guidance and his unsurpassed grasp of the hidden treasures in our nation's written memory. We also owe a debt of gratitude to other archives professionals: DeAnne Blanton, Michael Meier, Cindy Fox, and Stuart Butler.

Encouragement is a great motivator in any work involving so many hours of sifting tons of rock, in order to find a speck of gold. For their suggestions, enthusiasm, and encouraging words, I want to thank Paul Verduin, Scott Sandage, Thomas F. Schwartz, Michael Burlingame, Robert E. Denney, and Steven L. Carson.

As always, any errors, omissions, or ill-founded opinions are the sole responsibility of the author.

1

What We Know About Lincoln

In October 1863, Private Bernard McCloy of the 140th New York Regiment of Infantry got drunk, and in that condition he cursed and kicked his lieutenant. The next day, McCloy was penitent and apologetic, but it was too late: a court-martial sentenced him to wear a "twenty-five pound piece of iron" attached to his left leg for the rest of his enlistment and to forfeit part of his $13-a-month salary.[1] Mrs. McCloy wrote to Lincoln that she and her six children were starving, asked for mercy, and closed her letter saying, "I would beg to touch the hem of your garment as did one of old."

In 1863, the common people believed that good, personal good, could flow from the White House. Though this belief is much diminished today, in Lincoln's time an almost-mythic aura surrounded the man and his office, an aura which could inspire the foundering Mrs. McCloy to invoke the Biblical picture of a kneeling supplicant, reaching out for the slightest touch that might heal and restore. The faith of the common people was such that even the hint of access to Lincoln could lead to acts of desperation. For example, Lieutenant Edward King, of the 66th New York Infantry was sentenced to death for desertion. His wife, who kept a small grocery in New York City, was in the crowd which gathered on the White House porch. A man calling himself "Captain Parker" introduced himself, heard her story, and guaranteed a pardon—for $300. She handed over her life savings, and the "Captain" was seen no more.[2]

We know much about Lincoln, not because we must (like a student laboring over a required paper on the tax policies of Millard Fillmore) but because we want to, because we care. Fortunately, the impulse to know is met with a voluminous record and some remarkable handwriting, so crucial before the era of the typewriter.

Lincoln's hand is firm and bold. Unlike the thin vertical scratchings of Joseph Hooker, or the maniacal slashing scrawl of John C. Fremont, the "A. Lincoln" seen on so many thousands of documents is regular and consistent, readable today even by a generation weaned on word processors. Lincoln used good ink. That may seem a trivial point, but in many Civil War records, especially Confederate documents, the ink has badly faded. Not so the Lincoln records. The dark ink is still dark; the wide lines are still wide. The "A." of "A. Lincoln" is still clearly tied to the "L" by a consistent unifying loop, and the terminal six lower case letters are always slightly elevated. Always.

These strong and consistent characteristics are a boon to researchers but, sadly, over the past 150 years have inspired a hoard of souvenir hunters to vandalize documents, leaving gaping holes where the Emancipator's pen once touched the paper. Fortunately for those who treasure our nation's inheritance, current security measures at most archives have resulted in prison terms for many of these thieving despoilers.

Almost as soon as the assassin's shot ended Lincoln's life, there began a movement to collect, preserve and catalogue his writings. Some repositories hold great numbers, such as the National Archives, the Library of Congress, and Brown University. Some collections have only a single signature, proudly displayed by the owning institution. Other Lincoln documents are still in the hands of dealers and collectors, most of whom prefer anonymity. Such a vast number of documents, covering a long and productive life, and scattered at hundreds of sites, has called forth a variety of publications intended to reproduce and to index these documents in a way which will make them accessible to the public.

The first major venture in this endeavor was the 12-volume *Complete Works of Abraham Lincoln*, published over the period 1894-1905 and edited by Lincoln's two private secretaries, John G. Nicolay and John M. Hay.[3] This effort was followed in 1917 by Gilbert Tracy's *Uncollected Letters of Abraham Lincoln* and, ten years later, with *Lincoln Letters at Brown University*.[4] In 1930, Paul M. Angle, famous for his denunciation of Lincoln forgeries, produced *New Letters and Papers of Lincoln*, in which he published not only longer papers, but also "scraps" considered unworthy by other compilers.[5] Angle also remarked on how many documents showed Lincoln doing something to help someone. A publication in a somewhat different vein is the *The Abraham Lincoln Encyclopedia*, produced by Mark E. Neely, Jr., a very useful reference work clarifying issues and personalities which were widely known in Lincoln's time, but not in ours.[6]

Today, the definitive catalogue/index, edited by Roy P. Basler and two colleagues, is *The Collected Works of Abraham Lincoln*, whose ten volumes include an index and two supplements.[7] Basler attempted to include all the previous compilations, as well as documents discovered up to the time of his publication in the 1950s. But even here in this monumental work Basler seemed to have reached the limits of time, energy, and funding. He specifically excluded, for example, "routine pardon and clemency endorsements," which appear mostly in Record Group 153 at the National Archives, a complete collection of the approximately 80,000 general court-martials conducted by the Union Army.

Until 1994, there had been no systematic attempt to catalog and index the Civil War Union court-martials. The present author and his wife, Beverly Lowry, are creating such an index, which forms a computerized database capable of being searched by dozens of subjects in various combinations. In the course of reading these tens of thousands of cases, we have discovered these "unknown" Lincoln notations.

In the first 37,000 of these court-martials, 760 contain a notation in the hand of Abraham Lincoln. Of these, 543 do not appear in any of the three indices in the Basler catalogue. Some of these Lincoln writings are very brief, and some are a full paragraph, but certainly none are extended essays. These are the hurried notations of a very busy man. There are no legal briefs, no drafts of the Gettysburg Address, no philosophical musings; but every one of the signatures and comments changed someone's life.

Carl Sandburg tells of the night when the news came that General William H. L. Wallace had been killed at Shiloh. Two women relatives of General Lew Wallace, knowing only that a "General Wallace" was dead, called at the White House for information. When they learned which man was dead, they cheerily proclaimed, "Well, it wasn't our Wallace." Lincoln quietly rebuked them: "It was somebody's Wallace, wasn't it?"[8]

The cases that form this book are all "somebody's Wallace." Obscure or famous, private or colonel, wealthy contractor or hard-scrabble bushwhacker, a stroke of the President's pen made all the difference. For an officer, the alternatives might be disgrace so deep he could never go home, or a chance to redeem his name. For the common soldier, it might mean a return to his regiment, or years in the tropical sun at Dry Tortugas, or the Minie balls of a firing squad exploding his heart, tearing off his face, catapulting him into oblivion. For the convicted Confederate spy, the possibilities range from total freedom, to the sudden collapse of the gallows floor, the last moment of free-fall, and the terrible snap of the neck vertebrae as the rope goes taut.

True, from a compiler's view, faced with monumental stacks of longer Lincoln documents, cases of pardons and clemencies would indeed be "routine," but to the living, breathing, terrified men and women who awaited Lincoln's decision, they were the entire world, and that notation, however brief, was life or death.

Although the 543 previously unpublished notations, presented in this book, will tell us something of his beliefs and policies, they can only be a fleeting comet in the vast universe of Lincoln scholarship. There have been hundreds of books about Abraham Lincoln; some are limited in scope, such as those on his views on American Indians, on monetary policy, on religion. There have been studies and speculations at great length about his childhood, his love life, and his marriage. Psychohistorians have plumbed his psyche (a perilous task when the subject is as subtle and guarded as this one), and literally dozens of books have analyzed his role in Civil War military affairs.

Studies of Lincoln languished for a generation, as the nation was distracted by the twin calamities of the Great Depression and the Second World War, but in the mid 1940s, a vast archive, kept sealed for years by the terms of Robert Todd Lincoln's will, was opened at the Library of Congress. Out of this treasure trove came a fresh burst of primary source knowledge, organized into two volumes by David C. Mearns, and ushering in a new wave of studies based on untapped sources.[9]

Two historians have made particular use of the resources of the National Archives, that vast repository of original papers, sited six blocks west of the Library of Congress. Robert V. Bruce, in 1989, published a penetrating analysis of Lincoln's involvement in the technology of weaponry.[10] In 1991, Mark E. Neely published his study of presidential suspension of civil liberties and the resulting states of martial law.[11] By 1992, it appeared that the well had run dry, that no further original work would be forthcoming. Like many such predictions, it was premature.

In the early 1990s, following in the footsteps of Mearns, Harold Holzer read over 30,000 pages of letters received by Lincoln, and *Dear Mr. Lincoln* appeared, a useful addition to our knowledge of that era.[12] In 1994, Michael Burlingame published *The Inner World of Abraham Lincoln*, a compassionate and insightful study of Lincoln's anger, depression, hatred of slavery, and marital disappointments, based upon previously-neglected interview records and newspaper sources.[13] The following year, David H. Donald's prize-winning and widely acclaimed *Abraham Lincoln* appeared, and is currently the best-known one-volume study of the Great Emancipator.[14]

While finishing his *Inner World* book, Burlingame had one of those ideas which cause other writers to slap their foreheads and exclaim, "Why didn't I think of that?" Most authors collect more material than they use. Nicolay and Hay had published an enormous biography of their departed employer, but their work was done under the scrutiny of Robert Todd Lincoln, the President's surviving son, who was known to suppress any information possibly unfavorable to his father's memory. A little sleuthing on Burlingame's part turned up thirty-nine interviews of people who had known Lincoln, interviews conducted by Nicolay himself between 1875 and 1877. The result was the ground-breaking *An Oral History of Abraham Lincoln: John G. Nicolay's Interviews and Essays*, which appeared in 1996.[15] These interviews contained information that Lincoln's son almost certainly would have censored: the real reason why Lincoln broke his engagement to Mary Todd, new insights on his religious beliefs, and the quality of his legal knowledge. We learn of Lincoln's tears when he heard that Meade had not pursued Lee after

Gettysburg. Of particular relevance to the study of court-martials are the interviews with Joseph Holt, Lincoln's judge advocate general.

The cases which form the backbone of this book were filed away with only a name index. There has never been a survey of the court-martials before, largely because of the cost and labor of creating a useful subject index from nearly a million pages of hand-written material, some of it faded and stained. Although the entire project (under the auspices of the Index Project, Inc.) will not be completed until mid-1999, enough new trends and clusters have emerged to create the possibilities of useful quantitative historical research, based upon very large samples.[16]

But no elaborate statistical analysis is needed to grasp the depth and width of the passion and pathos that swept our nation in those years. In these records, we see the plaint of families, the clash of ethnic groups, the executions of Indians based upon a single paragraph of hearsay, the greed of contractors, the narrow obsessions of place and precedence among the officers. These records create a new view of the Boys in Blue, wracked with malarial chills, hurrying off the road as another round of cramps signals a fresh attack of diarrhea, reprimanded for straggling when their shoes had fallen to pieces. We see soldiers and officers assaulting one another. We see the smoking iron brought from the fire, the skin sizzling on the shoulder, on the face, or on the buttocks, as the red-hot branding iron descends: "D" for deserter, "T" for thief, "W" for worthless. We see a vast cavalcade of intemperance, passion, exhaustion, and desperation.

For the serious offenses, we see them reach their final destination, the President's desk. Harry Truman loved the motto "The Buck Stops Here," but Lincoln did not welcome this honor. But neither did he shrink from it. Since the army had almost two million men and employed tens of thousands of civilian workers, there was no way that any one man could attend to all the legal problems that such a mass will generate. Understanding the process by which the wheels continued to turn in the great engine of justice, requires a review of the court-martial process itself, of the Articles of War, of the governing authorities, of the upward channel of referral, of the role of the Judge Advocate General in analysis and recommendation, the travail of the White House secretaries, and the work of Lincoln himself.

Only then will the context and constraints under which Lincoln labored become visible, and it will be possible to begin to comprehend the tidal wave of military justice records which awaited "the pleasure of the President."

This picture of Judge Advocate General Joseph Holt was taken during the trial of the Lincoln murder conspirators. The grim bitterness on Holt's face reflects his admiration for the martyred President, and the lost hopes for an early North-South reconciliation.
Library of Congress

2

The Court-Martial Path

Armies, like all societies, need discipline. War is harsh; war is about killing. Thus, military justice has a different flavor from its civilian counterpart. However, the military version is not wild justice; on the contrary, it is based on clearly delineated rules.

This study attempts to answer the question: was Lincoln's legendary compassion, his willingness to forgive and pardon convicted offenders, real, or merely another myth? To answer this, it is necessary to study how court-martials were held, how their decisions proceeded up the path to review and appeal, and what happened to them at Lincoln's office in the Executive Mansion.

There were different disciplinary paths for officers and for enlisted men. The latter, for minor offenses, could be tried by the more informal tribunal of regimental or garrison court-martials, roughly the equivalent of civilian traffic courts and municipal courts. A smaller number of officers was needed to convene such a court-martial and the sentences were limited to modest fines and mild corporal punishment. The offenses tried in these courts were such things as losing part of a uniform, poor discipline at parade, or an untidy living area. (The so-called "drumhead" court-martials are difficult to study, as they may have been be held during active combat and records of such events are almost non-existent.)

Serious offenses, such as murder, desertion, striking an officer, robbery, arson, rape, and the all-purpose "conduct prejudicial to good order and military discipline," were tried by general court-martial, the highest military tribunal.

For commissioned officers, the lower level trials did not exist. An officer received a general court-martial or no court-martial at all. The most dreaded charge was "conduct unbecoming an officer and a gentleman." Conviction of this offense led automatically to dismissal (or to being "cashiered," which was almost identical).

Article 65 of the 1861 Articles of War specifies that any general officer commanding an army may appoint a general court-martial. As the war expanded the rules changed, but a commander of a department would commonly possess such power. This commander (usually through his adjutant) would then assign or "detail" certain officers for this duty. Article 64 specified that thirteen officers were the correct number for a court-martial board, while eight men was the absolute minimum. The trial records of court-martials with less than thirteen men contain the formulaic phrase, "the most that can be assembled without manifest injury to the Service."[1]

Officers who did not appear for this duty were required to account for themselves. The most common excuse was a note from the regimental surgeon that the officer was confined to his quarters with severe diarrhea. Many court-martials contain a note that the officer was unavailable because he had been recently killed in combat.

Article 75 prohibited an officer, whenever possible, from being tried by men of lesser rank. In a celebrated trial, such as that of Major General Fitz John Porter or Surgeon General William Hammond, a dozen generals and colonels might be occupied for months, enough even to impair the war effort, but the legal rights of the accused were protected.

The vast majority of Civil War general court-martials were not of famous commanders but of now-obscure officers and men; the rules were the same, whether the trial was held in an office building, a tent, an abandoned barn, or even under a tree. The accused was brought into court and the judge advocate read to him the order establishing the proceedings. The prisoner was then shown the members of the court and asked if he objected to any of them. Objections, though not common, were usually based on personal animosity between the accused and a court member, and were usually sustained. After any objection had been

considered and settled, the judge advocate, in the presence of the accused, swore in the members of the court. Then the presiding member of
the court swore in the judge advocate, and the charges were read. At this
point the accused was asked if he wished counsel, and his response was
recorded. If his requested counsel was not present, the court usually
adjourned the case until he could arrive.

The prisoner was asked to enter a plea. If he pled "guilty," the court
would confirm his plea and proceed to sentencing. If he pled "not
guilty," the trial began. If he remained mute, a plea of "not guilty" would
be entered by the court. When all the required persons were present and
accounted for, the witnesses withdrew so that each would not be con-
taminated by the testimony of the others.

This degree of detail regarding court proceedings may seem amiss
in a study of compassion, but any exercise of discretion, or insertion of
personal values (such as "compassion") could not exist in a vacuum, but
had to be firmly imbedded in a powerful matrix of rule, law, precedent,
and circumstance. The most practical aspect of these details of court
procedures is that, if they were mishandled, the verdict was nullified,
and scoundrels, including murderers and rapists, went free because of
procedural flaws.

At the conclusion of the trial, the verdict and all the testimony was
sent up to the general who had ordered the creation of this court-martial.
In most cases, he approved the findings of the court, and if it was for
acquittal, returned the man to duty. If the finding was of guilt, he usually
approved the sentence. Since most officers during the Civil War were
woefully ignorant of their new craft, there are many trial records where
the reviewing general disagreed vehemently with their procedures and
decisions, and wrote scathing reviews in support of his position.

Having passed the level of the appointing general, and usually reviewed by the general commanding the department (who might add his
own comments and opinions), cases of serious import—especially those
invoking the death penalty—were usually forwarded via the office of the
judge advocate general in Washington, DC, to the President. Cases at
this stage of the process were often described as "awaiting the pleasure
of the President." Either the Judge Advocate General's office or the
White House (called then the Executive Mansion) could become the

convergence point for letters from the condemned man, from his mother, his sister, his father, his friends, from members of his regiment, from his former neighbors, from the chaplain, and from senators, congressmen, and governors. Some men, from their jail cells, launched a veritable blizzard of correspondence on their own behalf. Others, illiterate and orphaned, might rely upon the crabbed scrawl of a cell-mate. This cataract of pleading did not all arrive at Lincoln's desk, nor did it go directly from a commander's hands into those of the President. The story of higher review involves half-a-dozen men, some almost lost to memory now, who were vital factors in these life or death decisions.

The first of these men is Joseph Holt, the army's Judge Advocate General. Holt is remembered now chiefly for his probably over-zealous prosecution of the conspirators in the Lincoln assassination, but that is to oversimplify the man and his career. He was Kentucky-born, a noted lawyer and orator. He had made a fortune in business and retired at age 35, but his greatest contributions lay ahead. He heeded the call of President James Buchanan and became Buchanan's Commissioner of Patents, Postmaster General, and Secretary of War. Although he was a Democrat and an anti-abolitionist, he became convinced of the evil of secession and served Lincoln well in keeping Kentucky in the Union. Lincoln was in increasing conflict with Congress over his treatment of political prisoners. Lincoln's immediate concern in appointing Holt to the newly-created post of Judge Advocate General was to deal with the courts and Congress regarding Presidential suspension of habeas corpus. Holt was very helpful to Lincoln in finding legal bases for the suspension of many civil rights. As these issues faded, the principal duties of the new Judge Advocate General (and his staff) were the receiving and recording of court-martials, followed by their analysis and the writing of an opinion and suggested course of action, which was then passed on to the President. This function of review and analysis applied to courts of inquiry and military commissions as well. The latter were military trials of civilians, and occurred chiefly in the border states; the accused men and women were usually tried on such charges as spying, smuggling, defrauding the government, bushwhacking, and pro-secession agitation. Courts of inquiry, which were rather rare, were fact-finding bodies; they did not prosecute.

Although Holt's biographers describe him as harsh and unyielding, a careful reading by this author of more than 15,000 court-martials, courts of inquiry, and military commissions suggests otherwise. Holt, though firm and unsentimental, was far from a tyrant and was quite alert to military abuses of power. Most of the cases that appear in this study have an opinion written or signed by Holt. His sharp, angular signature is usually the final word in a thorough, if brief, analysis.

Not visible in the records that form this book is the hand of Attorney General Edward Bates' pardon clerk, Edmund Stedman. "My chief soon discovered that my most important duty was to keep all but the most deserving cases from coming before the kind Mr. Lincoln at all," recalled Stedman, "since there was nothing harder for him to do than to put aside a prisoner's application, and he could not resist it when it was urged by a pleading wife and a weeping child."[2]

As to the Lincoln White House staff, it was so different from today's thousand or so chiefs, travel agents, spin doctors, advisors, pollsters, mail analysts, greeting clerks, protocol advisers, chefs, butlers, ad infinitum, that the presidential mansion of 1861-1865 might well have been on another planet. Not only was the White House frequently open to

> *Without more satisfactory evidence of his good conduct in the service, which should come from his company commander, to whom a reference might be made, a remission of the punishment imposed for his grave offence is not advised.*
>
> *J. Holt.*
>
> *Judge Advocate General.*

In the days before typewriters, administrators valued secretaries with good handwriting. Here we see part of a summary prepared by Holt's usual secretary (name unknown), followed by "J. Holt" in dark, angular script. *National Archives* mobs of supplicants, well-wishers, petitioners, critics, politicians, and insane inventors (with almost no hint of security), the actual work of the President was carried on by a staff of exactly four men, two of them fairly well known and two now quite obscure.

John G. Nicolay, a German immigrant, came from a very poor family and suffered chronic eye problems. He could not afford a formal education, but through his own efforts, which included reading the Bible in English for recreation, he was skilled enough at age 22 to become the editor of a small newspaper in rural Illinois. A few years earlier he had become friendly with John M. Hay. This cordiality lasted a lifetime and brought them together under the roof of the White House. After Lincoln was nominated for the Presidency, he sought a private secretary. Thus began his historic relationship, in which the 29-year-old Nicolay was Lincoln's one and only chief of staff. Nicolay's first duties were with the 250 pieces of mail which arrived every day, but in time, that was delegated to others and as the years progressed through the war, we see on many court-martials Nicolay's handwriting and Lincoln's signature. After Lincoln's death, Nicolay was U.S. Consul in Paris for four years, and in the 1880s prepared, with Hay, a ten-volume biography of Lincoln.

As a presidential candidate, Lincoln received about fifty letters a day, but as soon as he was elected, the volume quintupled. The mailbags bulged with offers of support, advice on the Rebellion, demands for Federal jobs, requests for commissions, hate mail for both President and Mrs. Lincoln, vulgar cartoons of the President, and ordinary business correspondence. Nicolay, understandably, soon asked for help. It came in the form of his old friend, John M. Hay, who at the age of 22 became the other half of the White House staff. At his graduation from Brown University, Hay had been class poet and his sprightly and witty ways were an odd counterpoint to his often-dour Teutonic friend, Nicolay. They had few ambitions for themselves, lived in one corner of the White House, in a wing separate from the Lincolns, and were utterly loyal to their employer. In later years, Hay enjoyed a distinguished career as an author and diplomat.

In the day-to-day work, Nicolay dealt with Congress while Hay supervised the correspondence, often writing letters which Lincoln would sign without reading. It was a measure of these men that history

A a wartime president, Abraham Lincoln had a staff of two: John G. Nicolay (seated) and John M. Hay, who was just twenty-two when he took the job. *Library of Congress*

records no instance where Hay wrote something which caused the President embarrassment, nor is there a record of Lincoln blaming any underling for something that went out bearing the Presidential signature.[3]

Soon, two staff members were not enough. The law required the President to sign not only letters and commissions, but also a veritable cosmos of other documents, including whaling licenses and land patents.

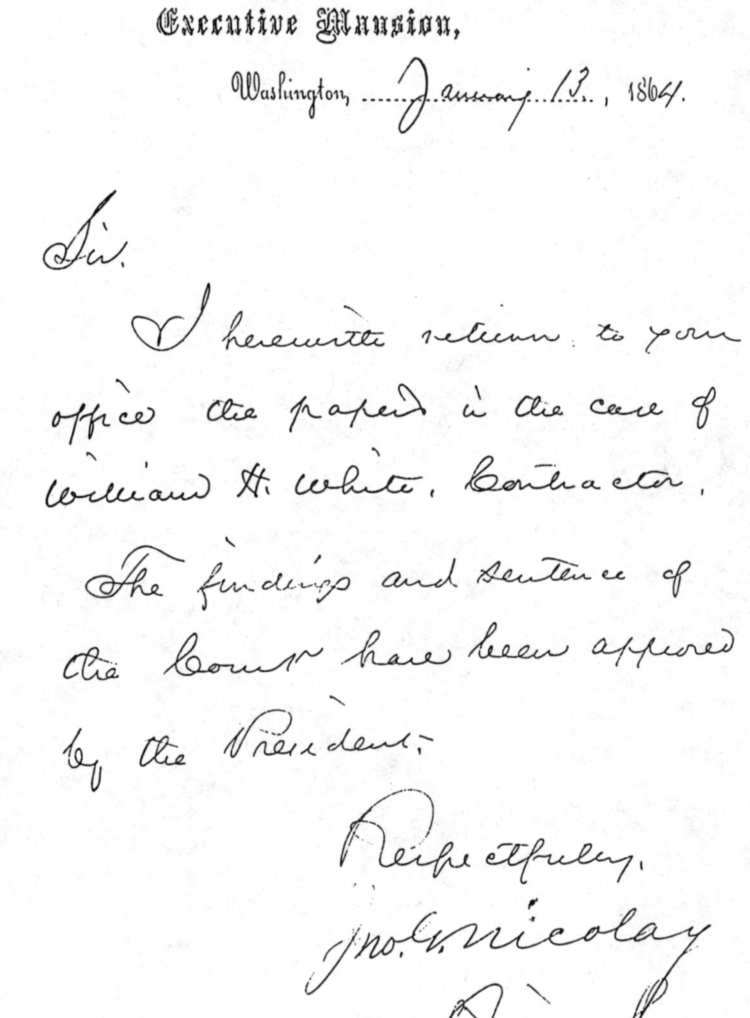

Executive Mansion,

Washington _____ January 13 , 1864.

Sir.

I herewith return to your office the papers in the case of William H. White, Contractor.

The findings and sentence of the Court have been approved by the President.

Respectfully,

Jno. G. Nicolay

Private Sec'y.

The Adjutant-General.

Many of the decisions were written by Nicolay or Hay, and signed by Lincoln. Even when there is no indication of which secretary sat at the table, the handwriting style was usually indicative of authorship. Nicolay wrote in a controlled, flowing hand, with even line space (as shown above); Hay's penmanship (opposite page) tended to be more angular and abrupt, with variation in line width, and much straying from the horizontal.

> The President directs me to
> refer the enclosed to the
> Judge Advocate General
> of the Army.
>
> John Hay,
> Major & A.A.G.
>
> April 23. 1864

William O. Stoddard, who had been angling for a White House job for several months, was hired in July 1861 and set to work signing "A. Lincoln" to 900 land patents a day. When this pile of unfinished documents was sent away, he was put in charge of opening the 250 letters that arrived every day, six days a week, an astonishing mishmash of business and personal letters intermixed with vitriolic attacks and lunatic inventions. (One writer, for example, proposed a double-barreled gun for cross-eyed soldiers.) Stoddard was merciless. The preprinted envelopes from the War Department (usually from Holt or Secretary of War Edwin Stanton) were carefully passed on to Lincoln, but the vast majority of hate letters, demands for favors, and other annoyances were hand-shredded and stuffed into an enormous waste basket. Stoddard estimated that Lincoln saw only one out of a hundred arriving letters; Nicolay's estimate was one in fifty.[4]

In 1864, Stoddard, now 29-years-old, was struck down with typhoid fever and was, for many months, too sick to work. His replacement was Edward D. Neill, a 43-year-old historian and ordained minister. By now, the daily input was closer to 500 letters and parcels, with the same mixture of assassination threats, well-wishing, straight business and favor-begging. Neill, like his predecessor, stood in awe of the President's patience, calm and productivity in the presence of his rambunctious children, vexatious wife (Hay dubbed her "The Hell-Cat"), pouting generals, hostile radical Republicans, and grasping office-seekers.[5]

Although Stoddard wrote several books about his years with Lincoln, and Nicolay and Hay authored a ten-volume biography and an even larger collection of Lincoln writings, there is precious little about the actual handling of court-martials in Lincoln's White House. Ten years after the war, Joseph Holt recalled his trying to convince Lincoln that more executions were necessary, that the soldier caught between the possibility of death in battle and certainty of death for desertion would do as he was ordered. He and Lincoln would spend hours arguing the subject, with Holt urging execution and Lincoln saying, "I don't think I can do it." Holt recalled, "His constant desire was to save life." John M. Hay noted in his diary in July 1863, "Today we spent 6 hours deciding on Court Martials, the President, Judge Holt & I. I was amused at the eagerness with which the President caught at any fact which would justify him in saving the life of a condemned soldier. He was only merciless in cases where meanness or cruelty were shown."[6]

These observations by Holt and Hay are very valuable for the light they shed on the review process, but they cannot be a substitute for a systematic analysis of all the factors which might impinge upon the President's decisions, and how these factors may have changed during the course of the war. To find this, we must seek elsewhere.

The court-martial records, in which most entries are dated, give a fairly accurate picture of the document flow into, through, and out of the White House. After a court-martial was analyzed at the judge advocate general's office, it received a written opinion and the signature of Holt, and went across the street to the White House. There Lincoln might write "Approved" and sign it. Or he might disagree and change the recommended sentence. It was his task and responsibility to make the final determination. Tradition holds that he overturned or lessened most penalties. The remainder of this study concerns itself with that very issue.

When the final decision had been made in a court-martial case, it was sent to the judge advocate general's office for filing. There, each was given a file folder number (actually a pair of letters, followed by a number) and a one-line entry in a huge ledger. Modern researchers are often puzzled by the file folder system, since any particular folder might contain one, or several, or even dozens of different trials. Probably because of the volume of paper work, a new series of folders was opened half way through war, so that there were at least five parallel sets of files (KK, LL, MM, NN, and OO), often covering the same time periods. The cases were filed in the order in which they were received, which is neither chronologically by trial date nor alphabetical. In many file folders there are cases tried a year apart. An extreme example is the file of Private Scott, "the sleeping sentinel." Although he was tried in 1861, his file was not entered into the registry ledger until 1865. It had been in some administrative limbo for four years and only by searching in the "wrong" place were these valuable pages unearthed. With the records in such an idiosyncratic pattern, any satisfactory survey can only be done by reading all the hand-written pages, in sequence, one by one. This book reflects the product of reading the first 37,000 court-martials, roughly one-third of a million pages.

This study, as far as the author can determine, is based upon cases not found in Basler's index. The assertion that a court-martial does not appear in Basler reflects the following factors: after Basler and his associates completed the first eight volumes of Lincoln writing, they received additional material, which was added to the eighth volume as two appendices (material received too late for ordinary inclusion, and material which was forged, or of dubious origin, or simply "routine.") An index volume, published in 1955, contains three indices: the main index, an index to Appendix II of Volume VIII, and an index of the location of Lincoln documents. In 1974, a supplement was published with its own index. A second supplement appeared in 1990. The work presented in this book is based upon cases which did not appear, by name, in the 1955 index volume, or in the 1974 supplemental volume.

In the first 37,000 general court-martials of the Civil War, 792 bear a notation in Lincoln's own hand. Of this number, 543 do not appear in the three above-described indices of Basler's compilation.

Of these 543 cases, approximately twenty percent (20%) were officers. This seems unusually high, since commissioned officers constituted not more than five percent of the Union army. Were officers really four times worse-behaved than enlisted men? Probably not. Some statistical artifact seems a better explanation. Perhaps lesser crimes by enlisted men were disposed of in the regimental court-martial system. Perhaps a higher standard was set for officers, or it might be that with their higher level of literacy, officers were more adept in obtaining higher levels of review. Perhaps an analysis of these 543 cases will provide an additional answer.

Among the enlisted men, forty-three percent (43%) of the trials were for desertion, seven percent (7%) for assaulting an officer; six percent (6%) for murder, and six percent (6%) for theft and/or robbery. The famous crime of William Scott, sleeping on sentry duty, accounted for only four percent (4%) of all court-martials of enlisted men.

In addition to understanding Abraham Lincoln and his handling of court-martial cases, we see in these 543 trials a new perspective of the Civil War. It is not the romantic dash into the cannon's mouth view, nor the officer charging forward on his noble steed, nor the private anxious to rush against the enemy, calling out his support of the Union. Instead, we become privy to a vast cavalcade of prohibited and disgraceful behavior, a diorama of fear, greed, lust, anger, pettiness, misunderstanding, rationalization, folly, grief, failure of nerve, fatigue, and sickness. These tales of things gone wrong, of missed chances, failed faith and violated trust are also part of the Civil War, just as much a part of our history as any deed of valor, just as much a reflection of the spectrum of human existence as were the wildest acts of heroism and courage.

In these not-so-long-ago stories, it is imperative to grasp the immediacy, the vitality of the events described, and to imagine not just the crimes that led to the court-martials and their outcomes, but the scene of the decisions as well. The usual meetings to review court-martials were held in the morning, at the Executive Mansion. The President and John Nicolay, who was the usual secretary for the meetings, both lived in the same building and thus did not have to travel. The other principal, Judge Advocate General Joseph Holt, commuted from his home near the corner of New Jersey Avenue and C Street North, to his office in the Bureau of Military Justice. The Bureau was housed in the Winder Building, located on 17th Street NW, near F Street. That office was but half a block from the Executive Mansion. Many of these sessions reviewed more than fifty cases, so Holt may have had help in transporting the day's paper to the rendezvous. There, Holt would present the case, summarizing the crime, the sentence, and the opinions of the generals who reviewed the papers before they reached Washington. He usually concluded with his own recommendations.

This written analysis is still found in most of the files that came before Lincoln. Fortunately for today's reader, Holt's usual clerk had excellent penmanship, and Holt's signature is very distinctive. Lincoln would read each file, discuss the various points with Judge Holt, and reach his own decision. The two men usually agreed, but often they did not. Whether the secretary (usually Nicolay, sometimes Hay) inserted his own opinion is unknown. The pattern of Lincoln's concurrence or disagreement with the verdict of the court, with the reviewing generals, and with Holt, is the essence of an objective measurement of Lincoln's "compassion," and forms the heart of this study.

The trials reviewed encompass such a variety of issues that several different schemes of organization have been used. The officers, who were also expected to be gentleman as well, occupy their own two chapters. Deserters, who were so frequent, occupy three full chapters, with one chapter devoted solely to Spring of 1863, where Union morale seems to have sunk to a critical low. Five chapters are organized around five different categories of crimes, while the border states, with their complex issues of spies, Confederate recruiters, guerrillas, and bushwhackers, have their own three chapters. A summary chapter addresses the overall pattern of outcomes and suggests a measure of compassion. Finally, there is a consideration of Lincoln's place in history.

When Holt, Lincoln, and Nicolay sat around the table, they were not acting in a vacuum isolated from their world. Quite the opposite. Outside the window was the jangle of cavalry, the shouts of carousing soldiers, the clouds of dust raised by wagons. The telegraph, the mail, and official dispatches brought into the capital a constant flow of news, alarms, and concerns, as nearly three million men clashed with each other in swamps, deserts, and forests, on rivers and on the high seas. After many of Lincoln's dated notations, we have added a highlight of that day's news (based on E. B. Long's *Civil War Day by Day*), in order to help convey the immediacy and the reality of these legal meetings. The world was very much with these men as they performed their task, and the implications of their decisions were palpable, not abstract.

The narrative begins with the officers. It could just as well begin with privates, or sergeants, or lurking spies, or murderous bushwhackers, but in the officers the issues seem more immediate. These men were more visible, were paid more, had more privileges, and usually had more education. The term "an officer and a gentleman" was not an idle sobriquet. More was given to them, and more was expected of them. Being higher, they had farther to fall.

Here are their stories—and Lincoln's decisions.

3

Generals, Colonels, Majors & Captains

Brigadier General James G. Spears was one of the many slave-owning but Union-supporting men from the border states, such as Maryland, Delaware, Kentucky, Missouri and Tennessee. When war came he organized the First Tennessee Infantry and fought bravely for the Union at Wild Cat Mountain and Mill Springs (both in Kentucky), and Murfreesboro, Tennessee. The Emancipation Proclamation was a turning point for him, since it threatened him with loss of his property—slaves. In February 1864, he was court-martialed for "disloyal language" and two lesser offenses. It was charged that at the home of George W. Mabrey of Knox County, Tennessee he said, "The administration intended to abolish slavery. They cannot interfere with a sovereign people. If they undertake such a game, I say God damn the government, let her go to hell. I will be found in the ranks fighting against her. It is the policy of the government to prolong the war, to free the slaves."

Spears was found guilty. Major General John M. Schofield forwarded the trial to the War Department, with the comment, "The evidence shows him to be in a criminal degree, regardless of his obligations as an officer of the government, and unworthy of the position he now holds." Holt reviewed the case and recommended dismissal from the service of the United States. The President's note was short and to the point: "Summary dismissal. A. Lincoln."[1]

Spears' faux pas was not nearly as egregious as Michael Corcoran's. The Irish officer resigned his commission in the British Army in 1849, in protest to a British policy in the Emerald Isle. By 1860, Corcoran was the colonel of the 69th New York Militia, where he was court-martialed

When slave-owning Union Brigadier General James G. Spears heard of the Emancipation Proclamation, he said, "God damn the government; let her go to hell!"

Generals in Blue

for refusing to parade his regiment during a visit by the Prince of Wales. The outcome of this trial was still pending when the war began. Corcoran was wounded and captured at First Bull Run and held as a hostage during a dispute over privateers. After he was released in August 1862, he dined at the White House and was made brigadier general of volunteers, strongly sponsored by the Roman Catholic Archbishop Hughes, of New York City. In May 1863, Corcoran was the subject of a Court of Inquiry. The subject: murder.

At two o'clock in the morning on April 12, 1863, Corcoran was ordered to place his command under arms within the next hour. As he rode to carry out his orders, a figure stepped out of the shadows and demanded the password. Corcoran asked who that person might be and by what authority he might demand the password. The reply was, "It's none of your Goddamn business." Corcoran identified himself and said that he must pass, as he had official business. The man on the road then drew his sword and shouted, "By God, we'll see about that!" Corcoran explained (four times, according to witnesses) who he was, what business he was about and the necessity that he pass, and each time the self-appointed sentinel replied with variations of this statement: "I will not get out of the way for any Goddamned Irish son of a bitch." After the fourth repetition, Corcoran fired his pistol and rode on by.

Four times, a drunken sentinel called Brigadier General Michael Corcoran a "Goddamned Irish son of a bitch!" Corcorcan shot him dead.

Generals in Blue

His Hibernophobic interrogator had been Lieutenant Colonel Edward A. Kimball of the 9th New York Infantry. The pistol ball had passed through Kimball's neck, killing him almost instantly. Witnesses at Corcoran's trial testified that Kimball had been drunk for at least several hours before the incident, and had no duty assignment that night, certainly not as a sentinel.

The Court of Inquiry found the shooting "censurable." Three months later, Corcoran's position was still not clarified. In early August he met with Lincoln, who asked Corcoran how he could help. The officer declined the President's assistance, but a week later on August 17, 1863, he wrote that he did not wish to trouble the President, but "I respectfully request that I may be ordered to some other command." On September 25, Lincoln passed his request forward with the endorsement "Submitted to the Secretary of War and General in Chief. A. Lincoln."

Corcoran's respite was a brief one. On December 22, 1863, his horse fell, killing him. Though the fall itself was beyond Presidential power, Lincoln certainly seemed willing to help an officer who had served faithfully.[2]

Joseph W. Revere, grandson of Paul Revere, had served 22 years in the U.S. Navy and two years as a colonel of artillery in the Mexican Army. Then the Civil War came. At Chancellorsville (Virginia), he held the rank of brigadier general. As Stonewall Jackson's attack on the Union right evolved, Revere marched his command to the rear "for the purpose of reorganizing and bringing them back to the field comparatively fresh." This unusual maneuver earned him a court-martial in May 1863, charged with "misbehavior before the enemy" and "neglect of duty," in that by this maneuver he allowed the Confederates to capture "189 muskets, 259 bayonets, 28,400 rounds of ammunition, 1,779 knapsacks and 2,000 tents." The court-martial board included Generals Winfield Hancock, John Gibbon and Romeyn Ayres. Revere was found guilty and ordered dismissed from the service. Major General Joseph Hooker approved the sentence and sent it on to the Judge Advocate General's Office. An opinion there, written in a barely readable microscopic script, and not signed by Holt, notes that Revere did regroup his men, picking up 800 stragglers, and returned to the battlefield, but only after an absence of several hours.

Analysis written by General-in-Chief Henry W. Halleck confined itself to legal technicalities. "If the conviction should be disapproved [on technicalities alone], I concur in the opinion of the Judge Advocate

General that Brigadier General Revere be dismissed from the service by the President,"wrote Halleck. Lincoln agreed with his military men and wrote, "August 10, 1863. Sentence of the court-martial approved. A. Lincoln"[3]

At the Battle of Chancellorsville, Brigadier General Joseph W. Revere marched his troops off the battlefield in order to regroup, leaving behind 28,400 rounds of ammunition.

Generals in Blue

In the case of the generals—Spears and Revere—Lincoln clearly endorsed their convictions. With Corcoran, he chose to ignore the Court of Inquiry's conclusion of "censurable," continued to meet with Corcoran, and tried to find him a change of assignment.

Colonel Frederick G. D'Utassy, commander of the Garibaldi Guards, had played a prominent part in the doomed defense of Harpers Ferry when Stonewall Jackson's forces fell upon the disorganized defenders in September 1862. D'Utassy particularly annoyed the Confederate officers by concealing his regimental colors rather than surrendering them. An investigation of the military debacle at Harpers Ferry exonerated D'Utassy.

He did not do as well in his April 1863 court martial, in which the charges and specifications alone total over 2,000 words. D'Utassy was charged with, among other things: advising three soldiers to desert, selling government horses and keeping the proceeds himself, opening private mail and stealing the contents, selling commissions, receiving kickbacks from the sutler's profits, cheating six of his officers out of their recruiting expenses, submitting $3,000.00 worth of false vouchers, changing the payroll of the band to profit himself, extorting $3.00 in gold from each of his enlisted men, and wrongfully dismissing several of his officers.

After a prolonged trial by a board of officers

Colonel Frederick G. D'Utassy, flamboyant head of the Garibaldi Guard, was convicted of fraud and theft. He fled the country to avoid prison.

USAMHI

headed by Major General Ethan Hitchcock (born in 1798 and no new-comer to military affairs), D'Utassy was found guilty of two of the three charges and was sentenced to be cashiered, imprisoned at hard labor for one year, disqualified forever from any Federal employment, and to have his name, crime, and punishment published in "at least three of the public papers of the State of New York."

Edwin Stanton wrote, on May 25, 1863, "The proceedings, findings and sentence of the court martial in the foregoing case are approved and the state prison at Sing Sing, New York is designated as the place of confinement of the prisoner." Two days later came the endorsement, "Approved. A. Lincoln."[4]

Another colonel who ran afoul of the military's laws was Jacob Van Zandt of the 91st New York. Van Zandt not only engaged in a three-year feud with his lieutenant colonel, Jonathan Tarbell, but was court-mar-tialed twice, once for his behavior at Port Hudson, Louisiana and again for his conduct at Pensacola, Florida. At the latter place, after demand-ing and receiving payment from the regiment, he opened their camp to liquor-peddlers and prostitutes. The resulting riot and debauchery re-sulted in one-third of the men being absent without leave and one-quar-ter of the regiment off sick with venereal disease. Further, he promised promotion to those officers of his regiment who "supplied his appetite and pandered to his lust."

At Port Hudson, he was acquitted of charges that he kept a "mulatto wench as his mistress," but was convicted of calling his captains ob-scene names while they were drilling their men, and of addressing "grossly vile and indecent language" to a lieutenant. In addition, Van Zandt was convicted of "neglecting to repress disorders in camp." He was sentenced to be dismissed, but in consideration of his recent good behavior in battle, the court-martial board suggested that he be allowed to resign. The reviewing officer, Major General Nathaniel Banks, rec-ommended instead that he be suspended from rank and pay for six months. The papers, including many petitions for and against Van Zandt, went upwards through channels to Judge Advocate General Holt, who recommended following General Banks' suggestion. Lincoln agreed, writing, "Recommendation of General Banks approved and ordered."[5]

Liquor also played a part in the near-downfall of Colonel Alfred W. Taylor of the 4th New York, who was tried in March 1862 for being drunk on duty. In the days before blood alcohol levels, being drunk was a matter of observation and opinion. One witness called him "not staggering drunk, but too drunk to issue commands," while another one said that the colonel was "not sober, but not what I would call drunk." Another man saw Taylor as "too drunk to draw his sword." A witness who had observed the colonel in the store of Russell and Company in New York City said, "The colonel was in full uniform; he was so drunk that his hat fell off and a stranger picked it up and put it back on his head." Still other witnesses, however, described Taylor as perfectly sober.

As part of his defense, Taylor's lawyer submitted a letter from Major General Winfield Scott, citing Taylor's bravery in the Mexican War, many years before. It did no good and Taylor was found guilty. These findings, plus dozens of pages of testimonials and observations, finally arrived on the Presidential desk. He wrote, "If, as stated within, the adjutant general has ordered Colonel A. W. Taylor to duty, the action of the court martial notwithstanding, let Colonel Taylor be pardoned, as within requested. A. Lincoln, April 15, 1862."[6]

Lieutenant Colonel Henry A. Cook of the 72nd Pennsylvania was apparently full of fun and frolic. On the night of January 25, 1864, well after "Taps" had blown, he encouraged the enlisted men of his regiment to assemble in and around his tent, "to carouse, shout, cheer and sing in a boisterous manner, thereby disturbing the quietness of the camp." Cook was sentenced to be "dishonorably dismissed." Major General George Meade, then Commander of the Army of the Potomac, approved the proceedings but noted "Under the circumstances of the case, however, it is considered that the sentence is more severe than is warranted by the facts. It is therefore suspended and the record respectfully forwarded for the order of the President, recommending that the sentence be commuted to a forfeiture of all pay. . .for the period of three months." Holt wrote, "The permission and encouragement given to the men in camp to assemble after 'Taps' and engage in boisterous entertainment were plain violations of the rules of the service, but General Meade was doubtless well advised of the necessities of the case and his recommendation is therefore concurred in." The President agreed: "Recom. of Gen. Meade approved and ordered. A. Lincoln April 21, 1864."[7]

Lieutenant Colonel John W. Stephens of the 11th Missouri Cavalry was tried for mutiny and insubordination. The trial revealed all the tensions of wartime Missouri: Stephens refused to obey the orders of his commander, Colonel W. D. Wood, circulated a petition among the officers asking to have Wood removed and carried the petition to Major General John Schofield and Governor Hamilton Gamble. At this time in history, Missouri had two governments, one in exile, headed by secessionist Governor Claiborne Jackson, and one then functioning in Missouri headed by Governor Gamble, who was pro-Union but opposed to the Federal draft. Colonel Wood had been appointed to his colonelcy by Gamble, but Stephens was convinced the appointment was invalid and that Wood was disloyal. General Schofield thought Wood's appointment was legitimate, but the tangle of Missouri politics was revealed in a broadside published shortly before by Colonel Wood and signed by him and four other men (who had since gone into the Confederate Army). In this publication, they referred to their being "dragged through the streets like convicts through our native city, scowled and derided at by men who could scarcely speak our language [presumably St. Louis Germans, who were strong Union men] and finally to be penned up like slaves in the Middle Passage."

Stephens was found guilty and sentenced to be cashiered. Schofield recommended that the sentence by commuted to three months suspension from rank and pay. When the case reached Holt, his office prepared a lengthy analysis, listing the historical factors and supporting Schofield's analysis. When it reached the President, he wrote, "Let the sentence of Colonel Stephens be commuted to suspension from rank, pay and emoluments for the term of one month from this date, November 17, 1863," recognizing that two months had already passed since Stephens had been found guilty.[8]

Several hundred miles east near Potomac Creek in late 1862, Lieutenant Colonel William Sackett of the 9th New York Cavalry ordered his men to "stand to horse" at 1:00 o'clock in the morning and then went to his own quarters and lay down. Later he was ordered to transport grain for the horses in his regimental wagons. Even though five of his wagons

Lieutenant Colonel Frederick F. Cavada of the 114th Pennsylvania Infantry disappeared for days during the December 1862 Battle of Fredericksburg and was accused of cowardice.

USAMHI

were empty, he refused. He was put under arrest, but left camp and proceeded over two miles before he was caught and returned.

At his court-martial, he was found guilty and sentenced to be cashiered. Major General Joseph Hooker recommended that the sentence be reduced to a reprimand and sent the papers on to Washington, D.C. Lincoln wrote, "The above sentence of Colonel Sackett is mitigated so that in lieu of cashiering, he be reprimanded by Major General Hooker. A. Lincoln. March 28, 1863."[9]

Lieutenant Colonel F. F. Cavada of the 114th Pennsylvania was charged with "misbehavior before the enemy" at the Battle of Fredericksburg, December 13, 1862. He had apparently hid in the rear while his regiment was engaged with the Confederates and did not return for several days. He was found guilty and cashiered. In February, Major General Joseph Hooker, who had replaced Ambrose Burnside after the debacle of Fredericksburg, reviewed the records and wrote, "The proceedings are respectfully forwarded in compliance with the 89th Article of War, for the decision of the President, with a recommendation that, from the circumstances of the case as established before the Court and the good character proven. . .that he be remitted." The President wrote on May 20, 1863, "Sentence remitted. A. Lincoln."[10] That same day, Lincoln pardoned Albert Horn, who had fitted out a ship for the slave trade.

Major Joseph Gilmer, of the 18th Pennsylvania cavalry was so drunk at Aldie, Virginia, that he could not tell Green Mountain boys from Confederates and ran away from the Vermont cavalry, thinking that they were the enemy. He was charged first with being drunk on duty and second with cowardice. His March 1863 trial found him guilty and sentenced him to be cashiered.

According to Judge Advocate General Hold, "Major Gilmer was acquitted of cowardice, but convicted of being drunk on duty and was sentenced to be cashiered. The proceedings were disapproved by Major General [Samuel] Heintzelman on account of fatal defects and irregularities, but the record is forwarded with the recommendation that the accused be dismissed by order of the President. The testimony shows that the accused was drunk on duty and brought disgrace upon himself and the service. The recommendation of General Heintzelman is therefore concurred [in]." Lincoln wrote on July 20, 1863, "Let Major Gilmer be dismissed as recommended by General Heintzelman."[11] As the ink was drying on Gilmer's dismissal papers, Federal troops were fighting Indians at Round Valley, California, forty miles north of Ukiah.

Major Rudolph W. Shenk of the 135th Pennsylvania avoided Gilmer's fate. Shenk was charged with conduct unbecoming an officer and a gentleman because he stole government food and liquor and was found drunk on duty. A trial record of hundreds of pages of accounting and requisitioning documents occupied the court for weeks. They concluded that Shenk was guilty and recommended that he be dismissed. The President came to other conclusions: "Being satisfied by the within that Major Shenk was misled to not make his defense against the charges in relationship to the trunks and being also satisfied that he is not guilty of the charges and is an honest and honorable man, I hereby remove the legal disability, so that the Governor of Pennsylvania may, in his discretion, re-appoint him. A. Lincoln."[12]

Major William H. Miller of the 2nd Wisconsin Cavalry saw the war through an alcoholic haze in southern Missouri. At Huntsville, he stole a quart of port wine from the hospital; at Dent County, he tore a corporal's chevrons off without a trial; in Wright County, he stole a quart of rye whisky from another hospital. In 1863, the railroad from St. Louis ended at Rolla, Missouri. On the long ride to Rolla, Major Miller blew kisses, for hours, to a Mrs. Whitset. When the train finally arrived he followed her along the street, blowing "lascivious" kisses. Despite these activities, the court martial acquitted him of conduct unbecoming an officer and a gentleman. Major General John Schofield disapproved the findings and sent the matter east for further review. The record shows that Miller was dismissed on Lincoln's orders, but the President's actual notation has been torn out of the record by a thief.[13]

Major Andrew Washburn of the 14th Massachussetts Infantry was tried for embezzlement. The record, almost 1,000 pages long, details approximately $130.00 in missing cash, as well as the theft of seven barrels of salt beef; in addition, several barrels of salt beef were bought or sold at improper prices. Washburn was cashiered. Lincoln wrote, "Judge Advocate General, please examine this case and report his opinion to me. A. Lincoln   Oct. 25, 1862." After reviewing the report, Lincoln re-instated Major Washburn, but that note is missing.[14]

Captains were not immune to transgressions which brought them the attention of the President. One of the more dramatic instances is Captain Bernard McMahon of the 71st Pennsylvania, who was tried for murder, after he fired his pistol at a Captain McManus. Captain McMahon was convicted of murder and sentenced to be shot to death by a firing squad. Holt, in an unusually long analysis (almost 2,000 words) laid out the story. McMahon, by his proven services in both the Mexican and Civil Wars, was certainly no coward. In fact, he had fought "gallantly" at Gettysburg between his trial

Major Andrew Washburn of the 14th Massachusetts was convicted of stealing seven barrels of salt beef. Based on Holt's legal analysis of the case, Lincoln reinstated Washburn.

USAMHI

and the Judge Advocate General's review. For reasons unclear, his victim, on many occasions, both verbally and in writing, had chosen to accuse McMahon of being "a coward and a loafer." Holt concluded, "The deceased must be regarded as having wantonly and wickedly thrown away his life. The outrage which he committed on the sensibilities and character of the accused would scarcely have been more aggravated had he applied a horse whip to his shoulders." Holt went on to say that if the accused had not resented these taunts, he would have shown "a want of spirit." Holt strongly recommended a full pardon. Lincoln's response: "Captain Bernard J. McMahon is hereby pardoned of the punishment and sentence above-mentioned."[15]

Captain J. K. Herbert, an assistant adjutant general, was tried for conduct unbecoming an officer and a gentleman. In Texas, he captured two men hiding from the Mexican authorities and returned them to Mexico to collect the reward. Herbert also profited by trading in stolen Confederate cotton. He was dismissed. Holt thought that he merited some degree of punishment, if perhaps not dismissal, but Maj. Gen. Ben Butler spoke well of the man. "Captain Herbert is hereby reprimanded upon the case herein shown," wrote Lincoln, "and all officers are admonished against similar acts. As General Butler has asked to have his services, let Captain Herbert report to General Butler. A. Lincoln."[16]

New York State, which furnished the largest number of soldiers for the Union cause, also provided twelve captains for this study. Captain Charles H. Roys of the 117th New

Captain Charles H. Roys of the 117th New York Infantry forged a pass for himself. Holt asked if an officer "whose perception of moral and legal right is so imperfect" should remain in service. Lincoln's answer was brief.

USAMHI

York used a leave of absence paper made out for a lieutenant, and also failed to show up when he was Officer of the Day. His admission that he knew the pass was not intended for him resulted in his dismissal, and the case went to Washington for review, where it inspired one of Holt's rare apoplectic fulminations. "It is for the President to decide whether an officer whose sense of honor is so blunt and whose perception of moral and legal right is so imperfect as to allow him to convert to his own use official papers, which he knew were not intended for him, possesses either the integrity or intelligence which would qualify him for military command." The President agreed: "Sentence approved. A. Lincoln July 18, 1863."[17]

Captain Charles Arthur of the 5th New York Cavalry was tried for being absent without leave for eleven days, with cowardice at Cedar Mountain on August 9, 1862, and with calling the President of the United States "a loafer and a traitor." He was sentenced to be dismissed. When the case reached Lincoln, some of the papers were missing and the President was not willing to judge a man without a proper review of the appropriate documents. He wrote, "If there is a record on file show-ing the evidence in this case, I will thank the Judge Advocate General to let me see it. November 12, 1862. A. Lincoln." After the President's review Arthur was, indeed, dismissed.[18] Major General Ambrose Burn-side, meanwhile, was assuming command of the Army of the Potomac, and preparing to lead it to slaughter and defeat at Fredericksburg.

Another New Yorker of some infamy, Captain Edward P. Jones of the 125th New York, was found guilty of being so drunk that he had to ride in an ambulance at Elk Run, Virginia, but was acquitted of coward-ice at both Gettysburg, Pennsylvania, and Auburn, Virginia. The court sentenced him to be cashiered and then petitioned for clemency. Major General George Meade recommended that the sentence be changed to the loss of three months pay. Holt thought that Jones had behaved dis-gracefully, but added that since the court knew his case very well, this would lead to "a more perfect comprehension of the case than an exami-nation of the pages of the record simply." Lincoln agreed: "General Meade's recommendation approved. A. Lincoln."[19]

At Morganza, Louisiana, each officer was allowed half a gallon of whisky a month. Thirsting for a more substantial apportionment, the creative but not particularly clever Captain Joseph Goodsell of the 176th New York altered a written whisky order to read, "One and a half gallons." He was convicted of conduct unbecoming an officer and a gentleman and dismissed. Goodsell immediately began pulling strings. United States Senator Edwin D. Morgan wrote, "Dear President, Cornelius Nelson, Postmaster at West Point, New York, writes to me very strongly in favor of Captain Joseph Goodsell who has been dismissed the service through a court martial for what Nelson considers a small offense. I think I cannot be mistaken that Captain Goodsell, who goes to you with this letter, is deserving of having his case reconsidered by you." The following day, Lincoln wrote, "Judge Advocate General please procure papers and reports on this case." The Army Register of the Volunteer Force lists Goodsell as "dismissed June 22, 1864"; it would seem that the Senator's plea was unavailing.[20]

Captain William S. Grantsyn (also spelled Gruntsynn) of the 140th New York was convicted of making a false return. On the morning report, he had listed Shadrack Jackson as absent with leave, when Jackson did not have such leave. The captain was cashiered. The court urged remission since Shadrack was on unofficial leave granted by the colonel, who wanted a man to care for his horse while on a journey. Major General George Meade recommended commutation to six months pay. Holt expressed no opinion. Lincoln's secretary Nicolay wrote: "Sentence of the Court commuted to forfeiture of pay proper for a period of six months from September 1, 1863." Lincoln signed Nicolay's note. This incident did not seem to have inhibited the career of Captain Grantsyn, since two years later he was a lieutenant colonel, and commanded the regiment.[21]

Captain Ross Deegan of the 162nd New York was tried for "conduct prejudicial to good order and military discipline." Enroute to Algiers, Louisiana, on the steamboat *Saint Maurice*, he played cards with enlisted men. Later, when his colonel asked him if his men had cooked their rations, as ordered, Deegan replied "in an impudent manner." When asked to sign a paper confirming that he had received an order, he refused. For these, and other offenses, Deegan was cashiered. Major General Nathaniel Banks concurred, but noted that the court-martial board contained two lieutenants. (Officers should not be tried by persons of inferior rank.) Banks asked for direct dismissal by the President, since the court-martial was probably invalid. Holt agreed with Banks. The final decision was "Judge Advocate General's recom. approved. A. Lincoln Feb. 9, 1864."[22] Lincoln spent all that morning with Holt, reviewing twenty-one cases, and in the evening attended the largest levee of the season.

Like many regiments of the Civil War, the 90th New York was consumed by internal bickering. At Key West, Florida, Captain Edward D. Smyth joined with thirteen other officers and all resigned on the same day. Colonel Joseph Morgan preferred charges against Smyth, who was convicted of joining in a mutiny, but since the court-martial board found "no criminality attached," Smyth was acquitted. Major General Banks reviewed the case and thought that Smyth should be dismissed. Holt, in reviewing the papers, noted that the captain had been "gallant in battle," and suggested reinstatement. Lincoln agreed: "Recom. of J. A. G. approved and ordered. A. Lincoln Feb. 15, 1864." In April 1864, the charging officer, Colonel Morgan, was himself dismissed from the army, while Smyth was honorably discharged at the end of his term of service.[23]

Captain Oliver Cotter of the 5th New York Heavy Artillery certified men as present when they were not, and drew rations for these non-existent men. He also confiscated smuggled clothing at Baltimore, Maryland, but did not turn them over to the government. He kept for himself four pairs of women's cotton hose, three pairs of lady's French kid gloves and some ribbons and laces. He was cashiered. Major General Robert C. Schenck (future Congressman and authority on draw poker) saw some ground for mitigation, but Holt thought the evidence so strong that he recommended against clemency. Hay wrote, "Report approved," and Lincoln, agreeing with Holt, signed on to the order. Cotter resigned January 28, 1865.[24]

Captain George W. Cothran of the 1st New York Light Artillery was in difficulty on several counts, including hiring a private as a regimental surgeon, for removing a ball and chain from a prisoner without authorization, and for keeping false accounts. The trial generated a huge file of strongly-contradictory testimony (Cothran was an attorney) and ended in a finding of guilty. Lincoln's opinion was different: "Let the sentence in this case be vacated, and let Captain George W. Cothran return to his duty as captain of Company M, First New York Artillery. A. Lincoln June 2, 1862." The previous day, Robert E. Lee had assumed command of Confederate forces outside Richmond. The contentious Captain Cothran served ten more months and then resigned.[25]

In the early spring of 1863, Captain James N. Root and the other soldiers of the 24th New York were marching to Falmouth, Virginia, to a new camp. The captains were ordered to stay with their companies, but Root, who was lame, turned his command over to a lieutenant and proceeded at a different pace. He was convicted of "disobedience" and dismissed. Major General Hooker thought the sentence "unduly severe, and it is suspended. The proceedings, in compliance with the 89th Article of War, are respectfully forwarded for the action of the President, recommending the sentence be mitigated." Holt had no objection to Hooker's views, and Nicolay wrote, "Sentence remitted, May 11, 1863"; Lincoln added his distinctive signature.[26]

That day Lincoln had many fish to fry, some larger than others. Not only did he rescue the career of the obscure and sore-footed Root, but he received the British ambassador, Lord Lyons, who brought official notice of the marriage of the Prince of Wales; Lyons also raised two naval questions, which Lincoln referred on to Gideon Welles, his Secretary of the Navy.

Captain Robert Jackson's crime was wholly unique when compared to his fellow New Yorkers mentioned within these pages: Jackson was tried for being too kind to a soldier. While on the march, a notoriously violent private of the 36th New York struck the captain with his rifle butt. The captain responded with a blow of his sheathed sword but positively refused to press charges against the private. Jackson was sentenced to be dismissed the service. Major General George McClellan thought that the captain's failure to have the private arrested was "reprehensible," but remitted the sentence based upon Jackson's previous good behavior. The case came directly to the Presidential mansion, where Lincoln wrote, "Submitted to the Judge Advocate General for report." The record contains no subsequent Lincoln notation, but regimental records show that Jackson was not dismissed from the service.[27]

Captain John W. Howland, a crooked Quartermaster with the US Volunteers, was charged with embezzling $16,470.04 (almost half a million present-day dollars) at Washington D.C. Not only was he cashiered, ordered to return the money, sent to prison for five years and forever disqualified from Federal employment, but his crime was published in three newspapers of his home state of Massachusetts.

The former Captain Howland remained at New York's Albany State Prison until his failing health was documented by three prison physicians who noted, "Night sweats, severe cough, and dullness over the upper lungs, confirming advanced tubercular consumption." Howland's family, anxious to have him die at home instead of in prison, petitioned Congressman Henry L. Dawes, who wrote to Lincoln asking for a pardon. Lincoln wrote: "Pardon granted as requested by Mr. Dawes. A. Lincoln Feb. 26, 1864."[28] That same day, Lincoln not only accommodated the Congressman and his moribund constituent, but issued General Order No. 76, which stated that all death sentences for desertion would be commuted to imprisonment at the Dry Tortugas until the end of the war.

Captain Christopher C. Owen of the 8th Missouri Militia Cavalry reflected the bitterness of that war-torn border state. It was charged that he had been drunk and disorderly at Newtonia and had ordered his men to drive a family from their home, which he then burned; that at Pittsburg, Missouri, he was ordered to reinforce the Federal forces at Centre Creek, but instead lay drunk for thirty-six hours; and that he failed to arrest deserters at Calhoun, Missouri, as he had been ordered to do. Owen was acquitted. Major General William Rosecrans disapproved the finding, recommended dismissal, and sent the record on to Washington. There, Holt reviewed Owen's defenses ("I wasn't drunk; I had diarrhea; I was ordered to destroy the homes of all known bushwhackers.") and dismissed them as verbal inventions. Holt concluded that the witnesses statements "are too clear, distinct and conclusive to leave it doubtful that Captain Owens is unfitted, by his private habits and his indifference to military rules, for the position he now occupies. General Rosecrans' recommendations are concurred in." The President turned the record over and wrote on the back: "Summary dismissal. A. Lincoln Aug. 17, 1864."[29]

Joseph G. Telford, a captain in the 3rd U. S. Cavalry was "disgracefully drunk" in the streets of Memphis and when put in arrest, left repeatedly. He was cashiered, but the court recommended clemency based upon prior good performance. Major General U. S. Grant passed the decision on to the President via Holt. The Judge Advocate General noted that because of some transmittal error, the record had taken five months to travel from Memphis to Washington, D.C.; all this time, Telford had been in arrest. Holt proposed no course of action, noting instead the humiliation of prolonged arrest. The President agreed: "Further punishment remitted. A. Lincoln April 16, 1864."[30]

As he wrote these words, a Confederate mine exploded under the steamer *General Hunter*, sending it to the bottom of Florida's St. Johns River.

Captain R. W. Thompson, a Commissary of Subsistence, had multiple responsibilities for feeding a large group of men. He had been ordered to remain at headquarters, but felt that he should be with the supply train seven miles away. He wrote a note to his commander requesting a change in his orders. For this, he was tried and convicted of "conduct prejudicial to good order" and sentenced to a reprimand and the loss of two months pay. Thompson's father wrote to Holt and to Lincoln protesting this decision. Holt described the captain's action as "hasty and indiscreet, but not culpable" and noted that Brigadier General Nelson Miles had certified that Thompson was "a most efficient commissary." The closing note on the case reads: "Unexecuted portion of sentence remitted. A. Lincoln Aug. 11, 1864."[31] U. S. Colored Troops were fighting at Kent's Landing, Arkansas; a week earlier, the Union victory at Mobile Bay had weakened the Confederacy.

The trial of Captain T. R. Dudley, a quartermaster, was an accountant's nightmare. Several civilian contractors at Winchester, Virginia, had supplied the army and Dudley paid them with vouchers worth less than the amount due. Thereafter, he was transferred to Stevenson, Alabama. He attempted to settle the accounts by sending money with various persons headed in the direction of Virginia, but this slap-dash method of payment failed. As a result, Dudley was charged with embezzlement, making false vouchers and attempting to pay debts with worthless Tennessee paper money. He was acquitted, but Major General George

Thomas disapproved this verdict and sent the case east. In May 1864, Holt prepared a lengthy summary of the sorry matter. "It is not believed that he intended to defraud these parties or the government," he concluded. "The case is therefore submitted for such action as the President may consider the honor and the welfare of the service requires."

It is astonishing that Lincoln found the time, in the midst of a vast national crisis, to insure justice for a junior officer 1,000 miles away. On June 6, 1864, as the Overland Campaign raged on between Generals Grant and Lee, Lincoln took a moment and wrote, "Please send by the bearer the papers in this case." Lincoln's burdensome insomnia may have enabled him to find the time to review this complex file, since two days later he wrote, "I think General Thomas mistakes the evidence when he says Capt. Dudley never intended to disburse the money covered by the vouchers. I think the evidence shows conclusively that he did intend to pay——I therefore decline to dismiss him from the service, but I also direct that he be assigned somewhere out of General Thomas' command. A. Lincoln."[32] While the President was busy rehabilitating Dudley's honor, a tumultuous convention unanimously nominated Lincoln to run for a second term.

The case of Captain C. H. Nichols of the 6th Connecticut, which fills a huge folder, is a tangled web of jurisdictions. At Beaufort, South Carolina, in January 1862, there were two Union commanders: Brigadier General John Brannan in overall command, and Brigadier General Rufus Saxton, who was ordered to seize and cultivate the local plantations and to muster 55,000 persons of "African descent," 50,000 as laborers and farmers and 5,000 to be trained and armed to defend those plantations. General Brannan had appointed Captain Nichols as provost marshal. Nichols found Dr. I. M. Hawks and some workmen tearing down an old shed preparatory to erecting a new stable for the doctor's horse. Nichols arrested the surgeon, who was wearing an officer's uniform. Hawks claimed to be a member of General Saxton's staff, and Saxton ordered Nichols to release the doctor. Nichols refused, and was himself arrested, convicted, and cashiered. The lengthy trial revealed that the doctor had never been commissioned and that General Saxton had no authorization for such a person on his staff, and further had no jurisdiction over Nichols. The case was succinctly closed by "Sentence disapproved. A. Lincoln July 18, 1863." Nichols was cleared of all charges and returned to duty; he served three more years.[33]

While the men employed to save the Union were squabbling over a horse shed, Lincoln and Holt spent six hours reviewing court-martials and their life or death implications. Later that July 18, just two weeks after the end of the Battle of Gettysburg, the President relaxed for a moment with John Hay and regaled his young secretary with the historic triple pun regarding Captain Cutts, the convicted voyeur, who had peered over a hotel transom at an unclad woman. Sweden's ambassador to the United States was Count Piper; Lincoln suggested to Hay that Cutts could become "Count Peeper and be elevated to the peerage."

Captain Cardinal Conant of the 31st Massachussetts was provost marshal for two Louisiana parishes. The trial record contains hundreds of travel passes, signed by him, allegedly issued upon the payment of a bribe. There are also allegations that he was never commissioned nor was he ever a captain. Conant was sentenced to three years at the prison on Ship Island, off the coast of Mississippi. Further evidence, and a detailed analysis by Holt and his staff, resulted in this final note, written in the hand of John Hay and signed by Lincoln. "Executive Mansion, Washington, January 6,1864. As the evidence upon which Mr. Conant was convicted of 'disobedience or orders in granting permits to travel

and trade beyond the lines,' now seems to have been based on a forgery, and the charge of 'embezzlement' is only sustained by evidence of irregularity in which no criminal intent appears, it is ordered that the sentence of the Court in the case of

At Skull Creek, South Carolina, Captain John Wilbur of the 3rd New Hampshire, against strict orders to the contrary, took his men into Confederate territory. When arrested, Wilbur said, "I've had enough of the service." His wish was granted.

USAMHI

Cardinal H. Conant be annulled and the accused set at liberty." Beneath this is the familiar signature, "A. Lincoln."[34]

Another incident from the Deep South worthy of note involved Captain John Wilbur of the 3rd New Hampshire, who was stationed in South Carolina. In November 1862, Wilbur commanded a work party "at Talbot's on Skull Creek." He took several men and crossed the creek onto Pinckney Island against the strict orders of Brigadier General Alfred Terry. When Wilbur was arrested, he told Dr. A. J. Buzzell, a surgeon with the regiment, "I have had about enough of the service; I would just as lief [i.e., as soon] get out of the service." The captain got his wish and was dismissed. Holt reviewed the case: "The testimony justifies the findings." Nicolay wrote, "Sentence approved in this case. May 11, 1863." Lincoln signed the note. Case closed.[35]

As General Grant was discharging his artillery on besieged Vicksburg, Captain John H. Behan of the 16th West Virginia was shooting off his rather foul mouth at Miner's Hill, Virginia. The bad-tempered captain referred to a lieutenant as "a half-assed adjutant," and urged his men to duty with these ringing words: "Turn out, you lazy sons-of-bitches, every goddamned one of you." At Alexandria, Virginia, he kept a stolen sword and defrauded a private of $23.00 (seven weeks pay back then). Behan was dismissed from the service. Holt agreed with the sentence, Hay wrote, "Sentence approved. June 24, 1863," and Lincoln signed the note.[36]

Joshua Lawrence Chamberlain, of Little Round Top fame, was on the court-martial board which tried Captain Judd Mott of the 16th Michigan. Mott was accused of overstaying his leave by ten days and was dismissed from the army. Major General Joseph Hooker approved the finding, but saw dismissal as "unduly severe." He sent the case on to the President with a recommendation that Captain Mott forfeit two months pay. An unidentified hand at the Executive Office wrote, "Approved but mitigated to forfeiture of pay for the period of two months." This was signed, "A. Lincoln, May 21, 1863."[37]

Captain James Starkey of the 1st Minnesota Mounted Rangers was convicted of making false muster rolls at Fort Snelling, Minnesota, and his conviction was approved by Brigadier General Henry H. Sibley. Holt noted that the findings were "fully sustained by the testimony," and as

Captain John H. Behan of the 16th West Virginia Infantry urged his sleepy-eyed men out of their tents with these stirring words: "Turn out, you lazy sons of bitches, every Goddamn one of you!" *USAMHI*

required by the 15th Article of War, Starkey was not only dismissed, but "forever disqualified to have or hold office or employment in the service of the US." Holt, however, noted that Captain Starkey's cutting corners was motivated by a wish to get his company into the field as soon as possible, rather than by any malign motive. The papers crossed the street from Holt's office to Lincoln's. There, Hay wrote "Sentence commuted so far as to remove the disability to hold office or be employed in the service of the United States. June 16, 1863." Lincoln signed.[38]

At Decherd, Tennessee, Captain William Wade of the 98th Illinois "purchased a bottle of Blackberry Brandy and drank of it too freely." He was convicted under the 45th Article of War and cashiered. His combat record showed him to be "a skillful and brave officer," and the court asked for remission. As the case meandered upward, General Joseph Reynolds disagreed with remission, General William Rosecrans endorsed remission, and Holt expressed no opinion. In the President's own hand appears: "Recommendation of General Rosecrans approved. A. Lincoln Nov. 7, 1863."[39] After spending that morning with Holt, Lincoln turned to much different work, officially receiving the new consuls from Prussia and Schaumburg-Lippe.

Confederate General John Hunt Morgan struck terror into the hearts of many Union men, including Captain Edward Fosha of the 91st Illinois, commanding the stockade at Elizabethtown, Kentucky. Fosha was so faint of heart he hung out a white flag and surrendered before he was attacked. At his trial, he said, "I had a report that a whole company had already been captured or killed. We could not stand Morgan's artillery." While Fosha was in arrest and awaiting trial, he went home to bury a dead child, which added the further charge of "breaking arrest." The court-martial board cashiered him, but recommended clemency. Brigadier General William K. Strong (a wealthy wool merchant in civilian life) gave his opinion: "It is doubtful whether the recommendation of the court [for clemency] should be complied with." The President disagreed with General Strong: "Sentence remitted. A. Lincoln Feb. 10, 1864."[40]

After a morning with Holt, Lincoln received the public, including eighteen men from Allegheny County, Pennsylvania, who wanted to change the Constitution. In the midst of the almost-endless demands for special favors and consideration, the smell of smoke entered Lincoln's office. Patterson McGee, Lincoln's coachman, who had recently been discharged for incompetence, had sent fire to the President's stables. Lincoln leaped over a hedge and pulled open the door, but it was too late to save the screaming animals. Tears streamed down the President's face as Tad's pony, two of Nicolay's horses, and two of the President's own burned to death.

Captain John Ganson of the 9th Ohio was untidy in his administrative affairs. He was absent without leave for a month while on recruiting duty; tried to resign without closing his clothing account; and was absent two months at Triune, Tennessee. He was cashiered, but the court urged clemency. General Rosecrans approved the cashiering, but Lincoln did not. An unknown hand wrote, "Finding and sentence disapproved. Feb. 10, 1864." The President's signature follows.[41]

Forty-five armed men under the command of Captain Milton Berry of the 5th Regiment of Enrolled Missouri Militia were guarding the Lamine Bridge in Missouri. When the Confederates attacked at midnight, most of the Union men were asleep. After a brief skirmish, the defenders surrendered and the Rebels burned both the bridge and the defender's blockhouse. Even though he had been warned an attack was imminent, Berry failed to post adequate pickets and was sound asleep when the attack came. In spite of this, he was acquitted. Brigadier General Egbert Brown disagreed with the acquittal and recommended "dishonorable dismissal." Holt prepared a detailed summary of the battle and concurred with General Brown. The President was of the same opinion: "Dismissed from service. A. Lincoln Aug. 16, 1864."[42]

Another border state case concerned Captain William Millar of the 23rd Missouri Infantry, which was camped at Harlem, Missouri. There, a slave woman and her four children came into his camp claiming their owner had abused them and asking for sanctuary. Millar arrested them, called for the owner and returned the five refugees, saying, "Here is your property." He also received a reward for returning the slaves. Millar was dismissed. Holt noted these offenses, as well as Millar's confiscation and sales of the property of fugitives and concluded that, "these are offenses which of themselves call loudly for this officer's dismissal." The final note says, "Sentence approved. A. Lincoln Feb. 15, 1864."[43] After a few early morning hours with Holt, Lincoln dealt with political patronage, selecting a new Collector of Customs for New York Harbor. In the evening, Mrs. Lincoln, Robert Todd Lincoln, and some of his Harvard friends, attended a tableau at Willard's Hotel, raising money for the Sanitary Commission.

Captain Emanuel Williamson of the 73rd Indiana was not a wise man. While traveling on a train with his company, he failed to maintain order, got drunk and surly, and proceeded to incite his men to mutiny by telling them to stack their arms and refuse duty. When arrested, he was very uncooperative (and likely still quite drunk). The court-martial acquitted him, which greatly inflamed the reviewing general. According to Judge Advocate General Holt, "The views of General [Orlando] Willcox are fully concurred in. The Court having failed to perform their imperative duty, it is recommended that Captain Williamson be dismissed by order of the President." At the bottom of the page is this brief note: "Capt. Williamson dismissed. A. Lincoln. Feb. 15, 1864."[44] (Willcox, Arizona bears the general's name, in remembrance of his role in the Indian Wars.)

Another Hoosier, Captain John A. Brewster of the 63rd Indiana, also had an uneasy relationship with the bottle. His "conduct unbecoming an officer and a gentleman" included being drunk while conducting a funeral at Sheperdsville, Kentucky. He also arranged to appear in the *Louisville Journal* as the commander of the regiment when, in fact, he commanded only *one* of the twelve companies of the 63rd Indiana. Brewster was cashiered, but the court recommended clemency. Brigadier General John Foster recommended dismissal and was seconded by Holt, who seems particularly disgusted by Brewster's conduct at the soldier's burial. The final note, in that strong, distinctive hand, reads "Recom. of Gen. Foster approved and ordered. A. Lincoln April 21, 1864."[45] Brewster was out.

Colonel Sanders was no Kentucky chicken. William Sanders of the 5th Kentucky Cavalry had been mortally wounded as he bravely lead his men into battle. At Nashville, Tennessee, in the spring of 1863, his officers were in a ferment over finding a replacement. Captain William Hoblitzel had been proposed for command. Captain John Glore (also spelled Glove) was one of the men who signed and circulated a petition which began: "Captain Hoblitzel. Sir. We have learned with deep regret that you are about to be appointed Lieutenant Colonel of this regiment and that it is your intention to accept same. We therefore earnestly request that you will decline the appointment, or, if commissioned, resign, inasmuch as your acceptance would be exceedingly repugnant to the undersigned officers. . ." Glore was tried for mutiny, convicted, and dismissed. When the papers arrived in Washington, Holt recommended disapproval of the sentence. The President wrote, "Sentence approved," then crossed out the second word. The final text reads, "Sentence disapproved. A. Lincoln Feb. 18, 1864."[46] That afternoon, when the court-martial reviews were finished, Lincoln wrote to the Governor of Massachusetts about a proposal to settle many freed black slaves in the Bay State. Back in Kentucky, Hoblitzel went on to command the regiment, and Glore remained a captain.

Captain Christopher Cheek had also signed the petition asking Hoblitzel to resign. Cheek, too, was convicted of mutiny and sentenced to be dismissed. After several exchanges of letters between Holt and Rosecrans, the case landed on the President's desk, where it received this brief note: "Sentence disapproved. A. Lincoln Feb. 15, 1864," thus confirming Holt's recommendation of remission.[47] Captain Asa Wells of the 5th Kentucky Cavalry was another signatory to the petition requesting that Hoblitzel resign. Wells, too, was found guilty and sentenced to dismissal. Again, Holt disagreed, and again, Lincoln wrote "Sentence disapproved."[48] Cheek rose to become the major of Hoblitzel's new command, while Wells stayed on as captain.

At the Battle of Stone's River on December 30, 1862, Captain William P. Egan of the 23rd Kentucky ran three miles away from his command and stayed away all day. He was tried for cowardice, convicted and sentenced to be dismissed. General Rosecrans approved the dismissal. Holt noted that the trial was technically invalid (the sentence had not been authenticated by the President of the Court), but concluded "the defect in the record should not allow the restoration of such an officer." Holt recommended dishonorable dismissal. The President's order itself, written in a different hand, is badly faded, but Lincoln's signature is bold and black. Captain Egan was finished as an officer.[49]

Captain David C. Stone of the 1st Kentucky Artillery was a strong Union man, did great service in raising troops in Kentucky and was a strict disciplinarian. The latter quality formed a background for his trial. His juniors in the 1st Kentucky Artillery charged that at Chaplin Hills, Kentucky, Stone hid in a position sheltered from enemy fire, that he was absent without leave for sixteen days in Louisville, and that he said of a lieutenant, "By God, that man is the damndest fool I ever saw." He was acquitted of the charge of cowardice and found guilty of the other charges and sentenced to be dismissed. When the case reached Lincoln, it contained twenty-five letters asking for remission. John Hay wrote, "Judge Advocate General, please examine and report to me on this case, with reference to my removing the disability now resting upon Capn. Stone." Lincoln signed the note on May 18, 1863. Holt's report and analysis was that the evidence did not justify the sentence, that Stone had been a patriotic and efficient officer, and that the root of the trouble was "the evident feeling of opposition and ill will entertained toward him by the subalterns of his late company." The President wrote, "The disability resting upon Captain D. C. Stone is hereby removed. A. Lincoln May 22, 1863."[50] Two thousand miles away at Vicksburg, Confederates repelled Grant's second direct attack. The almost-suicidal charge cost the Union 3,199 casualties and gained absolutely nothing.

Before the war, Captain John R. Breitenbach of the 106th Pennsylvania Infantry had been in business with his brother, who died in early 1863. The captain received a leave of absence to conclude their affairs; due to legal complexities and delays, he returned nine days late. On his return, he pleaded guilty to absence without leave, and was sentenced to be dismissed. The trial board recommended clemency because of previous "good character." This recommendation was endorsed by Brigadier John Gibbon, Major General Joseph Hooker, and the Judge Advocate General. The President agreed and wrote, "Sentence remitted. A. Lincoln July 18, 1863."[51]

In November 1862, another Keystone State officer, Charles Roescher of the 112th Pennsylvania, was convicted of making a false muster, of keeping the money paid to nonexistent soldiers, and of breaching his arrest for ten days. He was not only dishonorably dismissed, but was sentenced to a year of hard labor in the penitentiary. In December 1862, Holt noted no evidence that Roescher had profited from the false muster, thus "this portion of the sentence cannot be sustained." The wheels of justice turned slowly for six months, and in July, Holt observed that the Colonel Gibson who had ordered the court-martial had no authority to do so. Lincoln closed the matter on July 18, 1863: "Sentence as to dismissal approved, remainder disapproved."[52] Thus a quite pleased Roescher escaped a stretch in prison.

Captain Jacob Graeff of the 157th Pennsylvania was Officer of the Picket Guards at Union Mills, Virginia, and left his post for ten minutes. He was tried for abandoning his post and in spite of his plea that "I had no idea I had done wrong. I have only been in the army three months," was convicted and dismissed. The Court then petitioned for clemency, an idea endorsed by Brigadier General John Abercrombie, Major General Samuel Heintzelman, and Holt. This was an easy decision. Lincoln signed a note written in an unknown hand, which stated, "Approved. The sentence will be mitigated to a forfeiture of pay for the period of three months."[53]

A much more dramatic case was that of yet another Pennsylvanian, the drunken Captain F. M. Caldwell of the 157th Pennsylvania. At a Baltimore and Ohio Railroad depot, the inebriated captain seized a woman and said to her, "God damn you, you must sleep with me tonight." When her brother intervened, Caldwell pulled his pistol and shouted, "I'll blow your brains out." He was found guilty of conduct unbecoming an officer and a gentleman and dismissed. It would seem that in his sober moments he was better behaved, since both the court-martial board and many of the regimental officers sent petitions urging clemency and reinstatement. Holt noted that this outpouring of support "would fully justify the government in relieving him of the disability under which he labors and in authorizing the Governor of Pennsylvania to re-commission him." It would seem that Lincoln was unmoved by these suggestions, since his one recorded comment was "Application denied. A. Lincoln April 21, 1864." Lincoln had little sympathy for sex offenders. It was unusual for the President to endorse a harsher course of action than that urged by Holt, but this case contained all the elements that repelled Lincoln most.[54]

Captain George B. Chalmers of the 63rd Pennsylvania was assigned to be Regimental Officer of the Day. He refused this duty when he learned that the Brigade Officer of the Day on that occasion would be a lieutenant. He refused to do duty under someone of inferior rank, even under orders. Chalmers was court-martialed, found guilty of disobedience, and sentenced to make a written apology. The reviewer, Brigadier General David Birney, was inflamed by the triviality of the sentence and after further consideration, the court changed their sentence to dismissal. Major General George Meade approved the sentence with a recommendation of commutation to forfeiture of one month's pay, in view of Chalmer's previous good character. Hay wrote, "General Meade's recommendation approved. November 7, 1863," and Lincoln added his signature.[55] In the afternoon, politician Thurlow Weed dropped by for a chat; the two men discussed amnesty for Confederate leaders. Already, Lincoln's mind was turning toward reconciling a defeated Confederacy. With malice towards none. With charity for all; well, almost all.

Captain Conrad Eberhardt of the 1st Pennsylvania Cavalry illustrates the polyglot nature of the Union Army. Officers throughout the army were required to furnish their own rations. He and his lieutenants ate some of their meals from food designated for the enlisted men, and for this and related offenses, Eberhardt was convicted and dismissed. His defense was that he could not read English and depended on one of his lieutenants to translate the regulations for him. The court urged clemency on the basis of the captain knowing only German. Holt had some doubts about this excuse, but decided its validity "is left for the President to decide." Lincoln wrote, "Order of dismissal set aside and party to stand as honorably discharged."[56]

Joshua Reynolds, a captain of the 9th Pennsylvania Reserve Corps, was drunk at Rappahannock Station and again at Mountain Run, Virginia. He was cashiered, but applied for a pardon. In April 1864, Hay wrote and Lincoln signed, the following: "The Judge Advocate General will please give his opinion as to the propriety of the order desired." Holt's analysis showed that Reynolds had enlisted as a private and advanced to a captaincy based upon his "soldierly qualities," had a fine combat record, and no other offenses. Holt suggested that further proof be obtained that the captain was a valuable soldier. Four months passed. Proof arrived. The Chief Executive wrote: "Disability removed. A. Lincoln Aug. 17, 1864."[57]

With this first collection of fifty-seven officers, it is possible to begin an examination of Lincoln's legendary "compassion," defined here as a lessening or reduction of the severity of a sentence imposed upon a defendant. The traditional view is that Lincoln was tender-hearted, and that his decisions often went against the severe penalties recommended by courts of military justice and by his military advisors, including his judge advocate general.

That military justice might seem harsh to a man immersed in civil jurisprudence would not be surprising. Flogging, though officially pro-hibited, was still seen in the Union Army in 1861, and in the British Army was legal until 1881. As recently as 1740, it was still possible for a British soldier to be sentenced to more than 1,000 lashes, a punishment which usually resulted in a horrible death; Anglo-Saxon military justice has a rather recent history of severe brutality. Throughout the Civil War, Union miscreants could be, and often were, punished by branding with a hot iron. The most common location was the buttocks, though shoulder, hand, and face brandings were not rare. Death by firing squad was prescribed for desertion and sleeping on sentry duty, while rape and spying often led to the hangman's noose.

Whether Lincoln's inner moral compass was actuated more by genuine compassion, a wish to please his constituents, or by a natural reluctance to spill more blood than that already soaking the ground of America, it was inevitable that he, in the dual role of Supreme Civilian and Commander in Chief, would find himself torn between stern duty and the hopes of redemption through clemency.

As to measuring "compassion," the question immediately becomes a complex one. This is especially so since Lincoln might be in agreement or disagreement with the findings of the initial court-martial, or with the opinion of the officer authorizing the court-martial, or with the opinion of the general commanding the department, or with the judge advocate general (usually Holt), or with politicians who interjected themselves into the process, or with friends, comrades and family of the convicted man, or any combination of these possible interested parties.

Table One summarizes the answers to these questions, so far as they pertain to the generals, colonels, majors, and captains in our study. While Lincoln disagreed with the court-martial board in fifty-nine percent (59%) of the cases, he was by no means in conflict with the military justice system.

Opinion Maker	Lincoln Agrees	Lincoln Disagrees	% Agreement
Trial Verdict	23	33	41
Authorizing Officer	3	3	50
Departmental Commander	24	6	80
Judge Advocate General	41	4	91
Interested Politicians	2	1	66
Friends, Family & Comrades	1	0	100

In many of the cases, the lower levels of review had already suggested clemency, and Holt, his own judge advocate general, in spite of his reputation for harshness, often saw flaws in procedure or insufficient evidence to sustain a conviction. As will be seen in the aforementioned table, Lincoln and Holt were in agreement ninety-one percent (91%) of the time. For this group of court-martialed officers, at least, there is no strong tendency for Lincoln to oppose the weight of military justice opinion. Where there seemed any visible virtue in the defendant, the advisability of remission had already been pointed out by at least one prior reviewer before the case reached Lincoln's eyes. The President's final decisions in these cases seem more the endorsement of a prevailing opinion rather than a manifestation of a sentiment which could be labeled "compassion."

What appears most evident is that Lincoln considered each case on its own merits, rather than imposing any doctrinaire or idiosyncratic point of view. Here, as elsewhere, Lincoln was his own man.

4

Lieutenants, Chaplains, and Surgeons

The Civil War was, in some ways, the first modern war, both in scope and in technology, yet it was also the last of the ancient wars in its reliance on obsolete concepts—not only in tactics and strategy, but also in such mundane matters as personnel records. In brief, much of the time the Union army did not know where its men were or what they were supposed to be doing. The case of First Lieutenant John A. Gordon of the 85th Pennsylvania, who was tried and convicted for being absent without leave for five months, illustrates this problem.[1]

He had been stationed at Suffolk, Virginia, and failed to join his regiment in South Carolina. At the former place, he was in charge of the ambulance train of General John Peck's command, and responsible for 140 horses, 50 ambulances and 90 sets of harness. He was ordered to stay at Suffolk, supervising the ambulances, until his replacement could be found. When Gordon was free to join his regiment, he was court-martialed upon arrival, convicted, and dismissed. Holt recommended remission; Nicolay wrote, "Sentence disapproved, Feby. 10, 1864," which is followed by "A. Lincoln."

Several Pennsylvania officers ran afoul of military protocol. First Lieutenant Charles W. Mackey of the 10th Pennsylvania Cavalry, for example, left his company on December 13, 1862, when about to engage Lee's army at Fredericksburg. He was convicted of "misbehavior before the enemy" and dishonorably dismissed. General Heintzelman approved the sentence. Holt said, "The proof fully sustains the findings," and recommended approval. Nicolay wrote, "Sentence approved, as recommended by the Judge Advocate General." Lincoln signed the order.[2]

John H. Borden, a First Lieutenant with the 83rd Pennsylvania, left Falmouth, Virginia, on a leave of absence and returned ten days after it had expired. He was convicted of absence without leave and dismissed. General Hooker approved the proceedings, but felt the sentence too severe. He recommended mitigation to one month without pay. Holt gave no opinion. Beneath Nicolay's "Sentence commuted to forfeiture of pay for one month," is the President's familiar signature.[3]

Another First Lieutenant, Thomas Morton of the 81st Pennsylvania, refused picket duty at Salem, Virginia. He was convicted of disobedience and dismissed. The court then petitioned for mitigation. Major General Darius Couch suggested forfeiture of pay for three months, Holt agreed, and Lincoln wrote, "Sentence of dismissal commuted to loss of pay as above recommended. May 11, 1863. A. Lincoln." After a difficult morning of court-martial reviews, Lincoln was faced with cabinet problems: the ever-sensitive Salmon P. Chase, Secretary of the Treasury, submitted his resignation.[4]

First Lieutenant George W. O'Malley of the 115th Pennsylvania not only failed to be a gentleman, but committed the sort of crime that Lincoln rarely forgave. At Potomac Creek, Virginia, a "Mrs. Whippey" had come to see her wounded son, and Lieutenant O'Malley was asked to act as her escort at the camp. That evening, he came to her bed, lay on top of her and said, "What my wife doesn't know won't hurt her," and tried to have "carnal connexion" with her. At his trial, O'Malley gave this explanation, "I may have slipped and fallen on her, while I was covering her with a quilt, but I laid on her at most for two minutes." He received a dishonorable discharge and six years of hard labor at the District of Columbia Penitentiary. Hooker approved the sentence and Holt opined, "The crime is clear and the sentence is not in conflict with the Virginia Code in such cases and no reasons are apparent why the penalty pronounced should not be enforced." This was followed by "Sentence approved. A. Lincoln July 18, 1863."[5] That same afternoon, Colonel Robert Gould Shaw's blood soaked into the beach sand in front of Battery Wagner, South Carolina, the aftermath of a heroic charge which proved both the bravery of colored troops and the futile stupidity of frontal assault.

First Lieutenant John O'Neil of the 55th Pennsylvania had been confined to his tent by his bad-tempered commander, Colonel Richard White (who was later court-martialled himself for insolence to General Saxton). O'Neil had sauntered a mere fifteen feet from his tent when he was apprehended and charged with breach of arrest, convicted, and cashiered. The court urged remission, as did Brigadier General John Brannan. Holt saw a clear pattern of persecution by Colonel White: "It is proved that Colonel White had been in the habit of arresting his officers at the rate of two each day during a period of about two months." Not surprisingly, Holt agreed with the court and with General Brannan and recommended remission. Perhaps Lincoln sighed with impatience as he signed the following note by Nicolay, "Sentence of the prisoner remitted in accordance with the recommendation of the Judge Advocate General."[6]

Yet another first lieutenant, this one an Irishman named Septemo Ferguson of the 76th Pennsylvania, had imbibed one too many drinks at Hilton Head, South Carolina, when he was ordered to be Officer of the Guard. Septemo refused this duty and was insolent toward Lieutenant Colonel John W. Hicks. He was found guilty and dismissed, in spite of several character witnesses who described Ferguson as "one of the most industrious and faithful officers in the regiment." The court urged remission, as did Brigadier General Quincy Gillmore. Holt reluctantly recommended a forfeiture of three months pay instead of dismissal, adding "This suggestion is based wholly on the recommendations of the court and the commanding general, who from their opportunities of judging are best informed as to the necessities of the case." If Lincoln had doubts, they are not evident in his note: "Judge Advocate General's recom. approved. A. Lincoln Feb. 9, 1864." Ferguson went back to duty.[7]

Frank B. Smith, our final Pennsylvania first lieutenant, was a member of the elegantly-named Lafayette Cavalry. However, he was of little use to the Union. He announced that he was a Southern sympathizer, that he was opposed to emancipation, and that he planned to resign and join the Confederate army at Winchester, Virginia. His letter of resignation, which the court termed "insolent," included this sentiment: "I do not feel disposed to immolate myself for the gratification of others." He was dismissed on grounds of disloyalty and conduct prejudicial to military discipline. Holt recommended dishonorable dismissal. Lincoln wrote, "Lieut. Frank B. Smith is hereby dismissed the service. A. Lincoln April 26, 1864," but omitted the "dishonorable."[8] Hundreds of miles southwest in Louisiana, Union gunboats operating in conjunction with Major General Nathaniel Banks' luckless Red River expedition were trapped by low water and peppered by Confederate sharpshooters. Only the brilliance of a lowly engineer saved the fleet from capture.

In the spring of 1863, the 165th New York was stationed at New Orleans, Louisiana. There was bad blood between Lieutenant Colonel Abel Smith and First Lieutenant Edward G. Hoffman, who was under arrest. Hoffman obtained permission to take a bath, but did not mention that he planned to do so at the St. Charles Hotel, which was also the headquarters of the commanding general, Nathaniel Banks. Hoffman planned to see Banks and to prefer charges against his colonel. Hoffman's trial was filled with contradictory testimony. Although the court found him guilty of conduct unbecoming an officer and a gentleman—which carries automatic dismissal—it recommended clemency. General Banks was opposed to such clemency and referred the case to the President. Holt noted Hoffman's recent gallantry in the fighting at Port Hudson and recommended remission. Hay wrote, "The report of the Judge Advocate General is approved. Let the sentences of Lieutenants Hoffman and Vance be remitted." Lincoln signed.[9]

The "Lieutenant Vance" just mentioned was W. Henry Vance of the 165th New York. He had refused to drill his company while at New Orleans, saying that he was sick, yet he would not see the surgeon for a certificate. When under arrest at the Levee Steam Press, he left without permission. He was cashiered, but the court petitioned for clemency. Again, General Banks was opposed to clemency, and sent the case east, where it arrived five months later. In the interim, Vance was wounded in a charge against Port Hudson. Holt recommended remission as described above, and Lincoln signed.[10]

Another New York lieutenant in hot water was Eleazer Mulholland of the 98th New York. Mulholland, as it turned out, was his own worst

When Captain Edward G. Hoffman of the 165th New York was a lieutenant, an unauthorized bath at New Orleans' St. Charles Hotel nearly cost him his commission.

USAMHI

enemy. In North Carolina, he was drunk on the steamer *Cahawba*. When ordered to march off the ship with his company, he announced, "Jesus Christ, you aren't man enough to make me." On the steamer *United States* Mulholland had his Negro servant steal six bottles of beer from General Charles Heckman. The lieutenant was cashiered. Holt said, "No palliating circumstances are shown." Lincoln agreed, and signed a note which said simply, "Approved."[11]

A fondness for alcohol seems also to have been the bane of First Lieutenant John T. Shepard of the 90th New York, who was accused of being drunk on duty at Lighthouse Barracks, Key West, Florida. After much contradictory testimony, he was sentenced to be cashiered, with the court recommending remission. Colonel Good [first name and regiment unknown], who ordered the trial, disagreed with remission, while General Banks approved of it. Holt noted the contradictory testimony and supported Banks. The President wrote: "Sentence remitted. A. Lincoln Feb. 15, 1864."[12]

Adelbert Eddy, a first lieutenant of the 4th New York Artillery, was convicted of being absent without leave at Fort Ethan Allen, Virginia, and dismissed, in spite of medical testimony that he had been sent away to escape the air of the camp. Brigadier General John Abercrombie recommended commutation to two months suspension from rank and pay. Major General Heintzelman agreed, and sent the case to Washington, where it seems to have come directly to the President, who wrote, "Judge Advocate General please examine and report upon this case. A. Lincoln." Justice could move more swiftly in 1863 than today. The following day, the President wrote again: "Sentence commuted to suspension of two months rank and pay, to commence March 30th, 1863. A. Lincoln May 12, 1863."[13] As Lincoln was writing Eddy's fate, the Battle of Raymond, Mississippi, was raging as U.S. Grant moved inexorably on Vicksburg.

"I hold no commission under this damned Lincoln nigger government. . .I hold my commission from Governor Seymour, who is a gentleman," ranted Lieutenant Edward H. Underhill of the 1st New York Artillery. Was Lincoln's legendary patience sufficient to overlook such words? The trial board sentenced Underhill to two months suspension from rank and a fine of three months pay. General Couch thought this insufficient and requested a reconsideration. This time Underhill was dismissed. Couch approved, but suggested mitigation to a forfeiture of six months pay, because the words were uttered at a "time of great political excitement." Holt was less forgiving, noting that "there are many men. . .as well qualified. . .whose hearts are in the cause for which they are called upon to fight, and whose convictions and sympathies are so strong. . .that no language so comforting to its enemies and so damaging to the interests of the service. . .can be drawn out of them at times of 'great political excitement.'" Holt concluded with a recommendation for dismissal. The sorely-tried President again came down on the side of forgiveness: "Recom. of Gen Couch approved and ordered. A. Lincoln April 14, 1864." (With the advantage of hindsight, we now know that Lincoln's forgiveness was misplaced; the next year Underhill was sent to prison for a new crime—murder.)[14]

The next three cases were lieutenants from Regular Army regiments. First Lieutenant Robert H. Porter of the 14th U. S. Infantry did not report for duty as ordered and lied on a report. The court dismissed him and stated that the evidence clearly justified dismissal, but recommended clemency because brother officers had defended Porter's "integrity." Brigadier General Romeyn Ayres, who ordered the court martial, endorsed the recommendation. General Meade suggested commutation to forfeiture of six months pay. Holt, however, would have none of this clemency notion and stated, "The petition of the court clearly states that the evidence adduced fully justifies the conclusion of *criminal* intent [Holt's emphasis]. It is for the President to decide whether the interest of the service permits such officers to be retained in the army, when without a shadow of an excuse they have disgraced their position and dishonored themselves." It would seem that Lincoln had a higher tolerance for moral lepers than did Holt, since he wrote, "Recom. of Gen. Meade approved and ordered. April 27th, 1864. A. Lincoln"[15]

The pressure for political favors never ceased. After reviewing that day's thirty-six court-martial cases, Lincoln was confronted by twice-wounded Brigadier General Solomon Meredith, commander of the Iron Brigade. One of Meredith's sons has been dismissed from the army, and the general wanted him reinstated. It is but yet another example of the influential man who wants iron discipline—except for his boy.

First Lieutenant James Semple of the 15th U. S. Infantry was a man who should have avoided alcohol. While drunk at Chattanooga, the lieutenant went to the office of the Adjutant General and created such a scene and was so belligerent that he had to be carried to jail, where he was confined until sober. After his conviction of "conduct prejudicial," he was suspended from rank and pay for two years and removed from the promotion list for the same period. United States Senator from Ohio, John Sherman, (brother of William T. Sherman) wrote in support of remission. Holt strongly recommended the opposite. The President made his own decision, perhaps based upon Semple's good service at Shiloh, Corinth, Murfreesboro, Bowling Green, and Perryville: "But one act of intoxication appearing, and in view of his general good behavior and valuable services, the sentence of Lieut. Semple is rescinded [here Lincoln crossed out 'rescinded'] remitted. A. Lincoln July 9, 1864."[16] While the President was looking out for Semple's fate, Jubal Early's Confederate army was knocking at the gates of Washington.

First Lieutenant George Crossman of the 10th U. S. Infantry was a man with a short fuse. While stationed at the entrance of New York Harbor, he applied to Captain Clinton for permission to go to nearby Fort Hamilton for his supper. The captain approved, but asked him to return "within a reasonable time." The lieutenant replied that he had never been late. The captain shook his finger at Crossman and replied, "Yes, you have." Crossman then punched his captain in the nose and remarked, "I will allow no man to shake his fist in my face." Crossman was arrested, tried, convicted, and dismissed, but the court petitioned for mitigation, noting prior good service in the field. Brigadier General Edward Canby (of New Mexico fame) recommended suspension from rank and pay for two months, and Major General John Dix agreed. Holt expressed no opinion. Lincoln wrote, "Recommendation of Gen. Canby approved. Nov. 7, 1863."[17]

A first lieutenant of the 35th Missouri, with the distinguished name of Effingham T. Hyatt, was late with his reports, and when he did send them it was by a drunken orderly, which much delayed their delivery. Hyatt was even drunker and less restrained than his orderly. Aboard the steamboat *Rocket*, he not only denounced the President of the United States as a "damned abolitionist," and announced to his audience that

General George McClellan should have marched on Washington and seized the government, but Hyatt then stripped himself naked and danced on the deck of the ship, accompanying himself by singing bawdy songs. The court that convicted him was "inoperative" since the Judge Advocate had not been sworn. Major General U.S. Grant forwarded the case to Washington, D.C. Holt recommended dishonorable dismissal by direct order, since the trial was technically invalid. The final note reads: "Recom. of Judge Advocate General approved. A. Lincoln Feb. 15, 1864." Hyatt must have anticipated such an outcome: he resigned October 8, 1863.[18]

John Acker, a first lieutenant with the 24th Ohio, was escorting a group of Confederate prisoners from Louisville, Kentucky, to the prison at Johnson's Island, Ohio. Amazingly, while en route, he allowed them to enter saloons and drink without supervision. (Even more amazing is their failure to escape.) Acker was sentenced to be dismissed, but was recommended for mitigation because "he had been repeatedly and severely wounded while in the performance of efficient service." General Burnside recommended commutation to a fine of three months pay. Holt opined that Acker's offense "was a grave one and wholly without excuse," and that three months pay was an inadequate punishment. Lincoln signed the following notation by Nicolay: "Recommendation of Gen. Burnside approved in this case, Feb. 9, 1864." The much-wounded and overly hospitable Acker returned to duty.[19]

First Lieutenant Thomas Barber of the 10th Kentucky Cavalry had an imperfect grasp of military duty. When his company marched off to war from Crab Orchard, Kentucky, he persuaded several enlisted men to remain with him rather than follow their comrades. When asked by a "superior officer" to explain, he said, "Go to hell, God damn you, it's none of your business." He was convicted and dishonorably discharged. No one suggested remission. Beneath Nicolay's "Sentence approved," is the familiar "A. Lincoln."[20]

First Lieutenant John L. Walters was another Kentucky man not attracted to military responsibility. During his service with the 3rd Kentucky Cavalry, he twice evaded duty as Officer of the Pickets by rising before reveille and concealing himself. On the march to Clarksville, Tennessee, when ordered under arrest, he drew both his pistols and threatened to kill his arrestors. The trial which convicted him made so many procedural errors it was declared invalid. General Burnside noted the defects and suggested direct dismissal by the President. Holt agreed. The case ends with "Recom. of Gen. Burnside approved and ordered. A. Lincoln Feb. 18, 1864." Walters was out.[21]

Two Hoosier first lieutenants appear in this study. T. F. Dodd of the 73rd Indiana left the march at Bardstown, Kentucky, without permission. When queried about the incident, he claimed he was with a different regiment. He was dismissed, but remission was recommended by General William Rosecrans. Holt agreed and so did Lincoln, who signed an order which read, "Approved but sentence awarded by the court is remitted."[22]

James A. Miller of the 7th Indiana, serving at Rappahannock Station, Virginia, used coarse language to his captain and also to his lieutenant colonel. He was dismissed but, once again, there was a recommendation for remission based on provocations received by Miller. General Meade reviewed the case and recommended total remission. Lincoln signed the following order, which appears in Nicolay's hand: "The sentence of First Lt. and Ajt. James A. Miller, 7th Indiana Volunteers is hereby remitted."[23]

On New Years Eve, 1862 at Stone's River, Tennessee, First Lieutenant Hugh Norvell of the 3rd Eastern Tennessee Regiment was with the picket guard in the front line. He left and returned twenty-one days later. He said he was sick; the court decided that he had run away. His conviction was approved by General Rosecrans but was "inoperative" due to procedural flaws. Holt said, "Offenses of this nature should not go unpunished." Nicolay wrote, "Let Lieutenant Norvell be dishonorably dismissed the service to take effect January 24, 1863 as per order of Gen. Rosecrans." Once again appears "A. Lincoln."[24]

At Murfreesboro, Tennessee, First Lieutenant Henry Wright of the 25th Illinois got drunk. While not all witnesses agreed, several remembered that he had called Lieutenant Colonel James McClelland "a damned liar and a Goddamned thief." When put in arrest, Lieutenant Wright left his own tent and went to McClelland's tent, where he made a pest of himself with the usual surly mutterings of an unpleasant drunk. He was convicted of conduct unbecoming an officer and a gentleman and dismissed. The court saw mitigating factors and urged remission. General Rosecrans agreed, and Holt raised no objection. "Sentence remitted. A. Lincoln Nov. 7, 1863," ended the matter.[25]

An Illinoisian with the unique name of Hallet Spooner served as a first lieutenant with the 131st Illinois Infantry. Spooner was upset that his men had not been paid. At Fort Pickering, near Memphis, Tennessee, his method of encouraging his men was ill-chosen: "Boys, stack your arms and refuse duty. You might have to fight for what is right for you, but the sooner you refuse duty the sooner you will be paid." After his conviction for inciting mutiny, the sentence of dismissal was approved by General U.S. Grant. When the record reached Washington nine months later, Holt noted that the trial had fatal defects, that the sentence was invalid, and he recommended dismissal by direct order of the President. "Recom. of J.A.G. approved and ordered. A. Lincoln Feb. 15, 1864."[26]

Holt's insistence on the letter of the law is seen in the case of First Lieutenant George Hardy of the 2nd Delaware Infantry. He was convicted of overstaying a leave of absence and with denying that he was in the army when arrested. He was dismissed. The part about being absent without leave was caused by transportation delays. The second charge was based on the written affidavit of a Lieutenant Homer, who did not testify. Holt pointed out that "the record does not show that the accused waived his right to object to its reception. The court finding him guilty upon the strength of this evidence, it must be held that the proceeding was fatally irregular and the sentence is inoperative. The accused had no counsel, and was evidently ignorant of his right to object to the reception of the affidavit by the court. Such cases forcibly illustrate the necessity of strictly adhering to the rules against the admission of ex parte testimony." The President agreed. "Sentence disapproved. A. Lincoln July 18, 1863." A few such cases would furrow the brow of most men; that day, however, Lincoln and Holt met for six hours.[27]

First Lieutenant H. N. Hayes, Quartermaster of the 17th Connecticut, sold some of the food intended for his regiment. After a prolonged trial, he was convicted and dismissed. The court, sympathizing with the administrative difficulties faced by the lieutenant, recommended remission of the dismissal but retention of the order that he reimburse the government. The President agreed: "The above sentence of 1st Lieutenant H. N. Hayes is approved, except the dismissal from service, which is remitted. A. Lincoln March 28, 1863."[28]

At Morgan's Bend, Louisiana, First Lieutenant Phineas Clawson of the 20th Wisconsin allowed his men on picket duty to put down their guns and take off their cartridge belts while having supper. He was dismissed, but the court recommended remission because of ignorance of his duties. Major General Napoleon Dana was not impressed, and noted that accepting such an excuse "would be to suppose that Lieutenant Clawson was utterly ignorant of the duties of a commissioned officer or even those of a private on guard." While Dana opposed full remission, he did suggest mitigation to one month's pay. General Banks concurred. Holt noted Clawson's excuse that other officers had done the same, but pointed out that Clawson was being tried for his own acts, not those of others. Beyond this, Holt made no recommendation. Lincoln wrote, "Gen. Dana's recom. approved. Feb. 9, 1864." Clawson lost a month's pay, but kept his commission.[29]

The case of First Lieutenant Richard Cushman of the 14th Massachusetts Heavy Artillery contains little reason for evoking sympathy toward the defendant. At Fort Runyan, Virginia, a private died. Cushman was ordered to send home the man's valuables, in this case $14.88 in cash. Fifteen months later, the brother of the dead man wrote a letter of inquiry, at which point Cushman "discovered" that he still had the money. For this, and for gambling with the enlisted men, he was dismissed. Holt described the crime as "a heinous one," and recommended confirmation of the sentence. "Sentence approved. A. Lincoln July 18, 1863."[30]

Second Lieutenant Joseph B. Grice of the 5th New York Cavalry was charged with three offenses, each of them involving alcohol. He was absent without leave four days in Washington, D.C., drunk. At Fairfax Court House, Virginia, he was so drunk on New Years Eve, 1862, that he fell under his horse. At Chantilly, Virginia, he "disgraced himself" through intoxication. He was dismissed. Holt found "marked irregularities" in the proceedings and concluded that the testimony did not support the verdict. Lincoln agreed with Holt; a scribe wrote "Disapproved," and the President added his signature.[31]

August Knittle, a second lieutenant with the 174th New York was ill-tempered at Baton Rouge, Louisiana, and called a senior lieutenant "a coward and a scoundrel." He was convicted of conduct prejudicial to good order and dismissed. The court urged remission based on Knittle's combat record. General Banks agreed with remission and sent the record on to Holt, who wrote, "His offense was reprehensible to some extent, but under the circumstances as shown by the proof, it is not believed that the interest of the service would be promoted by his dismissal. General Banks is fully concurred in." The next line, "Sentence remitted. A. Lincoln April 26, 1864," returned Knittle to duty.[32] That same day, Federal Colonel Benjamin Grierson and his cavalrymen rode almost unopposed through Mississippi, demonstrating that the very heart of the Confederacy could not be defended.

A second lieutenant of the 71st New York, James W. Hoey, seems less virtuous. At Falmouth, Virginia, he was drunk at morning drill. He went absent without leave twice, apparently to avoid battle. When ordered before a Board of Examination, he refused once and when he finally appeared before the Board, he was drunk. While the court acquitted him, General Hooker was of a different opinion and recommended dishonorable discharge, noting that Hoey had disappeared and was presumably a deserter. Holt agreed with Hooker. Nicolay wrote, "Let Lieutenant Hoey be dishonorably dismissed in accordance with the recommendation of the Judge Advocate General," and the President added his usual signature.[33]

At Beverly Ford, Virginia, Second Lieutenant John McKinley was drunk and incoherent in the tent of "a brother officer." When told to be quiet and go to his own tent, McKinley replied, "God damn you, go to hell." He was convicted and dismissed. General Meade approved the findings but recommended commutation to the loss of four months pay. Holt analyzed the technical errors in framing the charges, but gave no opinion on sentencing. At the Executive Mansion, Nicolay wrote, "Recommendation of Gen. Meade approved and ordered." With the addition of "A. Lincoln," McKinley was returned to duty.[34]

Second Lieutenant George D. Wiseburn, of the 133rd New York, did not support the administration's political goals. At Baton Rouge, Louisiana, he submitted his resignation, stating, "I humbly beg to decline serving any longer in the Volunteer Army of the United States. The Executive has seen proper to make. . .the Emancipation of the Negro slaves and He has seen fit by his recent Proclamation to say that all colored persons of good condition will be received into the armed service. . .thus making the Negro my equal." Wiseburn was convicted of conduct prejudicial to good order and military discipline, and sentenced to be reprimanded and sent for two years of duty on Ship Island, off the coast of Mississippi. General Banks disagreed and recommended dismissal. Holt agreed with Banks. Lincoln's signature appears beneath Hay's notation: "Recommendation of Gen. Banks approved. Nov. 7, 1863."[35]

Folly Island, South Carolina, was an appropriately-named venue for the indiscretions of Second Lieutenant Francois Wallenus of the New York Independent Battery. After several hours of heavy drinking with the enlisted men (itself a crime), who consumed whisky provided by the Wallenus (another crime), he caught hold of a soldier's wife, put his hand under her dress and told the enlisted men that if they would hold her down, he would "force her." At the trial, she testified that his actual words were, "too indecent even to tell my husband." For reasons unclear the court found him not guilty. General Israel Vogdes, a former mathematics professor and the architect of the Folly Island fortifications, disapproved the acquittal, as did Holt, who described the court as "highly culpable for their dereliction of duty." The Chief Executive, who rarely tolerated sexual crime, wrote, "This officer is dishonorably dismissed. Feb. 15, 1864. A. Lincoln."[36]

At Big Springs, Tennessee, Second Lieutenant Joseph Pearson of the 11th Ohio went on a big drunk. Unfortunately, it was at dress parade. Such disgraceful behavior before his company caused the court to cashier him. However, because of his previous "good character and bravery in action," they also petitioned for remission. Major General George Thomas agreed with remission. Holt noted that there was no testimony about Pearson's good character, but conceded that "the court was doubtless well advised concerning his former character." The President concluded the matter: "Recom. of Gen. Thomas approved and ordered. A. Lincoln April 27, 1864." Lieutenant Pearson kept his job.[37]

Second Lieutenant Alfred Conklin of the 11th Ohio and the men under his command were guarding some prisoners on the march from Carthage, Tennessee to Rome, Tennessee. No doubt the Punic allusions evaded Conklin's attention, since the unruly behavior of his men at the bridge over the Cumberland River allowed many of the prisoners to escape. Conklin was convicted of disobedience, since he had been ordered to prevent such an escape. General Rosecrans urged remittal based on the lieutenant's good character, and Holt, in his review, commended Conklin's efforts to control his men. The final step toward restoration was, "Sentence remitted. A. Lincoln Nov. 7, 1863."[38]

The uncertainties of mid-Victorian transport are seen in the story of Second Lieutenant Ephraim Leach of the 5th Vermont. His regiment was on a steamboat in New York Harbor. There was no officer's mess, and Leach went ashore for breakfast; the boat left for Washington, D.C. He immediately went to the quartermaster's office in New York City, who refused transportation. After several hours he somehow obtained sufficient funds to buy a private ticket. He knew that his regiment was ordered to Culpeper, Virginia, and he was there waiting for them when his comrades arrived. In spite of his efforts, which brought him to Culpeper ahead of his regiment, he was cashiered for being absent without leave. To this sentence, the court added a plea of clemency. General Meade agreed, and suggested the loss of three months pay as an appropriate penalty. Holt took no position, but Lincoln did. Under Nicolay's "General Meade's recommendation approved," appears the President's signature.[39]

Under the stresses of war, some young men mature rapidly. Not Charles H. Smith, a second lieutenant with the 11th Vermont. He pled guilty to charges that he gambled with enlisted men, cheated a soldier by substituting a cheap watch for a good one, went absent without leave, lied about his absence, and allowed a prisoner to escape. His defense was unusual: "I am young and inexperienced. I thought I was in an easy situation, being away from home. I thought it would be like at school, where if you disobeyed and were not found out, it was all right. The men I gambled with were former schoolmates. I didn't realize my situation until I was arrested." He was sentenced to dishonorable dismissal. General Heintzelman, Judge Advocate General Holt, and the President were of the same opinion. "Sentence approved. A. Lincoln July 18, 1863."[40]

Second Lieutenant John D. Williams of the 9th Michigan was of similar mind. Williams played cards with enlisted men, stole a book from the mail, and said of Captain Samuel Wiggins, "I would have knocked the God damned son of a bitches head off." Williams was dismissed. General Rosecrans recommended commutation to loss of three months of pay. Holt passed the decision on to the Chief Executive, who wrote, "Recommendation of Gen. Rosecrans approved. A. Lincoln Nov. 7, 1863."[41] Two nights later, Lincoln attended the theater and watched actor John Wilkes Booth perform in *The Marble Heart*.

Stafford Court House, Virginia, was the scene of the downfall of Second Lieutenant William Colerick of the 1st Michigan Cavalry. There, he caroused drunkenly with enlisted men, was absent without leave for four days, cursed his superiors, and left while under arrest. The court dismissed him, but petitioned for clemency. Hooker passed the decision on to Lincoln, who had no sympathy with the accused and wrote, "Sentence approved. A. Lincoln June 24, 1863."[42]

Second Lieutenant Edward Lohmann of the 24th Illinois was another officer who should have avoided whisky. In an inebriated state, he entered the enlisted men's quarters and denounced them as "a God damned worthless lousey set of men," and then spoke in a "vulgar and contemptuous manner" of the Federal government, its printed currency, and its officers. He was cashiered. General Rosecrans, "in consideration of previous good character," recommended commuting the sentence to loss of a month's pay. Holt took violent exception: "An officer who carouses with the enlisted men, who in low, profane and vulgar language denounces the government and expresses his desire to get out of the service. . .is clearly unworthy of a commission." Holt noted the remarks of General Lovell Rousseau, who suggested that "this army is not the proper place for him. He should be with Jeff Davis." Holt concluded, "It is for the President to decide whether an officer who under any circumstances can so forget or violate his duty, as the accused is proved to have done, should remain in the service."

The President did decide. He gave Lohman another chance, with this decision: "Recom. of Gen. Rosecrans approved and ordered. A.

Lincoln April 21, 1864." Here, Lincoln's optimism bore fruit; Lohmann served another year and was mustered out at the end his regiment's enlistment. The President reviewed 72 court-martials that April day, and made 72 decisions that would affect the defendants the rest of their lives.[43]

Second Lieutenant James McCool of the 7th Illinois Cavalry was tried on three charges: calling Colonel Edward Prince a "son of a bitch," going into Memphis without permission, and breaching the limits of his arrest. He was acquitted of the first two charges. The third consisted of going to the hospital 150 yards away from his tent for medicine, an errand of under thirty minutes. He was cashiered, but recommended for clemency. Major General William T. Sherman agreed with clemency. Holt endorsed Sherman's position. The President had only to add "Sentence remitted. A. Lincoln Aug. 17, 1864," and McCool's name was cleared.[44]

Second Lieutenant James Clark had been commended by General Edwin Sumner for bravery at the Battle of Antietam. Richard Smith, the colonel of the 71st Pennsylvania, said, "There is no better officer in my regiment." These sentiments were what saved the lieutenant when he was convicted of drunkenness on duty. The sentence of dismissal was tempered by the court with the suggestion of mercy. The often-wounded General Alexander Webb recommended that a loss of two months salary would be sufficient punishment. General Meade withheld his opinion, citing the 45th Article of War, and passed the case on to the President. Holt also expressed no opinion. Lincoln placed his signature over this note by Hay, "Commuted as recommended by Genl. Webb. Nov. 7, 1863."[45]

William J. Briggs, a second lieutenant of the 75th Pennsylvania, was convicted of being drunk on duty. The court cashiered him, but recommended remittal because of Lieutenant Briggs' "high honor, especially in the battle of Bull Run." When the case reached the President's desk, he wrote, "The above sentence of Lieut. Briggs is mitigated so that in lieu of cashiering, he be reprimanded by the colonel of his regiment in the presence of the regiment. A. Lincoln Mar. 28, 1863."[46]

Second Lieutenant William F. Bragg, of the 24th Massachussetts was yet another officer who was drunk at dress parade. He, too, was cashiered and his court also recommended commutation. Holt's apparent reluctance may be seen in this double negative: "The recommendations of the court and of his commanding general are not without weight in his favor and it is for the President to decree. . ." The final word was, "Sentence commuted to loss of pay for three months. A. Lincoln April 14, 1864."[47] Not far from Washington, Generals Grant and Meade were preparing the Army of the Potomac to face Robert E. Lee. More than a thousand miles west, a Union expedition was making its way from Colorado Territory to Beaver Creek, Kansas.

James Barker, a second lieutenant in the 23rd Kentucky, left his regiment at Glasgow, Kentucky, and was gone four months. He said that he had been sick, but had little medical testimony to offer. General Rosecrans disagreed with the court's conviction and dismissal, and suggested six months confinement within the limits of the regimental camp. Holt disagreed with Rosecrans and recommended dismissal. At first, Lincoln wrote, "Gen. Rosecrans' recommendation approved. Feb. 9, 1864," but six days later, having apparently received further information, he wrote again: "And now full pardon is granted. A. Lincoln."[48]

A Minnesota officer, high on the hills above Harpers Ferry, Virginia, seemed to have stretched the limits of the army's tolerance. Second Lieutenant John A. Jones of the 1st Minnesota, on duty at Bolivar Heights, Virginia, not only released five prisoners without authority, but cursed and abused his superiors. He was dismissed. Three court members suggested mitigation, while the others did not. Holt said, "I see no grounds for this recommendation [of mitigation] and cannot concur in it." Nicolay's, "Sentence approved" is followed by the familiar "A. Lincoln," dated May 20, 1863.[49] The sentence may have saved Jones' life. Just a few weeks later at the Battle of Gettysburg on July 2, the 1st Minnesota was hurled headlong into a brigade of assaulting Alabamians—and suffered more than 82% casualties in but a handful of minutes.

Another Minnesotan, James K. Rochester of the 2nd Minnesota Infantry, chose a poor time to be drunk—when sitting on a court-martial board with a dozen other officers. It mandatory that an officer drunk on duty be cashiered, and he was. However, when sober he had made such a good impression that the court petitioned for remission. Others joined in this request. The Brigade Commander testified that when Rochester was sober, his character was beyond reproach and that "no officer could attend to his duties more strictly." The colonel of the 2nd Minnesota described Rochester as an excellent officer, "except as to his occasional tendency to indulge in drink." His major noted that Rochester had been in command of his company (a position usually held by a captain) and that Rochester's company was the "best-disciplined of any in the regiment." General Rosecrans recommended commutation to the loss of six months pay. Holt raised no objection. Hay wrote, "The above recommendation of Gen. Rosecrans is approved. October 20, 1863. Hay's employer added "A. Lincoln."[50]

The case of Second Lieutenant William S. Stewart of the 9th Maryland is particularly sad. The Marylander had been taken prisoner early in the war, and both his wife and child died during his nine months of captivity in Richmond. Following his release, he married again. In the fall of 1863, he received a letter that said his new wife was dying. He requested a leave of absence, which was refused. In his defense, he wrote, "My feelings of humanity and natural affection for my wife were something which I could not withstand and I was led to sacrifice the love and honor of performing my duty to the more natural feelings of the human heart. I could not bear the thought of losing my second wife while so near her, without being with her in her last hour."

Although his conviction was followed by dismissal, Brigadier General Benjamin Kelley (himself subject to the risks of love) recommended clemency, and even Holt gave weight to Stewart's "dictates of the heart." On January 30, 1864, Nicolay wrote, and Lincoln signed, "Sentence remitted in this case." A flurry of additional documents necessitated a second Presidential decision in the Stewart case and in his own hand appears the final notation, "Dismissal revoked. April 14, 1864. A. Lincoln."[51]

Second Lieutenant Joseph H. Brawner of the 8th Missouri was convicted of misbehavior before the enemy and of desertion. He was sentenced to be reduced to the ranks for three years. His record states that he left his company and went to the rear at Yazoo River and at Vicksburg, both in Mississippi. At Young's Point, Louisiana, he left and was gone six months. At Fort Hindman, Arkansas, he was wounded slightly in January 1863. A politician, whose name is illegible, writes of "this young gentleman" who is "incapable of wilful offense, " and asks remission. William T. Sherman approved the sentence, as did Ulysses S. Grant. On November 9, 1863, Hay wrote, and Lincoln signed, the following: "Will the Judge Advocate General please inform me whether there is any record on file in this case which seems to me a very unusual one? Please cause the answer to be sent to Mr. Hay." Holt wrote a two page analysis. "An examination of the record of Lt. Brawner's trial leaves no doubt but that the sentence of the court was warranted by the testimony." Holt further noted that "no surgeon thought the wound merited a certificate of disability," and concluded, "The accused is evidently unfit for command & well deserves the punishment he is now suffering." The final note is this: "Sentence approved & application denied. A. Lincoln Feb., 9, 1864."[52]

The white officers of the U. S. colored troops were supposed to set a good example. Not so Lieutenants Osborn and Benham of the Seventh Corps d'Afrique, stationed at Port Hudson, Louisiana. The day of the altercation, Benham had been pulling Osborn's whiskers, had pinned Osborn's suspenders to his shirt and later hid the suspenders. Benham denied any knowledge of the whereabouts of the suspenders and at this point Osborn punched Benham in the face and called him a "God damned liar," all this in front of the enlisted men. Second Lieutenant John W. Osborn was convicted of conduct unbecoming an officer and a gentleman, and dismissed. General Banks agreed with the court's recommendation of mitigation and referred the case east. Holt noted, "Lieutenant Benham's conduct was improper and irritating and was the cause of all the difficulty." Seven months after the trial, the record reached Lincoln, who wrote, "Sentence remitted. Feb. 15, 1864," and added his signature. Perhaps he silently debated whether this was an army or a kindergarten.[53]

More serious was the case of Second Lieutenant Charles Lewis of the 2nd U. S. Cavalry. Lewis was sentenced to hang when he was convicted of kidnapping and murder. At Memphis, Tennessee, he took a Negro man and a Negro woman beyond the picket lines and delivered them to two civilians. Later, Lewis, wearing a disguise, entered a Federal military prison, found a Confederate officer in a cell, called the officer by name and then shot him through the head. Major General Ulysses S. Grant approved the death sentence. In Holt's review, he found the kidnapping not sustained because "although the Negroes showed a disinclination to go," they had not been forcibly moved, thus not constituting kidnapping from the point of view of legal technicality. As to the murder, Holt noted that it was both premeditated and widely witnessed. Lieutenant Lewis' last hope evaporated with this brief note: "Sentence approved. A. Lincoln Feb. 10, 1864."[54]

Lieutenant Charles Gianini of the 55th New York was convicted of misbehavior before the enemy and was sentenced to be shot. At both Seven Pines, Virginia, and at Malvern Hill, Virginia, he disappeared either before or during the battle. Gianini said that he was sick and had nothing to eat for two days. General Darius Couch approved the death sentence, while Major General George McClellan recommended dishonorable dismissal. Lincoln wrote: "Let the sentence of death be mitigated to dishonorable dismissal from the service in the case of Lieut. Charles Gianini. Oct. 23, 1863. A. Lincoln."[55] That same day, Jefferson Davis, on a tour of the Western Theater, removed old friend and incompetent Gen. Leonidas Polk from command in Tennessee and sent him to a desk job; unfortunately for the South, he would again return to the field.

Lieutenant Jacob Garey of the 82nd Massachusetts probably qualified as an "old soldier," since he had served in the Mexican War. He also had a wife and seven children and had not been paid in five months, which may explain not only why he was gambling with the enlisted men at Falmouth but continued to do so when ordered to stop. Garey was convicted of disobedience and ordered dismissed. The court recommended mitigation based on "good character" and bravery. Brigadier General John Newton endorsed mitigation, as did Major General Hooker, who suggested a three-month loss of pay as the appropriate penalty. Holt's opinion was implied, rather than stated, in his review: "It is for the President to decide whether an officer who has thus disgraced himself should be retained in the service." The President did decide: "Sentence commuted to forfeiture of pay for three months. A. Lincoln July 18, 1863." Since Garey had seven children and hadn't been paid in five months, it is easy to imagine the effect of losing an additional three months of pay.[56]

Lieutenant William Wildman of the 88th Indiana was in charge of a fort-building party near Murfreesboro, Tennessee. Wildman lived up to his name by drinking to excess and becoming "boisterous and unofficer-like," and lost control of his men, for which he was court-martialed and cashiered. The court "earnestly recommended him to mercy" based on "excellent character and gallant bearing in the battlefield." General Rosecrans agreed with mitigation and suggested forfeiture of three months pay. Holt agreed. Hay wrote, "Recommendation approved," and his employer added "A. Lincoln."[57]

Lieutenant Newton W. Whitted of the 25th Iowa was not only drunk on New Years Eve at Van Buren, Missouri, but was also the author of an eloquent, if somewhat idiosyncratic, defense. He pled guilty and intro-duced the statements of two surgeons that a sick man, still debilitated, would be adversely effected by small amounts of alcohol. Then he added his own plea:

To General [John] Davidson,
Commander of the Army of Southeast Missouri.

General I was this day court Marshaled by a General court Marshal appointed by you. You General will allow me to set up the facts to you upon the honor of all to me that is sacred In a word the facts are these. On the 31st day of December 1862 In Company with Major [illegible] of the MO 24th Captain Walker of the Iowa 23 and Lieut. Huston of the Iowa 23rd I did in Company with these Gentlemen during the day take whiskey 3 or 4 times but not oftener than the latter number.

Whitted went on to explain that he had suffered from an "inflamma-tion of the head," and that he had always been a "strict temperance advocate," and that he would be disgraced forever if he were to be dismissed. Whitted's colonel, as well as Generals Davidson and Schofield all recommended remission. Holt had no opinion. Lincoln simply wrote, "Sentence remitted. Nov. 7, 1863," signed, and the matter was finished.[58]

Lieutenant James W. Weir, a recruiter with the 14th U. S. Infantry, did not do his paperwork, was dismissed, and inspired an unusually long note by the President. Over an eight-month period at Reading, Pennsylvania, Weir did not file any of the reports required by his position, although he was "furnished with necessary blanks and funds." In addition, he took several unauthorized vacations of a week each. He was dismissed.

The first Presidential note reads, "Will the Judge Advocate General please examine and report to me on this case! A. Lincoln March 17, 1863." The next entry, unusual in that it appears on Executive Mansion letterhead, reads: "March 28, 1863. Hon. Sec. Of War. Sir: I understand that Lieut. James W. Weir of the 14th US Infantry, has been dismissed by sentence of Court Martial—if Mr. Holt will say in writing that it is legally competent for me to restore him, I will do it. Yours truly, A. Lincoln." Lower on the same piece of paper is: "Let Lieut. Weir be restored. A. Lincoln March 30, 1863." The record leaves unclear the reasons for these administrative decisions.[59]

Lieutenant Albert Erskine of the 13th Illinois Cavalry sold eight bales of government hay, for which he received $15.00. The evidence showed that the regiment was leaving, had no use for the hay, and that the $15.00 had been put into the company fund. In spite of this evidence, Erskine was convicted of violating the 39th Article of War and was ordered dismissed the service. Major General Samuel Curtis urged remission, as did General Rosecrans. The President's impatience with this time-wasting legal exercise may explain why this notation is badly smeared: "Action of Gen. Curtis is confirmed. A. Lincoln April 14, 1864." A fateful anniversary-to-be.[60]

The army career of Lieutenant Michael J. Egan (170th New York) was a short one. As his mustering-in papers were being processed, he was assigned to be in charge of the pickets at Suffolk, Virginia; his response was, "If I can't get a pass to New York, I won't do any duty." At his trial, he told a different story: "My uniform wasn't presentable so I did not want to be in charge." He was dismissed. Major General John Dix added the provision that he should be dishonorably dismissed, an idea endorsed by Holt. Lincoln signed the note by Nicolay which read, "General Dix's recommendation approved."[61]

Delayed justice can have advantages, at least in the case of Lieutenant Charles N. Smith of the 90th New York, stationed at Key West, Florida. He had just come off a tour of guard duty and was reprimanded by Captain John Smart for having missed parade. Tempers flared. Smith was court-martialed and dismissed for saying, "What is the matter with you? If you want to fight me, God damn you, I will give you enough to do. I would have you know that I don't care a God damn for you." The case took six months to reach Holt, who noted that in the interim Smith had been wounded in a battle in which he had fought bravely. Holt urged clemency. Written on the margin of Holt's analysis is simply, "Sentence remitted. A. Lincoln April 14, 1862."[62] It was a Monday; in Tennessee, Federal mortar shells were falling on Fort Pillow.

Issues of life and death pervade the trial record of Lieutenant John P. Cole of the 144th New York. He left his regiment at Washington, D.C. and was arrested two days later, in civilian clothes, headed north. He was cashiered and forever disqualified from holding public office. Further, his crime was to be published in his hometown newspapers. The court was ordered to reconsider their verdict. It did so, and the new recommendation was that Cole be shot. He pleaded that he had left in response to his wife's letter about his sick child. The court recommended remission of the death penalty, as did General Heintzelman. Holt summarized the evidence and Nicolay wrote for the President, "Sentence commuted to dismissal, as recommended." Once again, we see "A. Lincoln."[63]

The prisoners at Schofield Barracks, Missouri, must have been surprised when the Officer of the Guard took them to a nearby saloon and got drunk with them. This officer was Lieutenant Alex Schrader of the 1st Missouri Militia, who was convicted of conduct unbecoming an officer and a gentleman and was dismissed. His court-martial members then petitioned for mitigation. John Schofield, the commanding general, endorsed such and Holt summarized the case without expressing an opinion. The man with the final responsibility wrote: "Recom. of Gen. Schofield approved and ordered. A. Lincoln April 14, 1864." Schrader was still in the army.[64]

At Brentwood, Tennessee, Lieutenant Henry K. Kelly of the 14th Michigan almost lost his new shoulder straps for being drunk. At his trial he said that the liquor had had an "unusual effect" and that he had not been informed that the enemy was approaching, otherwise he would have had nothing to drink. He expressed regret and contrition, but was cashiered in spite of that. General Rosecrans recommended commutation to the loss of six months pay. Holt offered no opinion. The President wrote, "Recom. of Gen. Rosecrans approved and ordered. A. Lincoln April 21, 1864."[65]

During the Civil War, there was no formal instruction in how to be a volunteer officer: no ROTC, no officer candidate school, no camps of indoctrination. This flaw lay behind the trial of Lieutenant LaFayette Butler of the 45th Massachussetts. At Fort Lyon, Virginia, he gave the password to an unauthorized person and gave two sergeants permission to leave camp. He pled guilty, but added that he had been unaware that these acts were improper. The court urged mercy, noting "his offense was the result of ignorance and want of proper instruction." General Heintzelman agreed and Holt passed the case on to Lincoln, who placed his signature at the end of this note, "Let the sentence be remitted and this officer restored to duty. April 29, 1863."[66]

Lieutenant William E. McLaughlin of the 65th Indiana was the officer in charge of guarding the forage train near Henderson, Kentucky. He pled guilty to being drunk on duty and was cashiered. Because of some irregularity in the proceedings, there began a long correspondence between Brigadier General Jeremiah Boyle, C. W. Foster and Thomas Vincent, both assistant adjutant generals, and Holt, the Judge Advocate General. Nine months after the trial, the case reached the Executive Mansion; Nicolay wrote, "Sentence disapproved for irregularity," and Lincoln signed.[67]

As should already be clear from several cases preceding, officers were to avoid "undue familiarity" with enlisted men. "You would make a better whorehouse pimp than any man in the regiment," was a remark addressed to Lieutenant Henry R. Curtis of the 14th New York Heavy Artillery by one of his enlisted subordinates as they drank wine together at the sutler's shop, near Fort Hamilton, at New York Harbor. For the crimes of socializing with enlisted men and not disciplining the man who made the remark, Curtis was sentenced to be dismissed. The court did recommend mitigation because of "faithful services." General Dix, in view of Curtis' "inexperience and good character," advised suspension from rank and pay for two months. Holt had no recommendation. The President made the final decision: "Recom. of Gen. Dix approved and ordered. April 14, 1864." Curtis lost two month's pay.[68]

Carrion Crow Bayou, Louisiana, was the site of conduct unbecoming an officer and a gentleman, in this case Lieutenant William J. Gannon of the 8th New Jersey. He was a little drunk and more than a little touchy, and when told to move his tent and control his men, he cursed the adjutant who brought these instructions. Gannon was cashiered but the court, as well as Generals William Franklin, and Nathaniel Banks, recommended remittal. Holt took no position, Nicolay wrote, "Sentence remitted," and Lincoln signed.[69]

Men holding traditional military ranks were not the only persons tried by court-martial. Among the first 40,000 men who appeared before court-martial boards were 108 surgeons, 79 assistant surgeons, six citizen surgeons, and 21 chaplains. Of these, three doctors and two men of the cloth came to the attention of President Lincoln.

George W. New, surgeon of the 7th Indiana, was tried for selling hospital brandy and whisky to the privates and keeping the proceeds. He said that the regiment was packing to move, that there was not room for all the liquor, and that he intended to give the proceeds to the brigade surgeon. Dr. New was sentenced to pay all the proceeds to the government and to be dismissed. General John Reynolds approved the sentence. When the case came to the Executive Mansion, the President wrote, "I am not satisfied with the sentence of the court in this case, so far as it dismisses the accused from the service. That he sold the liquor is unquestionable, but that he did so with any improper intention, or that he ever intended to appropriate the proceeds I think is not proven—I therefore wish to restore him to the service, if it is lawfully competent for me to do so. A. Lincoln December 31, 1861."

An opinion on this matter was rendered by Major John F. Lee, Judge Advocate of the Army. After lengthy analysis, Lee concluded, "The President's opinion on the record that the sentence is unjust, and restoration by the Governor [of Indiana] will satisfy the party, is all that can be done now." There is a final note on the record: "I think the law is correctly stated within. A. Lincoln June 3, 1862." (Dr. New went on to enjoy a long and honorable career.)[70]

George H. Mitchell, surgeon of the 88th Pennsylvania, seems a very different type of man. According to his record, he left the sick and wounded of his regiment without care for three days and expressed no

George W. New, M.D., was convicted of selling the 7th Indiana Infantry's whiskey. Lincoln's legal analysis of the case cleared New's name and returned him to duty.

B. R. Sulgrove, *History of Indianapolis and Marion County*, 1884

regret for his absence, took food intended for the sick, and quarreled loudly with the quartermaster. Instead of ending this quarrel when ordered to do so, he punched the quartermaster. Mitchell was dismissed. For him, there were no recommendations of mitigation. He appealed strenuously (and was still appealing in 1888), but on November 27, 1862, we see the following note: "Respectfully referred by the President to the Judge Advocate General. John Nicolay, Priv. Sec. Executive Mansion." Holt's reply noted that the offenses were fully proved, that Mitchell's dismissal was fully justified, and that "no further application for restoration of this officer should be entertained." Lincoln signed Nicolay's note, which said "Petition refused."[71]

John D. Johnson, Assistant Surgeon, U. S. Volunteers (a rank equivalent to Brigade Surgeon; such doctors did hospital or staff work), was in charge of a hospital at Chattanooga, Tennessee. A "small quantity of stimulants" (in this case, whisky) had been provided for the treatment of the patients. Dr. Johnson drank all of it. Testimony showed that the total amount was less than half a pint. Johnson told the court, "I drank it to correct the sick stomach created by the effluvia rising from the discharge, which was extremely offensive." In brief, the stench of rotting wounds nauseated him. Dr. Johnson was convicted and dismissed from the service. Later review showed that an angry patient had perjured himself to injure the doctor. Other doctors praised Johnson's competence. General George Thomas recommended commutation to a reprimand. Holt's review concluded: "The conduct of the accused was reprehensible but it is not believed that the interest of the service will be promoted by the dismissal of this officer." The final note, in the President's hand, says, "Recom. of Gen. Thomas approved and ordered. A. Lincoln April 26, 1864."[72]

In the first 40,000 general court-martials of the Union army, we find the trials of two chaplains received for review by Lincoln. Richard C. Christie of the 78th Pennsylvania was charged with being absent without leave five months at Chattanooga, Tennessee, during which time he performed no religious services and lived in a tent at Brigade Headquarters. He was dismissed from the service. General George Thomas recommended that the sentence be remitted. It appears there was a shortage of tents in the regiment. When his colonel was assigned to brigade command, Christie moved with him and continued to share a tent with Colonel William Sirwell. Holt agreed that the sentence should be remitted. The final entry reads, "Sentence remitted. A. Lincoln April 14, 1864."[73]

Nathan G. Axtell had been pastor of a large church in Oswego, New York before the war and joined the 30th New York as chaplain in 1861. He displayed such "soldierly qualities" that the field officers of his regiment recommended him for a command position, and he was soon major of the 142nd New York. As Field Officer of the Day at Falls Church, Virginia, he failed to visit the pickets and refused to dismount when challenged by a sentry. After voluminous testimony, he was convicted and dismissed. Holt's review noted the testimony of Major Alonzo Alden of the 169th New York Cavalry, who believed Axtell "free of all guilt whatsoever," as well as the opinion of General Heintzelman, who noted "mitigating circumstances which go far to relieve Major Axtell of any willful intent of disobedience." Holt recommended remission. An unknown hand wrote, "Approved, but in consideration of the mitigating circumstances exhibited by the record, the sentence awarded by the court is remitted. May 21, 1863." The familiar "A. Lincoln" follows.[74]

Table Two below summarizes Lincoln's decisions regarding the court-martials of lieutenants, surgeons, and chaplains. It is obvious that

Opinion Maker	Lincoln Agrees	Lincoln Disagrees	% Agreement
Trial Verdict	17	56	23
Authorizing Officer	10	3	77
Departmental Commander	49	3	94
Judge Advocate General	42	6	88
Interested Politicians	1	0	100
Friends, Family & Comrades	0	0	NA

the President usually disagreed with the original verdict by the court-martial itself, but it is also important to note that in forty-five percent (45%) of the convictions, the court-martial board had already attached a petition for clemency to the verdict of guilty, usually citing mitigating circumstances.

Thus, it is clear that when the petitions for mitigation are added into the equation, we find Lincoln in general agreement with the conclusions of the military justice system at every level—court-martial board, appointing authority, departmental commander, and judge advocate general. In this group of trials, we see Lincoln as compassionate and forgiving, but not much more so than the system he presided over. Except for sexual crimes, Lincoln was almost always willing to give a man a chance to redeem himself.

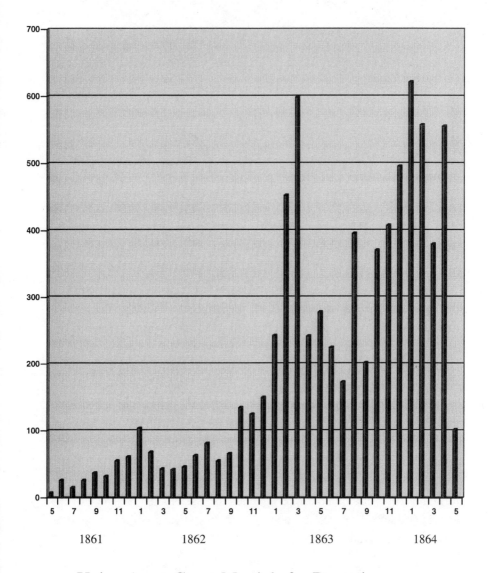

Union Army Court-Martials for Desertion
Trials per Month
May 1861 through May 1864
Data after April 1864 is omitted as incomplete, since indexing is not finished.
© The Index Project, Inc.

5

Deserters (1861-1862)

A soldier cannot resign. Once he is enlisted, he must stay until his term of obligation is completed. For many reasons, he may decide to leave without permission, and if he is gone long, or gone under suspicious circumstances, he will be in serious trouble.

During the first 180 years of American history, soldiers were governed by the Articles of War. In 1776, Section 6, Article 1, stated clearly, "All officers and soldiers, who having received pay, or having been duly inlisted (sic) in the service of the United States, shall be convicted of having deserted the same, shall suffer death, or such other punishment as by a court martial shall be inflicted." In the Revised Regulations of 1861, Article 20 is equally clear. "All officers and soldiers who have received pay, or have been duly enlisted in the service of the United States, and shall be convicted of having deserted the same, shall suffer death, or such other punishment, as by sentence of court martial, shall be inflicted. No officer or soldier shall be subject to the punishment of death for desertion in time of peace."

Major General George McClellan's orders relieving Private Scott—the sleeping sentinel—of death by firing squad was equally clear on such matters. "The duty of a sentinel is of such nature that its neglect, by sleeping upon or deserting his post, may endanger the safety of a command, or even of a whole army, and all nations affix to the offense the penalty of death."

In 1863, the anti-war Democrat politician Clement L. Vallandigham, who had urged citizens not to cooperate with Federal recruiting efforts, was arrested and convicted of treason. In response to New York Democrats who objected to these proceedings, Lincoln replied, "Long experience has shown that armies cannot be maintained unless desertion shall be punished by the severe penalty of death. The case requires, and the law and the Constitution, sanction this punishment." Here we see the iron hand of Lincoln, but the velvet glove shines forth in the succeeding passage. "Must I shoot a simple-minded soldier boy who deserts, while I must not touch a hair of a wily agitator [here Lincoln clearly intends Vallandigham] who induced him to desert?" In the final sentence, we see the Lincoln that tradition holds out to us: "I think that in such a case, to silence the agitator, and save the boy, is not only Constitutional, but, withall, a great mercy."[1]

At first view, the subject of desertion seems simple enough. One hundred men volunteer to fight for their country. One man, a moral defective, sneaks away, for his own selfish reasons, leaving his comrades to fight on alone, shorn of the deserter's strength, firepower, and team spirit. In the actual world of the Civil War, reasons for desertion ranged across a whole spectrum, from the wounded stalwart who is tried for desertion because slip-shod record-keeping failed to notice his months in the hospital, to the out-and-out criminal, who collected his bounty, changed his name, re-enlisted elsewhere, and collected a new bounty—all without the slightest intention of staying with any one regiment, much less of ever going into battle.

In the 1860s, there were no Federal allotment checks for the wives and children of soldiers. If the soldier did not send money home, his family starved. Many regiments were not paid for months on end, prompting some soldiers to travel home to earn bread for their children. There was none of the "compassionate leave" available to soldiers today. If a Civil War soldier received a letter that his wife or child was dying, he had little chance of getting a furlough and had to leave his regiment quickly if he wanted to see his family this side of the grave. (It was much easier for an officer to receive a leave of absence for "personal business.") There were dozens of reasons for a soldier to desert, but none of them were acceptable. In the first 42,000 Union court-martials of the Civil War, 14,146 were for desertion.

A graphic representation may help to illuminate the trends within this considerable number of desertions. Graph 1 suggests two patterns. The first is a seasonal variation, with increased desertion during the cold winter months (time usually spent in camp), and a decrease during the warm months of active campaigning. In winter camp, with time hanging heavy on his hands and plaintive letters from home arriving almost daily describing poverty, cold, and sickness, the soldier might see little virtue in Army life. As spring advanced, the Union army would move south, directing the soldier's attention to his main purpose: victory and a permanent return home. A striking increase in desertions as the war entered its third year is evident in the second pattern. By that time, visions of glory and a quick victory were replaced by the bitter reality of a long and bloody war.

Graph 2 focuses on 1863, the first year of heavy desertion. The shorter columns represent the cases reviewed by Lincoln, and it is clear that he saw only a small fraction of all desertion cases. An analysis of the April 1863 cases suggests the reasons. Excluding the cases seen later by Lincoln, there were 216 Union general court-martials for desertion in April 1863. In 32 cases, the verdict was for acquittal. Of the men convicted, 99 were imprisoned, usually at hard labor, for times ranging from ten days to five years, 65 received a fine or suffered a loss of pay. Eleven men were sentenced to be shot, but had the sentenced remitted, commuted, or overturned. Three men were sentenced to be shot and the court-martial record shows neither a remittal nor a review by Lincoln. Lesser sentences included one reprimand, one carrying of a large knapsack for several days, and two episodes of standing on a barrel six hours a day, usually for a week. Five of these men were noted to be mentally abnormal—although it did not change their sentence. Some of the sentences of hard labor contained additional provisions: fifteen men were drummed out, seven had their heads shaved, and six were branded with the letter "D." In April 1863, two captains were convicted of desertion; both were dismissed from the service and one was sent to the Dry Tortugas, a desolate fortified island miles from Key West.

It thus appears that the usual characteristic which brought a deserter to Presidential attention was a sentence of death. In general, less drastic punishments brought the review process to a halt at lower levels.

Lincoln issued two major proclamations which influenced military justice. The first, dated March 10, 1863, ordered all soldiers absent without leave to return to their respective regiments, and if they turned themselves in before April 1, 1863, they would escape punishment except for forfeiture of pay during their absence. Those who did not turn themselves in by the deadline were to be "arrested as deserters and punished as the law provides."

The second proclamation was issued February 26, 1864, and ordered that the death sentences of all deserters be commuted to imprisonment at the Dry Tortugas to the end of the war. The latter proclamation was, of course, far too late to account for the sudden rise in Lincoln-reviewed court-martials in the spring of 1863. The amnesty proclamation would also be unlikely to explain the steep rise in desertion trials which occurred a month before the amnesty. Further, there was frequently a considerable delay between arrest and trial, and the court records often speak of "long confinement, before proceedings." (On the other hand, some trials were held within days of the offense.)

The subject of desertions has not been a popular one. It offends the North, whose mythology describes the boys in blue as ever-stalwart in camp and combat, giving their all for the Union and to free the slaves. It offends the South, whose perhaps even-stronger mythology is that of the heroes of the Lost Cause, undaunted by the over-equipped, overfed Yankees, marching to barefooted glory for State's Rights, hearth, and home.

Even as late as 1928, Ella Lonn, the preeminent scholar of desertions felt the need to apologize for even studying the issue: "The few remaining survivors of the struggle, Northern as well as Southern, will be repelled by the very subject of this book; probably the average reader will question the worthwhileness of an exhaustive study of that which seems to record a nation's shame." Fortunately for students of the Civil War, Lonn overcame her fear of offending the graying veterans and produced a very valuable study on the subject.[2]

Having made that apology, Lonn enumerated the scope of desertions. Among the Confederate troops, 103,400 soldiers and 1,028 officers deserted. In August 1864, Union General Ulysses S. Grant estimated that desertion thinned the Southern ranks by one full regiment every day. Confederate General Sterling Price lost 500 men to desertion in a single day while crossing the Red River. General Braxton Bragg's forces often had 40 men desert each day—in spite of Bragg's policy of shooting as many deserters as he could find. Inchoate groups of Confederates, absent without leave, roamed the South as robber bands, despoiling their own countrymen.

North Carolina was the leader in Confederate desertions, with 23,694 Tar Heel men leaving without permission, while the Palmetto State, South Carolina, listed only 3,579 men as deserters. Virginia ranged in the middle with 12,071 men gone over the hill, along with 84 Virginia officers.

Vast as these figures may seem, Lonn's research concludes that they were overshadowed by the number of Union deserters, who totaled 278,644 by the end of the war. Morale and steadfastness seemed to reach a low in October and November of 1864; in each month, more than 10,000 Union men left without permission. New York led the pack, with a total of 44,913 deserters, with Pennsylvania a distant second, losing only 24,050 men. Being sick or wounded seemed to decrease men's martial ardor: over 33,000 Yankees deserted from Federal hospitals.

At least four variables play a part in complicating the patterns of offense, trial, and resolution. First, there are the dates and circumstances of the desertion. Did the soldier leave from a peaceful winter camp, or while marching into battle? How long was he absent—a week, a month, a year? Did he return voluntarily, or was he arrested and returned in handcuffs and leg irons? When arrested, was he in uniform, or had he switched to civilian clothing? When he returned, was he placed back on duty or was he locked up? Was his time away from his regiment largely from being shuttled from one jail to another as the local provost marshal tried to locate his moving regiment and send him to it? And what happened between his return to his regiment and the trial itself? In some cases, during that interim the soldier proved himself in battle which often earned him a much lighter sentence.

A further variable was the local commander's philosophy. Some generals shot as many deserters as possible as a deterrent to others, while in at least one jurisdiction nearly the opposite view prevailed. A mass-production court-martial of deserters, held in Alexandria, Virginia, in the winter of 1862-1863, gave nearly every soldier the same sentence: no pay while gone and a fine of $10 a month for a year. Not a single death sentence was issued, no matter how outrageous the testimony, and dozens of the men tried were clearly professional bounty jumpers.

All of these factors played a role in what cases might come to Lincoln, but he could not be concerned with every offender, and his recorded opinions on the cases actually brought before him are the only evidence we have, and that evidence commences in 1862.

Two of the first deserters to come to Lincoln's attention were Californians, and both cases were resolved by the President on the same day—with very different outcomes. Private Thomas Clifton of the 2nd California Cavalry deserted at Franklin, Texas, and took his horse with him. At his trial, he said, "I took an oath that as soon as the war was for the abolition of slavery, I would take no further part. At the first opportunity, I took my chance to remain neutral." Thomas was sentenced to be shot and Brigadier General James Carleton approved this decision. So did Holt. On July 18, 1863, Lincoln wrote, "Sentence approved," and signed his name.[3]

Private John Davis, another member of the 2nd California Cavalry, took his horse to Mexico, but the Mexicans returned him to the authorities at El Paso, Texas. He was tried for desertion, convicted in November 1862, and sentenced to be shot. Holt found "no palliating circumstances." The President wrote, "Sentence approved. A. Lincoln July 18, 1863." It had taken eight months for the papers to reach Lincoln. Fortunately for Davis, administrative matters traveling to the Southwest traveled just as slowly. In October, Davis was still alive and Holt wrote a new review. Twelve officers at Fort Craig, New Mexico, had written that Davis was repentant, that his brother had been killed fighting with General Alfred Pleasanton's cavalry, and that the condemned was the sole support of his destitute mother. Holt urged that these "circumstances justify his pardon." Davis had been in prison for sixteen months when Lincoln wrote, "Pardon. Feb. 9, 1864. A. Lincoln."[4] That same day, a tunnel out of the notorious Libby Prison in Richmond, Virginia, allowed 109 Union officers to escape their captors; 59 of the men reached Union lines.

Sylvester Buel, age 19, five foot six inches tall, enlisted in the 3rd New York and promptly deserted four times, aided by his ability to slip his handcuffs. Major General John Dix approved the death sentence, noting the need "to arrest and subdue this fearful element of demoralization." Holt agreed. So did the President: "Sentence approved. A. Lincoln February 4, 1863."[5]

Gottlieb Rittig was a lucky man. The 37th New York member dropped behind in the march because of a swollen ankle. He was captured and paroled by Captain Robert Randolph of the 4th Virginia Cavalry, CSA. Rittig, who spoke little English, was sentenced to death for desertion. Major General Joseph Hooker thought that the recent Presidential Proclamation should apply to the condemned and the President closed the case with one word: "Pardoned. A. Lincoln."[6]

Another private from the 37th New York, Ellis Fitters, was captured by the Confederate Black Horse Cavalry near Bank's Ford, Virginia. At his trial, Fitters was judged to be a deserter and was sentenced to be shot. Once again Hooker urged the application of Lincoln's Amnesty Proclamation, and once again Lincoln wrote "Pardoned," and signed his name, saving Fitters from a chest full of lead.[7]

Private Wesley Hawkins seems to have contributed to case law by deserting during the fighting at South Mountain, Maryland on September 14, 1862. Although he rejoined his 105th New York Regiment at Antietam a few days later, Hawkins was convicted of desertion and sentenced to be shot, a decision approved by Major General William B. Franklin. Holt noted that the court had been appointed by a divisional commander, Brigadier General James Ricketts, and that the approval of the commander of an entire army was required. Franklin, in a later note, complained, "If Colonel Holt's decision be the proper one, and I assume there is no appeal from it, all of the cases [involving death sentences or conviction of officers] ought to be examined by General [Ambrose] Burnside or the dismissed officers will probably get back again into service." The President's comment was limited to a single word: "Pardoned," and his signature.[8]

Henry Learned threw away his rifle and cartridge box and disappeared on the march to Sharpsburg, Maryland, site of the September 17, 1862 Battle of Antietam. After he was arrested and sent back to the 2nd

Massachussetts, Learned was convicted of desertion and sentenced to have the letter "D" tattooed on his hip, to have his head shaved, and to be drummed out. Fortunately for the Bay State youth, the court was ordered to reconsider this sentence; unfortunately, it arrived at a new penalty: the firing squad. The divisional commander approved the sentence but added, "The circumstances proved do not, however, in my opinion, justify the sentence of death." Hooker, again citing the March 10, 1863 Proclamation, recommended pardon and again, "A. Lincoln" appears below the word "Pardoned."[9] Henry Learned literally dodged a bullet, or more accurately, several of them.

Private George Bent left the 11th Massachussetts at Bladensburg, Maryland, was absent nine months, and was sentenced to die for desertion. Generals Joseph Hooker and Hiram Barry forwarded the sentence as approved, but in a revised opinion, Hooker again cited the Amnesty Proclamation and recommended pardon, which Lincoln quickly endorsed.[10]

Another deserter, Manuel Sidelinger of the 4th Maine, told the court, "I went for water and was captured and paroled with 250 other men at Bull Run Ridge, by [JEB] Stuart's men." Perhaps because he also deserted at Falmouth, Virginia, Sidelinger was sentenced to be shot. In his review, Hooker again cited the Proclamation and the President agreed with a single word, "Pardon," and the familiar "A. Lincoln."[11]

Another thirsty soldier caught up in the army's legal machinery was Richard Hamlin of the 90th Pennsylvania, who went for water at the Battle of Bull Run and was gone for six weeks. Hamlin claimed he had wrenched his foot and was taken to Alexandria, Virginia, by ambulance. One witness said that he saw Hamlin's foot "swollen," but another man testified, "Hamlin did not walk lame." The court-martial concluded that he should be shot. Holt voiced no direct opinion, but concluded his review rather tartly: "A mitigation of the sentence is recommended by Brigadier General Robinson, but upon what ground I am unable to perceive." That was enough for Lincoln, who placed his name below yet another one-word decision: "Pardon."[12]

George Hiner was court-martialed at Lexington, Kentucky, for quitting the 44th Ohio at its camp somewhere in Virginia and enlisting elsewhere for the bounty. His trial board concluded that shooting him was a proper punishment and the papers passed up the line to Holt, via Generals Quincy Gilmore, Gordon Granger, and Horatio Wright. Holt returned the papers, since Wright had failed to express an opinion. With Wright's approval of the death sentence, Holt undertook an analysis and found two technical flaws in the trial. Holt's employer closed the issue: "Sentence disapproved for irregularity. A. Lincoln July 18, 1863."[13] That day, Lincoln and Holt spent six hours on court-martials. Two days earlier, the steamboat *Imperial* had reached New Orleans from St. Louis; it was the first commercial run to New Orleans since the war began.

The November 1862 trial of Private St. Clair Lancaster focused on his behavior at the camp of the 7th Maryland, near Moore's House in his home state. The accused had not received his enlistment bounty and said that he would not fight until he received it. When no money arrived, he deserted. The death sentence was reviewed by Major General Robert C. Schenck, who remarked upon the "peculiar" and "mitigating" events by which Lancaster was "precipitated into error," and Holt agreed. Nicolay wrote, "Sentence commuted to imprisonment for one month from this date, May 11, 1863." There follows the familiar "A. Lincoln."[14] As Lincoln wrote, Federal cavalrymen at Crystal Springs, Mississippi, were tearing up the New Orleans & Jackson Railroad.

Robert Babbet of the 1st New Mexico Infantry departed from Las Vegas, New Mexico, riding a government horse. He was soon captured and sentenced to be shot for desertion. While Babbet languished in jail, his behavior was excellent, wrote Brigadier General James Carleton (a veteran of the 1839 Aroostook War, Stephen Kearny's Rocky Mountain Expedition, and the Mexican War), who added a recommendation for mercy. Holt said the entire court procedure had been totally inadequate, and urged that the members of the court be reprimanded and the prisoner freed. Babbet was more than a year older when Nicolay wrote "Proceedings and sentence disapproved, February 9, 1864," and Lincoln added his name.[15] That day, Union troops landed on St. John's Island, near Charleston, South Carolina, but fierce Confederate resistance forced them to withdraw.

In summary, the year 1861 contained no trials for desertion which came under the scrutiny of Lincoln, while 1862 contained thirteen court-martials for desertion reviewed by the President. Lincoln approved death for two men and pardoned or remitted eleven. One of the pardoned men had originally had his death sentence approved by Lincoln, but was later remitted after further review.

Table Three shows that Lincoln disagreed with the original decision of the court-martial in seventy-seven percent (77 %) of the cases, and agreed with Holt eighty-eight percent (88%) of the time. In brief, some degree of remission had already occurred at one of the three levels between the actual court-martial and Lincoln. The higher in the chain of command, the greater likelihood of a vote for mitigation. But will this trend continue as the war progressed?

Opinion Maker	Lincoln Agrees	Lincoln Disagrees	% Agreement
Trial Verdict	3	10	23
Authorizing Officer	3	4	43
Departmental Commander	7	1	88
Judge Advocate General	6	2	75
Interested Politicians	NA	NA	NA
Friends, Family & Comrades	NA	NA	NA

The President was quick to endorse capital punishment in his first few cases. The reasons for this can only be speculation. Did he fear being seen as "soft on crime"? Did he feel that the war would be brief, and he would have few such decisions to make? These were soldiers far away in the Southwest; perhaps they were easier to forget.

The real answer is that we don't know.

6

Desertion (January - March, 1863)

The spring of 1863 marked the first great surge of court-martials for desertions. President Lincoln received and reviewed eight trials which had been held in January of that year. The first case of 1863 was certainly "somebody's Wallace"; whether it did him any good, well, that is another story.

Louis de la Croix began his service with the 2nd New York Heavy Artillery on October 6, 1862. He needed less than twenty-four hours to determine army life was not for him, and deserted on October 7, 1862. Not only did he serve only a single day, but his name was not Louis de la Croix. Louis Robert, alias Dennis Robert, alias Louis Leon, alias Louis de la Croix, was a 24-year-old *Quebecoise* school teacher who, for reasons unknown, migrated to the United States. At his January 1863 trial, he pled guilty, entered no evidence on his behalf, and was sentenced to three years of hard labor with a 24-lb. ball and chain, to be followed with a dishonorable discharge.

After a year had passed, the prospect of dragging an iron ball across the prison yard for another two years galvanized Louis and his father to action. In March 1864, the United States Consul in Montreal forwarded a three-page petition signed by Louis Robert ("Flour Inspector of Montreal") and eight other worthies, including the mayor of Montreal. The document proclaimed that young Louis had deserted because he was "weak-minded," that he had behaved well in prison, and that he wished to be allowed to rejoin his regiment. The petition reached the Executive Mansion, where the President passed the case on to Edwin Stanton with this note: "Submitted to the Secretary of War. A. Lincoln April 1, 1864."

The War Department queried Brigadier General Albin Schoepf, commanding the prison at Fort Delaware, who affirmed that Louis' behavior had been "entirely satisfactory." For reasons not apparent in the record, Louis was transferred to Fort Jefferson on DryTortugas and from that hellhole he wrote the U.S. Consul in Montreal, inquiring about his case. The letter was eventually forwarded to William Seward, the U.S. Secretary of State. In November, Louis wrote again asking the same question, this time to Secretary of War Edwin Stanton. New Years came and went. In early 1865, Judge Advocate Holt wrote a review and recommended a pardon, but on April 27, 1865, changed his mind. Perhaps Holt was embittered by Lincoln's very recent murder. Certainly he was influenced by Colonel Joseph Whistler, commander of the 2nd New York Heavy Artillery, who gave his opinion that a man who enlists under a false name and deserts the next day is entitled to no consideration.

Louis de la Croix served his full sentence. In December 1865, he was issued a dishonorable discharge at Fort Jefferson. The following February, Louis and other ex-prisoners were being transported through Maryland when the Canadian disappeared and was not seen again. It is easy to believe that if Lincoln had lived, de la Croix would have been home sooner.[1]

The 1st Colorado Cavalry reflected the rude manners of the mining camps. Private Bill Smith told Private John Morrison, "Go to Central City and come back with my dog. If you don't, I will kill you." Taking his comrade at face value, Morrison left and was convicted of desertion and sentenced to hard labor with a ball and chain for the rest of his enlistment. Holt noted reports of "good moral character" and concluded, "It is for the President to determine whether his Proclamation of March last is sufficiently broad to cover this case." With an undated signature, the President decided: "Pardon. A. Lincoln."[2]

A Regular Army unit suffered a spate of unofficial absences during the bloody fighting at Stone's River in Tennessee. David van Sickle of the 15th U. S. Infantry left the battle on New Year's Day and was gone one week and a day. The court said he should be shot for desertion, but Major General William Rosecrans recommended commutation. The final note reads, "Recommendation of Gen. Rosecrans approved. A. Lincoln Nov. 7, 1863."[3] Two other members of the 15th U. S. Infantry left the same battle. Edgar Beatty was gone for a week, while Henry Moore was absent for 15 days. Both were sentenced to be shot, both were recommended for commutation by General Rosecrans, and both records bear the same notation: "Recommendation of Gen. Rosecrans approved. A. Lincoln Nov. 7, 1863."[4]

In the Eastern Theater, several events conspired to undermine Union morale in the early spring of 1863. At Antietam the previous September, Federal casualties had been over 12,000, with 2,000 dead and little gain to show for such a bloodletting. In mid-December at Fredericksburg, the North lost 12,000 more, 1,200 of them dead on the battlefield with even less to show for their efforts. This debacle was followed by another in early January when Burnside, attempting to get around the Confederate left flank, marched his troops up the north bank of the Rappahannock River. A three-day downpour mired wagons, cannons, and men in knee-deep muck. The infamous "Mud March" was enough to make many soldiers doubt the sanity, much less the wisdom, of their leaders. With the hospitals filled with men mutilated in fruitless battles, and not enough pay distributed to feed the families at home, demoralization was deep.

James Focht of the 139th Pennsylvania deserted at Falmouth, Virginia. A witness at his trial noted, "His general character is good, but he is very afraid and showed signs of the coward. He was induced by his tent-mate to desert." Hooker thought the death sentence should be mitigated by the March Proclamation. Nicolay wrote, "Pardon," and Lincoln wrote his name.[5]

Samuel Slingluff was 25 years old when he enlisted in the 51st Pennsylvania. He "abandoned his colors" and ran away at the Battle of Fredericksburg, Virginia. He, too, was sentenced to die. General John Sedgwick recommended commutation to "hard labor at the Rip Raps," but Major General Ambrose Burnside recommended execution. Holt agreed with Burnside. Nicolay wrote, "Report approved," and Lincoln signed, sending Slingluff to the firing squad.[6] Slingluff, however, cheated death by escaping from confinement and appears no more in the military records.

Two more Pennsylvania men complete the January list. Jacob Zerphy of the 79th Pennsylvania Infantry deserted at Louisville, Kentucky, saying, "One winter in the army is enough." Rosecrans suggested that the March Proclamation might save Zerphy from death. Holt noted that Zerphy did not return voluntarily and should not receive amnesty. Lincoln overruled Holt. Under Nicolay's words of "Sentence remitted, May 20, 1863," we see "A. Lincoln."[7] John Fisher of the 140th Infantry left his regiment near the mouth of Aquia Creek, Virginia. Eventually caught and tried, he was sentenced to die. General Winfield Hancock approved the death penalty but, again, Hooker saw the March Proclamation as applicable. Nicolay wrote, "Pardon," Lincoln wrote his name—and Fisher lived another day.[8]

February

As 1863 progressed, the pace of military justice began to accelerate and the month of February brought thirty-five trials which were to later receive the attention of the President. Although Regular Army troops formed only a small part of the Union army, in this month they accounted for almost one-third of the men tried. In one of those trials, Holt added a note which clarifies a point of military law.

Corporal Michael McGarvey of the 4th U. S. Infantry deserted in September 1862, at Frederick, Maryland, and returned voluntarily in November. He was sentenced to be shot. Major General John Wool urged commutation. Holt returned the papers, writing, "It has been the uniform decision of this office that the commutation of the sentence of death by a General Commanding is unauthorized and therefore inoperative. Under the existing laws, the President of the United States alone can exercise this power." Wool returned the file with his recommendation "that the sentence be remitted by the President of the United States." And so it was. "Sentence disapproved [Lincoln had written and then crossed out 'Remitted.']. A. Lincoln July 18, 1863."[9] Across the breadth of the nation, there was no peace. That same day at tiny Rio Hondo, in New Mexico Territory, Federal troops clashed with Apache Indians. At Battery Wagner, in the defenses of Charleston, South Carolina, 1,700 determined Confederate defenders endured hours of bombardment and then repulsed a charge by 6,000 Union troops.

Private John Kaim of the 4th U. S. Infantry had been in the United States only three days when he arrived on the battlefield at Fredericksburg, Virginia. He left, was gone five weeks and was tried for desertion upon his return, receiving a sentence of death. After this dramatic introduction to his adopted homeland, Kaim's luck turned for the better. Hooker cited the amnesty proclamation and Lincoln agreed. His "A. Lincoln" appears below Nicolay's "Pardoned."[10]

Four men of the 14th U. S. Infantry came to Lincoln's attention as a result of these February trials. All four deserted at Falmouth, Virginia. William Chapman told the court, "I was never mustered in. I never received any pay. I had no tent and lay in the cold two weeks before I deserted." General George Sykes endorsed the sentence of death.[11] Uriah Stahr said, "I'd had no shelter of any kind since December." Sykes recommended that Stahr also be shot.[12] John Doneho offered no defense, and his sentence of death was also approved by Sykes.[13] Louis Harbecker was also to face a firing squad, with Sykes' approval.[14] Hooker recommended all four for amnesty and Lincoln agreed, placing his signature below each of Nicolay's four inscriptions of "Pardoned." (If their stories were true, it did not speak well for the Union supply system.)

William Taylor and Joseph Steward, both of the 6th U. S. Infantry, deserted at Potomac Creek, Virginia.[15] Taylor offered no defense, while Steward said, "I have been ten months in the service and I have received no pay." Sykes endorsed death by shooting for both, Hooker recommended both for amnesty, and Lincoln placed his signature under Nicolay's "Pardon" for both men.[16]

Martin Albertson of the 7th U. S. Infantry also deserted at Potomac Creek. He pled guilty, was sentenced to die, had his death penalty endorsed by Sykes and was recommended for amnesty by Hooker. Again, "A. Lincoln" appears beneath "Pardoned."[17]

Lewis Abear of the 12th U. S. Infantry sensed the coming storm at Antietam, Maryland. As soon as the first shells dropped around him, he vanished and was not seen again for five months. His sentence of death was approved by Sykes. Hooker recommended amnesty. Nicolay wrote, "Pardon," and Lincoln wrote his name.[18] Sykes, who seems to have endorsed every death sentence that crossed his desk, was a West Point man with service in the Mexican War and along the desert frontier. A stickler for military protocol, his defensive performances at First and Second Manassas had won praise from superiors and subordinates alike.

Theodore Dunning ran away from the 15th U. S. Infantry at Murfreesboro on New Year's Eve and was gone sixteen days. His original sentence of six months hard labor was returned for reconsideration; his new sentence was a bit harsher: the firing squad. Rosecrans recommended commutation and the Chief Executive wrote, "Recommendation of Gen. Rosecrans approved. A. Lincoln Nov. 7, 1863."[19] That day, Federal troops marched on the defenders of Frog Bayou, Arkansas, and Jefferson Davis' Inspector General reported that the morale of Confederate troops in Arkansas was good.

The Granite State contributed one man to the February cases. Charles Heath of the 2nd New Hampshire was tried on several charges. In addition to refusing roll call and telling his sergeant, "If you arrest me, I will rip your Goddamn guts out and scatter them on the parade ground," he deserted at Yorktown, Virginia. Hooker approved this death sentence and forwarded it to Holt, who noted that Heath "deserves severe punishment." Taking note of the Amnesty, Holt then recommended commutation to hard labor for the rest of Heath's enlistment. In December 1864, Heath's wife wrote to Lincoln that her husband had been in prison for 31 of his 42 months in the service, and that "he has but one arm left." She seems to blame the President for her troubles: "If you could only know how much you make me suffer. . .if you have one spark of feeling or humanity left in your body, you must help me." Nicolay sent the letter to Holt, who noted that the President had pardoned Heath eighteen months earlier and wanted to know why Heath was still in prison. The answer to that does not appear in the court-martial records.[20]

New York, the most populous state, was the home of eight of the February soldiers. Richard Rush of the 137th New York deserted at Fairfax Station, Virginia. "I wanted to trade my gun for a citizen's suit and a cow." Later, he said that he was just looking for whisky at a better price than he had found at the sutler's shop. Rush was sentenced to die; Hooker cited the March Amnesty; Nicolay wrote, "Pardoned," and Lincoln wrote his name.[21]

Gideon Holmes of the 137th New York also deserted and was also sentenced to be shot. Witnesses stated that Holmes had been kicked in the head by a horse and had since suffered from "fits." He was described as "of unsound mind. . .unfit for duty. . .a lack of quickness of mind." Again, Hooker recommended pardon on the grounds of the Amnesty and the President concurred, adding his name to Nicolay's "Pardoned." This decision apparently sent back to duty a man remarkably unsuited for active service.[22]

John Baker of the 18th New York deserted in Stafford County, Virginia. He said that his feet were sore and that he had stayed at a house until his feet were better. He was sentenced to be shot; Hooker invoked the Proclamation, Nicolay wrote, "Pardoned," and Lincoln signed.[23] The complaint of sore feet was wide-spread, north and south. Men with bare feet suffered, but those who did receive shoes also suffered. Most had no arches, and the footwear was usually either too big or too small. It has been said that if either side had had modern athletic shoes, that side would have been victorious in the first year.

Landford Swan of the New York 50th Engineers deserted at Fort Ward, Virginia and joined a New York cavalry regiment, Scott's 900, where he served two months. His original sentence—seven days in solitary on bread and water, followed by hard labor for the rest of his enlistment—was overturned and he was ordered to be shot. Hooker invoked the Proclamation and Lincoln signed below the word "Pardoned."[24]

Ormsby Shevlin of the 1st New York deserted twice, once at Newport News, and again at Alexandria, both in Virginia. He was to be shot, which was approved by Brigadier General David Birney. Hooker cited his usual reason for pardon, and the President obliged. Nicolay wrote, "Pardoned," and Lincoln signed.[25] Hooker, whose military career and personal proclivities have been much studied, almost always sought a way to avoid carrying out the death penalty.

John Wilsey of the 121st New York left his regiment for three months while "marching to meet the enemy." He, too, was sentenced to die, saved by Hooker and pardoned by Lincoln, with the usual signatures.[26] Henry Dubois of the 165th New York left his regiment at New Orleans "for a few minutes." He was found drunk downtown that afternoon in civilian clothes and was charged with desertion. His defense—"I am French. I got something to drink"—while it had a certain Gallic *je ne sais quoi*, did not prevent a death sentence. Major General Nathaniel Banks remitted the sentence on a technicality; the final note reads, "Pardon. A. Lincoln Feb. 9, 1864."[27]

William Herbage and George Miller, both of the 117th New York, were convicted of desertion and sentenced to eighteen months hard labor on the Rip Raps.[28] In an unusually long note signed by Lincoln, Nicolay wrote of these two men: "They have the remainder of their sentences remitted, on condition that they make up by faithful military service in the field, the time lost to such service by reason of their imprisonment."[29]

The Garden State contributed seven men to the February group. Sergeant Henry McGaw of the 3rd New Jersey deserted at Falmouth, Virginia. Witnesses said that he had fought bravely at Gaines' Mill and Fredericksburg, Virginia, and Antietam, Maryland. McGaw defended his leaving during "Burnside's Mud March": "The mud was very deep and I was very tired. I hadn't been paid in six months and my sister, who depends on me, was starving." The court was unimpressed and sentenced him to die. Hooker disapproved and recommended pardon. Nicolay wrote, "Pardoned," and Lincoln signed.[30] Not all was glory during the war; the reality was usually wretched living conditions and bad food.

Corporal Thomas Matlack, also of the 3rd New Jersey, was a different story. Not only did he desert at White Oak Church, Virginia, but he persuaded three men to desert with him. He was also sentenced to be shot; he, too, was pardoned by the signatures of Hooker and Lincoln.[31]

Thomas Patton of the 5th New Jersey deserted, was arrested, tried, convicted, and sentenced to be shot. Hooker cited the Proclamation, Holt summarized the case without comment and the President wrote, "Pardon. A. Lincoln July 18, 1863."[32] Peter Post of the 5th New Jersey left at Falmouth, saying that his family was starving and needed him. The court sentenced him to be shot for desertion. Hooker cited the Proclamation; Nicolay wrote, "Pardoned;" Lincoln wrote his name.[33] (All of these similar cases provoke a logical question: might the whole process have been short-circuited by feeding the soldiers' families?)

David McManus, also of the 5th New Jersey, also deserted at Falmouth. He offered no excuse, but was saved from death by the same sequence of signatures.[34]

Another New Jerseyian, Thomas Guice of the 7th Regiment, left his regiment at Falmouth. His excuse offered at trial was, "I thought to go to Alexandria." This was not a very inspired defense and the court thought he should be shot, and so did General Hiram Berry. Hooker again cited the Proclamation and Lincoln signed Nicolay's "Pardoned."[35]

William Brant, yet another soldier of the 7th New Jersey, also deserted at Falmouth, for which he was sentenced to die. General Berry endorsed the sentence, Hooker recommended pardon, and Lincoln agreed. "A. Lincoln" brought the case to a close.[36]

James Stephens of the 12th Massachusetts had a fine sense of timing. By his two desertions he missed both the battle of Fredericksburg and the Mud March. The court thought that being shot might make up for this, but Hooker saw Stephens as entitled to the provisions of the Proclamation. Nicolay's "Pardoned" and the President's "A. Lincoln" closed the case.[37]

William Watson of the 32nd Massachusetts left at Potomac Creek, Virginia, after he had not been paid in nine months. He was convicted and sentenced to be shot. The same sequence of Hooker, Nicolay and Lincoln notes which reprieved the others also saved Watson from a violent death. A pattern of Presidential remission is certainly evident in all these cases.[38]

James Gleghorn of the 1st Maryland Artillery offered a different excuse for vacating the ranks without permission: he left at White Oak Church, Virginia, in order to see his parents. His death sentence was also pardoned by the notations of Hooker, Nicolay and Lincoln.[39] William Angell of the 2nd Rhode Island left at the Battle of Antietam (perhaps he had seen enough blood) and simply went home. He had not been shot by the Confederates, but the court thought he should be shot by his own comrades. General John Newton said he did "not see anything sufficiently aggravated in this case to justify the infliction of the death penalty." The Chief Executive agreed and directed Nicolay to write, "Pardoned," to which he affixed the presidential signature.[40]

Joseph Rodgers of the 20th Indiana said that he was wounded in the shin and taken prisoner by JEB Stuart at Bull Run. As happened so often, there seemed to be no documentation proving or disproving either the wound or the capture, and the court was not in the mood to look at his shin. Instead, it ordered the Indiana man shot for desertion. Again, Hooker interceded and was confirmed by Lincoln, writing under Nicolay's "Pardoned."[41] Another Indiana soldier, Marion Linville, was accused of deserting at Pratt's Point, Virginia. He denied any intent of deserting from the 7th Indiana, only that he planned "to take French leave." Since this meant being absent without leave, it only substituted one crime for another. This defense carried no weight with the court and he, too, was to face a firing squad. Again, we see the handwriting of Hooker, Nicolay and Lincoln. Linville was not shot.[42]

George W. Castleberry of the 122nd Illinois had "urgent family matters," but was refused a furlough. When arrested, he was fifteen miles from his camp. Castleberry was to be shot. Major General Ulysses S. Grant recommended pardon and Holt concurred. The President wrote, "Prisoner pardoned. A. Lincoln Nov. 7, 1863."[43] Castleberry had waited nine months in prison for that decision. During that time his comrades had served at Corinth, Tuscumbia, Salisbury, and Iuka. As Lincoln was signing Castleberry's pardon, Confederate forces were capturing Union pickets at Warrenton, Virginia.

Samuel Moore, who deserted the 9th West Virginia and joined the Confederate Army, was to be shot on February 20, 1863. The trial record failed to note the required "two-thirds of the members concurring." The papers were passed from one office to another for many months in an attempt to remedy this administrative error, to no avail. Holt's analysis concluded, "The sentence is inoperative." Nicolay wrote, "Finding and sentence void for informality." The last entry reads: "A. Lincoln Feb. 10, 1864."[44] Moore had missed a year of the war.

March

The third month of the third year of the war was a banner month for trials of Union deserters. In the records reviewed thus far, 54 March cases came to Lincoln's attention. Remarkably, 24 of these cases involved Regular Army soldiers as opposed to state volunteers. Even more surprising, 14 of these men from a single regiment, the 11th U. S. Infantry, which had been raised in Boston, Massachussetts. This regiment had been through the battles of Antietam and Fredericksburg, as well as the Mud March. Ten of these men deserted at a single location (Potomac Creek, Virginia): Privates Michael Fitzgibbons, John Quinlan, John Mehan, Michael McCluskey, Francis Gillis, William H. Brown, William Kellison, Martin Jillson, John McKinney, and John Robbins.[45] All were sentenced to be shot. On all of them Hooker's note reads, "The President by Proclamation has pardoned all deserters that rejoin before the 1st of April. As it would seem unjust under these circumstances to enforce the extreme penalty of the law on those who differ from others simply in having been apprehended, I recommend a pardon be extended in this case." On every one, Nicolay wrote "Pardoned," and on every case is the signature "A. Lincoln." The Civil War is an endless fountain of questions to be answered. What was happening in the 11th Infantry? Were they mostly Irish immigrants, as the names suggest? Was it the battles which had caused them to lose heart, or were other factors at work?

Private William Kellison's records are different from those of the other nine deserters in that they contain a note about his mental condition and a letter from his wife. One witness observed, "He seemed abstracted, walking around." Mrs. Kellison addressed her husband as "Absent Companion," and described hardship: "Well you have rote a number of times that you was agoin to draw your pay but that aint agoin to cloth the children if you cant support them thare I wish you would come home and support them here." After describing a few recent marriages in the neighborhood, she went on to tell her husband that the children had no shoes (the letter was written in December) and no credit at the store. Once again glory was in short supply.

Samuel Murphy of the 11th U. S. Infantry deserted at Antietam, Maryland.[46] David Albertson deserted at Falmouth, Virginia.[47] Both were sentenced to be shot. They received the same Hooker, Nicolay and Lincoln notations, as did their comrades, which stopped their executions. The case was identical for Seth Knowles and Charles Watkins, also of the 11th U. S. Infantry, whose place of desertion is not noted.[48]

Charles W. Hayford, John P. Martin, William Quinn and William Pender, all of the 17th U. S. Infantry, also voluntarily separated themselves from their comrades. They, too, were sentenced to be shot but were ultimately reprieved by the signatures of Hooker and Lincoln. Martin left during the Mud March.[49] Quinn also bogged down in that terrible muck and left for drier climes.[50] Hayford deserted at Antietam.[51] Pender pled guilty and offered no defense.[52]

Charles Campbell of the 14th U. S. Infantry was gone for four months after Antietam. The court-martial sentenced him to death. Lincoln put his signature in a corner of the crowded court-martial paper and Campbell was pardoned. [53] One scrawled signature, a mere eight letters, and Campbell lived on.

Four men whose regiment is given as "US Engineers" deserted at Falmouth, Virginia, and escaped sudden death by firing squad by means of the familiar signatures of Hooker and Lincoln. According to Edward Currier, he was "just taking a ramble. I crossed the river in a rented skiff to buy a canteen of whisky and some food from a farmer," which at least offered the court a story.[54] George Bean said that he had been on the schooner *Waterman*, which made no impression on the men trying him, since he had no business being on any schooner.[55] Neither of the other two men, John Iott nor Henry W. Perkins, had much to offer as a defense. It seemed not to matter, for all four escaped an untimely death.[56]

Lincoln reviewed fifteen March cases from the Empire State. Fernando Smith and Edward Pryor of the 21st New York both deserted at Brook Station, Virginia, and were sentenced to two months hard labor.[57] Henry Adams, also of the 21st, deserted from a hospital in Washington, DC.[58] All three men were recommended for pardon by Hooker, a view which was confirmed by the President.

The Troy regiment, the 2nd New York, had three men tried for desertion in March. John Russell and John Cunningham both left at Fair Oaks, Virginia. General Berry agreed with their being shot. Hooker recommended pardon, using the same words as before, and Lincoln added his signature.[59] James Ferrill left during the fighting at Fredericksburg; his death sentence was also confirmed by Berry, disagreed with by Hooker, and disposed of by "A. Lincoln," with the single word "Pardon."[60]

Amos Treat, August Greiner, and John McCarty, all of the 20th New York State Militia, were charged with desertion. Treat said that he was captured and paroled at Warrenton, Virginia, but was fined two months pay anyway.[61] Greiner said that he was captured and paroled at Gainesville, Virginia; he was sentenced to hard labor in prison to the end of his enlistment.[62] McCarty left Fredericksburg the day before the battle; he was fined three months pay.[63] In each case, Lincoln endorsed Hooker's recommendation for pardon.

Reuben Fagan and James Dilks of the 73rd New York both ran away at Fredericksburg and were both gone for three months. Both were sentenced to be shot.[64] Several exchanges of letters between Hooker, Holt and Berry over legal technicalities in the proceedings were brought to a halt by Lincoln, who wrote, "Sentence disapproved. A. Lincoln May 11, 1863." The South at this time was in mourning for Stonewall Jackson, but that seemed little consolation for the dispirited Union soldiers.

The case of William Durnin of the 50th New York is rather unusual. The New Yorker had never been paid. At Aquia Creek, Virginia, he went to the paymaster and complained about his plight. The paymaster told Durnin that there was no record of his ever having been enlisted, and therefore no reason to pay him. Durnin, naturally enough, went home. At his trial, he was sentenced to prison at hard labor for the rest of his enlistment—plus the loss of most of his pay—pay which he had never received, for an enlistment which officially had never taken place. Hooker asked the court to reconsider its verdict. It did, and the new verdict was that Durnin should be shot to death, which was probably not what Hooker had in mind (Durnin either, for that matter). Holt rightly urged mitigation, Nicolay wrote "Sentence commuted to imprisonment for three months, May 11, 1863," and Lincoln signed.[65] This sad comedy of private miseries and nearly fatal errors may have seemed to Lincoln a strange counterpoint to his receiving official notification that same afternoon of the splendors of the recent marriage of the future Edward VII to the lovely Princess Alexandra of Denmark.

"I have a wife and six children," was Barney Fitzpatrick's reason for deserting at Camp Rufus King. The excuse may have saved the part-time member of the 35th New York from the firing squad, as he was sentenced to hard labor for the rest of his enlistment. Hooker recommended pardon and Lincoln endorsed this wish.[66] Moses Tompkins of the 76th New York ran out of patriotism on the Mud March and went home. He was arrested, tried, convicted, and sentenced to die, a fate he'd managed to escape at Antietam and Fredericksburg. Hooker urged pardon, Nicolay wrote the word, and "A. Lincoln" sent Tompkins back to duty.[67]

Even the undeserving received kind treatment. James Free of the 150th New York deserted not once but twice, threatened to kill the Officer of the Day, and boasted that he would desert as often as he could. He was to be shot. Free complained that he was prevented from returning under the Presidential Proclamation because he was already in custody elsewhere. Major General Robert Schenck approved shooting Private Free for desertion, but said he "feels constrained under the Acts of Congress to refer this case to the President, as the conviction is not alone for desertion but also for a violation of the Fourth Article of War. A sentence of death for a violation of this Article cannot carry into execution. Otherwise, such an evil in our army has desertion become, [I] would be disposed to order the execution of this man." Holt noted the same issues, discovered defects in the wording of two of the specifications, and concluded "the sentence should not be enforced." Lincoln remitted the sentence and freed Free.[68]

Another scoundrel, John Dorris of the 154th Pennsylvania, sorely tried the patience of the authorities. As soon as he collected his enlistment bounty, he went on an extended drunk and then deserted. He evaded arrest for a while by calling himself "Lieutenant Dorris" and exhibiting a fake commission. When arrested, he persuaded a sympathetic civil judge to "release" him from the army on habeus corpus. When he was finally tried, he appealed on the grounds that the court had sat past 3:00 p.m., which could invalidate the trial. After his conviction for desertion (and a sentence of two years of hard labor) the case came first to the President, who wrote, "Will the Judge Advocate General please examine and report on this case. A. Lincoln June 1, 1863." Holt wrote a lengthy analysis, concluding "the remission of his sentence could not fail to be highly detrimental to the service and is not advised." Lincoln added, "Conclusions of the Judge Advocate General approved. June 3, 1863. A. Lincoln." Even Lincoln had lost patience with Dorris.[69]

Little else seemed to be going right that day. The Democrats, led by the Mayor of New York, Fernando Wood, met and demanded that Lincoln sue for peace; at Sheffield, England, a large rally was held to honor the recently-deceased Stonewall Jackson, and in Virginia, Lee's army had begun its march towards Gettysburg.

Closer to home, things were no better. John Cleary, a lance corporal of the permanent party at Fort Columbus, New York Harbor, was not only a deserter but was also a thief, making off with tents, knives, blankets, a telescope, and twenty-four pairs of trousers. He was given a dishonorable discharge and sent to the penitentiary. Stanton asked to see the record. Nicolay wrote "The President saw the proceeding and decided that sentence must be executed." Lincoln's actual notation has been stolen out of the Federal records. Why the Secretary of War wanted to see this thief's papers is unknown.[70]

Musician Christopher Flake of the 99th Pennsylvania deserted at Washington, DC and was gone five months. His death sentence was reviewed by Hooker, who recommended pardon, which was granted by "A. Lincoln."[71]

Belle Plain Landing, Virginia, a busy Federal steamboat landing on an indentation of the Potomac River northeast of Fredericksburg, was where three men of the 24th Michigan (part of the vaunted Iron Brigade) deserted. Andrew Wanbeck said he had size nine feet and was issued size seven shoes. "It hurt too much to march. I could not keep up." He was to be shot.[72] Frederick Wright was fined $10.00 a month for ten months for his desertion. The case was returned to the court for reconsideration; Wright's new sentence was death by firing squad.[73] Anthony Brabbon deserted at the same place and was also sentenced to die.[74] For all three men, the notations of Hooker, Nicolay and Lincoln spared their lives and restored them to duty.

It was not just Michigan boys who were unhappy at Belle Plain Landing. Romanzo Harbronck and Henry Dunn, both of the 6th Wisconsin (another Iron Brigade regiment), deserted there. The latter said he had no clothes and it was way too cold to be a naked soldier. Harbronck offered no excuse. The death sentence of each was remitted by "A. Lincoln," as he endorsed Hooker's views on clemency.[75]

Edward Harrison came to grief at Falmouth in the rain. "It was very wet where we were camped. I went up the hill to a drier place, near a fire. In the morning, the regiment was gone." Several men testified as to his "good character," but he was sentenced to be shot anyway. Again, the familiar handwriting of Hooker, Nicolay, and Lincoln pointed the way to life and a full pardon.[76]

Three men of the 117th Ohio were not happy at Ashland, Kentucky. Charles Brundridge deserted twice and said he would desert again as soon as he was paid.[77] Jackson McFann deserted once at Ashland and twice at nearby Catlettsburg.[78] Joseph Cole was in the hospital at Ashland but he, too, left this town.[79] Major General Ambrose Burnside approved all three death sentences, but considered the men covered by the Proclamation; thus he sent the cases on to the Executive Mansion, where the occupant wrote, "Sentence remitted. A. Lincoln April 29, 1863." The continent from Virginia to Mississippi seemed at war that day, with action at Kelly's Ford, in the Wilderness, Deep Run, White Oak Run, Brandy Station, Fairmont, Grand Gulf, Snyder's Mill, La Grange, Brookhaven, Castor River, and a dozen other spots.

Not many lieutenants were sentenced to be shot, but Second Lieutenant Charles Conzet of the 123rd Illinois achieved that distinction. He not only deserted at both Nashville and Stone's River, but encouraged, both verbally and in writing, other men to follow suit. This was not why the army paid lieutenants. Conzet was sentenced to be stripped of his badges of rank and then shot. Generals William Rosecrans and John Reynolds both approved the execution. Letters and petitions for clemency fill the file. September 24, 1864, John Hay wrote, "Let the prisoner be released from confinement and dishonorably dismissed the service of the United States." Below that is "A. Lincoln."[80] It was a Saturday. In the Shenandoah Valley, General Philip Sheridan was carrying out his orders to remove the valley as a source of Confederate food; the smoke from burning barns and crops filled the air. Hundreds of Virginia farmers were ruined and thousands of Southerners would go hungry.

Elijah Peacock of the 8th Indiana Artillery deserted at Nashville. When he was arrested a year later, he pled guilty and was sentenced to die.[81] Rosecrans considered Peacock to be under the provisions of the Proclamation. Under the word "Pardon" is "A. Lincoln July 18, 1863."

That day, at New Albany, Indiana, a leader of the Knights of the Golden Circle, a secret society of pro-slavery men, was arrested by Federal agents; at Charleston, South Carolina, Union siege guns began to pound Confederate forts into rubble—despite the valiant efforts of their defenders.

Logan Fraim not only escaped the death penalty, but was still corresponding with the Pension Bureau in 1894. When he was a private in the 14th Indiana, marching through our nation's capital, he dropped out of the ranks and stayed in Washington for three months. While it is likely that he spent his time in the saloons and bawdy houses of that city, the record is silent on that point. He was to be shot, but Hooker's opinions on the Proclamation and Lincoln's signature brought a full pardon.[82]

At South Mountain, Maryland, Private William Fitzgibbons of the 28th Massachusetts fled while under fire with grape shot and canister. After Fitzgibbons was arrested, tried, convicted, and sentenced to die, General Winfield Hancock approved the outcome. Hooker passed the case on to the President, saying that the offense occurred before he took command. The outcome is brief: "Pardon. A. Lincoln July 18, 1863."[83]

James E. Verdier is the final defendant tried in March 1863. This 24-year-old laborer (height 64 inches, dark hair and complexion) deserted from the 2nd Pennsylvania Artillery at Fort Thayer, Washington, DC, and was sentenced to a year without pay at hard labor on the Rip Raps. Verdier was most emphatically "somebody's Wallace." On June 2, 1863, one A. N. Rankin of Chambersburg, Pennsylvania, addressed a letter to Hon. Edward McPherson, Deputy Commissioner of the Internal Revenue Service: "Dear Sir, Enclosed you will find a petition which you will greatly oblige a large number of the best citizens of Quincy Township in this County, by presenting to the President for the pardon, and the restoration to his regiment of James E. Verdier. . .I never knew a case in which a whole community took so deep and interest. Major Hughes, proprietor of Mont Alto iron works, supposing the case within reach of Gov. Curtin, makes an especial appeal to that functionary as you will see, over his signature."

Rankin continued with the thinly veiled threats so reflective of the political process: "Please give the matter your personal attention and thereby call down upon your own and to the President's head the blessings of very many excellent people." Two days later, McPherson wrote to Lincoln, enclosing Rankin's petition signed by "many of the most respectable citizens of Franklin County, Pa., who testify to Verdier's fine personal qualities, and appeal for your clemency." McPherson concluded, "I beg to commend the subject to your consideration." Verdier's case is but another example of local dignitaries demanding iron discipline in the Army—except for their hometown boy. One can easily sympathize with the President, who wrote, "Judge Advocate General please report on this. A. Lincoln June 26, 1863." The following day, Holt replied, "This case was reported on to the President, on 22nd inst." There Verdier's court-martial record ends; fortunately, we have other records, which tell of a happy ending.[84] He was released by order of the President in October 1863, promoted to corporal four months later and to sergeant in January 1865. Two months after the Confederate surrender, he was mustered out with his regiment. His only further crime was the loss of a cartridge box plate, for which he was charged fourteen cents.

These nearly one hundred cases may seem repetitive and perhaps not worthy of comment. A recent newspaper article may put a different light on such a conclusion. Since 1976, the various states have executed over 500 criminals. One Texas official was quoted as saying, "We've got it down to a science. It's routine." Routine perhaps to the guards and administrators, but it is much to be doubted that the matter is "routine" to the person being executed. Each person's life is of enormous consequence to that person. Lincoln's signature on a pardon was everything to that condemned man.

What is at issue in this study is the extent of Lincoln's reprieves, and the pattern in which it agreed or disagreed with his professional military men. Looking at Table Four (next page), we see that Lincoln disagreed with the sentence pronounced by the court in ninety-six percent (96%) of the cases. However, the reviewing general, most commonly Hooker or Rosecrans, usually felt as Lincoln did; the agreement between the President and his departmental commanders in this set of trials is ninety-seven percent (97%). For the spring of 1863, at least, Lincoln granted a pardon to nearly every desertion case presented to him, and in doing so he was almost completely in harmony with his military leaders.

Opinion Maker	Lincoln Agrees	Lincoln Disagrees	% Agreement
Trial Verdict	4	99	4
Authorizing Officer	2	22	8
Departmental Commander	91	3	97
Judge Advocate General	7	1	88
Interested Politicians	1	0	100
Friends, Family & Comrades	NA	NA	NA

Lincoln was compassionate, or at least forgiving, but so were many men with general's stars upon their shoulders.

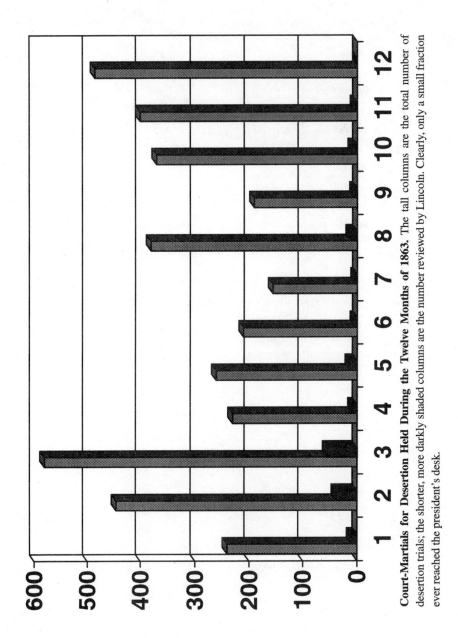

Court-Martials for Desertion Held During the Twelve Months of 1863. The tall columns are the total number of desertion trials; the shorter, more darkly shaded columns are the number reviewed by Lincoln. Clearly, only a small fraction ever reached the president's desk.

Desertion (April 1863 - April 1865)

Within the first 43,000 court martials of the Civil War, the records with entries by Abraham Lincoln are concentrated in the years 1861-1863. Due to the chaotic filing system (or lack of system) that developed during the hectic war years, however, a given folder might contain records from both 1862 and 1865. Thus, in this chapter the majority of the records are from 1863, but there are a few from 1864 and one—a poignant one at that—in which Lincoln's entry was made just hours before he was murdered by John Wilkes Booth.

The first April 1863 case illustrates both the bitter nature of border warfare and the limits of Lincoln's forgiveness. Henry Estep of the 14th Kentucky deserted on the march to Cumberland Gap and joined the 5th Kentucky Infantry of the Confederate Army. He was arrested a year later and convicted of desertion and of aiding the enemy. The death sentence was approved by General Ambrose Burnside and concurred in by Holt. The President wrote, "Sentence approved. A. Lincoln July 18, 1863." Estep was shot on Friday, November 13, 1863. He left a wife and four children.[1] The day of his execution, Federal shells still rained down on Charleston Harbor, and along the South Fork of California's Trinity River, Federal troops clashed with Hoopa Indians, displaced from their ancestral homes.

Eight other "Lincoln cases" were tried that April. Daniel Nihne of the 2nd Massachusetts Cavalry was sentenced to a year at hard labor for desertion. By accident, it was discovered that he was also known as Daniel Andrews of the 11th Infantry, US Army, who was sentenced to death for desertion from that regiment. Major General John Dix wrote,

"His character is highly spoken of by all his officers." Dix suggested that Andrews/Nihne be returned to duty. Holt passed that decision on to the Chief Executive, who wrote, "Pardon. A. Lincoln Feb. 9, 1864."[2] The same day, a Union expedition made its way up Florida's Nassau River, and Federal troops occupied Yazoo City, Mississippi.

Frederick Blanchard deserted from the 34th Massachusetts at Fort Lyon, Virginia, and was sentenced to be shot. General Heintzelman recommended commutation to a sentence of dishonorable discharge and hard labor for the rest of his enlistment. Holt concurred. So did Lincoln, who signed his name to that sentence.[3]

The convoluted workings of the legal process seems to have saved the life of Jackson Floyd of the 5th West Virginia. He escaped from the guard house and joined a band of Rebel guerillas, where he was captured carrying a gun and wearing the butternut-dyed clothing of a Confederate soldier. Floyd was convicted of deserting to the enemy and was sentenced to be shot. Holt reviewed the case and noted that Floyd had claimed temporary insanity resulting from being struck on the head by a gun in the hands of his Union lieutenant colonel. Holt felt that the death penalty was warranted, but because the court had not properly admitted testimony about the alleged insanity caused by the blow to the head, the President must decide whether the proceedings should be approved. Lincoln did not, and the case concludes with the words, "Sentence disapproved. A. Lincoln Feb. 9, 1864."[4]

William Drake of the 12th Ohio deserted at Fayetteville, Virginia. He was captured, convicted and sentenced to be shot. General Benjamin Kelley (who was captured by Confederate partisans during a visit to his fiancee at Cumberland, Maryland) recommended "mercy" based on Lincoln's Proclamation. Holt made no recommendation, but his employer did: "Pardon. A. Lincoln Feb. 9, 1864."[5]

The impending Battle of Perryville, Kentucky, held no attractions for Richard Hembree, who left the 5th Indiana and did not return for seven months. He pled guilty and offered no defense. The two-page trial record concluded that he "is to be shot to death with musketry." General Rosecrans approved the sentence, but a flurry of letters and petitions—"He is of no information or education. . .has a wife and five children"—in the days before his date with death resulted in "Pardon. A.

Lincoln July 18, 1863."[6] That Monday, John Bell Hood assumed command of the Confederate forces outside Atlanta, with fateful consequences. Four months later he would effectively destroy his valiant army's morale and command structure by hurling it against Union defenses at Franklin, Tennessee. Over 1,700 Southern men were killed, including six generals.

George Wentworth of the 20th Massachusetts deserted at the Battle of Fredericksburg. His death sentence was approved by General John Gibbon, but Hooker invoked the Proclamation, Nicolay wrote, "Pardoned," and Lincoln signed.[7]

A private of the 14th Michigan, William Dodge, deserted at Camp Big Springs, Mississippi. He also stole a month's pay from a comrade. Dodge offered no defense and pled guilty. He was sentenced to be shot. Rosecrans approved the sentence but believed that the Proclamation protected Dodge. Nicolay wrote, "Sentence remitted according to the recommendation of Major General Rosecrans." Lincoln added his signature, and Dodge lived on to tell the tale.[8]

May 1863 brought fifteen cases, including seven which give unusual insight into the decision-making process in Civil War justice. Six of these privates were from the 157th New York: Bradford Butler, George Carpenter, James Fox, Michael Miller, Simon Nesler, and William Waggoner. All had deserted at Hartwood Church, Virginia, except Carpenter, who left his regiment at Stafford Courthouse, also in Virginia. The seventh man was Peter Schalowsky of the 45th New York, who deserted at Kelly's Ford, Virginia. All these men were convicted and sentenced to be shot. Their records arrived at the Executive Mansion in one large batch. Lincoln wrote in his own hand, "Let execution of the persons within named be suspended until Gen. Meade can act upon the cases who will dispose of them according to his judgment and discretion. July 24, 1863. A. Lincoln."[9]

These six cases generated an unusual amount of interest. That same day, Secretary of War Edwin Stanton appointed a colonel as special investigator and wrote, in his own hand, an unusual document addressed to General Herman Haupt, the Chief of Military Transportation for the Union Army. "The Superintendent of Railroad Transportation will give transport by express to Colonel [Phillip] Brown of the 157th New York

Regiment from Washington to Gainesville with the utmost dispatch and the officer commanding at Gainesville will give him transportation and escort to secure him safe arrival at General Howard's Headquarters at New Baltimore." Colonel Brown and the aide-de-camp of General O. O. Howard interviewed numerous witnesses and made these paraphrased observations: Fox and Carpenter were both age 19 and of "good character." Miller was age 46 with a wife and four children and also of "good character." Nesler, age 22, had "good character;" Waggoner had not only "good character," but also a wife and four children. Schalowsky's officers presented a petition for clemency, stating that he was "barely age 19, led astray, and is the sole support of an aging mother."

Butler, on the other hand, had been tried for homicide before the war and was described as "turbulent, insubordinate and of bad character." Unlike today's endless litigation, events usually moved swiftly in the war between the North and the South. On July 27, General Howard wrote, "These men are all guilty and the only adequate punishment is death. But I regard it as better for the Corps at this time to confine the executions to the worst case and to pardon the rest. I believe the remaining six will return to duty and strive to regain the character they have lost. This opinion upon a full and careful reconsideration of the cases involved."

Howard's opinion was endorsed by Major General George Meade. On July 31, 1863, Hay wrote "The recommendation to mercy made by General Meade is approved." Lincoln signed. The first six men were pardoned, but the "turbulent" and "insubordinate" Butler was shot the next day, August 1, 1863, at Warrenton, Virginia.

Two New Jersey soldiers were tried for desertion in May and reviewed by Lincoln. Private John A. Thompson of the 13th New Jersey deserted at Tennallytown, Maryland. "I was very tired on the march. I lay down and slept and my equipment was stolen. I went home and missed the Proclamation as I had the measles." He was to be shot. Hooker cited the Proclamation and Lincoln wrote his name under Nicolay's "Pardoned."[10]

The other New Jersey soldier, Private John Leeson of the 3rd Regiment, was convicted of desertion and cowardice: he left while under fire at Antietam. On his return eight months later he was tried and sentenced to be shot—in spite of his claim to have been in the hospital. (Once again, there seemed to be no way to confirm or deny his stay in the hospital, nor did the court express an interest in doing so.) Holt reviewed the transcript and recommended commutation. Hay wrote, "Sentence commuted as recommended by the Judge Advocate General within." After that is "A. Lincoln."[11]

Private Justus Brockett of the 15th Connecticut deserted at Washington, D.C. and was arrested in his home town four months later. The court sentenced him to meet a firing squad, but recommended mitigation. So did Brigadier General George Getty and Major General John Foster. "It is believed that the prisoner," wrote Holt, "comes within the class that since the first of April have uniformly received the pardon of the President." Holt was right. The next entry reads, "Pardon. A. Lincoln Feb. 9, 1864."[12] The next morning at the French port of Brest on the Bay of Biscay, the Confederate warship *Florida* slipped by the Union blockade and escaped into the open sea.

Private John Hoffman of the 16th West Virginia did not see any combat as his regiment waited in the defenses of Washington, D.C. for an attack which never came. He was in the guard house for some offense, escaped, and deserted. When caught, he pled guilty and was sentenced to be shot. General Heintzelman recommended mitigation. Holt, somewhat testily, noted that no grounds for mitigation appeared in the record and that shooting Hoffman would be quite appropriate. However, the President did not agree and placed his signature under Hay's note: "Sentence commuted in accordance with the recommendation of Gen. Heintzelman."[13]

Private Paris Rollins, another soldier of the 16th West Virginia, celebrated Christmas of 1862 by deserting. When arrested, he was held in the Old Slave Pen in Alexandria, but escaped and was gone three more months. When recaptured and tried, he pled guilty and was sentenced to die. Heintzelman disapproved the findings on the grounds that the location of the crime was unspecified in the charges. Holt disagreed: "The court was fully justified in sentencing him to be shot." The final decision was Lincoln's, who wrote in his own hand "Sentence commuted as recommended by Genl. Heintzelman. July 18, 1863."[14] That day, Lincoln spent six full hours on his court-martial cases.

A border state soldier with the 26th Kentucky deserted once in January and again in February. Private John W. Boyd pled guilty, offered no defense and received the death penalty. General Ambrose Burnside agreed and set the execution for noon on July 3, 1863. Holt reviewed the record: "Boyd has never been mustered into the service of the United States. He is therefore not subject to punishment for desertion." (In the recent Leeson case, the army didn't know whether he'd been in the hospital; in Boyd's case the army didn't know he wasn't in the army.) The final word appears thus: "Report approved. A. Lincoln July 18, 1863."[15]

The final case of May 1863 was William Polson, a private in the 8th Kansas who appears to have been a one-man crime wave. Not only did he desert, but at Fort Leavenworth, Kansas, he stole Major Stephen Todd's horse, kept it for three days and then shot the animal. A few days later, he stole a pony from a "Mr. Titus." Following Polson's sentence of death, the President received letters from the soldier's "respectable and loyal" parents, the captain of his company, the Lieutenant Governor of Kansas, and from United States Senator Lane, all urging some degree of clemency, varying from three years in prison to total pardon. Holt offered no opinion. Lincoln signed this entry, in the hand of Hays: "Sentence commuted to imprisonment during the war. Nov. 7, 1863." Polson, too, was certainly "somebody's Wallace," even if he doesn't seem to merit such loving concern.[16]

June, the month of the summer solstice, brought three trials which ended on the President's desk. Jacob Strang of the 2nd Pennsylvania Artillery deserted from the defenses of Washington. One of the Lincoln legends was his ability to tell an honest man from a phony. Strang may have been among the latter. In the summer of 1863, he was defending his nation's capital at Fort Thayer, now 25th Street Southeast, near Irving Street in the District of Columbia. Unable to read or write, he defended himself before the court in this statement written by a scribe: "Private Wolf and myself started for Fort Bunker Hill to get some ale, but being unable to procure any, we continued on to Fort Stevens for the same purpose, but were still unable to obtain any. I knew where there was a rum shop above Fort Stevens and we went there, but were refused liquor. Meeting two 'darkies' they told us we could get something to drink up the road and we went on until we came to the house where we were arrested. I had no idea of deserting, but was in search of liquor."

The court noted that he had been arrested fourteen miles north of Fort Thayer and noted further his plea that, "If I had not been ill-used I would have stayed," and decided he was, indeed, a deserter. It sent him to the Dry Tortugas, that hell hole off Key West, Florida, for the rest of his enlistment with the loss of six months of pay. This meant, of course, no income for his wife and five children. Strang wrote two letter asking for clemency, one to Andrew Curtin, Governor of Pennsylvania and one to Lincoln.   Each was written in an entirely different hand, but the message was identical: prison is a very unhealthy place and I should be let out. As to being fourteen miles from his camp, Strang explained to Governor Curtin, he "had left camp to go but a short distance to a house where they sold liquor. That is all there is to my case."   Lincoln made the following note, "If there are papers in this case, please have them sent to me. A. Lincoln Oct. 30, 1863." The following day, Holt provided the required records. After a careful review, Lincoln declined to pardon Strang, who experienced some difficult months in an unforgiving clime.[17] (Aaron Strang of the same regiment, who was probably Jacob's brother, also served time for desertion; perhaps it ran in the family.)   In Charleston Harbor, Confederate defenders of Fort Sumter gamely held their position as the continuing Union bombardment reduced the brick structure to rubble, confirming that the day of the masonry fort had passed.

The Union's 9th Kentucky Cavalry had not received their promised bounty. When ordered to march to war at Nicholasville, Kentucky, they would not move. Instead, they stood chanting "Forty dollars!" until they were arrested. Sergeant Robert Lynn said to the officers, "Well, you did not arrest me, but I'll go to the guard house too because I promised to stick with the boys." When the group was released, Lynn left and en-listed in an Indiana artillery regiment. He was arrested eight months later and was sentenced to be shot. The court petitioned for clemency, as did his Indiana officers, who described him as skillful, gallant and coura-geous. General Burnside "earnestly" recommended commutation. In Holt's review, he noted that Lynn had been in prison for four months awaiting a decision, and ended by writing, "It is believed that a pardon might be granted in this case without injury to the service." Lincoln's reply avoided the passive voice: "Pardoned. A. Lincoln."[18]

"Insane or idiotic, non compos mentis," is the way Patrick Murphy of the 2nd California Infantry is described in his trial record. He deserted at Portland, Oregon, only to enlist in the 6th California Infantry. He was sentenced to be shot, but the court recommended clemency, stating that Murphy was manifestly "not perfectly sound." General George Wright forwarded the papers without comment on September 1, 1863. Holt urged discharge from the service "if the man is insane or an idiot." The 3,000 miles separating the two coasts delayed administrative matters, but when the final entry came to this record, it was poignant, indeed. "This man is pardoned and hereby ordered to be discharged from the service. A. Lincoln April 14, 1865." A few hours later, Lincoln put on his hat and headed for Ford's Theater. During the winter of 1998-1999, Murphy's papers formed part of a new public exhibit of "Treasures" at the National Archives. Fame comes to men in many strange ways.[19]

"A wanton and atrocious murderer," was how Joseph Holt described John Kestison of the 11th Illinois Cavalry. He deserted at Christmas 1862 and joined a Rebel guerilla band. In Mississippi, he shot an unarmed prisoner from the 12th Michigan and also shot an unnamed civilian fleeing north. General Grenville Dodge approved the death sentence and urged immediate execution. Holt was puzzled by General U. S. Grant's recommendation for commutation, and saw no basis for such. Neither did the Chief Executive: "Sentence approved. April 26, 1864."[20]

Eleven trials, held in August 1863, came under the President's review. Privates Andrew Bans and Jacob Barth, both of the 82nd Illinois, deserted and were sentenced to be shot. General Hector Tyndale, twice wounded hero of Antietam, recommended commutation and noted that the 82nd Illinois was not fully organized when Bans left. General Meade recommended commutation to hard labor for the duration of the war. Holt took no stand and Lincoln wrote, "Gen. Meade's recom. approved. Feb. 9, 1864." Bans went to prison.[21]

Barth was described as a man who would keep drinking until he was out of money. The chaplain saw it as his "sacred duty" to tell the court martial board that Barth was "almost an imbecile," a point reinforced by

Barth's behavior in Cincinnati. He stopped people on the streets to tell them how he deserted, a spectacularly idiotic activity which supported the chaplain's view of Barth's mental condition, but also led to his capture. Nineteen officers signed a statement that Barth was "deranged." General O. O. Howard agreed and recommended commutation. Holt passed his summary on to Lincoln, who wrote, "Pardon & discharge. Feb. 9, 1864."[22] From a Darwinian point of view, wars kill the best and the bravest, leaving the defectives and the cowards to reproduce. It seems strange to celebrate such an activity.

At the Battle of Fredericksburg, 18-year-old Eugene Sullivan of the 20th Massachusetts stood shoulder-to-shoulder with his father, who a moment later was struck dead by a Rebel bullet. On the first day of the Battle of Gettysburg, Eugene ran. He was sentenced to be shot for "desertion in the face of the enemy." The court petitioned for clemency, noting that young Sullivan "is shocked and terror-stricken at the prospect of a battle," although he had carried himself well at Chancellorsville. There was further testimony that when the regimental commander, Colonel Paul Revere, was badly wounded at Gettysburg, he asked Eugene to stay close to him, which he did until Revere's death on July 5. Five officers of the 20th Massachusetts submitted this petition: "Sullivan is but eighteen years old. . .he has been in several battles and behaved with proper courage previous to the offense for which he is now sentenced. He has never been vicious nor generally insubordinate." Every level of command endorsed the concept of clemency for Sullivan. Holt summarized the case, without making a recommendation. This must have been an easy decision for Lincoln, who wrote "Sentence remitted April 27, 1864," and signed his name.[23] That day, President Jefferson Davis sent two men on a mission to Canada to see if the United States might agree to a negotiated peace.

Patrick Berrian had troubles aplenty. He had performed bravely in several battles, but was undone on the home front. His wife had been jailed for adultery and had sold all of Patrick's belongings to pay for her lawyer. "The children were going to the Poor House to be bound out [sold into semi-slavery]. I was half crazy thinking of my children." Berrian got drunk, left the 16th Massachusetts, and headed home. He was arrested, convicted and sentenced to die. The court-martial board and General Meade both recommended clemency. Holt had no opinion. Fortunately for Barrien, Lincoln did. The Chief Executive wrote, "Pardon Feb. 9, 1864."[24]

Robert Myers and John Watson, both of the 90th Pennsylvania, deserted at Rappahannock Station, Virginia. They were both absent for three days, and they were both sentenced to be shot. Major General John Newton recommended commutation to six months hard labor and no pay for 12 months. General Meade agreed and Holt summarized but did not comment. On both, Hay wrote, "General Newton's recommendation approved. Nov. 7, 1863," and Lincoln signed.[25]

Seventeen-year-old James Burnell of the 10th Kentucky deserted on the way to a battle near Elizabethtown, Kentucky. He was unable to read or write, but he told the court, "I was broke down and could go no farther." The court, noting his youth and prior good conduct, recommended remission of the death sentence. General Rosecrans agreed, suggesting a fine of six months pay. "Gen. Rosecrans' recom. approved. A. Lincoln Feb. 9, 1864."[26]

Gabriel Dougherty was in the end a lucky man. The 27th Kentucky was pursuing Confederate General Braxton Bragg near Bardstown, Kentucky, when Dougherty left his regiment and did not return for ten months. He was sentenced to be shot between noon and 3:00 p.m. on October 16, 1863. A telegram citing "extenuating circumstances" (but giving no details) halted the process. The final note in this case reads, "Pardon. A. Lincoln Feb. 9, 1864."[27]

Nineteen-year-old Benjamin Wilson of the 81st Illinois was in Memphis, Tennessee, when he deserted. He was to be shot, but the court recommended clemency based on youth and prior good behavior. General U.S. Grant, who obviously took a fairly grim view of the case, changed the sentence to life in prison. Holt said that such a sentence is "contrary to law" and recommended hard labor for the rest of his enlistment. The response from the Executive Mansion? "Recommendation of Judge Advocate General approved. A. Lincoln Nov. 7, 1863."[28]

After he was captured in August 1862, at the Second Battle of Bull Run, Virginia, Robert Bartman of the 1st New Jersey was paroled and sent to the Federal camp at Annapolis, Maryland. There, bored with inactivity, he returned home to his family in Hoboken, New Jersey. In

December 1862, he applied for transportation back to his regiment but was told there were no funds, so he stayed home until arrested. In August 1863, he received a sentence of death. Generals Horatio Wright and George Meade recommended commutation to hard labor to the end of the war, at no pay, a plan endorsed with the words "Gen. Wright's recom. approved. A. Lincoln Feb. 9, 1864."

A year later, the president received a letter which began, "An unfortunate wife and mother, I crave your official clemency for my husband who has been held confined since April 1864 at Tortugas. . .I humbly beg Your Excellency to interpose your clemency, to revoke this sentence and to permit my husband to return to his company ('F') there to serve out his term as a soldier and enable him to provide his starving family. . . it is a very hard task for me to support by the work of my hands alone myself and. . .four small children." Her letter was endorsed by ten local dignitaries. The next entry in this record is this note: "Respectfully referred by the President to the Judge Advocate General for report. Jno. G. Nicolay Priv. Sec. March 2, 1865." No further note by Lincoln appears. In May 1865, Bartman was released from the Dry Tortugas with the condition that he serve out the rest of his enlistment.[29]

Six months after James Vaughn deserted from the 13th Ohio at Franklin, Tennessee, he was convicted of desertion and sentenced to be shot. The court cited "mitigating circumstances" and asked for mercy. General Horatio Van Cleve recommended prison at hard labor for three months for this 20-year-old former farmer. Rosecrans suggested the same penalty as that offered by Van Cleve. Hay wrote, "The recommendation of General Rosecrans is approved," and "A. Lincoln" follows.[30]

The 8th U. S. Infantry generated three unusual trials in September 1863. The wife of one man wrote that her husband had been lured into a house of ill-fame (prostitution), drugged and, in this narcotized condition, enticed into desertion. The unlucky man fortunate to have such an understanding spouse was Charles H. Boirs (also spelled Boyce and Boyers), stationed at Fort Columbus in New York Harbor. When he returned five weeks later, he was tried and sentenced to be shot. His company commander described Boirs as "as a general thing, a good man, but at times was refractory and had been in the guard house several times." General Canby recommended mitigation to hard labor for the rest of his enlistment.

In November 1863, Mrs. Boirs wrote to Lincoln as follows:

"Honored Sir:

I take the opportunity to ask you a great favor that I have hardly any hopes will be granted and knowing that you are a generous and kind-hearted man, I can only hope that you will pardon me for my assurance in writing to you in hope of getting my husband pardoned for what is considered by his country a great offense a case of desertion. He belongs to the 8 Infantry he was lured into a house of ill fame and there had been druged and while in that state was persuaded to desert. He was taken in Washington and I can only hope that you will pardon my husband Charles H. Boyce as he is my only support. I am now entirely destitute of means but manage to get along.

I am you humble servant,

Cora Boyce."

The final note is "Recom. of Gen. Canby approved and ordered. A. Lincoln April 14, 1864." Since Canby's recommendation was for hard labor the rest of Boirs' enlistment, it appears that Lincoln gave the distressed Mrs. Boirs—nothing. Perhaps the President was put off by a man so easily lured into a bordello.[31]

Henry Connolly had been in the army for eighteen years and had served with Braxton Bragg's battery of artillery in the Mexican War. When the 8th U. S. Infantry arrived at Park Barracks in New York City, Connolly disappeared but returned voluntarily nine weeks later. The isolated life of a soldier (or at least this soldier) is revealed in his statement to the court: "When we arrived in New York City I decided to see my family. I found my wife had died, my son was in the army and my daughter had moved to Oswego, New York. I went there to find her but could not. I would never desert because in 18 months I will have a pension for life." The court sentenced him to be shot, but asked for leniency because "he has grown gray in the service and now he is old."

On February 9, 1864, Lincoln wrote, "Sentence remitted." Connolly no longer had a family—but he had Father Abraham.[32]

Corporal James Benson, also of the 8th U. S. Infantry, was gone for twenty days and was charged with desertion. He told the court, "I didn't desert, I just went to see friends. I have been in the army eight years." He was sentenced to be reduced to the ranks, confined at hard labor to the end of his enlistment and then dishonorably discharged. Holt, in an unusually warm note, wrote:

> This man was one of those whom Gen. Banks in General Order No. 34, so justly lauded for having, while undergoing severe hardship and suffering brutal treatment as prisoner of war (surrendered by traitor commanders) withstood all attempts to seduce, persuade or force them from loyalty to their government and fidelity to their flag. In view of this and the fact that the prisoner voluntarily returned, it is recommended that he be pardoned by the President.

Holt's discussion referred to an incident involving the regiment at the outbreak of the war, when it was stationed in Texas. Secessionist officers, betraying their oaths of allegiance, surrendered the troops and forts under their command. It is no surprise to read: "Pardon. A. Lincoln Feb. 9, 1864."[33]

Two men of the 1st Missouri State Militia deserted: John Finnerty at Lawson's Station, Missouri, and Henry Bergemeyer at Big Pine Railroad Bridge in that same state. Both were sentenced to be shot. Neither Finnerty nor Bergemeyer made a defense, but General John Schofield recommended commutation to six months in prison for each. Holt had no objection, and on each record appears "Recom. of Gen. Schofield approved and ordered—A. Lincoln April 14, 1864."[34]

William Hays was to be shot at noon, October 23, 1863. He had deserted twice from the 122nd Illinois, and was charged with threatening the arresting officer with an ax. Hays offered this brilliant defense: "I don't give a damn what you do with me." Holt noted in the affidavit of the arresting officer that Hays had offered no resistance, much less brandishing an ax, and also noted a favorable letter from a Mr. Wills of the Christian Commission. Holt seems to hint at remission in his final sentence: "In view of all the circumstances of the case, it is for the President to decide what punishment shall be inflicted in this case." Along one margin of an already-filled page (paper was in short supply) we see, "Pardon. A. Lincoln April 14, 1864." In spite of his thumbing his nose at the process, Hays was a free man.[35]

The tenth month of the year brought ten trials. Another case from the 8th U. S. Infantry, still at Fort Columbus, New York Harbor, illustrates the snares of the big city. William Cobb was gone four weeks. "It wasn't my fault," he explained. "A friendly stranger got me drunk and sold me as a substitute." Even with this plausible story—substitute brokers were notoriously unethical—Cobb was sentenced to die. His company commander wrote, "This man served under me on the frontier and was a faithful and true soldier and appears penitent." Holt passed this summary on to the President, who probably had not a moment's hesitation as he wrote, "Sentence remitted. A. Lincoln Feb. 9, 1864."[36]

In the 1860s, the U. S. Army enlisted boys as young as age 12 for three-year tours of duty and sent them to a music school at Fort Columbus on Governor's Island, New York Harbor. They belonged to Company B, "The Music Boys." These boys were subject to normal military discipline. In fact, two of them were sentenced to face a firing squad: Frederick Bristley (or Brüstley), a German-born nail maker who was four feet, seven inches and 15 years old when he deserted for six months. Generals Canby and Dix concurred in the court's recommendation of remission. The President wrote, "Sentence remitted. A. Lincoln Feb. 9, 1864."[37]

Henry Wilmott, whose age is given simply as "extreme youth," was also sentenced to be shot for desertion from music school. At his trial, this Music Boy offered no excuse, and neither defense nor prosecution entered evidence. The court, after passing sentence, made petition for clemency with these remarks: "for the reason of his extreme youth and his short period of service previous to his desertion being not (to a boy of his age) sufficient to impress on his mind a full understanding of his duties as a soldier." He, too, was spared by the recommendations of Canby, Dix, and Lincoln.[38]

William Camp, a new recruit of the 9th Ohio Cavalry, got drunk at Newport, Kentucky, and spent three days in jail. Someone told him that he could escape punishment for being AWOL if he enlisted in the Regular Army, which he did. Someone lied. Camp was listed as a deserter, tried, convicted, and sentenced to be shot. General Burnside recommended that the sentence be commuted. Holt noted that Camp had already been locked up for three months, and recommended a small fine, followed by a return to duty. Lincoln signed Nicolay's note, which said, "Judge Advocate General's recommendation approved. Feb. 9, 1864."[39]

Two more Buckeye boys were tried in October. Christopher Seinn of the 117th Ohio left at Catlettsburg, Kentucky, because "My family was in a suffering condition." He returned voluntarily after providing for them. Burnside recommended commutation to three years hard labor. Holt went further: "It is believed that a pardon might be extended in this case." It was. Once again, in that firm, dark, and distinctive hand, we see "Pardon. A. Lincoln April 14, 1864." Lincoln had exactly a year to live.[40]

William Aughenbaugh of the 44th Ohio got drunk and deserted at Danville, Kentucky; he was to be shot. General Milo Hascall, a district attorney before the war, noted that of the six deserters tried by this court, only Aughenbaugh had received a death sentence. Hascall saw no reason for this inconsistency. General Burnside chided the court for "carelessness" and recommended pardon and return to duty. This found a ready audience, who wrote, "Recommendation of Gen. Burnside approved. A. Lincoln Feb. 9, 1864."[41]

Wounded veteran George E. Clifford of the 1st Maine Artillery seems to have been a victim of a Boston substitute broker. After a substantial drunk, he woke up many miles away at Concord, New Hampshire, and was told that he had enlisted in a New Hampshire regiment. He wrote to his old commander regarding the situation. He was returned to his old regiment, was tried and was given a death penalty. Seven of the eight court members recommended executive clemency. The lone dissenter was T. D. Chamberlain, Joshua's less famous brother, who was apparently more hard-hearted than his portrayal in the movie *Gettysburg*. General Dix agreed with the majority, as did Lincoln: "Sentence remitted. Feb. 9, 1864."[42]

Lieutenant Chamberlain was more generous in the case of Alonzo Long, a Maine draftee, who left Camp Berry on Mackey's Island in the harbor of Portland, Maine, and went downtown for a four-day drunk. The court, after sentencing Long to die, recommended remittal, as did

Dix and Holt. Nicolay wrote, "Sentence remitted," and his employer signed.[43]

Lincoln often referred to his "leg cases," i.e., where men whose legs carried them away from danger led to a trial for desertion or cowardice. Never were these issues clearer than in a statement delivered by Mathew Smith. "I have a good heart," explained the soon-to-be-convicted soldier, "but my cowardly legs will run. I returned to my regiment even though I may be shot." As a member of the 72nd Pennsylvania. Smith had fought well at Yorktown, Fair Oaks, Savage Station and at Malvern Hill. He had also done his duty on the first two days at Gettysburg, but on the final day, July 3, 1863, his legs ran. He was sentenced to have his head shaved, be drummed out of the regiment and to spend four years at hard labor. After a long exchange of letters and reports, Lincoln forgave every one of the penalties and restored him to duty. Hay wrote, "Nov. 25, 1863. Let the within named Mathew H. Smith 72nd PA Vols be pardoned and relieved of the penalties of desertion." Lincoln signed.[44] Even as he put pen to paper, Union forces in Tennessee were sweeping the Confederates off Missionary Ridge and ending the quasi-siege of Chattanooga.

Being lost in a bureaucratic maze can have advantages. Robert Campbell was sentenced to be shot. His papers, sent for review, took a whole year to reach Washington, D.C. Campbell had deserted from the 26th Kentucky, taking with him six stolen blankets and six stolen shirts, and enlisted in the 52nd Kentucky. His state of sobriety at that time was described as "tolerably tight." When these papers finally appeared in Holt's "In" basket, the Judge Advocate noted that Campbell had been waiting in prison for a year and that his company commander thought Campbell "would make a good and faithful soldier." Holt recommended "that the sentence be mitigated to imprisonment in the penitentiary for one year," presumably the year already spent, and the President wrote, "Report approved and ordered. A. Lincoln Jan. 23, 1865."[45] Campbell lived; Lincoln would be dead in three months.

The last three 1863 trials in this sample were all in November. Luther Butler joined the 1st Maine Cavalry when he was a minor and without parental consent. When he deserted a few weeks later and returned home, his dying mother begged him to stay at home and his father forbade him to return to the army. Two years later, he was arrested, tried and sentenced to be shot. He, too, was certainly "somebody's Wallace." His company commander testified that Butler's father had a right to keep his son at home. Two members of the State Executive Council wrote letters testifying to the loyalty and integrity of both the father and the son. The Assistant Provost Marshal of the State of Maine endorsed these opinions, and General Dix urged mercy. Holt concluded, "It is believed that the sentence might safely be commuted to forfeiture of all pay and allowances now due and make good the time lost." The Chief Executive wrote: "Judge Advocate General's recom. approved, order accordingly. A. Lincoln Feb. 9, 1864." It is unclear why Butler was tried at all, since his original enlistment was illegal.[46]

James A. Philips had enlisted for two years. When his time was up, instead of being released home he was transferred, much against his will, to the 44th New York. With his new comrades he fought through the three days of Gettysburg, and when the smoke cleared set out for home. Ten weeks later he was brought back to the 44th New York, tried, and sentenced to be shot. General Charles Griffin recommended clemency "on the grounds that there was great dissatisfaction among the transferred men." General Meade forwarded the papers, suggesting commutation, to the addition of ten weeks to his service, and a penalty of eight dollars a month (60 percent of his pay) for the rest of his enlistment. Lincoln softened the blow still further: "Commuted to making good of lost time and omitting loss of pay. Nov. 7, 1863."[47]

The trial of Edward Rookey of the 92nd New York reads like a detective story. The private and two companions took a canoe trip up a creek near Fort Anderson, North Carolina, with the stated purpose of checking some fish lines. When they did not return, a search found the empty canoe and their distinctive footprints headed towards Confederate territory. A search of their tent showed that they had taken their best clothing with them. Nine days later Rookey reappeared and said that he had been captured by the Confederates, taken to Richmond, then sent to Fort Monroe, Virginia, and then to Parole Camp at Annapolis, Maryland, from which he was sent back to North Carolina. It was highly unlikely—and in fact impossible—that all this had happened in nine days. The court did not belieeve Rookey, even though a witness claimed to have seen him in Annapolis! He was convicted of desertion to the enemy. General Ben Butler approved the death sentence and sent the record to the President. Holt noted only that there were "grave doubts" about several aspects of the case. The final arbiter resolved the doubts with a single word: "Pardon," followed by "A. Lincoln April 14, 1864."[48]

It takes a thief to catch a thief, runs an ancient cliché. Henry Capron, who deserted from the 7th Rhode Island, was employed by the provost marshal as a private detective to—catch deserters. When he surrendered himself, he pled guilty and was sentenced to five years hard labor, the first year with a ball and chain, all without pay, of course. Yet, like Wallace, he was not devoid of friends. The provost marshal said that he was most useful in catching other deserters. Numerous neighbors back in Rhode Island petitioned for mercy to aid his starving family; even the governor endorsed their plea. Holt recommended remittal. Lincoln wrote: "Pardon for unexecuted part of sentence on condition that he go to, and serve out his term, in his regiment. Jan. 23, 1865."[49]

Capron's trial and five others were held in January 1864. Joseph Advena was not just "somebody's Wallace," but received concern and support from 65 members of the Pennsylvania Legislature. Advena, who spoke mostly German, had deserted for almost a year from the 41st New York. (Why he lived in Pennsylvania and joined a New York regiment is unclear.) At his trial, he said that his wife and two children had been sick and he went to be with them. He was sentenced to five years of hard labor in the Dry Tortugas (at no pay) and a dishonorable discharge. His wife wrote Lincoln from Philadelphia on January 27, 1865:

> Sir: Allow me to bring my misfortune to your memory. My husband Joseph Advena of Company K, 41st NYV having been convicted of the crime of desertion, better than a year ago, is since confined in one of the forts in Florida, where his health is failing, which is adding very much to my trouble and sorrow; besides this I have lost the little we had saved and I am not able to support and maintain my little children, who are crying for their daily wants, as well as for their beloved father. Your Excellency! I most respectfully beg You to pardon my beloved husband the father of my poor little children and make a parted family once more happy. Your most obedient servant,
>
> Emmy Advena.

The crowded pages of this trial contained one small corner not yet written upon. It was filled with this: "Pardon for unexecuted part of sentence. A. Lincoln Feb. 24, 1865."[50] The rendezvous at Ford's Theater lay just forty-two days ahead.

Henry Phillips of the 106th New York deserted at North Mountain, Virginia, and made his way to Canada. While there, he heard that men in Canada would be forgiven if they returned to their regiments. He did so and was put at hard labor for two years, at no pay. The court was "lenient" because Phillips was close to age fifty. A note dated June 30, 1864, in a hand both elegant and illegible reminded the Bureau of Military Justice about the Canadian returnees policy. The Fourth of July may have been a holiday for many, but not for the President, since the last entry in the records is: "Pardon for unexecuted part of punishment. A. Lincoln July 4, 1864."[51] In Congress, Lincoln was confronted this day with the radical Republicans' plan for the post-war South, plans which would greatly limit the political participation of anyone who had ever served in the Confederate Army.

At Maryland Heights, high above Harpe's Ferry, Virginia, Thomas Linton received a letter telling him that his wife was very sick. He left his regiment, the 7th Maryland, and was gone five months. On his return, he was sentenced to 18 months hard labor. When the case came to Lincoln, he wrote, "Pardon for unexecuted part of sentence. Dec. 7, 1864," and signed his name.[52]

There are many ways of celebrating Christmas. Milford Torrence of the 11th Missouri Cavalry stole two greatcoats and two army Colt revolvers at Springfield, Missouri, then went to a dance. After that, he deserted. At his January 1864 trial, he was sentenced to three years in prison and a dishonorable discharge. Three months later, his case passed across Lincoln's desk and received the words "Sentence remitted."[53]

Simeon Smith belonged to the 2nd Invalid Corps. In January 1864, he received word that one of his children had died. He was unable to obtain a furlough to attend the funeral, so he forged a pass and was gone for two weeks. He was sentenced to hard labor, with a ball and chain, to the end of the war. His home town prepared a petition for mitigation and it was forwarded to Lincoln with this note by the Governor of Indiana: "I have no doubt the statements in the citizen's memorial are true and feeling confident that the prisoner Simeon Smith was guilty only through his natural anxiety to take care of his sick children, and has already suffered more than the character of his offense can justly require, I hope the remainder of his term of punishment may be remitted." It was. The President's notation appears more hurried and fatigued than it had been four years earlier, but the hand is still distinctive. "Pardon for unexpired part of sentence, and party to go to his regiment. A. Lincoln Jan. 6, 1865."[54]

Daniel Kelly seems to have had venereal disease and lung trouble when he deserted from the 4th Rhode Island. He told the trial board, "I was sick with pleurisy and then the bad disorder broke out upon me and I did not want folks at home to know it, so I left." In spite of his ailments, he was sent to Hard Labor Prison at Norfolk, Virginia, where he was to wear a 24-pound iron ball attached to his right leg by a three-foot chain. General Ben Butler approved this sentence. Lincoln did not. "Pardon for unexecuted part. A. Lincoln Jan. 23, 1865."[55] As he signed, the Confederacy was unraveling. John Bell Hood had resigned his command of the Army of Tennessee, most of his men were being sent to Georgia for shipment to the Carolinas, and the forces that remained were evaporating from disease and desertion.

"When sorrows come, they come not single spies but in battalions." (Hamlet, 4:5) Rachel Lake of Williamsport, Pennsylvania, might have agreed. When the Civil War opened, she had a husband and five sons. Her son John was killed on picket duty at Waterloo Creek, Virginia. Her sons Ellis and Joseph were killed when the powder magazine exploded in the attack on Fort Fisher. Her one son at home was age fourteen and badly crippled. Her husband became insane and unmanageable, leaving Mrs. Lake at home with a son and a husband both totally dependent upon her care and supervision. She wrote to her one son remaining in the army, Henry Lake of the 107th Pennsylvania, to come home and help her. Unable to obtain a pass, he left without one and was gone for a year. After his father's insanity ended in death, he returned to his regiment, was sentenced to serve an extra year and to lose ten dollars of his $13.00 monthly pay for four months. A petition signed by fifty neighbors asked that Lake be released from the service to care for his destitute family. Lincoln asked Holt for his opinion.

In a reply unusual for its warmth and minimal use of the passive voice, Holt replied: "In view of the patriotism of the prisoner's family his three brothers having fallen in the military service and of his own distinguished character for courage and faithfulness as a soldier previous to his offense and considering that his voluntary return to duty justifies the conclusion that he was guilty not of desertion but simply of absence without leave under strongly extenuating circumstances, it is recommended—as his term of enlistment has expired—that the prayer of his mother, left destitute and helpless by the death of her husband and three sons, be granted, and that the unexecuted portion of the prisoner's sentence be remitted." Lincoln could not have written it better. Hay wrote "Pardon for unexecuted portion of sentence. March 10, 1865." The President signed.[56] In a month, the war would be all but over. Robert E. Lee wrote to President Davis, urging immediate enlistment of Negroes into the Confederate Army. Neither Davis nor the Confederate Congress was ready for such a move, although nearly every grain of sand had run through the Southern hourglass.

Two March 1864 desertion trials came to Lincoln's attention. The President pardoned sinners as well as saints. James Walsh of the 3rd Delaware deserted twice, once from the guard house where he was serving time for a previous sentence and once at Hanover Switch, Maryland. When in camp, he stole $4.00 (ten days pay) from a comrade. One night, claiming that he was a captain, he entered the house of a "colored man," cursed and abused the family and stole their chickens. He was sentenced to five years at hard labor without pay. The convicted man wrote to Lincoln, who examined the record on January 4, 1865, and wrote: "Pardon for unexpired part of imprisonment. A. Lincoln," saving Walsh from another four years of confinement.[57]

Henry Spicer of the 4th West Virginia Cavalry deserted at Camp Piatt in his native state and was gone for nine months. He financed his trip by stealing two Colt revolvers. A court-martial found him guilty and sentenced to hard labor until the end of the war, while wearing a ball and chain. When his time was up, he was to be branded on the left hip with the letter "D," have his head shaved, and be sent off with a dishonorable discharge. General George A. Custer approved the sentence. Spicer must have definitely been "somebody's Wallace," because on January 30, 1865, Lincoln received a petition from Hon. K. V. Whaley, F. P. Blair and W. G. Brown, asking pardon. The recipient replied, "Pardon for unexecuted portion of the sentence. A. Lincoln March 21, 1865."[58] In North Carolina, the three-day Battle of Bentonville was drawing to a close. Appomattox was 16 days away. Booth's rage and sense of destiny were coming to a boil.

Politics and sickness. Private Michael Sheehy of the 5th New York Heavy Artillery was saved by one and laid low by the other. He was on duty, escorting Confederate prisoners, when he became absent. His captain had given him permission to visit home for one day. He returned nine months later. A certificate from his doctor said that he had been sick with "cholera morbus," and too sick to travel. Sheehy was convicted, however, and sentenced to a year at hard labor at no pay. He had a wife and five children, ranging from age ten to a newborn, the latter apparently the product of his homecoming. A week after his conviction his congressman, Aaron Herrick, wrote to Lincoln on Sheehy's behalf. Lincoln said that he would pardon the prisoner if Herrick would produce a letter from Sheehy's colonel promising to take him back. On June 25, 1864, the congressman wrote a long letter to Colonel Samuel Graham, ending with a plea for "an immediate response to this note and a favorable view of poor Sheehy's case, expressive of your readiness to receive him back into your command will be well appreciated by the many friends of the man, will console an afflicted family, and very much gratify your obedient servant, Aaron Herrick, MC, Ninth District, New York." With the war drawing to a close, many colonels had an eye on a future in politics. On July 1, Herrick wrote to Lincoln again, enclosing the colonel's favorable reply. Four days later, Hay wrote, "Let the pardon requested within be granted." Lincoln signed.[59]

William Mahoney, a bugler with the 8th Pennsylvania Cavalry, was discharged and sent home by his first colonel. Two years later, he was arrested and tried for desertion. He entered into evidence his discharge papers and a witness told the court, "He is a bugler, not a soldier." In spite of this, he was convicted and given two years at hard labor. (Truly, the left hand knew not what the right hand did.) Two months later, the case reached the President, who wrote, "Pardon for unexecuted part of the sentence. A. Lincoln Sept. 19, 1864."[60] That day, at Cabin Creek, in Indian Territory, Confederate forces captured 202 wagons, five ambulances, 40 horses and 1,253 mules.

Private Benjamin Hall of the 14th Veteran Reserve Corps left his regiment at Pottsville, Pennsylvania, and was gone for five months. "My wife was confined [in childbirth] and very low." The court was not impressed. It added five months to his enlistment, gave him a year of hard labor, and removed most of his pay for a year. From prison, he wrote to Lincoln and applied for pardon. Hall cited his "tyrannical" captain, noted that during the "Rebel invasion of Maryland" he was released, armed and sent to the defenses of Washington, and that he had been denied new clothing. "I assure Your Honor, I stand in great need of." Hall even brought politics to bear: "My captain said that my sentence should not be read until after the election & if that be true I infer that he anticipates my sentence might prove an acquittal & then Little Mack would loose a vote." Whatever Hall meant by this, it didn't work. "Application denied. A. Lincoln Jan. 25, 1865."[61]

In August 1864, Private Albert Griswold was tried for desertion. He had left the 12th Massachusetts Light Artillery at Port Hudson, Louisiana, and when captured, offered this as his only excuse: "I desired. . .to obtain liquor to appease a burning thirst." He was given hard labor for the rest of his enlistment. He clearly had friends who overlooked his need for alcohol. Both the commissioned and noncommissioned officers of his regiment signed a petition asking for his release, and Congressman Henry Deming wrote the President the following note: "I respectfully request the pardon of Albert E. Griswold a deserter." Griswold himself wrote the President on Christmas Day from the guard house at Port Hudson: "Honorable sir. I have the honor to address you in my own behalf. Having committed the act of Desertion from our army and as the accompanying plea which was presented by myself to the court martial fully expresses my reasons or rather lack of reasons for said act, I will simply entreat for a mitigation of my sentence. Faithfully promising that if such leniency is shown me that the future shall show how sincerely I regret the past and I will strive to make my every action hereafter be in atonement for the crime committed and be worthy the soldier and the man." Whatever might be the reasons, Griswold's plea succeeded where Hall's did not. On the papers of the former is "Pardon. A. Lincoln Feb. 20, 1865."[62] In North Carolina, Federal troops were closing in on the vital port of Wilmington.

Private Timothy McMahon of the 147th New York said that he was in the hospital and was not a deserter. Once again, hospital records seemed unavailable. The court fined him $10.00 a month for 12 months. His lieutenant wrote to Lincoln on McMahon's behalf, with good effect: "Sentence remitted as to loss of pay. A. Lincoln Nov. 7, 1864."[63]

The dreadful trench warfare around Petersburg, Virginia, killed and wounded tens of thousands of men. One of those injured, Private William Elliott of the 1st Maryland (Union), left his hospital at Washington, D.C. and was gone for five weeks. He was fined $10.00 a month for six months. He could not read or write, but his mother could. She arrived at the Executive Mansion from Baltimore carrying this letter, signed by herself and seven friends:

> The bearer of this, Mrs. Elliott, has lost her husband and two sons in this war. The husband died in one of the prisons of Richmond. One of her sons was killed at Vicksburg and another died at home from wounds received in battle. She had two other sons now in the army, both of which have been wounded. She is in much reduced circumstances and stands in need of the aid and assistance of one of them; she therefore asks that you will assist her in this her time of need, by ordering the discharge of her youngest son William or have him transferred to the Invalid Corps. By so doing, you will confer a very great favor on a worthy person and for which you will ever be held in grateful remembrance.

Lincoln requested a report on young William. Ten days later, satisfied of the truth of this petition, he wrote, "Let this man be transferred to the Veterans Reserve Corps [a later name for the Invalid Corps]. A. Lincoln Oct. 15, 1864."[65]

In the era before social security numbers and telephone directories, the system to locate citizens was close to non-existent. (Privately-owned city directory services were the nearest equivalent.) James Hope had been in Washington, D.C., working on an army supply boat as a civilian when he was arrested as a deserter and a draft dodger. His induction papers had been left at a house in Philadelphia, a place he had left over a

year before. At his trial he pointed out that he had never received a draft
notice. Further, he displayed a doctor's certificate describing inflamma-
tion of the kidneys, making him "entirely unfit for military duty." He
was also the sole support for a wife and four children. The court sent
him to hard labor in prison for a year but asked for review. The trial was
in October 1863; the petition reached Lincoln three months later. He
wrote, "Judge Advocate General please procure records and report on
this case. A. Lincoln Jan. 7, 1865." Nine days later, in the same hand
appears "Pardon and discharge." Hope, who had never been in the army,
was now out of the army.[66]

The same day that Hope was pardoned, Francis Preston Blair, Sr., a
powerful political figure who had just returned from Richmond, described to Lincoln his meeting with Jefferson Davis, and his presentation
of the Blair plan for peace. Its provisions were a sort of truce between
North and South, during which they would jointly invade Mexico. The
sheer weirdness of this plan suggests how desperate people were for a
stop to the bloodshed.[67]

The final two "Lincoln cases" of 1864 were in the month of November. A private of the 72nd Pennsylvania, Private James Huffnagle, had
suffered much for his country. He was wounded at Savage's Station and
Antietam, and wounded even more seriously by a bullet in the groin at
Gettysburg. As soon as he was able to move around, he was put to work
in the hospital. He deserted and was gone for a year. When brought back
and put on trial, he said, "At the hospital I was assigned duties beyond
my capacity. I went home to be prescribed for by my own doctor." The
verdict was guilty, the sentence was to serve a year at hard labor, followed by a year in the field on active duty. When the case came to the
President four months had passed. Lincoln wrote: "Pardon. March 10,
1865. A. Lincoln"[68] In thirty-four days, he would belong to the ages.

Private Charles H. Harris was in the 11th U. S. Infantry. He deserted
and assumed the name of John H. Loveland. When arrested ten months
later, he was sentenced to be branded with the letter "D" and receive a
dishonorable discharge after his five years of hard labor in prison. His
appeal to the Executive Mansion was only a partial success. Hay wrote,
"Sentence remitted as to branding." The President added "A. Lincoln
Jan. 18, 1865." Harris would not carry a "D" on his hide, but he still had

five years of prison ahead of him.[84] The next day, Sherman's troops began their march from Georgia into South Carolina, the "Cradle of Secession," where they would do terrible and deliberate damage.

Private Hugh Kerr of the 14th U. S. Infantry deserted at New Baltimore, Virginia and was found five months later. He was sentenced to be shot. General Joseph Hooker wrote, "It would seem unjust under these circumstances to enforce the extreme penalty of the law on those who differ from the others simply in having been apprehended. I recommend a pardon be extended in this case." In a tiny space at the bottom of the page, barely visible, are the words: "Pardoned. A. Lincoln."[70] (The President's favor was not returned: a year later Kerr was convicted of mutiny after trying to break a musket over his lieutenant's head. After his time in prison, Kerr was tattooed with the letter "M," had his head shaved, and was drummed out of the service.)

Private Andrew Squibb was a person of questionable worth. He had deserted seven times from the 72nd Pennsylvania and, it was said, "associates with criminals." Nevertheless, he, too, was the subject of a flurry of letters praising his splendid character and urging remission of his two-year prison sentence. One missive began, "Dear Sir. Mrs. Squibb of Philadelphia the bearer, a really deserving lady, is the wife of Andrew Squibb, Co. F, 72 PA Vols—sentenced to two years imprisonment for desertion. He has now been five months in confinement and his officers state that his conduct has been excellent since he has been under their charge. . .he has been ill a long time and his family are destitute." Other men such as Squibb had been branded with the letter "W" for "worthless," but Squibb fared better. On February 1, 1865, Lincoln wrote and signed the following: "Pardon for unexecuted part of sentence."[71] That day, Illinois became the first state to ratify the Thirteenth Amendment, which abolished slavery. In the South, Sherman's forces were approaching the capital of South Carolina, much of which would soon burn to the ground under mysterious circumstances.

The final deserter in this series was Private Stewart St. Clair of the 12th Pennsylvania Cavalry, who deserted at Washington, D.C. and was gone five months. He offered no defense for his crime and was sentenced to lose $10.00 of his pay each month and serve an extra five months on his enlistment. Even this relatively mild sentence did not sit well with the home folks, and the prisoner's mother arrived at the Executive Mansion carrying the following letter, signed by twenty noteworthies, including Governor Andrew Curtin:

> The undersigned, citizens of Johnstown, Penn., would recommend to your favorable notice the bearer of this letter Mrs. Thankful D. St. Clair who visits you in relation to the case of her son, who is confined in prison at Alexandria on a charge of desertion. Mrs. St. Clair is a widow, a woman of unimpeachable character. She has but two sons of the proper age for military service. The younger one is now in the army and the one now in prison was amongst the first to respond to the call for 75,000 men. After being honorably discharged from the three-month service he immediately enlisted for three years in the 12th Pennsylvania Cavalry. There are said to be mitigating circumstances connected. . .with his desertion which will be explained to you by the mother in a personal interview, which we hope, your many and pressing official duties, you may find time to favor her.[72]

The President did see her and, perhaps doubting that her son possessed all the virtues described by the Widow St. Clair, wrote the following: "If the colonel commanding this man's regiment will say in writing on this sheet that he is willing to receive him back to his regiment, I will pardon him upon condition of his serving out his term. A. Lincoln Jan. 19, 1865."

Colonel Marcus Reno, whose name a decade later would be forever associated with Custer's Last Stand on the Little Bighorn), replied. "The within named man is now with his regiment. The pardon would effect only his pay—inasmuch as there appear palliating circumstances he should be pardoned from the forfeiture of his pay on condition of his serving faithfully the time lost by desertion. His original term expires March 4, 1865." Once again, as the historian Paul Angle has remarked, Lincoln was doing something for somebody. The concluding note reads, "Pardon & if competent for me to decide, let him have his pay. A. Lincoln March 8, 1865." There is no way to know if Private St. Clair was grateful, but we know that his mother was Thankful.

Table Four on the following page illustrates clearly Lincoln's trend toward mitigation. In 93 percent (93%) of the cases, the President overturned the original sentence of the court—but his actions did not fly in face of the system. The opinions of the various levels of review do not always appear, or at least not legibly, but from what is recorded we see Lincoln was in agreement with the general convening the court-martial 86 percent (86%) of the time, and with the departmental commander's opinion 89 percent (89%) of the time. Again, we see a trend toward clemency, mitigation, and commutation on the part of the Union's generals. Some, like Meade and Sykes, were less forgiving, while Hooker nearly always looked for a reason to mitigate. The overall trend in this series of cases was that Lincoln was concurring with already-existing opinions, rather than breaking new ground.

Opinion Maker	Lincoln Agrees	Lincoln Disagrees	% Agreement
Trial Verdict	5	69	7
Authorizing Officer	12	2	86
Departmental Commander	40	5	89
Judge Advocate General	23	2	92
Interested Politicians	9	1	90
Friends, Family & Comrades	19	0	100

Holt did not always take a position on a verdict; sometimes, he only summarized the salient points and passed them on. Where Holt had an opinion, he and Lincoln were in agreement 92 percent (92%) of the time; where they disagreed, it was usually Lincoln urging a mitigation and Holt pushing for a stronger penalty. The influence of outside parties, which occurred in about one out of every five cases, was considerable. Where politicians asked for clemency, Lincoln obliged them in 90 percent (90%) of their requests. When family or comrades petitioned for relief, Lincoln met their requests in every case.

8

Mutiny and Violence Against Officers

America is built on turbulence, dissension, and dissatisfaction. Deeply displeased with the restraints of class-bound England, famine-wracked Ireland, the oppressive regimes of the German states, the pogroms of Czarist Russia, the strictures of state religions, and the forced military conscription prevalent in most countries, immigrants have sought the New World, where each group could practice its own version of true doctrine and correct behavior.

In 1776, those who favored the status quo and were loyal to the Crown became refugees and, by differential migration, further established the United States as a land of revolutionaries, deeply suspicious of central authority and regulated behavior. From such a bouillabaisse of individualistic opinions and prickly attitudes the Union attempted to fashion a reliable and obedient army. The fact that they were volunteers made it even more difficult, since volunteers tend to feel that they should have a voice in how things are run.

The same system of military organization that produced those who must obey also creates those who must be obeyed. If those in command are unreasonable, or sadistic, or given to displays of power for the sake of inflating their own senses of self-worth, it is not long before mischief is afoot. All these currents flowed together to produce incidents of mutiny or physical resistance to superior officers.

Of the previously-unknown cases of mutiny and violence to officers which came to Lincoln, as found in the first 50,000 court martials surveyed, fourteen cases were tried in 1862, thirty in 1863 and twelve more in 1864.

It will be no surprise to find that fifty-three percent (53%) of the cases mention alcohol as a factor in the conflicts which led to court-martial, and a lesser degree of intoxication may well have played a role in those cases where it is not specifically mentioned. (Reading between the lines of thousands of military trials, it is plain that a certain degree of alcohol intake almost every day was far from rare.)

A common question in Civil War trials was, "Has this soldier heard the Articles of War?" Regulation and tradition held that a soldier could not be responsible for forbidden actions if he was unfamiliar with the Articles of War, which were supposed to be read to all troops at least once, particularly in the early phases of their training.

The Articles pertinent to the subject of this chapter include Number Six (any soldier who shows disrespect to a superior shall be punished,) and Number Seven (any soldier who begins or joins in a mutiny shall suffer death). Article Eight holds that any soldier or officer who fails to suppress a mutiny shall suffer death, while Article Nine is of even more ominous import for our subjects, as it states that any soldier who strikes his superior, or threatens his superior with violence, shall suffer death.

In the Civil War, the proverbial "irresistible force" of the individualistic soldier would meet the equally proverbial "immovable object" of the Articles of War.

1862

Private Adolph Schramm illustrates both the turbulent soldier and the difficult officer. Schramm was court-martialed twice and both his cases were reviewed by Lincoln. Schramm was a member of the New York Volunteer Engineers, and at Hilton Head, South Carolina, refused to embark for Tybee Island, Georgia. Once on the island, he refused all duty and used threatening language to, or about, a variety of generals, colonels, captains, lieutenants, and sergeants. He urged four comrades, Privates John Henreri, Carl Frantz, Conrad Pilzer and John Wilson to kill Generals Quincy Gillmore and Alfred Terry. Saving the best for last, Schramm had this to say about Lieutenant Colonel James Hall: "I have a stick which I brought from Key West and I think I can take care of Colonel Hall with it, the son of a bitch, and if the stick fails, why his

—— ain't very large and I think I can take it off with a jackknife." On Another occasion, Schramm and his friends also refused to embark for St. Helena Island, South Carolina. Schramm was found guilty and sentenced to be shot. The court made a recommendation for mercy, apparently based upon widely-held feelings of disenchantment with the regimental commander.

Major General David Hunter agreed with the court, but added—in a most unusual addendum—the following: "From a very full knowledge of all the facts in this case, I regard the colonel of this regiment [Edward W. Serrell] as mainly responsible for all the repeated offenses of mutiny and insubordination of which the men have been guilty." Hunter's statement is followed by a long note in the President's own hand: "Colonel Serrell complains of the above expression of General Hunter being published in this order, saying that he has been tried by a court martial and fully acquitted of the charges embraced in General Hunter's censure. Will the Judge Advocate General please examine and report to me whether he has been so tried and acquitted? A. Lincoln May 14, 1863."

Colonel Serrell had indeed been court-martialed (in July 1862) for making a false muster, causing sedition, conduct unbecoming an officer and a gentleman, and conduct prejudicial to military discipline and good order. In spite of much damning testimony, Serrell was acquitted. In regards to Schramm's first death sentence, Lincoln apparently remitted it in a note not evident today in the court-martial.

Though fortunate to be alive, Schramm did not know when to quit. A few months later, he was tried again on similar charges, and was again sentenced to be shot. Five prominent German-Americans wrote to Lincoln, "to bear testimony to the previous good and unblemished character" of Schramm. "He has been a resident in this country for the past 13 years, has a family and five children and has heretofore been esteemed by all who knew him." Holt noted the various recommendations for mercy and endorsed them. So did his employer. "Sentence remitted. A. Lincoln April 24, 1863."[1] Schramm was a slow learner, but he finally got the message.

Sergeant Charles Braffitt of the 5th Ohio Cavalry was drunk at Corinth, Mississippi. He told Major Charles Hayes, "I don't give a damn for you or for the whole rest of the whole God damned battalion." After

Braffitt was arrested, he escaped the guard house by waving an axe, then seized a "Colt's Revolver" and went to Hayes' tent, where he interrupted the major's dinner with a variety of threats and two attempts to fire his pistol. Braffitt was sentenced to be "shot to death." As his case awaited Presidential review, Braffitt's family and the Governor of Ohio both wrote and asked for clemency. Holt noted the influence of liquor, the previous good behavior, and "the fact that neither life was taken nor blood shed," and judged the sentence "too severe." Nicolay wrote, "Sentence in this case commuted to imprisonment for three months from this day. May 11, 1863." In darker ink, we see "A. Lincoln." (In a touch of irony, Braffitt lived when the Articles prescribed death, while Major Hayes was killed in action three weeks before Lincoln signed the reprieve.)[2]

Private James Keefe said not a word during his trial for punching and kicking his commanding officer. This private of the 8th Wisconsin Infantry, thought to be "deranged" by one witness, was sentenced to be shot. General William Rosecrans agreed with the sentence but ordered Keefe to "be confined in some prison north of the Ohio until his case or his friends can have time to show if he is insane." The President wrote, "Suspended according to the suggestion of Gen. Rosecrans. A. Lincoln Oct. 24, 1862." Lorenzo Thomas, the army's Adjutant General, noted that "The record is defective in not stating that two-thirds of the members of the court concurred in the sentence of death. (Section 87, Rules and Articles of War)." On this technicality, Keefe was returned to duty.[3]

Frank Kelly was a private in the 18th U. S. Infantry, camped near Columbus, Kentucky. Kelly, drunk once again, stood in the doorway of his captain's tent and began to curse. When a lieutenant standing nearby ordered Kelly to go to his own tent, the reply was, "Kiss my ass, God damn you." Kelly clung to the captain's tent-pole while being expelled, pausing only to punch a sergeant. The court concluded that shooting Kelly was a proper response to such behavior. Rosecrans forwarded the case without comment. Holt noted that "The testimony is very meager; the finding rests almost wholly on the plea of guilty. The prisoner is represented to be of an unruly temper and to be much addicted to intoxication." The Judge Advocate General agreed with "severe" punishment in this case, but not a sentence of death. Nicolay wrote, "Sentence in this case commuted to imprisonment in one of the military prisons for the term of three months from this date. May 11, 1863," and Lincoln added his signature.[4]

Corporal William Flynn, another citizen from the Emerald Isle, serving with the 17th U. S. Infantry at Sheppard's Ford, Maryland, was drunk on picket duty and tried to shoot the sergeant sent to arrest him. Flynn, too, was to face a firing squad. Brigadier General Daniel Butterfield (the composer of "Taps") passed the decision upward. Major General George Meade agreed with the court's plea for mitigation. Holt agreed with Meade, and Nicolay wrote, "Sentence commuted to one year's imprisonment. May 20, 1863." In darker ink again appears the familiar "A. Lincoln."[5]

Private John Sullivan was not only drunk, but intentionally shot his lieutenant in the left leg. The 27th Michigan member was sentenced to die. Major General Horatio Wright agreed with the death penalty and sent the case upward. Holt noted that the "two-thirds concurrence" was missing from the proceedings, and Nicolay wrote, "Sentence disapproved for informality. May 11, 1863." The third man at the table added his signature and Sullivan, like Private James Keefe a few months earlier, was saved by a technicality.[6]

James Dolan was drunk on picket duty at Sharpsburg, Maryland. When admonished by his lieutenant, Dolan knocked the man down and threatened him with a loaded pistol. This star of the 105th New York was sentenced to be shot. One witness described Dolan's pattern thus: "When intoxicated, he is perfectly crazy and. . .afterwards repents." Dolan himself pled for mercy on the grounds of having a wife and four children. Major General William Franklin noted the suggestion of clemency by five court members and recommended hard labor for the rest of his enlistment, at no pay except a clothing allowance, without which Dolan would soon have been naked. Major General Joseph Hooker agreed with Franklin. Holt noted Dolan's "faithful services and personal bravery in several engagements," and recommended a "greater mitigation" than that proposed by Franklin. The final note, again in Nicolay's hand, reads, "Sentence commuted to six months imprisonment at hard labor with loss of pay. May 20, 1863." Perhaps, as he signed his name,

Lincoln was thinking of the unfortunate Mrs. Dolan and her four children, left penniless by their father's ruinous alcoholism.[7]

Private Josiah Sears was also fortified with liquid courage at Washington, D.C., and had a further supply in his army canteen when his lieutenant took steps to stop the flow of refreshment. Sears violently resisted this effort, shouting, "It will take eighteen men to take me to the guard house." This private of the 112th Pennsylvania Infantry was sentenced to spend a year in the District of Columbia Penitentiary and then to be drummed out with half his head shaved. Lincoln, perhaps thinking of the cost of feeding Sears for a year without receiving any work in return, instructed Nicolay to write, "So much of this sentence as subjects the accused to confinement in the penitentiary of the District of Columbia is disapproved. May 20, 1863." Lincoln's signature is hurried and smeared, perhaps reflecting the President's workload. Presumably, Sears was soon taking one last turn around the parade ground, the drums thudding out the shame of the Rogue's March, while one side of his newly-shaved head gleamed white in the sunlight.[8]

Private James Weldon of the 7th Illinois Cavalry was apparently cold sober when he stole four boxes of tobacco, threatened to shoot a sentinel, and tried to shoot his own captain, all near Tuscumbia, Alabama. No recommendation for mercy appears in the record, but Holt discovered that "This case is fatally defective in not showing that the Judge Advocate was sworn." The only note that follows is written bold: "Not approved. A. Lincoln Oct. 24, 1862." James Weldon may have been an undeserving wretch, but he was protected by the rule of law in the Union Army.[9]

Patrick Finlan of Scott's 900 (later the 11th New York Cavalry) saw fit to celebrate the birth of his child by becoming drunk, trying to leave Camp Relief (District of Columbia) without permission, and firing a shot at his captain. For this, and three days of being absent without leave, he was sent to the Dry Tortugas, via Old Capitol Prison, to spend the rest of his enlistment. His wife Eliza, apparently a more practical person than her husband, set about freeing him since, with him in prison, she and her infant were utterly without support. "My husband bore a good character until September 1862," she wrote the President, "when, I having a child born to me, my husband, then the worse for liquor. . .so far forgot himself as to attempt to shoot the captain. . .this misfortune has left me alone and destitute." She then joined the flood of supplicants who filled the Executive Mansion and extracted from the President a promise that if she would obtain favorable letters from her husband's superiors, he would free Patrick.

William P. Wood, Superintendent of Old Capitol Prison, wrote, "The conduct of Patrick Finlan during his confinement. . .was good. I believe he would endeavor to redeem his character as a soldier if he were pardoned." Finlan's commander, Colonel James B. Swain (who himself was soon to dismissed in disgrace) added, "Until about two months previous to the assault, Finlan was a good soldier. His wife is very anxious to have him pardoned and returned to the Regiment, she believing that he will hereafter be steady and faithful. I have no objection to try the experiment." The final entry in the record reads, "Let Michael (sic) Finlan, named within return to his regiment and resume his duty therein, upon doing which he is pardoned for the unexecuted part of the sentence of the court Martial mentioned within. A. Lincoln June 2, 1863." The graceful phrasing of the Gettysburg Address is absent; Lincoln has substituted one Irish first name for another, and there are two blots and a word crossed out. The President was clearly tired and hurried—but he kept his word to Eliza.[10]

Private Hugh Shaw, apparently sober, struck his major with a club at Decherd, Tennessee. This action certainly disrupted things in the 58th Indiana Infantry and led to Shaw's trial for violating the Ninth Article of War. He was sentenced to be shot, a decision supported by the area commander. However, when the papers reached Washington, Holt noticed that there was no record of the judge advocate having been sworn, which left the case fatally irregular. Lincoln instructed Nicolay to write: "Sentence disapproved for irregularity. May 20, 1863," and the President added his signature.[11]

The mutiny trials of 1862 closed with Martin Finley of the 5th New York Cavalry. By now, his regiment had fought up and down the Shenandoah Valley. It was charged that on November 18, Finley threatened Captain George C. Morton with an ax, saying that he would chop Morton's head off, and then promised to shoot most of the officers of his regiment. Finley himself was sentenced to be shot. In their petition for mercy, the court noted that he waved the ax but did not attempt to strike the captain and concluded,

> Private Finley is very sensitive about his nationality. When he heard the orderly sergeant call a comrade an 'Irish son-of-a-bitch,' he became very excited. He threatened to shoot the officers only after they had knocked him down, choked him and tied him up tightly [and painfully]. Finley is one of the bravest and most devoted soldiers in the Army and behaves with courage under fire. In the charge, he is always foremost. His example in courage encourages his company in hand-to-hand combat with the enemy.

Holt concurred in the court's recommendation for unconditional pardon. Lincoln signed Nicolay's note, which read, "The sentence in this case is remitted. June 23, 1863."[12] Lincoln had other things on his mind when he signed the pardon: Lee and the Army of Northern Virginia were marching through Maryland on the way to Pennsylvania.

1863

The workings of a citizen army loom sharply in the mutiny trials of eight non-commissioned officers from the 11th Illinois. At Lake Providence, Louisiana, they stacked their arms and said they would do no more duty until their lieutenant resigned. All pleaded guilty and all were sentenced to be shot.

These men were D. W. Mathews, Henry C. Carnes, Noah Shrigley, John N. Storm, Mathew Evans, John Evans, William Wilcox and Thomas Griffith. The latter's father, Parris Griffith, wrote to Lincoln from Effingham, Illinois:

> Having heard that my son, T. Griffith, has been condemned to be shot on the ground of stacking his arms, etc. Now my son may have done wrong, but when he is shot you do not know that you have approved the shooting of as fine a man as lives, the one first in this county to encourage all to put down the Rebellion. He supported the present Admin. and many called him an Abolitionist for voting for you. He was a prisoner eight months in the South, but because he desired to have a voice in selecting his officers he must be shot. Hoping to induce you to pardon my son or to delay the same until you investigate the matter.

Major General Stephen Hurlbut suggested remission to one month hard labor and reduction to the rank of private. For reasons unclear, eleven months passed before these eight cases reached Washington, D.C. for review. Holt suggested full pardons since the men had been confined for a year. On every one, the President wrote: "Pardon. A. Lincoln Feb. 15, 1864."[13]

Far from the steaming swamps of Louisiana, Private Robert Babbitt of the 1st New Mexico Infantry took his horse, gun and cartridge box, departed from "Monton de Alarmos," and did not return. After he was arrested and tried, he was sentenced to be shot. He waited half a year in jail at Fort Stanton, New Mexico, until his case arrived back east. Holt noticed the shocking lack of testimony or evidence and described the quality of the court-martial as "manifest ignorance or indifference." He recommended disapproval of the sentence, Nicolay wrote, "Proceedings and sentence disapproved, February 9, 1864," and Lincoln signed.[14]

Private John Killeen of the 96th Pennsylvania has a trial record with six separate charges. He had been drunk at Windmill Point, Virginia, in March 1863, and refused to go on guard duty. When admonished to do his duty, he cursed his sergeant and his captain, struck the captain, and failed to shoot the latter only because he had not loaded his musket correctly. Killeen was to be shot. Hooker, who routinely sought mitigation, endorsed the shooting and sent the case on to the capital. Holt noted that Killeen had used the excuse of being drunk. The Judge Advocate General sniffed, "The alarming frequency with which Drunkenness is urged in extenuation of great criminality and atrocity calls for a rigid adherence to the principle of law that it aggravates rather than excuses the offense. It is recommended that the sentence be enforced." Here Lincoln disagreed with Holt: "Sentence commuted to imprisonment during the war. A. Lincoln July 18, 1863."[15] The previous day, at Honey Springs, Indian Territory, Indian Confederate troops and black Union troops battled until the Confederates ran low on ammunition and withdrew.

Private John Hoy was an English-born, 45-year-old blacksmith and a member of the 9th New York Artillery. He refused to drill or do fatigue duty, saying, "I was promised $104.00 in advance money and received only $2.00. I was never mustered in." (With a wife and six children, he doubtless needed the money.) Hoy was sentenced to a year at hard labor. There is a note, in Lincoln's hand, saying, "Judge Advocate General, to be pardoned." And there the record ends. There is no explanation and no signature.[16]

William T. Boyle of the 1st New York Mounted Rifles exceeded even the patience of Lincoln. Boyle was absent without leave for five hours at Dillard's Farm, North Carolina. When arrested and returned to camp, he burst into his lieutenant's room and said he was "not going to be guarded by a lot of Dutch hounds." He refused to be tied up, brandished a knife and swore, "I will bury this knife in the breast of the first man who lays hands on me." He then raised his knife above the lieutenant and said, "I will bury this in your heart." After several legal twists and turns, Boyle was convicted of mutiny and sentenced to be shot.

Major General John Peck, who ordered the trial, expressed his own views clearly: "The interests of humanity, the good of the service and the majesty of violated law, demand the prompt and public execution of this sentence." The President agreed: "Sentence approved. A. Lincoln April 14, 1864." However, Boyle had the final word: he escaped into Confederate territory. Major General Benjamin Butler commented that Boyle gave the enemy information which stopped an expedition against Richmond, Virginia, "which adds treason to his crimes." The file ends with the recommendation that Boyle be shot if he was ever caught again.[17]

In early 1863, two Californians, both serving in the southwest, contributed to the Golden State's reputation for turbulence. Private Thomas Boylan of the 1st California Infantry was at Tucson, Arizona, when he called his captain a "damned hump-backed son-of-a-bitch," and struck both the Officer of the Day and a guard with a shovel. Boylan said that he was only preserving his own life—"the first law of nature," according to Boylan—since the guard had just bayoneted him in the groin. Although Boylan vigorously pled this injury to his manhood, it availed him naught, and he was sentenced to die. After the papers made their way across the desert to Washington, D.C., Holt noted that the record failed to "show that two-thirds concurred in the sentence and it is inoperative." John Hay (Lincoln's other principal secretary) wrote "Report approved. July 18, 1863," which is followed by "A. Lincoln." Boylan was spared.[18]

Private John O'Brien of 1st California Cavalry was at Mesilla, New Mexico, when the captain called roll. Eschewing subtlety, O'Brien took a shot at the captain. He, in turn, was sentenced to be shot. Holt, however, noted the same "two-thirds" problem seen in the Boylan case. The same words by Hay and Lincoln which spared Boylan also returned O'Brien to duty. Whatever his personal merits, he had, for the moment, escaped the jaws of death.[19]

A family reunion was nearly the death of Private John Mulvany of the 42nd New York. He was stationed at Fort Hamilton, on the southwest shore of Brooklyn, New York, and without permission left to visit his brother, whom he had not seen in two years. That night, as he returned on board a train, Private Mulvany was in a state of near-paralytic intoxication. The lights in the car were dim. Next to him sat a man in civilian clothes. Apparently more sleepy than forward, Mulvany put his head down on the knees of the stranger, who protested vigorously. Words were exchanged and blows followed. The stranger turned out to be Lieutenant M. H. Stacey of the 12th U. S. Infantry, who preferred charges against Mulvany for striking a superior officer, contempt for a superior officer, and being absent without leave. Mulvany was convicted and sentenced to be shot to death. Major General John Dix approved the death sentence. Lieutenant Stacey, apparently struck with remorse, wrote a letter in favor of Mulvany, stating that it is most probable that the erring Irishman did not recognize him as an officer due to a combination of intoxication and poor lighting. Holt tended to agree that a sentence of death was "not justly incurred" and disagreed with General Dix. In the unmistakable firm dark hand, we see "Sentence remitted. A. Lincoln April 14, 1864."[20] The Compassionate Heart would stop beating in exactly one year.

Michael Duffy was "out of his mind" with whiskey when he stabbed his captain in the neck, "inflicting a dangerous wound." Their regiment, the 3rd Rhode Island Artillery, was stationed at Beaufort, South Carolina. The evidence was clear and brought a verdict of guilty and a sentence of death. In mitigation was a letter from the captain saying that he would accept Duffy back into the regiment—suggesting that the captain was a man of considerable courage. A note by Brigadier General Rufus Saxton approved the sentence, but added a recommendation of commutation based on "previous good character." Holt favored the firing squad in this case, but conceded that General Saxton, "is probably possessed of a more intimate knowledge of all the circumstances connected with the affair than the record conveys." The next step was an easy one for Lincoln. He wrote, "Sentence remitted. A. Lincoln July 18, 1863."[21]

At Corinth, Mississippi, Private Edward Shaw of the 7th Iowa was tied up for misbehavior. Franklin Hessey, of the same regiment, tried to excite a mutiny for the purpose of releasing Shaw. Hessey was convicted and sentenced to eight months at Alton Prison, Illinois, at no pay, with a ten-pound ball and chain on his left leg. The court suggested some mitigation. In the file is a petition to the Governor of Iowa, Samuel J. Kirkwood, signed by Colonel George W. Kincaid, seventeen other commissioned officers of Hessey's regiment, and Chaplain J. H. White, saying: "We ask to have him released and returned to duty." Governor Kirkwood referred the papers onward to the Secretary of War with an endorsement, adding that a governor had no power to remit a sentence of court-martial. Holt reviewed the case, noted that Hessey had already served six months, and concluded, "It is for the President to determine if this is an adequate punishment." Lincoln wrote, "Pardon for remainder. Feb. 15, 1864 A. Lincoln," but by then Hessey's sentence was almost completed.[22]

Kansas soldiers could be very rowdy. At Somersville, Tennessee, a crowd of men from the 7th Kentucky Cavalry were "roving the place and becoming disorderly." Of course, the men were drunk. Several officers went into town and ordered the men back to camp. They not only refused the invitation, but drew their pistols and jostled and struck one lieutenant, trying to provoke a conflict. The visible leader in this provocation was Private James Heusel. For disobedience and for striking a superior officer, he was sentenced to be shot. Major General U.S. Grant recommended commutation to life in prison. Holt observed that such a sentence is not available in military law, and noted that much of the trial record was missing. Lincoln put an end to the matter: "Sentence commuted to confinement at hard labor in the penitentiary for five years. A. Lincoln April 26, 1864."[23] Four days earlier, President Jefferson Davis had advised his commander in Alabama that any captured U. S. Colored Troops should be placed as slaves.

Private John C. Shore (also spelled Schorr and Shorr) of the 109th Illinois was leader of a 40-man lynch mob near Memphis, Tennessee, and urged the others to hang some arrested deserters. It was not a wise course of action, as evidenced by Schorr's own trial on grounds of mutiny. There were many sworn statements that he was a bad man, including one from a man who had known Schorr for twenty years: "His reputation for truth and honesty is exceedingly bad." (His enlistment papers describe him as a blue-eyed farmer, with fair hair and complexion, but he seems to have been no one's "fair-haired boy.") Major General Ambrose Burnside approved the sentence of death.

A large envelope regarding Shore was sent by Adams Express addressed to "Abraham Lincoln, Prest., U.S. of America, Washington, D.C., for immediate attention—a case of death." On the envelope is an unsigned note in Lincoln's hand: "These papers reached me at 1:00 p.m., June 6, 1863." There is no explanation in the records, but Shore's death sentence was mitigated to a stay at the Dry Tortugas. Also unexplained is why he was released from prison in August 1865 from Johnson's Island, Ohio.[24]

Richard Green, a private in the 1st South Carolina Infantry (African Descent), was part of an expedition on the steamer *Saxon* about to land at St. Simeon's Sound, Georgia. He and other men refused to go ashore and described the venture as "hopeless." In the brief mutiny which followed, two men were shot dead and two wounded. Green was convicted of mutiny and sentenced to be executed. He was not alone in his opinion about this expedition. According to a colonel's testimony, "The man in charge of this expedition is insane." The court urged clemency, as did General Quincy Gillmore. Holt said that a year at hard labor would be "suitable and sufficient." The final note reads, "Report approved. A. Lincoln July 21, 1863."[25]

Private Michael Fitzgibbons of the 24th New York was certainly drunk and disorderly, and when ordered to his tent to the colonel, replied, "You God damned bald-headed old son-of-a-bitch, I'll go to my tent when I want to." A sentence of death seems surprising for this offense, and equally surprising was Major General Joseph Hooker's approval of the firing squad, as he almost always found reasons for remission. In this case, it was Holt who took the initiative to lessen the blow. The Judge Advocate General noted testimony that several officers had already failed to quell the disturbance, and called attention to the court's plea for clemency. Holt recommended "lesser punishment as the President may deem just." In this case, the President directed Nicolay to write, "Sentence of Michael Fitzgibbons commuted to imprisonment for one year. May 20, 1863," and added his own signature.[26] The following day, in Louisiana, Federal troops began the siege of Port Hudson.

Private Christian Thompson and his friends thought they were enlisting in a Home Guard unit to protect the city of St. Louis. They were soon told that they were, in fact, in the 2nd Missouri Light Artillery and about to march to Pilot Knob, Missouri, some sixty miles to the south. They refused to cooperate with this plan, and shouted, "We have been humbugged." Thompson was sentenced to be shot for mutiny, but the court recommended clemency, noting that the men had been "influenced by the German press in St. Louis." Major General John Schofield agreed with the recommendation of clemency and sent the case up to the President. Holt concluded that the recruiting officers had lied to the men and on February 15, 1864, Lincoln closed the matter with a single word: "Pardon." Thompson was not to be shot, but neither was he in the Home Guards, where he wanted to be.[27]

Private Rayran Tiernay (also spelled Kayran Turnay) of Company A, 34th Massachusetts Infantry, was engaged in a quarrel at Harpers Ferry, in western Virginia. The Officer of the Guard ordered him to go to the guard house, and Tiernay struck the officer in the face. General B. F. Kelly approved the sentence of death and sent the record to Holt, who passed it on without comment. No one seemed to have a good word for Tiernay. Even the President did not extend himself very much: "Sentence commuted to confinement at hard labor during the war under the direction of the Secretary of War. April 14, 1864. A. Lincoln."[28] Two days earlier, Nathan Bedford Forrest's men captured Fort Pillow, Tennessee. Union sources reported that the U. S. Colored Troops who surrendered there were massacred.

The file in the case of William C. Johnson, Quartermaster Sergeant of the 2nd Nebraska Cavalry, contains an unusual note by the surgeon.

Johnson was convicted of threatening and then striking Second Lieutenant Robert Mason at Camp Cook, Dakota Territory. Johnson was sentenced to two years at hard labor, with no pay, to be followed by a dishonorable discharge. In his letter, Dr. Ardius Bowen, Regimental Surgeon and Medical Director of Nebraska Territory, began with a general plea for order and discipline among the troops, but soon turned his attention to Lieutenant Mason:

> No man in our regiment has set a worse example than the complainant against Johnson. We had all supposed Lieutenant Mason to be a man of some character and respectability. The whole town where he belongs has been shocked with indignant surprise at his conduct since he entered the service. Leaving an amiable and intelligent wife, an interesting family of children, and a fair character all behind him, he has entered into a course of dissipation and disgusting licentiousness. He has been as forward as anyone of his company in drinking to excess and directing sprees. He has openly and shamelessly taken a courtesan from a brothel in Omaha into his tent.

The doctor remarked further that Johnson was no angel, but that rather than a conflict between a sergeant and a lieutenant, the offense should be seen as a "drunken brawl between two dissipated men," with both equally to blame. The final note, in Lincoln's hand, reads: "Submitted to the Judge Advocate General with the request that when the record in the case—that of William C. Johnson—shall return, the case may be brought to my attention—these papers are left with me by Hon. M. Daly of Nebraska. A. Lincoln July 25, 1863." There, the court-martial file ends.[29] A day after Lincoln's note, the hero of the Texas War for Independence, Sam Houston died at Huntsville, Texas. He had spoken out against secession, but had been overruled by younger politicians.

The 1st Ohio Light Artillery was camped near Salem, Tennessee, when Private Henry Stackhorn, drunk and belligerent, struck Lieutenant Nathaniel Newell in the face. Stackhorn was to pay for his aggression against a commissioned officer by facing a firing squad. He had been noisy in his tent and refused to exit when ordered to the guard house. Lieutenant Newell had gone into the tent, and at this point the witnesses told different stories. Some said that Newell was also himself drunk, punched Stackhorn first, and then threatened Stackhorn with a knife.

Others completely contradicted this story. Whatever the truth, the private was sentenced to be shot for violence against a commissioned officer. Major General George Thomas thought Lieutenant Newell had "pursued an improper course," and sent the record on to the President with a recommendation of commutation to hard labor to the end of Stackhorn's enlistment, at no pay. Holt had no opinion on the matter. In a small margin space, with spatters from the nib of the pen, we see "Recom. of Gen. Thomas approved and ordered. A. Lincoln April 14, 1864."[30] Lincoln spared a life; in 365 days, Booth would not.

Ladies were visiting the camp of the 13th Pennsylvania Cavalry, chatting with Major William Bell, when Private George Stetter of the same regiment leveled his pistol and took a shot at Bell. Although the ball went wide, the visitors were perturbed. Earlier that day, Bell had quelled a drunken brawl and in the process had punched Stetter, who then swore that he would kill the major. At the trial, Stetter claimed diminished responsibility and introduced testimony that he was "of unsound mind and occasionally acting in a strange manner. . .as though suffering mental disease and infirmity." He was sent to prison for five years, a plan endorsed by the President when he wrote, "Sentence approved. A. Lincoln Feb. 15, 1864." The almost forgotten war in Florida continued. As Lincoln was sending the seemingly deranged Stetter off to prison, blue and gray forces clashed at Woodstock, a town no longer on the map.[31]

Ludwig Dessyn, a German in the 1st Regiment of the Missouri State Militia, was described as a "willful, passionate, turbulent man" during his trial for mutiny. (His wife may have been equally dismayed by him, as she had left him.) At Victoria, Missouri, Dessyn entered a tent "used by officers for private purposes," and refused to leave. As the major threw him out, Dessyn struck a captain and seized the major. The enlisted men of the company were summoned to arrest their comrade, but were slow to do so until forced to their duty at gunpoint. When he was tied to a tree, Dessyn called out to the men to rise up and free him, but now they ignored him, even when he shouted, "Hurrah for Jeff Davis!" (Of course, he was drunk.) General Schofield recommended commuting the death sentence to six months at hard labor. Holt agreed, and Nicolay wrote, "General Schofield's recommendation approved." The President wrote, "A. Lincoln Mar. 15, 1864."[32] Nathan Bedford Forrest was beginning a four-week foray into Kentucky.

The 99th Ohio Infantry was marching to McMinnville, Tennessee, when Private George Snyder fell behind. When ordered to catch up, he struck both his sergeant and his lieutenant with his gun butt and then tried to punch the major. Under the Ninth Article of War, Snyder was sentenced to die. General Rosecrans approved the proceedings, but suggested commutation to hard labor for the rest of Snyder's enlistment. Holt saw no reason not to shoot Snyder, and passed the decision across the table, where Lincoln wrote and signed, "Recom. of Gen. Rosecrans approved and ordered. April 14, 1864." The hurried scrawl, crammed into a marginal space, with crossed-out words and smeared ink, brings to mind the vast flow of decisions passing through the Presidential offices. It meant life or death for someone, and all received Lincoln's undivided attention—if only for their moment.[33]

In 1863, the 11th U. S. Infantry was stationed at Potomac Creek, Virginia, where Private John Creardon struck Sergeant John Garside and then disappeared for eleven days. He pleaded guilty and asked for mercy on the grounds that he had been drunk Major General George Sykes approved a sentence of death. General Hooker cited Lincoln's Proclamation, and Nicolay wrote, on a sheaf of trial records bound together with red ribbon, "Pardoned." Below this, undated, is "A. Lincoln."[34]

John A. Chase, a sergeant in the 24th New York Infantry, was "crazy drunk" when he struck his captain and then loaded his gun, threatening to finish the job with a bullet. His death sentence was approved by Generals Joseph Hooker and John Reynolds. Chase's many friends petitioned the Chief Executive for mercy; even his doctor wrote to say that the man was too sick to stand imprisonment. Holt thought that even severe illness could "hardly be deemed sufficient of itself to justify his immediate release." Lincoln thought otherwise and signed this entry by John Hay: "Unexecuted portion of the sentence remitted. Nov. 7, 1863."[35]

The term "conscientious objector"was not part of the Civil War military vocabulary, but the act existed all the same. Private Daniel Putnam was drafted into the 16th Maine and joined the regiment at Raccoon Ford, Virginia. He was handed a musket, which he refused, saying, "I am a Second Adventist; it is against my religious principles to take arms. I am sorry to disobey orders, but I cannot carry arms." His own arms and legs were tied tightly and he was left in this painful condition all night. The next day, in spite of aching limbs, he said that he would do any other duty, but would not carry a gun. He was tied up again. At one point, his gun was strapped to his back; nevertheless, when he marched away with his regiment, he was still unarmed. (He also refused to accept any pay, saying that he had not earned it.)

His lieutenant recorded that Putnam was a sober, temperate and obedient person in every other way. Putnam's colonel tried to use "logic" on Putnam, to no avail. Although his court-martial sentenced him to be shot, the members recommended clemency. Holt noted that "General Meade concurs in the recommendation of the court and forwards the records for the action of the President, stating that like cases will probably occur among drafted men." While Holt had no opinion on Putnam, the President certainly did: "Sentence remitted. A. Lincoln Feb. 15, 1864."[36]

Private Charles Williams was supposed to be shot, but was saved by the incompetence of the court. The 6th New Hampshire was at Covington, Kentucky, where Williams punched and cursed his sergeant, bit the man's thumb, and tried to shoot him. Williams was convicted of "violence against a superior officer" and sentenced to die. Holt cited the standard authorities on military jurisprudence to show that "a superior officer" means a commissioned officer. Holt pronounced the case to be "fatally defective and the sentence pronounced void." In the last remaining space on the page is "Sentence remitted as illegal. A. Lincoln April 27, 1864." As Lincoln wrote, Southern troops were attacking at Taylor's Ridge, Georgia, and thumb-biter Williams was headed back to duty.[37]

The martial arts seem to be useful for commissioned officers in dealing with men like Private Joseph Wolf of Battery G, 1st Regiment of Pennsylvania Light Artillery. First Lieutenant Belden Spence told the story:

> We were camped near Frederick City, Maryland. Around noon, Wolf was making a lot of noise and was insolent when I told him to be quiet. I ordered the Corporal of the Guard, to confine him, but he ran away. Our surgeon [Dr. M. F. Price]

persuaded Wolf to come back, but then he ran at Lieutenant [C. B.] Brockway with a knife and tried to stab him. I took a saber from one of the guards and was going to cut him down, but instead I grabbed him from behind. He tried to get me with a backward cut of the knife, but with an effort, I raised him off the ground and threw him on his back. Then the others disarmed him.

Lieutenant Spence shed this light on Wolf's drinking habits: "That day, Wolf was insane drunk. He only drinks when liquor is to be found. In battle, however, he is very good."

General Gouverner K. Warren reviewed the death sentence and suggested mitigation to half pay ·for the rest of Wolf's enlistment. General Meade agreed. So did the final arbiter: "Recommendation of Gen. Warren approved. A. Lincoln Nov. 7, 1863."[38]

1864

John Mitchell may have been only a private in the 3rd Illinois Cavalry, but he had friends at home. Bound from Port Hudson, Louisiana, to Memphis, Tennessee, aboard the steamer *L. M. Kennett*, he was ordered to guard duty. He said that he was too sick for such duty. For refusing, he was punished by being told to carry a 40-pound weight for six hours. When the officers ordered this, Mitchell absolutely refused. At the Memphis levee, two guards escorted Mitchell toward the Provost Marshal's Office. Perhaps his health had improved, because when he took to his heels, they could not catch him. Four days later, he was brought in and jailed. Mitchell was convicted of "conduct prejudicial to good order and military discipline" and sentenced to two years in prison and a dishonorable discharge.

Within a few weeks, Lincoln received several missives related to this case. Sixty citizens of Sangamon County, Lincoln's home ground, signed a petition stating that Mitchell was "a poor man and had served his country faithfully for three years." This petition was forwarded to Lincoln by Richard Yates, Governor of Illinois. Two days later, John Williams, President of the First National Bank of Illinois (Lincoln had been a champion of a national bank), wrote to Congressman John T. Stuart (Lincoln's first law partner), asking for an investigation of the Mitchell case. Eight days later, Lincoln wrote, "Pardon for unexecuted part of sentence. Dec. 23, 1864," and added his signature. It never hurts to have friends in the right places.[39] At Fort Fisher, North Carolina, Benjamin Butler's secret weapon intended to level Fort Fisher—an old ship filled with gunpowder—exploded without doing a bit of harm.

Ripley, Ohio, is forty miles upstream from Cincinnati. On August 20, 1863, the Ripley *Bee* published an advertisement headed by a cannon belching smoke and a breeze-tossed Stars and Stripes, with the following text:

> HEAVY ARTILLERY! 25 more men wanted. $402 bounty. Lieutenant David Cozad is recruiting for the Second Ohio Heavy Artillery, Captain H. G. Whiting, a company for the defense of Cincinnati. This regiment is to be recruited expressly for the purpose of garrisoning the forts in the vicinity of the city. The advantages are thus apparent—men being near home in case of sickness.

The attractive offer of being a soldier while still close to mother attracted nearly a dozen young men. A few weeks later, these young men found themselves at Bowling Green, Kentucky, 150 miles from Cincinnati and with no bonus in sight, and certainly not any $402.00. Being new to military life, Lucien Stevens, Calvin Shaw, Henry Washburn, and John Steele assumed that their obligations were now at an end. After all, a deal is a deal. Their trial for mutiny soon disabused them of this notion, as did their prison sentences, which varied from six to 24 months. A few weeks later, the President received a letter from a former Cincinnati lawyer, Salmon P. Chase (who also happened to be Lincoln's Secretary of the Treasury) conveying a petition signed by nearly a hundred citizens of Ripley, including many doctors, judges and military officers. The wheels of administration now turned more quickly. The next entry reads, "If this petition is true, as it probably is, these men should be pardoned—can the J.A.G. throw any light upon it? A. Lincoln April 25, 1864." Four days later, Holt issued a lengthy legal opinion in which he found that the recruits had been "deceived and misled," and described Lieutenant Cozad as deserving "severe reprehension." Soon, all the men were released from prison—and returned to duty with the same unit. Apparently, fraud in recruiting is not reversible.[40]

Privates Alexander Miller, Cornelius O'Connor and John Gibbons went on a wild drunk in Vicksburg, Mississippi. These three men, of the 5th Illinois Cavalry, roamed the streets, snapping their revolvers at strangers and, when ordered by an officer to behave, cursed the lieutenant and urged others to shoot the officers. Convicted of mutiny, they were sentenced to five years of hard labor in a military prison. The passage of a few months of sobriety and the undoubted need for soldiers at the front may be the reason for the following entry: "The men named within are pardoned for the unexecuted part of their respective sentences. A. Lincoln Sep. 28, 1864."[41] Meanwhile, Sterling Price, a former governor of Missouri, continued his ill-fated raid into his home state.

At Clear Creek, Mississippi, Private Joseph Dunn of the 11th Illinois Cavalry cursed his sergeant and threatened his captain with a revolver. For this, he was sent to prison for a year. A few months after the trial, the former colonel of the regiment, Robert G. Ingersoll, wrote to Lincoln, saying that the captain had provoked the incident and urged Dunn's release. A familiar hand wrote: "Pardoned for unexecuted part of sentence. A. Lincoln Feb. 6, 1865."[42]

A young boy was in tears in a saloon in Ironton, Missouri, a victim of the bullying and abuse of Bugler John Gooch of the 3rd Regiment of Cavalry, Missouri State Militia. Sergeant John Whitmore intervened on the lad's behalf and reprimanded Gooch for terrorizing the child. For his efforts Whitmore was stabbed and seriously wounded by Gooch, who was then charged with striking a superior officer and attempted murder. He sentence was three years at hard labor with a ball and chain. Holt noted that the sergeant was not a commissioned officer, but thought the punishment just.[43]

Gooch's mother wrote to Lincoln and asked for a pardon for her son on the grounds that he was her sole support. Besides, she added, "he is a good boy." Gooch was not Father Abraham's notion of a good boy, and he wrote, "Application denied. A. Lincoln Jan. 23, 1865." Far around the globe in Australia, the Confederate raider *Shenandoah* entered a harbor for supplies. She continued to sink Yankee ships until four months after the war was over.

"I have nearly killed one damned nigger this morning and I expect to kill another before night," shouted Union officer Lieutenant William Striblen of the 9th Louisiana (African) Infantry. The regiment was camped near Memphis. The day before, an order had been issued to send the soldiers' women across the Mississippi River to the Arkansas shore, an order in Holt's words, "apparently unexpected by them and regarded as an intrusion upon their rights."

During the morning of January 28, 1864, a black man (not of the regiment) had been severely beaten by Lieutenant Striblen. Later that afternoon, the lieutenant advanced on his angry company of armed men with a revolver up his sleeve. In the melee that followed, Striblen fired into the crowd, Private Sterling Bradley ran his bayonet into the lieutenant's lung, and Private Charles Davis struck Striblen a blow on the head with a musket.[44]

Davis and Bradley were both sentenced to be shot for mutiny. Major General James McPherson urged immediate execution. Holt agreed and wrote: "It is vitally important to the success of the great and promising experiment of employing Negroes as soldiers that—while no unjust distinctions should be made between them and other troops—neither benevolence nor sympathy should deter us from the enforcement of a rigorous discipline—the good of the whole sometimes requires the infliction of severe punishment in individuals."

The President differed with the court, with the reviewer, and with the Judge Advocate General. "Sentence commuted to confinement at hard labor for six months. A. Lincoln July 9, 1864." Outside Lincoln's office, the city was buzzing with anxiety as Jubal Early's raid drove deep into Maryland. Even as Lincoln wrote, Early was imposing a $200,000 ransom upon the city of Frederick, nearly $80 million in today's dollars.

Expelled from a whorehouse at bayonet point, Private Martin Smith evaded the guard and was soon back in the Martinsburg, West Virginia, bordello, conveniently located near the camp of the 12th West Virginia Infantry. For this, and for trying to shoot his captain, for refusing duty, and for breaking his musket into pieces on the Fourth of July, Smith was given a dishonorable discharge and ten years in the penitentiary. Neither the commanding general nor Holt saw reason for clemency. It is hard to know which of these many crimes offended Lincoln the most, but his overall conclusion is summarized in very few words: "Sentence approved. July 8, 1864. A. Lincoln."[45]

Like many drunks, Private Charles Benning claimed he didn't remember anything. However, his sergeant in the 14th U. S. Infantry, who was punched in the face in a brawl at Bealton Station, Virginia, remembered the incident very well. Benning, who had refused to stop fighting, was convicted of mutiny and ordered to face a firing squad. His captain spoke of "previous good behavior," and General Romeyn Ayres (incidentally, one of the few generals fluent in Latin) suggested clemency, as did Major General Meade, who recommended prison to the end of the war. Holt had no opinion, and passed the papers on to the Final Authority, who wrote, "Recom. of Gen. Meade approved. A. Lincoln April 26, 1864."[46]

Francis Standley of the 1st Nebraska Cavalry took a horse without permission, rode the beast into Batesville, Arkansas, and as night follows the day—got drunk. In this condition, he cursed, punched and stoned his sergeant, for which he was given two years at hard labor. Six months after the crime, his company commander wrote to Lincoln asking for mitigation. Standley returned to duty after Lincoln wrote: "Pardon for unexecuted part of sentence. Dec. 29, 1864."[47]

.   The Union Army had little money to spare on well-built guard houses, as seen in the case of drunk and disorderly Private Gilbert W. Conner, who knocked down the guard house at Point of Rocks, Maryland. He was also charged with refusing to obey the provost marshal, an offense under Article 9, and for this was sentenced to three years at hard labor with a 20-pound ball and chain. A few months later, Conner's commander, the colonel of the 1st Potomac Home Brigade, wrote to Washington, D.C., asking for clemency. The reply came. "Let this boy be discharged and restored to his duty in his regiment as his Colonel requests. A. Lincoln Oct. 3, 1864."[48]

How do you treat a hungry soldier? Cut his rations in half. That was the court's answer to John Chatten of the 7th West Virginia Cavalry, a re-enlisted veteran. After the skirmish at New River Bridge in Virginia, Chatten's regiment marched nearly a hundred miles with nearly no food or rest. During this time, Chatten, glancing toward Rebel territory, said, "If I don't get something to eat shortly, I'll go where I can get it." On the basis of this remark, he was convicted of mutiny and sentenced to nine months at hard labor on half rations of bread and water. Several prominent citizens of West Virginia, including Governor Arthur I. Boreman, wrote Lincoln asking for clemency. The Judge Advocate General agreed with them. On August 16, 1864, Lincoln wrote his shortest opinion: the single word, "Pardon."[49]

The band of the 1st Michigan Infantry (Colored) was presenting a "promenade concert" at Detroit's Merrill Hall, on February 16, 1864. Private James Chancellor had downed a few whiskeys and interrupted the festivities by his drunk and disorderly behavior. When hushed by Lieutenant Edward Cahill, Chancellor raised his bayonet to strike, but was subdued by a bystander At the trial, the defendant claimed he remembered nothing. Memory or not, Chancellor was convicted of trying to kill an officer and was sentenced to be shot. The court recommended clemency as "it was midnight and Chancellor was off duty."

In mute testimony to Lincoln's lack of need to stand on ceremony or to call attention to his good works, we see his life-saving notation crammed into the lowest corner of the transcript, nearly obscured by the superimposition of a clerk's notation and a "date received" rubber stamp. Blots and smears are seen in every word, but the meaning is clear: "Sentence commuted to confinement for six months. A. Lincoln Aug. 17, 1864." Private Chancellor, like so many before him, would have a chance to redeem himself. It was always Lincoln's hope that every man might have his chance.[50]

An analysis of Lincoln's decisions in the mutiny cases is seen in Table Six on the following page. Once again, two trends are manifest. First, Lincoln overturns the sentence of the court-martial in the majority of the cases; second, and perhaps most important, however, is that he is in agreement with his generals and his legal advisor most of the time.

The President upheld the sentence, usually death, in only eight percent (8%) of the mutiny cases he reviewed. However, he was in agreement with his commanding generals seventy-seven percent (77%) of the time, and with Judge Advocate General Joseph Holt eighty-eight percent (88%) of the time. In other words, the lessening of the punishment, in most cases, originated at levels below Lincoln. That he agreed with these mitigations does not detract from his compassionate views; after all, it was within his discretion to ignore the requests for clemency and insist on a harsher tone in military justice.

Opinion Maker	Lincoln Agrees	Lincoln Disagrees	% Agreement
Trial Verdict	4	44	8
Authorizing Officer	6	2	75
Departmental Commander	20	6	77
Judge Advocate General	30	4	88
Interested Politicians	5	0	100
Friends, Family & Comrades	6	1	86

In cases where politicians intervened regarding a case of mutiny (or assault on an officer) Lincoln agreed with their requests one hundred percent (100%) of the time. Where family members or comrades pled for mercy, he turned down only one request and agreed to the other six. In mutiny and violence to officers, as in most other crimes, Lincoln was validating the recommendations of others. He was hardly a solitary voice crying in a wilderness of harsh military justice, but rather the stopping point in a system where he had the final say. Given the choice, he usually supported a recommendation that a man have a chance to redeem himself.

When Lincoln served briefly as a captain in the Black Hawk War, he quickly found that his rank did not impress other volunteers. His authority extended no further than his fellow citizen-soldiers were willing to concede such authority. Since he learned more from experience than most men, and tended to remember such lessons, he probably understood quite well the relationship between volunteer officers and volunteer soldiers. One Lincoln anecdote, in which he seems to stretch the realistic limits of Army discipline to make a point, describes his response to a Pennsylvania Congressman who visited to request clemency for a boy who had struck his captain. Lincoln told his visitor that Congress could remedy this type of problem with a single piece of legislation: "Pass a law that a private shall have a right to knock down his captain."[51]

Lincoln's choices in mitigation might also be ascribed to political expediency, or to a wish not to diminish the Union Army by shooting its soldiers (the Confederates were adept enough at that). Taken in the context of all his actions over a lifetime, a belief in redemption and an innate feeling of compassion seem to most readily explain his actions. He liked to give men an opportunity to rescue themselves from their own follies.

9

Murderers

Amidst the vast and wholesale slaughter that took place on the battlefields of the Civil War, there were also the small-scale, individual murders, which were tried under that name. In the first 45,000 court-martials studied, there were 910 cases of murder, of which sixteen came under Lincoln's review. One of these was tried in the first year of the war, three in 1862, eight in 1863, and four in 1864.

The first murder took place in Mendocino City, on the fog-bound coast of northern California. Private John Carrigan of the 6th U. S. Infantry, had seven prior arrests for intoxication and was known to be a "mean drunk." He was drunk once again and locked in the old sawmill which served as guard house, where his incessant talking disturbed the other prisoner. Sergeant Thomas Hall was sent to move Carrigan to a different room. Hospital Steward Charles A. Drummer testified, "I heard a cry as if a man was in extreme fright. When I reached Sergeant Hall, I found a four-inch wound in his left side, with the intestines protruding." Despite the efforts of Surgeon Pascal Quinan, Hall died eight hours later.

In the trial, held at Alcatraces Island (now known as Alcatraz), in San Francisco Bay, Carrigan was sentenced to be hanged. The decision was approved by Brigadier General George Wright, who commanded the Pacific coast during the war. Holt's review states, "There is reason to infer that the wound was inflicted without notice, as it was certainly without the slightest provocation." Lincoln approved the hanging. Eighteen months after the crime, Nicolay wrote, "Sentence approved in this case, May 11, 1863." The last barrier to Carrigan's execution was removed by the words "A. Lincoln."[1]

The Minnesota Sioux uprising produced many death on both sides. Toon-nan-na-kin-ya-chatka was convicted of "participation in murders, robberies and outrages, at Fort New Ulm, Birch Coolie, and Wood Lake," and sentenced to hang. One of the witnesses listed (although his testimony does not appear) was David Faribault, whose name now graces a city of 18,000 people. The defendant made this statement, recorded by a translator: "I fired one shot at the fort and two through windows at New Ulm. I fired [a total of] three shots at New Ulm." This is the sum of the recorded testimony. In January 1863, the case came to Holt, who opined, "This record is altogether too imperfect to justify the government in carrying the sentence into execution." Five months later (the delay is not explained in the record), a note was recorded, "Sentence disapproved. A. Lincoln May 11, 1863."[2]

At Camp Hamilton, Virginia, Frederick Letz, a civilian teamster, got into an argument with "an old colored man" whose name does not appear in the record. Letz was driving a team, and the old man, who was loading the wagon, asked Letz to bring the vehicle closer. Letz refused, which prompted the "colored man" to voice a complaint. Letz replied, "You damned black son-of-a-bitch, if you don't shut up, I'll shoot you." The other man was not intimidated: "I'm not afraid of any damned white man, especially of a cripple like you. I'll mash your brains if you try to hurt me."

A few hours later, Letz appeared with a rifle and shot the old man dead. A "colored" witness named John Butler told the military commission: "I saw Letz shoot him with a rifle. It was very mean. He told me he didn't give a damn if the old man was dead." Major General John Dix approved the verdict of guilty and the sentence of death. The entry, "The foregoing sentence is approved. A. Lincoln Dec. 17, 1862," endorsed the hanging of a white man for the death of a black man, not a common thing in Old Virginia in 1862.[3]

The next trial contains a sketch of the dying victim lying in the road next to his mule cart. The killer was Private William Dormody of Battery H, 1st Pennsylvania Light Artillery. The regiment was at Yorktown, Virginia, when Dormody left his post to "pillage and plunder." Citizen Hezekiah Stokes provided a death-bed deposition. "I was driving my mule cart to the mill. They seized my mule and beat me with clubs.

Private William Dormody of the 1st Pennsylvania Artillery was tried for the murder of
Hezekiah Stokes, an elderly civilian. This
sketch, which was submitted into evidence,
shows Mr. Stokes' cart and mule, with the
victim lying by the right wheel. The numbers
indicate the position of each assailant. Lincoln
approved Dormody's hanging.

National Archives

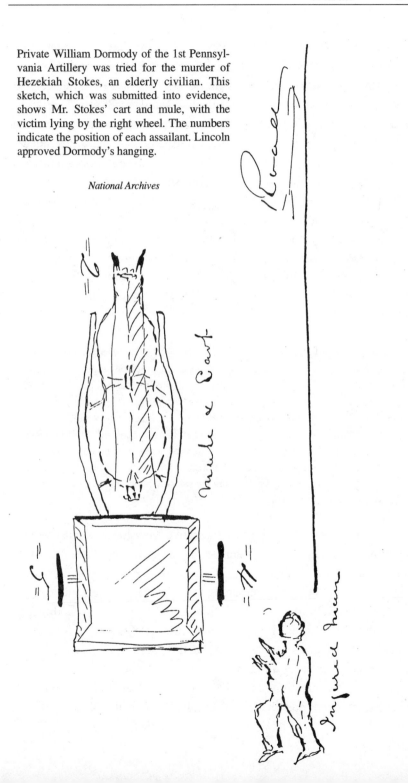

Some said, 'Kill him, kill him.' They knocked me down. Then the man I know to be Michael Slaven stepped up and stabbed me with his knife. Another struck me on the head with his revolver and I lost all recollection. I have always been a loyal citizen." Margaret Stokes, Hezekiah's widow-to-be, told the court, "I was there when my husband pointed out Dormody as the man who assaulted him. My husband knew he was dying." And he was correct. Nine days after the assault Stokes journeyed into the next world in spite of the efforts of Dr. Robert H. Powers, who described "contused wounds on the head, and a suppurating [draining pus] stab wound just below the shoulderblade."

The court sentenced Private Dormody to hang by the neck until dead. General Erasmus Keyes passed the decision on to "higher authority." Major General John Dix approved the death sentence and sent the case to Washington, D.C. There, Joseph Holt had much to say in his review:

> The testimony fully sustains the sentence. The murder, as the commanding general remarks, was 'one of great brutality.' It was committed by a gang of soldiers from motives of revenge on an unarmed senior citizen, who had never wronged them or offered them the slightest offense. Mistaking him for another, or being indifferent as to who he was, they fell upon their unresisting victim and with clubs and knives beat and stabbed him to death in a most cowardly and atrocious manner. The prisoner was the first to point out the deceased to his comrades, who at once set upon him and although it is not shown that he struck him, he joined in the pursuit with those who were dealing their deadly blows and evidently was an active participant in the crime.

The man then occupying the Executive Mansion was least sympathetic to crimes involving meanness and cruelty. He wrote, "Sentence approved. A. Lincoln Feb. 2, 1863." Thirty days later, at Fort Yorktown, Virginia, Dormody's body fell through the trap door of the gallows.[4]

Cornelius Collins, of the 20th New York State Militia was drunk on picket duty at Windmill Point, Virginia. Instead of watching for Rebels, he and his comrades set to quarreling. In the fracas that followed, Collins fatally stabbed one peer and wounded another. The court ordered Collins hanged, but in mitigation noted that the officers had earlier supplied the whiskey involved, and that no officer had visited the picket post that entire night. Major General Joseph Hooker promised that charges would be brought against the officers involved; he also leaned toward mitigation. Holt noted all these factors and concluded, "It is for the President to decide whether the interests of the service and the good of society would be better subserved by pursuing any other course than the enforcement of the penalty pronounced by the court." In spite of Holt's obvious distaste for commutation in this case, the President wrote, "Sentence commuted to imprisonment during the war. A. Lincoln July 18, 1863."[5]

Telling a drunk that he has "had enough" is risky business. Gideon Hodson, a private with the 1st Colorado Cavalry, was drinking in the Exchange Saloon on Second Street in St. Joseph, Missouri. His drinking partner was Captain Charles Mast of the 25th Enrolled Missouri Militia. Mast was also proprietor of the saloon. As the evening wore on, Hodson began to talk of shooting someone named "Zimmerman," whom Hodson was sure was a Rebel. Although Zimmerman was nowhere in the vicinity, Hodson became more boisterous, flourishing his cavalry pistol and shouting incoherent threats. Mast told his customer-drinking partner that he'd "had enough" and that he should put away the pistol. For this effort to maintain the peace, Mast was shot dead.

Sentenced to die, Hodson wrote to the Chief Executive: "Mr. Abraham Linken, Presadent of they Unites States or America, I have the honor of addressing a few lines to you stating they reason of my intrusions on your time." In this missive, Hodson claimed that he was on guard duty and that Mast, without authorization, tried to disarm him. "Mr. Presadent, was it not my sworn duty while on guard to refuse to give up my armes to any person except they officer of they day...?"

Hodson was not above enlisting a somewhat gullible chaplain in this campaign of misinformation. The Reverend S. P. Ives, Chaplain at Gratiot Street Prison at St. Louis, wrote a long letter to Lincoln in which he admitted that he had "no knowledge of the evidence in his case, but he assures me he had no intention of killing the man."

A very different note was struck by Colonel John Williams, commanding the Seventh Military District of Missouri. "I am informed that the statement made by the soldier to the President is basely false," wrote Williams. "Instead of being on guard, as he states, he was in a grocery [liquor store], drunk and raising a disturbance." For whatever reasons,

Lincoln acted to spare Hodson's life. "Sentence commuted to confinement at hard labor in the penitentiary for five years. A. Lincoln Feb. 15, 1864."[6]

An utterly different case was that of Private James McGee of the 2nd District of Columbia Infantry, who ran into trouble on the bright afternoon of June 17, 1863. The private was stationed on Long Bridge, which ran from the foot of 14th Street across the Potomac River to the Virginia shore. McGee, with the feckless inattention of youth, pointed his musket at Private August Sembling and clicked the trigger of an unloaded gun. Unfortunately, it was not unloaded. An instant later a heavy lead ball traversed the twenty feet between the two men, entered the back of Sembling's head and exited his forehead, taking with it a large piece of the skull and most of Sembling's brain.

Private William Page of McGee's regiment told the court, "He put his hands on my shoulder and said, 'Oh, God, I have shot him. It was an accident. When he fell, I thought it was just part of a joke. I did it and I am really sorry I did it. Please call a doctor.'" Page added, "Neither man was drunk. McGee is a humble and good-hearted man." The careless soldier received two years of hard labor for manslaughter. At the Presidential Office, Nicolay wrote, "Sentence approved. Feb. 10, 1864," and the President's well-known signature follows. A year later, McGee was returned to duty.[7]

A quarrel over hay and oats, followed with some hot words, was concluded with the flash of a knife. On an autumn day at Culpeper, Virginia, Private Edward Brandingham of the 6th U. S. Cavalry stabbed and killed Sergeant Schwaggers of the same regiment. The murderer had been quarreling loudly with some other enlisted men over forage. The sergeant approached the group and told Brandingham to be quiet or he would be tied up. The noisemaker cursed the sergeant, who then punched the rowdy private. In a moment, the blows were returned with the cut of a knife. Brandingham was convicted of murder and of drawing a weapon against a superior officer. He was convicted and sentenced to be hanged.

Major General George Meade disapproved the first charge, saying that the act had been manslaughter, not murder. When the case arrived on Holt's desk, the conviction was overturned on the basis that an officer was a commissioned officer, and that murdering a sergeant did not count as a violent act against a "superior officer." Further, Holt noticed that the sergeant had struck the private and threatened punishment, both of which are out of the powers of a noncommissioned officer. "For those reasons, it is recommended that the proceedings be disapproved." The President took his lawyer's advice: "Sentence disapproved. A. Lincoln Feb. 9, 1864." A killer went free.[8]

What scene could be more congenial to a painter's eye: a group of cavalrymen sitting in a circle around a morning fire at Chalk Bluff, Arkansas, coffee in their mugs, and breakfast in their mess kits. The only flaw in this idyll was Private Richard O'Connor stepping forward from his tent, raising his pistol and blowing out the brains of Private Thomas Gray, who tumbled backwards from his log seat, his last cup of coffee wildly spilled. Both men had belonged to a Missouri cavalry regiment called Merrill's Horse, and both had quarreled earlier over guard duty. Gray, so went the testimony, had "struck the prisoner two or three blows, punishing him somewhat, and marking him about the nose." Gray then sat down by the fire and a few minutes later was gunned down by O'Connor, who told the court, "I am the butt of the company. . .Gray continually annoyed and tormented me."

O'Connor was sentenced to be hanged. General John Davidson reviewed the proceedings and believed it to be a case of manslaughter, not murder. Davidson recommended mitigation to five years in prison. Holt disagreed strongly in a 1,500-word opinion complete with multiple citations. The crucial point to the Judge Advocate was that the combination of malice and prior reflection made the crime murder, rather than the lesser manslaughter. Holt's concluding paragraphs touch the heart of the matter:

> The provocation under which he was laboring at the time of committing the deed, therefore rests upon the subsequent threats and acts of the deceased, in advancing toward him and threatening to tear him to pieces if he did not stop talking. Upon this provocation, the prisoner proceeded several yards to his tent, provided himself with a pistol from his holster, turned and advanced several steps toward the deceased, who, unsuspecting and unarmed, was then engaged in drinking a cup of coffee, and, taking deliberate aim at the head of the deceased, fired at him this deadly weapon.

These acts of the prisoner show that he had formed a deliberate, willful design and purpose to take the life of the deceased, and though such design had not been long entertained, still it was fully formed, and carried into effect, and evinces on his part a wicked and depraved heart, and that premeditation and malice, which constitute the crime of murder. It is believed that the distinguished Generals who urge a mitigation of the sentence for the reason that in their opinion the court erred in considering the offense to be murder, entirely misapprehended the law applicable in this case. It is therefore recommended that the sentence be carried into execution.

In spite of Holt's impassioned plea for the hangman's noose, the President felt otherwise: "Recom. of Gen. Davidson approved and ordered. A. Lincoln Aug. 16, 1864."[9]

Lincoln was much less sympathetic to Private John Campbell of the 16th Indiana, who also murdered a comrade at breakfast, this time at Pilot Knob, Missouri. The victim was Moses Hughes. Witness Charles Matthews, age 19, recalled: "I was at breakfast, sitting around the fire, next to Hughes. Campbell came up and shot Hughes. The ball went in an inch above his right eye and came out about his left ear. Campbell put the gun down and said, 'I have killed one son-of-a-bitch.'" Other witnesses said that Campbell had been drinking heavily for a month and the night before had come into camp with a full canteen of whisky.

Campbell defended his actions, claiming that Hughes had stolen from him while he slept. Although the court recommended the firing squad, for reasons unstated it suggested mitigation. Major General Nathaniel Banks saw no reason for clemency. "The discipline of the Army," he intoned, "and the interests of justice require the sentence to be enforced." Holt agreed. "The proof is clear that it was an atrocious murder, committed in cold blood and with premeditation." Two generals, two thumbs down for Campbell. The man with final decision power turned his own thumb to the floor as well and added, "Sentence approved. A. Lincoln."[10]

"I don't fool with a darky!" With these words, Private George W. Johnson plunged a dagger into the heart of a "colored barber" at Gloucester Point, Virginia. The outcome was fatal for both. Johnson, a member of the 4th Delaware Infantry, and several other men were gathered at the "Old Water Battery," drinking and quarreling. The barber,

George Holland, was well known to them. Johnson gave Holland 60 cents and sent him for a fresh bottle of whisky. Holland protested that whisky could not be purchased with so little money. Hot words were followed by blows. The autopsy showed a knife wound clear through the left ventricle of Holland's heart. At the trial, there was no evidence in Johnson's favor, and he was sentenced to be hanged.

With this verdict, his family sprang into action with letters and petitions. Johnson's mother, father, sister and brother-in-law wrote that Johnson should be pardoned because he was from a good family! Thirty-four other people added their names to the petition. His sister also wrote to "Abrm. Lincoln," that "his mother and father are ready to drop in the grave with grief," and concluded, "Oh, my brother, my baby brother, cannot his life be spared?" The tears of the killer's family were unavailing. The final note reads, "Sentence approved. A. Lincoln July 18, 1863."[11]

Private John Flippin of the 2nd Illinois Artillery was tried for murder, robbery, and forcing a safe guard (certificate of official protection). The latter had been issued by General Stephen Hurlbut to A. P. Parrish of Randolph Forges, Stewart County, Tennessee, and stated that all persons and property at the Forges were to remain unmolested under penalty of death. Witness Charles Canby, described only as "colored," said that Flippin came to the Forges, "shot two hogs, stole my shirt and bedclothes, and stole my coat with the gilt buttons, which were given out by the government when we worked for them last winter." Nathaniel Cockrill, also "colored," recalled that "After he shot the hogs, Flippin and another man went to John Washington's house and fired into the house. They killed Washington."

Flippin was found guilty and sentenced to be shot, but the court recommended clemency because of "extreme youth [Flippin was 18] and previous good character." Major General George Thomas recommended commutation to six months pay. Holt noted that the fatal shot had been fired by a man other than Flippin and recommended a $75.00 fine. Lincoln wrote, "Gen. Thomas recom. approved & ordered. Feb. 10, 1864," and signed his name.[12]

"The evidence showed that the accused. . .visited the house of a colored man. . .for the purpose of having sexual intercourse with a woman living there." Thus begins Holt's review of the murder trial of Sergeant Arthur Woods of the 12th New York Cavalry. About 10:00 o'clock on an April evening at New Berne, North Carolina, Woods and three other men banged on the door of Edmund Smith, "a negro." What happened next was a matter of dispute, but at least several witnesses said that Smith fired from inside the door, that the soldiers broke in, and that Woods shot Smith in the head. Woods' excuse? "I didn't know the other barrel was loaded." It swayed the court, which convicted him of man-slaughter and sentenced him to a year of prison. General Innis N. Palmer, who reviewed the case, was not happy with the ruling and wrote, "It looks to me like deliberate murder."

Woods soon began to work towards reducing his sentence. He had his captain write a letter describing "excellent character." Woods' colonel, James Savage, wrote that Woods was of good character and suggested strongly that four months in prison was sufficient punishment (for killing a man). At Woods' request, a John R. St. John of Lockport, New York, wrote to Lincoln, urging clemency. This man must have been of some influence, as we see this entry: "Let execution in this case be suspended and the record of trial be sent to me. Also allow Mr. St. John to go to New Berne, NC and return, for the purpose of attending to this case. A. Lincoln July 27, 1864."

Holt's position in the matter was clear from his recommendation: "It is a question for the President whether a year's hard labor and forfeiture of pay is too severe. . .for a reckless misdemeanor, which resulted in a homicide." Lincoln's decision in Woods' case, one involving murder and illicit sex, seems strangely lenient: "Sentenced reduced to imprisonment and loss of pay up to October 20, 1864. A. Lincoln Aug. 18, 1864."

This slap on the wrist was not the last of Woods (or of the Lincoln name) in the Federal records. In 1881, a Washington D. C. attorney named A. A. Harwood requested a copy of the earlier proceedings "to discredit Woods, who is a witness in a murder case." Ironically, the letter of reply was signed by the Secretary of War, Robert Todd Lincoln, the son of the late President.[13]

The case of Jasper Laster is another one of puzzling leniency. Laster was a private with the 3rd Missouri State Militia Cavalry. Two days before Christmas 1863, he was on the road from Farmington to Pilot

Knob (both in Missouri) when he met a "Mr. Larbe," who had a goose for sale. Laster offered "two bits," but the owner said he would not sell the goose for less than fifty cents. After a brief quarrel, Private Laster shot the owner of the goose; the victim's pistol was still in its holster as he lay dead. Larbe's goose was cooked—twice.

Laster was convicted and sentenced to face a firing squad. General John Schofield recommended commutation to ten years in prison at hard labor. Holt concluded that the "crime was doubtless a willful, unprovoked murder." For reasons wholly unknown, Lincoln saw fit to spare a man who murdered a stranger over a quarter, and wrote, "Sentence commuted to confinement at hard labor in the penitentiary for ten years. April 21, 1864." That day, the President reviewed 72 court-martials. Perhaps the volume of work impaired his judgment.[14]

"Good evening, Johnnie," were the fatal words spoken by a private named Fitzgerald, out for a stroll near Black River, Mississippi. He addressed this greeting to Private John Ford of the 20th Illinois Infantry, who pulled out a pistol and shot Fitzgerald. Ignoring the dying man's cries for help, Ford walked on. When arrested, he said, "I thought the man was secesh and I don't allow any secesh to talk to me in that way."

Ford employed a pair of defenses. "I didn't know the gun was loaded," was his first effort, followed up with, "I had two glasses of cider and didn't know what I was doing." The court did, however, and sentenced him to life in prison. Holt offered no objection to the sentence, and the President agreed: "Sentence approved. A. Lincoln July 9, 1864."

Over the following five years, Ford used every wile of the jailhouse lawyer. He invented several new stories of the shooting—I was only carrying out orders, I was on duty as a guard, it was an accident—and concluded with the masterful, "I am as innocent as a child." He inspired twenty-four farmers of Dewitt County, Illinois to send a petition begging for his release. He wrote to Andrew Johnson, Ulysses S. Grant, Edwin Stanton, Congressman J. W. McClurg, and Thomas Fletcher, Governor of Missouri. Joseph Holt, when asked to review all these requests, wrote, "He has made six or seven petitions for clemency, each one a new fabrication." Lies they may have been, but the murdering private proved once again that the squeaky wheel gets the grease, and was pardoned in 1869.[15]

Private Richard Cooper of the 10th New Jersey was stationed at Pottsville, Pennsylvania. He and three comrades came into town with murder in their hearts, seeking a man they felt had wronged them. They pursued an unarmed citizen, Charles Mendham, through the bar of Leonard's Hotel at Second and Market Streets and shot him down in cold blood. The killing created quite a sensation and the Pottsville *Miner's Journal* of October 10, 1863, devoted thousands of words to the testimony. In spite of a vigorous defense, the evidence (which included two hand-drawn maps of downtown Pottsville) was overwhelming and Cooper was sentenced to hang. General Darius Couch, who reviewed the matter, approved the decision. However, in the face of petitions and protests by "leading citizens" of New Jersey, Couch backed down and suggested three years in prison instead.

One of the petitions is a study in obfuscation. The thirteen signatories urged clemency because of the "known virtues of Jerseymen," and contained no reference either to the crime or to Cooper's character. Cooper prevailed upon the commander of his prison to recommend clemency based upon three months of good conduct. Holt saw through this razzle-dazzle: "This was a brutal and cowardly murder of an unarmed man. There is no basis for a recommendation of clemency." The die was cast with the words "Sentence approved. A. Lincoln July 9, 1864." A few weeks later, the hangman at Fort Mifflin, Pennsylvania, sent Cooper hurtling into eternity.[16]

Table Seven on the following page shows a much different pattern than Lincoln's treatment of deserters. With the murderers, Lincoln endorsed severe sentences in half the cases he reviewed, and was far less amenable to the pressures and entreaties of family and politicians than with other sorts of crimes. Lincoln was in complete agreement with his departmental commanders in these cases, and with Holt in two-thirds of them. He was clearly more lenient than Holt, who had little patience with cold-blooded killers. This difference is not surprising, since Holt was a strong believer that criminals must pay for their crimes, while Lincoln, in some of these cases seems strangely willing to offer clemency.

What we learn about Lincoln in this study of murder cases is that his legendary "compassion" was tempered by the need for justice. He hated intentional meanness and cruelty. In most (but not all) murder cases with those traits, he was quite willing that the defendant swing from a rope or face a firing squad.

Opinion Maker	Lincoln Agrees	Lincoln Disagrees	% Agreement
Trial Verdict	8	8	50
Authorizing Officer	1	2	33
Departmental Commander	11	0	100
Judge Advocate General	9	4	69
Interested Politicians	1	1	50
Friends, Family & Comrades	1	2	33

10

Confederate Recruiters, Spies & Soldiers

In addition to the court-martials described at length in preceding chapters, there were military commissions. This unusual form of justice was used in areas where civil law had collapsed, such as Missouri and parts of Tennessee. Military commissions were also used in the trials of civilians accused of military crimes, such as spying and smuggling of weapons. Guerrillas who attacked Union troops and Union sympathizers were tried by military commissions, as were recruiters sent north to sign up men for Confederate service. Many men arrested within Union lines claimed to be Confederate soldiers, operating on orders from duly commissioned Confederate officers. The implications of being a "real" soldier will be discussed shortly.

Court-martials had eight to thirteen officers sitting in judgment; military commissions usually had only three. During the war, approximately 4,500 military commissions were held.

A frequent defense raised by persons thus tried was that a military commission had no authority to conduct such trials or to pass sentence. Who is entitled to try whom is a question which still vexes Constitutional scholars, just as it did during the war. What is clear is that military commissions were a central fact of life in the border states. (To further confuse the issue of jurisdiction, some civilian employees of the Federal government, and some civilian contractors, were tried by court-martial rather than by military commission.)

There were few military commissions held in New England or in the upper northwest states, such as Michigan and Minnesota, for the obvious reasons that the civil law was functioning in those areas and there were very few men from those states who fought for the Confederacy. Quite the opposite was true in Missouri and Tennessee. There, Union and Confederate sympathizers lived side by side. Tolerance and compassion were notably absent, and there were daily murders, threats, insults, robberies, and retaliations. Unlike the neatly divided lines of butternut and blue in traditional pitched battles, the border states were a patchwork of blood, feud, and hatred.

While Maryland, Missouri, and Tennessee were officially in the Union, thousands of men from those states fought for the Confederacy. In order to visit their homes, they needed to cross into Union territory. If they were captured there, they were likely to be tried as spies. Thus the important question: when is a soldier not a soldier?

A man in uniform, acting under the orders of an organized government, one authorized to appoint and commission a military hierarchy, is a soldier, and if captured, is entitled to be treated as a prisoner of war with the traditional rights accorded such prisoners. However, the woods and valleys of the Ozarks (and other border regions as well) were filled with armed bands of dubious legality. If a man is wearing Union pants, a butternut blouse, and a civilian hat, and is riding a stolen horse and bears allegiance to "Smith's Company" or "Mitchell's Band," is he a Confederate soldier, or just a common cutthroat wrapping his pillage and murder in the cloak of Southern patriotism? This confusion will be seen in the court-martials and military commissions described in the next few chapters. As we shall see, the system of justice under military law struggled not only to determine guilt or innocence, but to determine if an event was an act of war or simply a crime. One hundred and thirty-some years after the fact, it is no easier to answer these questions.

The military commission trials of thirty-two Confederate soldiers (trials not indexed in Basler) came to Lincoln's attention in the records we have reviewed thus far. Here are their stories and the part that Lincoln played in their encounters with wartime justice. . . .

Army recruiters for the Confederacy operated in the North as well as the South. The Union did not take kindly to such activity above the Mason-Dixon Line. The tenor of the times was expressed by General

Burnside's General Order No. 38, dated April 13, 1863, at Cincinnati, Ohio, which recommended death for Confederate recruiters found north of the lines. The same fatal penalty was prescribed for carriers of Confederate mail, for the writers of such mail, for men going south to join the Confederate army, and for anyone who sheltered or fed the enemy.

Sergeant William Corbin (regiment not given) met these criteria when, in Campbell County, Kentucky, he recruited eight men for the Confederate army. When arrested, he was carrying not only mail, a Colt's revolver and a large knife, but also a letter from Confederate Brigadier General Humphrey Marshall authorizing Corbin to "raise a company of mounted men into the service of the Confederate States." (In late 1862, Marshall commanded the Confederate District of Abingdon.) Additional evidence showed that Corbin had helped burn bridges on the Kentucky Central Railroad. He was sentenced to be shot May 15, 1863, at Johnson's Island, Ohio. The President reviewed the case and wrote, "The foregoing sentence is approved. May 4, 1863. A. Lincoln." Corbin is almost unknown today, but those few words on a piece of paper were, for him, life or death. And it was death.[1]

(Many of the cases Lincoln dealt with on this subject originated in Missouri, where the organization of troops, both Union and Confederate, is a very confusing subject. The state had two governors, one Union and one Confederate, and a wide variety of independently-operated military units whose names, designations, and officers are not found in the usual reference books. In order to avoid adding to this confusion, the designations used in these chapters are *verbatim* those used in the trial record.)

On November 24, 1862, Colonel S. D. Jackman, commanding Jackman's Independent Partisan Regiment (Confederate), wrote a letter authorizing Captain W. G. Watkins to "enlist and swear into the service of the Confederate States. . .one company of men to serve as cavalry. . . to operate in the state of Missouri." Watkins was carrying this letter and his Confederate captain's commission when captured. The military commission sentenced him to be shot. The President did not have much difficulty playing a role in ushering these individuals into the next world. The Chief Executive wrote, "Sentence approved. A. Lincoln August 9. 1864," and Jackson was history.[2]

James R. Kirby was a true child of the border. This native of Missouri joined the Confederate army in December 1861, fought at the Battle of Pea Ridge, and was discharged in June 1862. He returned home, took the Oath of Allegiance to the Federal Government, and joined the Enrolled Missouri Militia (Union), from which he deserted. He then accepted a commission as a recruiter for the Confederate army. He was captured, tried in August 1863, and sentenced to be shot. The case took a year to reach the President. His decision? "Sentence approved. Aug. 9, 1864. A. Lincoln."[3]

T. G. McGraw was at Rouse's Mills, Pendleton County, Kentucky, when he was arrested for recruiting for the Confederate army. He was carrying a rifle musket and his holster bulged with a Colt's revolver. McGraw's defense was not well thought out: "I regret I did not burn any bridges." The verdict was guilty and he was sentenced to be shot. The case reached Lincoln a few weeks later. Over his signature is "The foregoing sentence approved. May 4, 1863." Nine days later, a firing squad ended McGraw's life.[4]

Spies were not welcome in the North. Mount Washington, Kentucky, was the location of the undoing of James. W. Hodges. There, he struck up a conversation with two men named Coleman and Giles. After convincing himself that they were Southern sympathizers, he disclosed to the pair that he was in the Confederate army and was also a Knight of the Golden Circle (an underground brotherhood sworn to defeat the Union and uphold slavery). Giles and Coleman responded with the secret counter-sign of the Golden Circle, and Hodges gave them further details of his work as a Confederate spy. He had chosen his new friends unwisely, for they were Federal detectives. Arrested and tried, Hodges was sentenced to hang. He escaped briefly and was recaptured. Judge Advocate Holt noted some technical difficulties in the framing of the charges, but felt that they were not "fatal" to the prosecution. The final decision went to Lincoln, who wrote, "Sentence approved. Aug. 16, 1864," and signed his name. (This matter might be one of the cases Basler described as "routine endorsements." For the condemned Hodges, it meant dropping through the floor of the gallows and the snap of his neck vertebrae. Routine? Not to Hodges.[5])

Major General John A. Schofield was the commander of the Department of Missouri, and reviewed hundreds of trials of bushwhackers and guerrillas.

Generals in Blue

Confederate soldiers, other than recruiters and spies, were more likely to receive mercy from Lincoln. Twelve Missouri cases prove that point. Thomas F. Sanders burned Deck Bridge, in Missouri, and when tried, admitted his guilt. The reviewing general in this matter was John M. Schofield, an 1853 graduate of West Point and the commander of the Department of Missouri during the war's middle years. Schofield is better known to students of the Civil War because of his defeat of John Hood at Franklin, Tennessee, in November 1864. (Schofield's other contribution to American history was his post-war recommendation to convert swampy Pearl Harbor into Hawaii's major naval base, which set the stage for the dreadful news of December 7, 1941.) The general examined Sanders' case and recommended that the sentence "hang by the neck until dead" be commuted to imprisonment to the end of the war. Holt saw "no ground whatsoever" for mercy. The President offered no reason for his decision, and simply wrote "Recom. of Gen. Schofield approved and ordered. April 27, 1864. A. Lincoln."[6]

Charles Clifford, when arrested at Springfield, Missouri, said he was a major in the Confederate service visiting his dear wife. His lack of a uniform and inability to produce such a wife led to a conviction and sentence of death by hanging. Holt found no ground for clemency, but his superior wrote, "Sentence commuted to confinement in one of the military prisons for during the war. May 11, 1863. A. Lincoln." Here the stroke of Lincoln's pen meant life, not death.[7]

Benjamin Singleton robbed two Missouri citizens at gunpoint, in each case taking a saddle. He confessed to his crimes and stated that he was in the Confederate army. He was sentenced to three years at hard labor. General Schofield, not being authorized to confirm such a sentence, submitted the issue to the President, who wrote, "Sentence approved. April 14, 1864. A. Lincoln."[8] In one year to the day, Lincoln would be attending a play at Ford's Theater.

David F. Sigler of St. Louis took the Oath of Allegiance in April 1862. Thereafter he accepted a Confederate commission as captain of Company I, Stein's Regiment, Missouri Infantry, and fought with the Confederate forces at Prairie Grove, Arkansas. He was charged with violating his Oath of Allegiance. At his trial, Sigler blundered badly when he submitted his March 18, 1863 resignation from the Confederate army, which only added to the evidence against him. He was sentenced to be shot. Hope remained for his wife and four children when the President wrote, "Sentence commuted to hard labor for during the war. April 14, 1864. A. Lincoln."[9]

Lloyd Daniels, another St. Louis citizen, took the Oath of Allegiance and then joined Captain Serge's Company of the Third Missouri Cavalry (Confederate). He was arrested after he robbed three Union soldiers at gunpoint, taking their clothes. When tried in October 1863, Daniels said that he was age 23, had a wife, two children, and no slaves. He readily admitted his Confederate enlistment and his robberies. He was sentenced to hang, a decision endorsed by Schofield. On April 14, 1864, Lincoln wrote and signed this note: "Sentence commuted to imprisonment at hard labor in the penitentiary for five years."[10]

Alfred Yates served on both sides. After a time in the First Nebraska Infantry (Union) he traveled south and joined Company F of Colonel Green's Regiment (Confederate). When Yates was arrested in Washington County, Missouri, "at the home of a Rebel sympathizer," he told his captors that he had only come north to see his mother. He was convicted of lurking and spying and was sentenced to hang. Schofield recommended commutation to prison to the end of the war. Holt suggested that a spy was entitled to little consideration, but his employer wrote, "Commutation as recommended by Gen. Schofield approved. A. Lincoln. Nov. 7, 1863."[11]

Illegal mail was expensive in 1863. William Bamberge, a 17-year-old sergeant in an unnamed unit of the Confederate army, charged $5.00 a letter when he crossed the lines from Union to Confederate territory. In addition to smuggling, he had fought in three battles: Pea Ridge, Farmington, and Murfreesboro. This St. Louis native was arrested with twenty-five letters in his pockets, but claimed they had been left there by someone who had borrowed the coat and he had not noticed them. His sentence was death by the hangman's noose. Schofield recommended prison to the end of the war, while Holt merely opined that Bamberg was a liar. Lincoln wrote and signed, "Gen. Schofield's recommendation approved. Feb. 9, 1864." Bamberg was saved from a hemp tie.[12]

Mrs. Columba Musgrave wrote to Lincoln in November 1863 upon hearing that her 23-year-old husband was to be shot. "Allow me to most earnestly implore pardon for my young and misguided husband, whom, I am satisfied, if he is restored to liberty, will deport himself as a good and loyal citizen. . .he was induced to go south by false and pernicious representations." The "misguided husband" was Francis Musgrave, a citizen of Pulaski County, Missouri, who had violated his oath by joining "Pickett's Regiment," in which he served for four months. The Military Commission sentenced him to be shot. Schofield recommended prison to the end of the war, and Lincoln's secretary John Nicolay wrote, "Recommendation of General Schofield approved and ordered. Feb. 10, 1864," and Lincoln signed.[13]

Thomas Bryant of Lawrence County, Missouri, would have fought for the Rebels at Prairie Grove—but he had the measles. When he was captured and tried in October 1863, he was charged with violating his oath by joining "Colonel Mitchell's Regiment of Guerrillas." He pled guilty to all of the charges, but objected to the word "guerrilla." He was convicted and sentenced to prison during the war. Nicolay wrote, "Sentence approved. February 9, 1864." The "A. Lincoln" is smeared, but still clearly readable.[14]

George Casey's mother said that he came home to Potosi, Missouri, in a "worn-out" Confederate uniform and she "provided him with a new suit of jeans." He had no furlough papers, but told the commission that he had taken "French leave," which he described as customary in his Confederate unit. (French leave simply means leaving without permission.) It is unclear what regiment he belonged to, but he was convicted of "lurking within the U.S. lines," and sentenced to be hanged by the neck. The reviewing general suggested prison to the end of the war. John Hay wrote in a cramped hand along a narrow margin of the page, "Sentence commuted according to the recommendation of Gen. Schofield. Nov. 7, 1863." In the last remaining space is "A.. Lincoln," one of the few times when such double punctuation is seen.[15]

At age 44, Ephraim Harris was older than most Missouri soldiers. On his farm was his wife, one child, and one slave. After taking the Oath of Allegiance to the United States, he joined the Rebel forces as a first lieutenant in Co. K of "Burbridge's Regiment." When captured, he was tried and sentenced to be shot. Schofield recommended commutation to prison during the duration of the war; Holt made no recommendation. The final notation is, "Recom. Gen. Schofield approved. A. Lincoln, Feb. 15, 1865." (The horizontal bar of the "A" is left undone.) [16] That day, William T. Sherman's forces were entering the suburbs of Columbia, South Carolina. The long war was winding to a conclusion; luckily for Ephraim Harris, his period of incarceration would be relatively brief.

James Holton had been a stonemason in St. Louis before becoming a sergeant in Co. B, Second Missouri Cavalry (Confederate). He fought for the South in the battles of Wilson's Creek, Pea Ridge and Corinth. When arrested at Manchester, Missouri, he gave a false name. He did not comport himself well or wisely at his trial, where "in a boastful and defiant manner" he said that he had a right to come and go as he pleased, that he had obtained much information about Union troop dispositions, and that, given the chance, would convey this intelligence to the Confederate service. He was sentenced to hang.

Once again, Schofield recommended commutation to imprisonment during the war. In this case, Holt voiced strong disagreement. "A clear case, as charged, was made out, and there is no reason why the full penalty of the law should not be executed." Holt went on to notice the almost-universal excuse of Rebel spies ("I was just visiting my family, wife, mother, etc."), a practice which has been "dangerously prevalent and it is believed should be prevented by the rigid enforcement of the laws of war." Lincoln did not agree, and wrote, "Recom. of Gen. Schofield approved, and signed and ordered. April 26, 1864. A. Lincoln."[17]

James A. Powell, a member of "Captain Powell's company" of Missouri Confederates, shot and killed a Union soldier who was on picket. Powell was sentenced to face a firing squad, but Schofield added a note recommending commutation to prison for the duration of the war, The president wrote: "Recom. of Gen. Schofield approved and ordered. Apl. 27, 1864 A. Lincoln." The hurried scrawl and the smeared date suggest a man with a desk deep in papers.[18]

Muse Kirby took the Oath of Allegiance in September 1862, and a month later joined Wicks' band of (Confederate) outlaws, where he joined in plundering citizens at Hartsville, Missouri. When captured, he was surly, hostile, and defiant. Kirby did provide the information that he was unable to read or write, was unmarried, and owned no slaves. His sentence "to be shot to death with musketry" was strongly endorsed by Holt, who noted that Kirby "robbed those people who remained steadfast in their loyalty and fidelity. . .citizens who have suffered unprecedented outrages from such outlaws." As to Schofield's suggestion of commutation, Holt saw no reason in the records for mercy. Neither did the President: "Sentence approved. A. Lincoln August 4, 1864."[19]

Benjamin Simpson, although a member of Confederate "Major Livingston's Company," came north dressed in a Union uniform and with several companions stole three horses and a mule. He was arrested, tried, and convicted of the charges of "being a spy" and "being a brigand," and sentenced to be shot. Schofield agreed with this decision; Holt was of the opinion that "The findings were justified by the proof and the execution of the sentence called for." Wearing a false uniform is one of the surest ways to a firing squad. In spite of this factor, and against the judgment of the commission, the commanding general, and his own legal adviser, the Chief Executive chose a different course: "Sentence commuted to imprisonment in Penitentiary at hard labor for five years. A. Lincoln Feb. 15, 1864." One wonders if Simpson thereafter felt anything positive about the man who spared his life.[20]

Tennessee Confederates and Bushwhackers

Five Tennessee Confederate soldiers came to Lincoln's attention. Silas Worlds of the 20th Tennessee Infantry came north disguised in civilian clothing. At LaVergne, Tennessee, he attacked the sutler of the 1st Ohio Infantry and was unhitching the sutler's horses when driven off by Union cavalry. A few miles away, Worlds stole a civilian's horse at gunpoint, saying, "I have a right to take away the horse of any damned Lincolnite!" The commission acquitted him of the "Lincolnite" charge, but found him guilty in the sutler incident and recommended that he be shot, a decision endorsed by General Rosecrans. Holt reviewed the case and concluded, "His participation in the robbery fully justifies the sentence of death." Worlds' end came with the notation, "Sentence approved. A. Lincoln. Nov. 7, 1863."[21]

William Andrews had been in the Confederate army (the unit is not specified in the records) but went to Gallatin, Tennessee, and took the Oath of Allegiance. The Union post commander, a "Captain Noble," warned Andrews before administering the oath that the penalty for violation was death. Nevertheless, when Confederate General John Hunt Morgan attacked Gallatin, three months later, there was Andrews, carrying a gun and fighting with the Rebels.

Captured, Andrews was sentenced to prison for the duration of the war. Rosecrans was deeply distressed: "The punishment is entirely inadequate and should have been death." He referred to such oath-breakers as "hypocritical and perjured villains," but approved the sentence nontheless. Holt was of the same sentiment: "Such perfidy merits the severest penalties of the law. . .the punishment declared by the Court is inadequate." Lincoln simply wrote, "Sentence approved, Feb. 8. 1864," and signed his name.[22]

David Martin was a soldier in "Braxton Bragg's army," in the early winter of 1863. He obtained his captain's permission to go home (which was near Spencer, Tennessee) and procure a new horse. However, Martin did not return to his previous regiment, but instead joined "Captain Carter's" band of guerrillas and bushwhackers. When captured, Martin was charged with highway robbery and the murder of an unnamed civilian at Bledsoe County, Tennessee. It was not proved that he pulled the trigger at the fatal shooting, but the evidence showed him to have been with the gang that did the killing. He was sentenced to hard labor at a Tennessee prison until the end of the war. Holt agreed with the conviction, but thought that a Tennessee prison offered too much chance of escape. The President agreed: "Sentence approved and imprisonment to be at Albany, N.Y. A. Lincoln April 27, 1864."[23]

James Fraly, described as "a straggler from the Confederate Army," was tried by a military commission in February 1864. After becoming separated from his unit in a raid on Sparta, Tennessee, he joined up with "Captain Carter's notorious band of guerrillas," the same outfit that carried our last subject, David Martin, on its rolls. Fraly returned to Bledsoe County, where he had once lived, and set to robbing his old neighbors of their horses and guns. In one of these nighttime raids he "brutally murdered" a man trying to escape out his own back door. General George Thomas approved the sentence of hanging, as did Holt. Along the margin of the papers appears, "Sentence approved. A. Lincoln April 14, 1864."[24]

James F. Johnson was a surgeon in the Confederate army. He was arrested at Clarksville, Tennessee, where he was paroled after giving his word that he would not go south again. However, Johnson traveled to Richmond, Virginia, to collect his back pay, and thence to Georgia, where he looked into some real estate. Upon returning north the doctor failed to report to the Provost Marshal. Johnson claimed to be ignorant of such a requirement, but his being in the delirium tremens during his return may account for his inattention.

The court sentenced the doctor to hang, but urged clemency based upon his mental condition when arrested. Rosecrans agreed and recommended a $1,000.00 fine and prison to the end of the war. Several "respectable Union men" petitioned for Dr. Johnson's release, and Holt recommended that the sentence be reduced to taking the oath and posting a $1,000.00 bond. Lincoln wrote, "Recom. of J.A.G. approved. Feb. 15, 1864," and added the well-known signature. (One cannot avoid wondering how useful the doctor had been to his Confederate patients when he was so saturated with alcohol.)[25]

While many Confederate soldiers were tried by military commission, the vast majority of such commissions dealt with civilians. The state of Tennessee contributed thirteen cases of civilians for Lincoln's consideration.

The rather unsavory Carney brothers of Montgomery County were both tried for murder for shooting their wealthy secessionist uncle. On the day of the killing the issue was fishing rights in the local stream. The victim, Lawson J. Murphy, lived about forty-five minutes after being shot and named Richard Carney as his assailant. As a result, Wright Carney was found not guilty but Richard was convicted and sentenced to be hanged. Citizens flooded the President's desk with petitions asserting Richard's fine qualities. Holt thought none of their arguments relevant and saw no grounds for clemency. Neither did the President. "Sentence approved. A. Lincoln Feb. 9, 1864."[26]

Timothy Sisk was tried at Clarksville, Tennessee, for taking two horses at gun point. He was sentenced to fifteen years in prison. Holt concurred, and Lincoln approved the sentence on April 14, 1864, in his familiar handwriting.[27]

On Christmas Day 1863, Pres Pollock retained a "Mr. Albright" as a guide. When they were deep in the woods of Dixon County, Tennessee, Pollock shot Albright in cold blood. When brought to trial before the commission, his own witnesses implicated him in two other brutal murders—as well as confirming his role in the killing for which he was charged. Holt noted Pollock's much-violated Oath of Allegiance (still in the file), his local reputation as "a terror," and his membership in the notorious "Perkins gang," and endorsed hanging. So did the President, who wrote "Sentence approved. A. Lincoln August 16, 1864."[28]

Andrew Bartee bought a mule from "a Yankee soldier" for $20.00, and a few days later sold it for $75.00, saying that he had owned the mule for two years. He was convicted of obtaining money by false pretenses and sentenced to three years in the penitentiary. Holt, in his review of the matter, cited four precedents in case law and two authorities, all of which would have led to a reversal of Bartee's conviction. Holt's conclusion, however, shines the brightest light on the law in wartime Tennessee:

The case under consideration seems to be covered by the decisions and opinions recited, but the reasons for such subtle distinctions as to what constitutes the offense in question, are not perceived. They are mere technicalities, by the interposition of which, the ends of justice are frequently frustrated and criminals permitted to escape merited punishment. In a country where. . .the ordinary civil courts are not open and the condition of things are unsettled and individuals are left dependent upon military tribunals for protection. . .there are especial reasons why such technicalities should be disregarded.

The recipient of this opinion, another experienced lawyer, agreed: "Sentence approved. A. Lincoln Aug. 16, 1864."[29]

In Robertson County, Tennessee, John Holmes and Jesse Pilant had been feuding. In July 1862, as Pilant was plowing his field, Holmes shot him in the left arm, inflicting a severe wound. Healing was slow and difficult and the pain was excruciating. A few weeks later, Pilant died of "fever." The charge of murder was not sustained, as no medical witness would say that the gunshot was the cause of death. For the shooting, Pilant was sentenced to four years of hard labor in the penitentiary. Holt offered no opinion, but Lincoln had one: "Sentence approved. April 27, 1864."[30]

Alexander Black, a "free colored man" of Stewart County, Tennessee, described himself as "old and feeble." However, he did have sufficient energy to beat his wife. He also had the stamina to shoot his friend "Mike," when the latter told Black to stop beating his spouse. Among those distressed by Mike's death was Mrs. Susan Pugh, his owner. The sentence was ten years at hard labor. Holt said, "A sentence of death would have been fully justified." Lincoln simply wrote, "Sentence approved. Feb. 9, 1864," and signed.[31]

Smuggling articles South, even love letters, could bring the death penalty. Imagine what the military commission thought of Memphis citizen Mathew A. Miller, who was caught smuggling swords to the Confederacy early in the war. His appointment with the firing squad was delayed by his many influential friends who bombarded the authorities with pleas for clemency and testimonials as to his fine character. In November 1861, Holt recommended commutation to a prison sentence. Seven months later (the delay is not explained), Nicolay wrote: "Sentence commuted to confinement in one of the military prisons during the war. May 20, 1863," and Lincoln signed. On May 28, Holt wrote that, upon review, the record of the Commission was "fatally defective," since it did not show that the members of the commission had been sworn. Presumably, Miller went free.[32]

It was only luck that saved the victim's life. In Memphis, John Wright robbed a man at gun point and then shot him. Wright's aim was poor and the bullet passed through the man's hat, barely missing his head. Ulysses S. Grant approved the sentence of death by hanging. Holt noted that the commission had not been sworn properly. Nicolay wrote, "Report approved. July 18, 1863," and Lincoln added his name. Wright was free, even if undeserving.[33]

He came as a thief in the night. Alfred Etherly, of Cheatham County, Tennessee, had taken the oath of allegiance. He violated that oath by guiding a band of Rebel guerrillas to a Union man's house, where they stole a horse, $350.00 (close to $14,000.00 in today's money), and kidnapped two men. The commission sentenced Etherly to ten years of hard labor in prison. General George Thomas recommended reduction of the sentence to imprisonment until the war was over. Holt thought that the evidence was overwhelming and saw "no extenuating circumstances" which might call for the reduced sentence. Lincoln was more charitable than Holt, and he signed his name to this note by Nicolay: "Recommendation of Gen. Thomas approved. Feb. 10, 1864."[34]

The terror along the border sometimes matched that of other vicious civil wars, such as in the Balkans. Union man John Ryan and his family were asleep in their isolated cabin in Coffee County, Tennessee, when a band of bushwhackers broke in, took him, his wife and their child, and marched them three miles into the woods. The woman and child were sent home alone, while Ryan was forced to walk another nine miles. Suddenly, the group halted and Ephraim Summers, its leader, ordered the other men to shoot Ryan. They did as instructed and rode away, leaving Ryan for dead. Much to Summers' dismay, however, Ryan survived the brutal attack and gave the testimony which sent Summers to prison for five years. At the Executive Mansion, the five-year sentence was confirmed by, "Sentence approved. A. Lincoln April 27, 1864."[35]

Are horses more valuable than people? Ephraim Summers received five years for attempted murder. James Dodson, a horse thief from Robertson County, Tennessee, got ten years at hard labor. Dodson had gone to the home of Lemuel Ayres and offered $600.00 in Confederate money for a fine horse. Ayres, however, said that he did not take Confederate money. Two nights later the horse disappeared. Within a week Dodson was stopped at midnight riding the stolen animal. He received ten years at hard labor, but made application for clemency. Lincoln answered, "Application denied. Feb'y 9, 1864."[36]

Twenty-eight-year-old John Davis was a single man with no slaves and a 30-acre farm. After taking the oath, near Memphis, he joined "Colonel Clark's" command of guerrillas, and when arrested was carrying a letter of commendation from Clark. As might be expected, Davis was sentenced to be shot. General Schofield, once again recommended commutation to prison for the duration of the war. This note—"Gen. Schofield's recom. approved. A. Lincoln Feb. 9, 1864"—ended the case and saved Davis' life.[37]

When Judge Jackson's mother named him, she may have foreseen a career in the law. She was right, but this Judge was in the defendant's seat, not on the bench. The reason for his predicament was his use of a shotgun on James May, which created wounds in the chest, shoulders, hands, and abdomen. May and Jackson had quarreled for years and many in the community had taken sides. Although Jackson received only two years in prison, he felt wronged by serving any time at all and inspired a flurry of petitions from his wife, from six of his ten children, and from many local "prominent citizens." The Chief Executive was not impressed. "Application denied and sentence affirmed. A. Lincoln August 9, 1864."[38]

Franklin S. Williams was convicted of "being a guerrilla" in Stewart County, Tennessee, and sentenced to be shot. However, the commission suggested a commutation to imprisonment until the end of the war. Major General George H. Thomas endorsed this recommendation and sent the papers east "to await the pleasure of the President." Holt examined the evidence and concluded that Williams had been forced to join the group of bushwhackers known as "Dunbar's Horse," that he had escaped from their company, and that he had gone voluntarily to the Union authorities. Holt's conclusion? Williams was innocent. There was no disagreement on this case: "Sentence disapproved. A. Lincoln July 9, 1864." Six months after his trial and sentence of death, Williams walked out of his cell a free man.[39]

"Doc" James was sentenced to hang. In Dickson County, Tennessee, along the west bank of the Cumberland River about ten in the morning, a party of Union cavalry from the 8th Kentucky was searching for Confederate guerrillas. The bandits were said to be assembled at the "Irish Shanty," a grog shop run by an old French woman near the Western Railroad. The Union men were under the command of Captain John Dever, who sent forward a "Lieutenant Curry" (not in the Army Register) and several soldiers. As the advance party approached the clearing, "many horses" were seen to be hitched outside the little building. Just then, a customer at the grog shop (they were called "groceries" in the 1860s) spotted the cavalrymen and began to fire. Soon the little opening in the woods was filled with gun smoke, shouting men, and calls for surrender.

The principal man arrested, said to be the captain of the guerrilla group, was Dr. Aaron J. James, a "well-respected" local medical practitioner nicknamed "Doc." He was convicted of being the captain of a guerrilla band, shooting at Union soldiers, and violation of the oath of allegiance. He was sentenced to end his life on the gallows, an outcome endorsed by Major General Rosecrans.

Holt however, took a different view. In a long and careful review of the testimony, which was full of contradictions, he noted that only three shots had been fired, and that the smoke around the shanty was mostly likely from the "old Frenchwoman" cooking some eggs for the doctor. Holt went further, finding that there was "not a particle of evidence" that the doctor was a guerrilla, much less a captain of guerrillas. In fact, continued Holt, the evidence suggested James was at the shanty with two friends having a drink to celebrate the sale of a wagon. The fact that the doctor emerged from the cabin and fell down three times was not an act of evasion, reasoned the Judge Advocate, but merely the result of the doctor's well-known habit of heavy early morning drinking. In brief, there was no case. Lincoln agreed, and the record closes with: "Sentence disapproved. A. Lincoln Dec. 12, 1863."[40]

Cases From Other States

One Virginian was in the ranks of soldiers tried by military commission. He was John Manaydier, arrested near Sir John's Run, Virginia. His revolver and gun belt were concealed under his clothes. Testimony showed that he had spent two weeks at his in-laws home (behind Union lines) visiting his wife and children and resting his injured feet. The commission ordered him hanged for spying but, based on the testimony about his family, recommended mitigation to "punishment only less severe than death." After a lengthy legal analysis, Holt arrived at the same conclusion, and the President added, "Let the punishment of death in this case be commuted to imprisonment during the present war. A. Lincoln January 8, 1864."[41]

The much-reviled General Benjamin Butler must have surprised his Rebel detractors with his actions in the case of Charles H. Harris, a private in Company G, Crescent City Regiment (Confederate) from Louisiana. Harris was arrested in the vicinity of "General Davis' Plantation," near New Orleans, and tried as a spy. "I have known the prisoner since he was quite young," one witness said. "If I had any business of importance, I would not trust it with him. I do not think his mind is quite right." Harris made a long, rambling, and somewhat incoherent statement in which he described his stay in Confederate hospitals, his many attempts to desert from Confederate service, and his picaresque journey from Corinth, Mississippi to the outskirts of New Orleans.

The commission convicted him of being a spy and sentenced him to the gallows, but then petitioned for clemency. The case went to Major General Benjamin Butler, who wrote that he "is of the opinion that the prisoner has not either that force of character or depth of guilt which will require a capital execution and therefore orders that the sentence be commuted to imprisonment at hard labor at Ship Island during the war." Holt agreed; the case was closed with these words: "Sentence commuted to confinement at hard labor on the Island or some other military prison for during the war. May 11, 1863. A. Lincoln."[42]

The sound of a quail filtered through the woods near Gurley's Tank, Alabama. Answering the call was not another quail, but Robert L. Welsh, a soldier of the 3rd Arkansas Infantry (Confederate) operating as a member of Hughes' band of bushwhackers and guerrillas. Welsh congratulated the two men who had mastered the Confederate guerrillas' secret signal (the sound of a quail). This was a mistake on Welsh's part, since the men who were able to imitate the bird's call were Union agents. At his trial by military commission Welsh admitted that he had helped place a torpedo (mine) under the tracks of the Memphis and Charleston Railroad. Welsh was sentenced to be shot, an act strongly endorsed by Holt, who commented that blowing up a railroad is "so monstrous and denotes such a heartless disregard for human life. . .passengers and troops who may be slaughtered wholesale by the act of an assassin. . .that the death of the offender can scarcely atone for the magnitude of his guilt." In this case, Lincoln overrode all of his advisors and ordered: "Sentence commuted to imprisonment to ten years in the penitentiary. A. Lincoln July 8, 1864."[43]

Confederate soldier George P. Sims was charged with spying in Kentucky in May 1863, and sentenced to be hanged. On May 28, Lincoln received some of the papers in the case and wrote, "If the Judge Advocate General has a record of this case, he will please send it to me with those papers." Two months later, Holt noted that the petition regarding Sims asked merely that the execution be suspended for thirty days, not for pardon, and that almost sixty days had elapsed. Here, the record is unclear as to whether Sims was indeed executed.[44]

Neophytes in Civil War history are surprised to learn that there was a slave state north of Washington, D.C. That, of course, was Maryland, which came close to seceding. It also provided soldiers for the Southern army, some of whom came to Lincoln's attention.

Three Marylanders were captured at the Rappahannock River, Virginia, in April 1863. Although in Confederate uniform, they were Marylanders and thus tried for treason. The three men, James Rider, James Oliver, and Samuel Betts, were all sentenced to hang. The decision was endorsed by General Joseph Hooker, a man usually known for citing the President's amnesty proclamation as a means of avoiding death sentences. Holt reviewed the cases and concluded, "The sentences cannot be enforced. The record shows clearly that the parties were prisoners of war and should be treated as such and exchanged under the cartel."

Lincoln echoed these words in all three cases in a note written by an unknown scribe, dated May 21, 1863. The President signed his name.[45]

Andrew Laypole (alias Isadore Leopold, alias Andrew Layopole) was quite a different Marylander. He was an exchanged prisoner who had served in the Confederate army. Laypole returned to his old neighborhood in the Shepherdstown–Harpers Ferry area, where he committed several murders while moving with a gang commanded by one Burke, "a notorious brigand." Laypole's first victim was a ferryman named Entler, whom Laypole shot in the victim's own doorway. The second to fall was a Mr. Crokers, who was helping an old man ferry his goods across the Potomac River. Crokers survived the first fusillade, but was shot through the head while attempting to swim to safety. Laypole later went to the door of a man named Hudson, living in Shepherdstown, and knocked. When Hudson opened the door, he was shot at close range, but only wounded. Laypole was sentenced to hang. Holt noted, "The prisoner. . . formerly lived among the people whom he robbed and murdered, and justice, and the security of society, demand that such atrocities should be summarily and adequately punished." Immediately follows, "Sentence approved. A. Lincoln April 24, 1864."[46]

The pattern of Presidential decisions in these cases of Rebel recruiters, spies, bushwhackers, and guerrillas, is very different from his decisions in the cases of desertion and mutiny. The men tried in this chapter will be considered in two different groups, since Lincoln's degree of leniency is so different for the two. The first is that of men commissioned to come North to recruit for the Confederate army (and is reflected in Table Eight at the top of the next page). Using the usual criteria for inclusion in this study (reviewed by Lincoln and not in Basler's index) we find four cases of Confederate recruiters. All four were sentenced to death. In every single instance Lincoln approved the death sentence. No other category of crime received one hundred percent (100%) endorsement of capital punishment by the President of the United States. While Lincoln made no comment as to his reasons, one might speculate that he was deeply affronted that men would come into states, officially loyal to the Federal government, to recruit men to subvert that government.

Opinion Maker	Lincoln Agrees	Lincoln Disagrees	% Agreement
Trial Verdict	4	0	100

The second category is "all other," which includes spies, non-recruiter Confederate soldiers found in Union territory, and civilian criminals in locations where civil law had collapsed. These figures are reflected on Table Nine in this chapter, reproduced below. Here also we find a very different pattern from his decisions regarding desertions and mutiny. With these spies and bushwhackers Lincoln endorsed forty percent (40%) of the sentences—a rather high figure for Lincoln, but much less strict than his decisions regarding recruiters. He agreed with his departmental commanders sixty-eight percent (68%) of the time, which is not as high as usual; even more important, he disagreed with his own judge advocate general in thirty-five percent (35%) of the cases. In these reviews Holt usually urged the harshest possible penalty, while Lincoln took the more liberal stance. Holt had deep roots in Kentucky and a keen feel for the divided loyalties in that part of the country. Perhaps he felt that the strongest possible measures were needed to prevent a complete breakdown of mid-South society.

Opinion Maker	Lincoln Agrees	Lincoln Disagrees	% Agreement
Trial Verdict	14	21	40
Authorizing Officer	NA	NA	NA
Departmental Commander	13	6	68
Judge Advocate General	15	8	65
Interested Politicians	0	1	0
Friends, Family & Comrades	1	1	50

11

Missouri Spies and Bushwhackers

Missouri in the 1860s was the very heart of ill-will, hatred, resentment, and dissension. The state seethed with mutual accusations of treason and treachery. It had rival state governments and more than a dozen military organizations operating under as many authorities. Nor were its civilian disturbances limited to the border with Confederate Arkansas. In every corner of Missouri and, indeed, in its center, there was armed resistance to Federal authority. The following cases of Missouri civilians, men who came to Lincoln's attention, represent only a small fraction of that state's suffering during the War of the Rebellion.

New Madrid County, in the southeast corner of the state, produced a champion horse thief in John Webb. On at least three occasions he stole a pair of horses from civilian supporters of the Union cause. Webb's trials occupy three different folders in the National Archives. He received the unusual sentence of hard labor at a military prison to the end of the war, with an additional year in a state prison, to be served whenever the war ended. Holt summarized the case, but made no recommendation. The words "Sentence approved. A. Lincoln July 8, 1864," closed the proceedings.[1]

Dunklin County, Missouri, protrudes into the northeast corner of Arkansas. There, the illiterate but woods-wise James Smith guided Bolin's band of bushwhackers through the swamps, helping them steal horses and guns. Holt reviewed the testimony, noting that Smith's "character was shown to be notoriously bad." The President spared the defendant from the firing squad with, "Sentence commuted to confinement at hard labor in the Penitentiary for five years. A. Lincoln April 14, 1864."[2]

Another Dunklin man, George Caldwell, was convicted of being a guerrilla in Kitchen's band of horse thieves. Holt noted Kitchen's role in the Round Pond Massacre, a notorious bit of Missouri brutality where Confederate bushwhackers killed twelve unarmed Union soldiers returning to their units from a hospital. Caldwell was sentenced to be shot for his association with Kitchen. Schofield recommended commutation to hard labor to the end of the war. Lincoln wrote, "Recom. of Gen. Schofield approved & ordered. April 14, 1864. A. Lincoln" Caldwell lived another day.[3]

Cass County is on the Kansas border and contributed two men to this study: John W. Wilson and James Williams. In August 1863, both were convicted of violating the oath of allegiance and of plundering as guerrillas. Both were sentenced to die. Holt thought that "no lesser penalty than hanging would be adequate." On February 15, 1864, Lincoln wrote on both trial records "Sentence commuted to confinement in the Penitentiary at hard labor for five years," and added his signature.[4]

The case of Henry Ogle shows clearly that the Union system of justice was not a mere kangaroo court. Ogle was convicted of murdering two men in Andrew County, of stealing a large sum of money from a woman he had just made a widow, and of setting fire to a home. He was sentenced to ten years at hard labor. Holt's original review endorsed the sentence. However, three weeks later, on the basis of additional information from the provost marshal at St. Joseph, Missouri—information which indicated massive perjury helped convict Ogle—Holt wrote, "The recommendations made in the former report are withdrawn and it is advised that the prisoner be pardoned by the President." This must have been a welcome change for Lincoln, as he wrote the single word "Pardon," signed his name, and added the date, "July 9, 1864."[5] That day in Georgia, the Confederate Army of Tennessee moved in reverse again, its back to the gates of Atlanta.

Another Andrew County man, Joseph Lanier, was convicted of setting fire to a mill, causing substantial damage (over a million dollars in 1999 money). In addition, he shouted, "Hurrah for Jeff Davis." He was convicted and sentenced to be shot. Lanier's action seemed to have taxed the patience of the President, as he wrote, "Sentence approved. Feb. 10, 1864."[6]

The far north of Missouri was not immune to secessionism. In Sullivan County, almost on the Iowa border, Nathan Wilson and John Eller each faced the unusual charge of "being a bad and dangerous man." In addition, Eller had killed a man and stolen his horse, and Wilson had hanged one of his neighbors. They were both sentenced to be shot, but the Commission failed to add the necessary words "two-thirds of the members concurring." For this reason, Holt advised the President that the sentences could not be carried out. Under Hays' notation were penned the words "Report approved. July 18, 1863," Lincoln wrote his name, and two dangerous felons went free.[7]

The current fashion of romanticizing the Civil War might be dampened by stories such as this little drama, played out in Barry County, Missouri, on the Arkansas border. Two guerrillas decoyed a Union lieutenant into the woods, where they captured, disarmed, and stripped him. He was forced to kneel naked in front of his captors, who then shot him to death at close range. The man who pulled the trigger escaped, but his accomplice, Smith Crim, was caught and tried. He admitted having been there, with a loaded gun, but denied any responsibility. The Commission thought differently, found him guilty and sentenced him to be shot. Holt agreed with the death penalty, Nicolay wrote, "Sentence in this case approved. May 11, 1863," "A. Lincoln" closed the case, and, it would seem, Crim's life.[8]

In Schuyler County, right on the Iowa border, Daniel Lyle and thirty others robbed store owner Christian Figgy at gunpoint, taking calico, silk, and shoes. Lyle and his friends returned a few weeks later, robbed Figgy again, and fired shots at Figgy's wife and children. Witnesses testified that when Lyle was down on his luck, poor and sick, Figgy had befriended him and brought him food. Perhaps it was the crime itself, or perhaps it was the extraordinary lack of gratitude, but the military commission, General Schofield, and Judge Advocate General Holt all recommended death by hanging. Once again, Lincoln extended clemency to a man who seemed to deserve very little. "Sentence commuted to imprisonment at hard labor in the Penitentiary for five years. A. Lincoln. Feb. 10, 1864."[9]

Twenty-one-year-old Francis Norvell of Saline County thought he was joining the Confederate Army. When he learned that his new companions were actually bushwhackers and common thieves, he left them and turned himself in to the United States authorities. He was tried for being a guerrilla and sentenced to be shot. General Egbert Brown, however, recognized the unfairness of the sentence and took note of Norvell's "good character and extreme youth." Norvell, he recommended, should be released upon the condition that he take the Oath and post bond. Holt posed no objection, and the other man at the table wrote, "Recom. of Gen. Brown approved & ordered. A. Lincoln April 27, 1864."[10]

At Waverly, today a village of eight hundred souls, Rees McNiel hid a stolen Union Army wagon. For this, and for helping local guerrillas, he was sentenced to be shot. Holt thought the death penalty too severe for these crimes. Lincoln agreed. He wrote his signature under this note by Nicolay: "Sentence commuted to imprisonment in one of the military prisons for one year. May 11, 1863."[11]

Near the banks of the muddy Missouri River in Platte County, James Meek shot and killed a Union soldier. Meek was sentenced to hang, but the "circumstances of the shooting" caused Schofield to recommend mitigation to prison to the end of the war. Once again, John Nicolay picked up his pen: "Recommendation of General Schofield approved and ordered. Feb. 10, 1864." Once again, his employer signed. It was almost certain that Meek did not inherit the earth, but at least he had an opportunity to redeem himself.[12]

In Nodaway County, William McDaniels and several secessionist friends opened fire on a group of men going to a Union meeting, wounding one man and killing a horse. McDaniels claimed self-defense, but the commission did not believe him. Its ruling: death by firing squad, a fate approved by Schofield and Holt. Only Lincoln disagreed. He directed Nicolay to write "Sentence commuted to imprisonment at hard labor in Penitentiary for five years. Feb'y. 10, 1864." The familiar signature stands distinct on the paper.[13]

However, Lincoln was less lenient with guerilla Thomas Caldwell of Dade County, who shot and killed two Union soldiers (a "Captain Beard," and a private named Jacob Paris). Caldwell defended himself by saying that Federal forces were plundering and looting just as bad as the guerrillas. The efficacy of this defense is shown in the sentence: death by firing squad. This concept was endorsed by Generals Brown and Curtis, and by Holt. Lincoln's note was brief. "Sentence approved. July 18, 1863."[14]

Joseph Englehart did not limit his thievery to only horses and mules. In Pettis County, he moved up in the world of crime by stealing and hiding an entire mail coach. The authorities were not amused. Following the May 1862 trial, his sentence was to be "shot to death with musketry." Holt read the record and noticed that the proceedings were invalid since the military commission had not been sworn in the presence of the prisoner—a technical "fatal defect" for the legal validity of the proceedings. Lincoln signed Nicolay's note, which said, "Sentence disapproved for informality." Whether Englehart continued his robbing ways is unknown.[15]

Boone County, in central Missouri, had its share of neighborly conflict. John Skaggs, who had been in the Confederate army, was captured and paroled with the provision that he no longer fight for the Confederacy. However, he soon enlisted in "Porter's Command." He said that his secessionist neighbors forced him into this act; the commission did not believe him and sentenced him to be shot. General Schofield had a different opinion. He recommended mitigation and the President wrote, "Recom. of Gen. Schofield approved & ordered. A. Lincoln. April 14, 1864." Exactly a year of life remained for the President.[16]

William McGinnis told his military commission, "I hold the militia as my enemies." He was a man of his word: at Wright City, he had shot and killed a member of the Enrolled Missouri Militia. McGinnis' excuse was the rather lame, "I was forced to do it." Since he would not reveal the names any of those alleged to have forced him to kill, the commission was not impressed with his claim of Union loyalty and sentenced him to ten years in prison. Lincoln agreed: "Sentence approved. April 21, 1864." After Lincoln's death, McGinnis wrote to President Andrew Johnson, who pardoned him.[17]

John Nicols was described by one witness as "the most notorious scoundrel, thief, and robber that ever infested our county. He is a terror." On at least six occasions, Nicols and his gang broke into Union families' homes at night, terrorized the inmates, and stole money, clothes and horses. Nicols boasted that he had killed many Union men, but at the trial, denied having said such, much less having done it. He was convicted of "being a guerrilla" and was sentenced to death. His legal defense was that there was no such crime as "being a guerrilla," certainly none in the statutes, and therefore, he could not be held guilty of such a charge. Holt's long legal analysis is a rebuttal to Nicols' argument. Lincoln simply wrote: "Sentence approved. Sep. 10, 1863." Nicols was a dead man.[18]

John F. Cook was convicted of violating the oath of allegiance. He said that he was a soldier in "Captain Casey's Company, of Green's Regiment, under [Confederate Brigadier General John S.] Marmaduke." The commission described Casey's unit as "a band of guerrillas, insurgents, and outlaws. . .not soldiers." General Schofield reviewed the sentence of being shot to death and recommended prison for the duration of the war. In what appears to be a hurried scrawl, we see, "Recommendation of Gen. Schofield approved. A. Lincoln Nov. 7, 1863."[19]

The steamer *White Cloud* was puffing her way up the Missouri River past Saline County when Moses Fornshall opened fire. He claimed before the military commission which held his fate that he was a regularly enlisted Confederate soldier, ordered by his officers to shoot. Some witnesses said that he merely belonged to a group of guerrillas and bushwhackers under the leadership of a man named "Jackson," while other witnesses supported Fornshall's claim of legitimate soldiering. Late in 1863, Fornshall was captured hiding in the rafters of a friend's home; he was eventually sentenced to death. The condemned wrote to Lincoln claiming that he was about to surrender himself when he was discovered.

The President also received a letter from the defendant's wife, Sophia, who began, "to Mr. Abraham Linkon Presedent of the Unired States: Deare Sir do not get angry at mee fore trynge to pledd for husban." According to Sophia, the government witnesses against her husband were all his personal enemies, men that he had known before the war, and that they used the trial for perjured vengeance. She feared for her young child if Moses was shot, and added, "I havent hurd of your haven eny man kild yet. Oh pity me and Babe." Her prayers were answered: "Sentence commuted to confinement during the war. A. Lincoln Feb. 10, 1864." Mrs. Fornshall's grammar may have left something to be desired—but it spared her husband's life.[20]

The Hannibal and St. Joseph Railroad ran straight across the top of Missouri, west from Tom Sawyer's legendary fence, to the terminus on the east bank of the Missouri. At Palmyra, William J. Livingston created havoc by derailing the train and fatally shooting one of the passengers. Livingston, in turn, was sentenced to be shot. Holt noted that the derailer had been captured as a prisoner of war, and was thus eligible to be exchanged. Lincoln agreed with his legal adviser and directed Nicolay to write: "Sentence disapproved, May 20, 1863."[21]

Missouri bushwhacker James Anderson and his friends opened fire on a group of Union soldiers, wounding five of them. Anderson was sentenced to be shot, which produced a flurry of letters attesting to his excellent character and pleading for clemency. General Brown, apparently swayed by such an outpouring of support, recommended commuting the death sentence to confinement until the end of the war. "Recommendation of Gen. Brown approved. A. Lincoln Feb. 9, 1864."[22]

Martin Adams was a member of Tom Reeve's gang of Missouri outlaws, men who made their living robbing recently-discharged Union soldiers. (After all, they had money!) Adams' sentence of five years hard labor was approved by "A. Lincoln," appearing under Nicolay's note: "Sentence approved in this case. Feb'y. 9, 1864."[23]

Guerrilla James Johnson "ravished" his women victims, according to one witness; others said he only terrorized them. For this, for breaking his oath of allegiance, and for multiple robberies at gun point, Johnson was sentenced to ten years at hard labor. The commission was asked to reconsider its verdict. It did. Johnson, came the new decision, should be shot. Lincoln agreed and Nicolay wrote, "Sentence approved."[24]

One walked, one rode. Henry Sipes and William Roberts were tried together. Both were convicted of joining a band of outlaws and guerrillas, and of stealing a horse, saddle, and bridle. When arrested, Roberts was riding the stolen horse. In their November 1863 trial before a military commission, both men were sentenced to be shot. On the trial record is this note: "Sentences in these cases each commuted to imprisonment in Penitentiary at hard labor for five years. A. Lincoln Feb. 15, 1864."[25]

Today, the word "Jayhawker" is associated with University of Kansas athletic teams. During the mid-Nineteenth century, it was applied to the abolitionist thugs and villains who terrorized secessionist and pro-slavery inhabitants at the Kansas-Missouri border. James A. Stoker, of Springfield, was tried for stealing two horses and terrorizing families in southwest Missouri, "in company with other jayhawkers and bush-whackers." His conviction led to a death sentence by hanging.

Holt's lengthy review noted Stoker's claim to being a Confederate soldier: "There is not the slightest indication that he was performing any military service. The proof is full that he was one of a band of 'jayhawk-ers,' thieves and robbers who went from house to house, stealing, seiz-ing everything on which they could lay their hand, down to the very quilts that covered the women and children. . .if he is not shot [he was actually sentenced to be hanged], as he well deserves to be, he should certainly be subjected to some prolonged and infamous punishment." (Anyone familiar with the labor that goes into a quilt would agree with this punishment.) Lincoln did not take this opportunity to redress the wounds inflicted upon "Bleeding Kansas" by the violence of the pro-slavery and anti-slavery factions. Instead, he wrote his well-known "A. Lincoln," under Nicolay's "Sentence commuted to imprisonment at hard labor during the war." (Here, the term "jayhawker" seems to be used in a very general sense, rather than that of an anti-secessionist guerrilla.)[26]

J. P. Holland is described in the records of the military commission that tried him as a guerrilla with Thornton's band of horse thieves, and as "having enlisted in the army of the so-called Confederate States of America." This characterization makes it difficult to determine whether the commission considered him a soldier or an outlaw. The question seems to be settled by his conviction for being a horse thief and guer-rilla. His sentence of death on the gallows inspired several letters and petitions to be sent to the Executive Mansion—all of them suggesting Holland was a splendid fellow, worthy of the President's finest senti-ments.[27]

Tried with Holland were John Utz and Henry Highsmith. They, too, were charged with being members of Thornton's band. In addition,

Highsmith stole two horses and Utz was accused of murder. Both were sentenced to hang and both were reprieved by the same words that spared Holland from the hangman's noose. Whether it was the petitions, the evidence, the political situation, or Lincoln's compassion that spared their lives—or a combination these things—is unclear. The record shows only this: "Sentence in these three cases commuted to imprisonment in the Penitentiary at hard labor during the war. A. Lincoln. Jan. 11, 1865."

"I am a secessionist, heart and soul." That impassioned cry from William Vittenhof of St. Louis, seems a fitting way to conclude this recitation of Missouri murderers, malefactors, and marauders. Vittenhof's publicly expressed opinion, described as a violation of the oath of allegiance, seems to be the sole basis for his sentence of death by a hemp necklace. Holt, as we have seen, could send defendants to their deaths when necessary, but he never allowed an illegal sentence to stand. He wrote: "Nothing is proved against the prisoner except the utterance of very disloyal sentiments. No acts are shown which warrant this sentence of death." The sixteenth President of the United States was quick to agree: "Sentence disapproved or remitted. A. Lincoln July 18, 1863."[28]

Opinion Maker	Lincoln Agrees	Lincoln Disagrees	% Agreement
Trial Verdict	8	23	26
Authorizing Officer	2	0	100
Departmental Commander	6	2	75
Judge Advocate General	10	6	63
Interested Politicians	NA	NA	NA
Friends, Family & Comrades	5	0	100

As evidenced in Table Ten above, Lincoln reduced the severity of seventy-four percent (74%) of the Missouri military commission cases presented to him for final judgment. Many of the men who benefited by his oversight were spared the death penalty. In the few cases where the authorizing general's opinion appears, Lincoln was in agreement. He also agreed with his departmental commanders seventy-five percent (75%) of the time. Lincoln and Holt agreed only sixty-three percent (63%) of the time—with Holt urging severe penalties for serious crimes, and Lincoln often being rather lenient on an unusual assortment of border ruffians.

This group of cases shows a Lincoln unusually influenced by pleading letters from friends and family of the accused. This was true even when their assertions directly contradicted the evidence presented in the case, and even when their claims of the condemned man's virtues seemed self-serving (and not entirely true). Missouri was a harsh and bitter land during the Civil War. Perhaps Lincoln thought his mitigations might create a feeling of gratitude in the lucky recipients or create a climate of reconciliation for the future. Perhaps he hoped his actions would foster his vision of a nation of mutuality and shared interests, that it might bind up the wounds of the nation's soul.

If he was thinking along those lines, and had he lived, he would have been disappointed. The South did not succeed in becoming an independent nation, but some of the goals of the Confederacy—which it could not win on the battlefield—were accomplished in the post-war century through Jim Crow laws, the Ku Klux Klan, poll taxes, the rise of the Southern Democrats, and the policies of segregationist presidents, such as Woodrow Wilson.

But that is a different book.

12

A Potpourri of Military Commissions

Military commissions were held for dozens of reasons and in every state. The defendants ranged from supercilious British blockade runners to former slaves accused of rape, from quinine smugglers to arsonists. All had in common their civilian status and their trial under military law. The cases presented in this chapter are from the outer limits of the country: the far west, the deep south, the Atlantic coast—and even include a case involving a British citizen, with whom we shall begin this chapter.

Richard M. Hall was a loyal subject of Her Royal (soon to be Imperial) Majesty, Queen Victoria, the sovereign of Great Britain and a wide variety of other possessions. He was charged with violation of the laws of war because he ran the Union blockade, traveled throughout the South, and traded with the enemy. His trial record is full of exhibits documenting his travels: telegrams from the New York, Troy, and Saratoga Telegraph Company, and a card entitling Hall to unlimited free dispatches on the wires of the Southern Telegraph Company. A permit from the Confederate War Department grants Hall ("Age 45, height 3 ½ feet [that's what it says!], complexion Caucasian") authority to travel to Charlottesville on the Central Railroad, providing he reveal no Confederate military secrets.

The evidence and testimony was air-tight. Hall was convicted and sentenced to four months locked up in Fort McHenry, plus a fine of $6,000.00. It did not take long for the letters of protest to pour forth. The British Ambassador to the United States, Lord Lyons, asked Lincoln for Hall's release, as did the mayor of Montreal. Two months after the military commission rendered its verdict, a note by Nicolay dated July 9, 1864 reads as follows: "Respectfully referred by the President to the Honorable the Judge Advocate General of the United States." Lincoln signed the note. The unflappable Holt was not impressed, and his legal analysis may be paraphrased thusly: "Hall is clearly guilty, hides behind his British citizenship, and deserves no clemency." The record closes with an unsigned pencil note in an unknown hand: "The President decides to do nothing in this case."[1]

Friday the 13th of February 1863 was not a good day for Granville, a former slave accused of rape. The native of Thibodeaux, Louisiana, was tried in November 1862 for his assault on Louise Leufrene, age twelve-and-a-half. Through an interpreter (she spoke only French), she told the commission:

> I was fetching tomatoes for my brother. That man held a knife to my throat. There were five of us; he made the others leave and separated me from them. He tried to do the thing with me. He raised my dress and endeavored to have connexion with me. I cried out. He exposed his person. He took out his you-know-what. He did not accomplish his purpose because I was too small. He tried to strangle me. I had pains in my secret parts after.

When the case came to Lincoln, he agreed with the sentence by writing the simple word "Approved," signed his name, and added the date, "Jan. 20, 1863." Twenty-four days later on Friday the 13th, Granville swung from a rope.[2]

"Dave, a colored man" is part of a much different story. Dave (who was also called David Lamb) was sentenced to hang. He was convicted at Memphis, Tennessee, of the crime of aiding "John J. Glover, alias Jake, in committing a murder." The victim was George Redman, whose plantation stood on the Arkansas side of the Mississippi River in Crittendon County (Dave lived on the Tennessee side of the river). The defendant's two daughters, ages 14 and 16, were former slaves of Mr. Redman, and he swore publicly that he would never let them go—despite Lincoln's Emancipation Proclamation. Dave and Jake crossed the Father of Waters in a skiff at midnight (no easy feat in itself) and brought one girl down to the riverbank. It was now two in the morning. When they went back for her sister, Redman appeared with a pistol in hand and confronted the rescue party. Jake fired once and fatally wounded Redman. Although Redman's own son testified that the slave owner had fired first, the military commission found both Dave and Jake guilty of murder. William Tecumseh Sherman approved the death penalty for Dave, his crime being that of an accomplice to murder.

In another display of clear thinking and sound legal analysis, Holt noted that Dave had crossed the river "with no purpose except to get his children, unlawfully held from him. . .the rescue of his two young daughters from illegal restraint and servitude. It is not thought that. . .the prisoner should be held responsible for the acts of his companion and it is recommended that he be discharged from custody." Was William T. Sherman not capable of reaching such a just conclusion, or had he not taken the time to seriously examine the facts before affirming the original sentence? Holt's opinion is followed by "Sentence disapproved. A. Lincoln July 8, 1864."

Jake, the man who fired the fatal shot, was also sentenced to hang. Holt noted the purpose of the midnight visit and the firing of the first shot by Redman. He also took notice of the testimony of Redman's daughter, who told the Commission that her father had sworn to shoot any man who came after the two girls. One witness told the Commission that Redman was a "kind and indulgent master to his slaves," but that carried little weight with Holt, who concluded, "It is believed to be a case in which a strong and armed man has rashly thrown away his life in an endeavor to enslave a feeble young woman in defiance of the Proclamation of the President, which had declared her free."

(If one takes an interest in the science of graphology, it might be possible to make much of the President's conclusionary note in Jake's case. "Sentence disapproved," is in a scrawl, quite unlike Lincoln's usual bold autographic writing; the last four letters of "disapproved" are simply a puddle of black ink. The paper is torn, destroying much of the date. There are two dots above the "i" in "Lincoln," and the last two letters of the President's name are smeared. A reflection on the difficulties of emancipation? Suppressed anger over the captive girls? Sadness over an unnecessary death, or simply fatigue and the crushing burdens of office? Or perhaps it means nothing at all.)[3]

The other cases in this assembly of military commissions span most of the continent, from the frontier territories, to the deep south, and on up into New York. An Alabaman secessionist, Bradford Hambrick, hunted loyal citizens with hounds to compel them to join the Rebel army, threatened to shoot the wife of a man who did not want to wear the gray uniform of secession, and hanged a Union man until he was almost dead. For these crimes, Hambrick was sentenced to spend a year in the penitentiary and pay a $2,000.00 fine. From his prison cell, he wrote to the President. Perhaps Hambrick was surprised when his papers received this notation: "Pardoned. A. Lincoln April 14, 1865." Perhaps Hambrick was grateful that one of Lincoln's last acts as President was to grant him a pardon. Perhaps Hambrick became illuminated by the same inner light of compassion and forgiveness that flowed from Lincoln—but that seems unlikely in a man willing to hang his own neighbor.[4]

A flower of Southern manhood, Frank Marigold, was only eighteen years of age when he was arrested in Vicksburg with 300 ounces of quinine destined for the South. Since five or six grains of quinine a day will keep a man safe from malaria, Marigold's cargo—if it had reached its destination—would have kept a full-strength Confederate regiment healthy for a month. The medicine was thus of considerable military significance to the South, since whole populations were often incapacitated by freezing chills, alternating with burning fever, all accompanied by severe fatigue. The military commission confiscated the quinine and sent Marigold to prison for three years. The immediate result: a wave of petitions urging the President to show clemency and insisting that Marigold, a mere youth, was only the dupe of unscrupulous men, a mere pawn in the hands of wealthy and powerful secessionist smugglers.

Marigold's record contains two responses by the President. The first reads, "Judge Advocate General please procure record & report on this case. A. Lincoln Nov. 14, 1864." A month and a day later, he wrote again. "Pardon for unexecuted part of sentence. A. Lincoln."[5]

Currituck County, North Carolina, is bounded on the north by Virginia and on the east by the waters of the Atlantic Ocean. There, a military commission found Simeon Kight guilty of being a member of a gang of guerrillas who took a Union man into the woods, produced a

LL 2953

Pardon.

A. Lincoln

April 14. 1865.

Respectfully referred to the Adjutant General, U. S. Army, for the execution of the orders of the President.

BY ORDER OF THE PRESIDENT:

Jas A Hardie

Inspector General, U. S. A.

WAR DEPARTMENT,
April 14 1865.

See letter to C.O.
Nashville Tenn.
April 14 1865.

Recd. a.g.o. Apr. 17. 1865
Letter to Maj. Gen. Thomas
April 27. 1865 —

Previously unknown to Lincoln scholars, on the last day of his life the President pardoned two offenders.. Bradford Hambrick, an Alabama secessionist who had hanged a Union neighbor, was set free by one word from Lincoln: "Pardon." Patrick Murphy, a mentally defective private from a California regiment, received the longer note (see next page). Lincoln did not stand on ceremony—he wrote wherever there was blank space on the page. Both cases were located by Beverly Lowry. *National Archives*

This man is pardoned, and hereby ordered to be discharged from the service.

April 14. 1865   A. Lincoln

rope, and said that they would now hang him. The proposed victim escaped, in part because of the incompetent marksmanship of the guerrillas who had fired three shots without hitting him. Kight was sentenced to hang and the case came to Holt's desk. His review showed that three witnesses had said the victim was a liar, while three others swore they would have no difficulty believing his testimony. Holt concluded, "As the case stands, it is believed that the death sentence is not justified by the testimony as recorded." As the law required, the final decision was the President's. "Sentence commuted to confinement at hard labor in the penitentiary for five years. A. Lincoln April 21, 1864."[6]

Far from the gray-green breakers of the Carolina coast is Fort Kearney, a post buried deep in the Nebraska Territory. There, on May 5, 1862, martial law had been declared by Brigadier General James Craig. (He had been a Democratic Congressman and was given his commission by Lincoln to keep Craig's Missouri Democrat supporters from bolting to the Confederacy.) The proclamation began: "In consequence of the absence of all proper civil officers, and the almost utter disregard of all civil law, which has led the people along the line of the Overland Mail Route to believe there is no law by which crime can be punished. . . ." Craig went on to cite the dangers to immigrants and traders, and to declare that Colorado and Nebraska were now under the jurisdiction of the United States army.

Civilian William Kirby was foolish enough to test the limits of military justice under Craig's jurisdiction. At the stagecoach station near Fort Kearney, he stole a $50.00 silver watch from a man named McCartney, and a $100.00 gold watch from a Mr. Hook. He completed his little crime wave by stealing a horse from the corral of the Overland Stage Line, all of which earned him five years at hard labor in the penitentiary. Kirby protested that martial law was illegal. Holt said that Kirby was wrong, and the Chief Executive ended the argument: "Sentence approved. A. Lincoln April 26, 1864." Kirby was indeed in error.[7]

Two cases from Kentucky move our venue back to the border state region. William Morris of Fulton County, in the furthest southwest tip of the Bluegrass State, violated his oath of allegiance by joining an armed party of Confederates along the Obion River. Ulysses S. Grant approved Morris' sentence: "To be shot to death with musketry." Holt's analysis showed Morris to be a prisoner of war, not a guerrilla, Nicolay wrote, "Sentence commuted to confinement for one year from this date. May 20, 1863," and his employer added, in a large, bold hand, "A. Lincoln."

One of the men traveling along the Obion River with Morris was Samuel Johns. He, too, was convicted of treason and violation of the oath of allegiance, and sentenced to be shot. Holt's attention was caught by testimony showing that Johns was "fleeing the rumor that border state men were to be handcuffed and used as breastworks." He also noted that Johns was not only unarmed, but sick. The notes by Nicolay and Lincoln are identical with those in the case of Morris.[8]

Unwanted by the Confederacy and hanged by the Union, a sad legacy for Joseph Leddy. He was convicted of being a spy, of smuggling a large quantity of letters into St. Louis from the South, and of trying to ship quinine, morphine, and revolvers to the Confederacy. During his trial, he insisted that he was a captain in the 5th Missouri Infantry (CSA), but then admitted that he had been cashiered (dishonorably discharged) from the Confederate army. Major General Frederick Steele approved the sentence. So did the President: "Sentence approved. A. Lincoln July 9, 1864."[9]

Thomas Brackenridge was equally unlucky. With his guerrilla comrades, he robbed two homes in Lawrence County, Arkansas, of horses, furniture, and blankets. General Steele approved his death by firing squad, and Holt added, "His outrages were at gun point, with threats and curses." Brackenridge's journey had come to the end of the line: "Sentence approved. A. Lincoln Aug. 9, 1864."[10]

In Norfolk, Virginia, Alexander Spence burglarized a building near the waterfront, hid the stolen goods in a false bulkhead of his schooner, and set fire to the building to conceal his crime. The flames spread and destroyed seven adjacent buildings, some of which were occupied. A military commission convicted him of arson and sentenced him to hang. Holt noted that the Virginia statutes prescribed the death penalty for burning an occupied building, and was careful to explain that the decision of the commission was consonant with existing Virginia laws. Nicolay wrote, "Sentence approved. May 11, 1863," and Spence's appeal ended with "A. Lincoln."[11]

John W. Sailor seemed certain to hang. In Page County, Virginia, he had shot and killed ten men—two civilians and eight Union soldiers. But when Sailor's death sentence reached Holt, events took an unexpected turn: "This record is regarded as fatally defective. It does not appear that the General Order convening the Commission was read to the prisoner," noted the Judge Advocate, "or that he had an opportunity to object to any member of the Commission, nor does it appear that the charge against him was in writing. . .or that he had any knowledge of the offense of which he was to be tried." It was also not shown, observed Holt, "that the prisoner was allowed to plead to the charge against him. . .in a proceeding involving life, [and] such irregularities are wholly inexcusable and make the execution of the death sentence legally impossible." Lincoln agreed. Under Hay's note, "Report approved. July 18, 1863," the President signed his name. Thus a mass murderer walked away a free man.[12]

J. G. Smith, a citizen of the District of Columbia, forged a voucher and received $1,032.00. He pled guilty and was sentenced to five years in the penitentiary. A few weeks after his conviction, the following note in Lincoln's hand, with no other explanation, appears in the record, written on Executive Mansion letterhead: "March 25, 1864. Hon. Sec. of War. My dear sir, You see I have written 'pardon' at the bottom of the Judge Advocate General's report in this case. Yours truly, A. Lincoln."[13]

Three young men from Baltimore were tried together, each charged with spying and treason. At the outbreak of the war, they had made their way south and now, after a two-year absence, had returned secretly to see their families. Two of them, Pierre Dugan and John Scott, were clerks in the Medical Department of the Confederate Army. The third, Simon Kemp, when arrested, was carrying many letters from the South, destined for citizens of Maryland. All three were sentenced to be hanged. Eleven months elapsed before their cases came to Holt and Lincoln for review. Holt concluded that they were not really spies, and Lincoln took care of them with a single note: "Sentences commuted to imprisonment during the war. A. Lincoln Feb. 15, 1864." Their war, and Lincoln's as well, would be over in less than fourteen months.[14]

Pennsylvania's 22nd Congressional District was where Henry Moul ran afoul of the law when he helped his brother desert from the army.

After Henry began his six-month sentence at Allegheny County Prison, some question was raised as to his sanity. R. B. Simpson, Surgeon for the Enrollment Board was asked to make an examination; he summarized the results in his February 13, 1864, report:

> I am satisfied he is of a defective mind. When spoken to slowly, he appears to understand and can answer correctly, but a question put rapidly disconcerts him and the movement of his eyes shows his dullness of comprehension. From his appearance and statements, I have little doubt his conviction arose from his misunderstanding the questions put to him by the Special Officer who called at the house to arrest his brother.
>
> He seems quiet and inoffensive, and however much I would be opposed to showing leniency to one who would in any way interfere with the efforts. . .to crush the present rebellion, I deem this a case in which after the punishment Moul has already received, the President would do well to extend his pardon."[15]

(It is not possible to pass by this last phrase without reflecting on its implications. The men occupying the White House today, shielded from the world by bullet-proof windows, heavily armed Secret Service men, and an enormous staff, which screens the mail and electronic communications, have no time for the miseries of individual citizens. Today, the rare afflicted "nobody" may be trotted out for a photo "opportunity" and then be quickly shown the door, but such visitations are for a special purpose and are hardly the usual pattern. The sheer availability of Lincoln is astonishing.)

Holt briefly summarized the case and the doctor's report and concluded, "This poor stupid culprit has already suffered months of imprisonment, of which he perhaps could scarcely appreciate the criminality. . . it is extremely doubtful whether any good purpose will be answered by inflicting. . .further punishment." The President could hardly have received an easier decision. "Sentence remitted. A. Lincoln April 27, 1864."

Just plain crooked. That was James B. Dawson, sometimes of Pittsburgh, Pennsylvania. This swindler and confidence man traveled about the east coast posing as a Union officer on secret duty. He presented forged orders at the offices of various quartermasters—allegedly signed by Ulysses S. Grant—and obtained a total of $1,357.00 (nine year's pay for a private).

Like a fly which has to be swatted twice, he was tried and convicted on one set of frauds, and soon thereafter tried and convicted a second time based on a whole new set of deceptions. Holt was not patient with this man: "This [new] sentence, if confirmed, will make his [prison] term six years, which is believed to be fully justified by proof and the character of his crimes." The President shared this opinion: "Sentence approved. A. Lincoln Feb. 9, 1864."[16]

The court-martial of James E. Pierce is one of the anomalous proceedings that confuse the study of military justice in the Civil War. Although he received a general court-martial, he was not a soldier but a civilian. And not just any civilian, but the 12-year-old Negro servant of Captain George F. McKnight of the 12th Battery of New York Light Artillery. At Culpeper, Virginia, it was discovered that Pierce had been opening much of the unit's mail and removing cash and valuables. He was convicted and sentenced to a year in prison. The case was reviewed by Major General William French, who thought Pierce too young for prison, and suggested he be sent to an "isolated Contraband Camp, where, placed beyond the reach of temptation, he may become encouraged to become honest and useful." The President concurred in this optimistic plan: "Recom. of Gen. French approved & ordered. A. Lincoln April 27, 1864."[17]

What use had the Federal Government for 50,000 defective haversacks? Civilian contractor William H. White did not have a good answer to that question. Like Pierce, White was a civilian tried by court-martial. The government had provided a sample standard haversack and White's associates submitted the low bid to make them—53 cents each. When the time came for delivery, the haversacks were too small and had the straps sewn on improperly. White was convicted of neglect of duty and ordered to pay a fine of $3,000.00. The court noted that White had been treated leniently, and it soon became clear that a "Mr. Shattuck" was the real villain in the crime, using White only as a front. The prolonged trial, which generated thousands of pages of testimony and exhibits, was finally brought down to a single key word: "Approved. Jan. 13, 1864. A. Lincoln."[18]

Table Eleven summarizes the outcomes of these military commissions (and anomalous court-martials) we see that Lincoln's legendary lenience is still at a low ebb. While it true that he lessened the penalties in sixty-four percent (64%) of the cases, conversely he let the full weight of the penalty fall upon over a third of the malefactors. More remarkable is his agreement with Holt: 100 percent, a total congruence of opinion.

Opinion Maker	Lincoln Agrees	Lincoln Disagrees	% Agreement
Trial Verdict	8	14	36
Authorizing Officer	NA	NA	NA
Departmental Commander	3	3	50
Judge Advocate General	16	0	100
Interested Politicians	NA	NA	NA
Friends, Family & Comrades	1	0	100

Some of the cases were ones where Lincoln rarely forgave the crime—rape would certainly be in that category—but complete concord between Holt and Lincoln was a rare thing. Most photographs of Lincoln show him looking benign or a least neutral; the few images of Holt reveal a brooding scowl. This group of evil-doers has brought them, if only for a moment, into perfect harmony.

13

Thieves and Robbers

There were almost two million men in the Union army. Some were not exactly stalwart defenders of the Union, dedicated to clean living and good behavior. Away from the constraints of wives, parents, church, and the ethos of their hometown, some men acted like just plain criminals. As will be seen, such behavior was not confined to any one group, but included men from every corner of the Union. The ones presented here were all men who came to Lincoln's attention and were not catalogued in Basler's great work. Was Lincoln's sympathy for thieves and robbers any different from his willingness to extend leniency to spies, murderers, deserters, and the other miscreants presented earlier?

The first case is of a soldier from Maine whose mother wrote to Lincoln: "In every instance that a Widow made supplication to Jesus, to a Prophet or King, or even an unjust Judge, they were granted," explained the distraught woman. "The Presedent is the Father of our Country & he is my Father in whom I confide." Her son, Private Daniel A. Conant of the 17th Maine, was convicted of stealing money from mail at Camp Parole, near Annapolis, Maryland, and of stealing a revolver and mailing it home. He was sentenced to six months of confinement at Fort Delaware and the loss of most of his pay for the same period. "The Court is thus lenient believing the accused to have acted more from thoughtlessness than from a knowledge of the serious character of the offense he was committing," was what was written in Conant's file.

In addition to writing to the President, Conant's mother also wrote to Mrs. Lincoln: "Do not think me an intruder—altho in one sense I really am so," and went on to describe in great detail her son's legal difficulties. His home town, Temple, Maine, had at considerable expense sent a delegation to represent Conant at his trial, but without success. Conant's mother and the other citizens of Temple asserted the following: Conant had found the revolver on the road and could not find its owner. An officer had told him, "It's yours as much as anyone's." So, the lad mailed it home. His wife would have sent it back express, "if she had known a crime had been committed." The mother continued for four closely-packed pages to urge her case upon both Mrs. Lincoln and the President. The prisoner himself also wrote to Lincoln, covering many of the same points. Three months after the trial, Conant's papers received this note: "Pardon for unexecuted part of sentence. A. Lincoln Feb. 28, 1865." Mom's supplications, and those of her neighbors, were successful.[1]

Private Patrick Welch of the 28th Massachusetts Infantry, a regiment in the famed Irish Brigade, chose his victim most unwisely: Welch stole from his own captain while the regiment was camped at Falmouth, Virginia. The private waited until late at night, slipped into the captain's tent, and "stole a pair of pantaloons." He also took a pocketbook with $60.00 in Treasury notes. General Meade, who rarely saw the necessity for mitigation, was certainly not going to remit this case, and he did not. Welch had been sentenced to have his head shaved and be drummed through the regiment wearing a large sign which read "Thief." This humilating display was to be followed by a year in the penitentiary. The President's decision? "Sentence approved. A. Lincoln Nov. 7, 1863."[2]

Private John Murray of the 6th Connecticut was not just a drunk, but a vicious and disorderly inebriate. The regiment was traveling from New Haven, Connecticut, to Riker's Island in New York Harbor aboard the steamer *Charles Osgood*. With a companion named John Kelly, Murray beat and robbed several comrades. When ordered to desist, he called the captain a "son of a bitch." Murray assembled a number of thugs and villains around him and not only told the officers that they, too, would be beaten and the ship set on fire if they interfered, but concluded the evening's festivities by shouting, "Hurrah for Jeff Davis," and "continued to sing and dance until dawn." This display of Hibernian insouciance did not sit well with the President, who wrote, "Sentence approved. April 14, 1864. A. Lincoln." Thus the final arbiter of such things confirmed Murray's three years at hard labor and his dishonorable discharge.[3]

Private James McMoran of the 7th New York Artillery was stationed in the District of Columbia, keeping the citizens safe from the Confederacy. Unfortunately, the citizens were not safe from McMoran. The New Yorker entered the home of Miss Emma Clokey on the pretense of looking for deserters, punched her around awhile, and then robbed her of $11.00. McMoran was given five years at hard labor and a dishonorable discharge. The President, who was slow to forgive crimes involving cruelty or meanness, wrote "Sentence approved. A. Lincoln April 27, 1864."[4]

"Let's go to Cherry Alley for beer and have some fun with the girls." To the ears of Private John Rice, this must have sounded like a plan for a splendid evening in Georgetown, District of Columbia. What Rice did not know was that Private Thomas Boyd, also of the 9th New York Heavy Artillery, planned to mug his comrade. A few hours later in one of Georgetown's dark alleys, Boyd and three companions beat Rice and took his $18.00. The court sent Boyd to the grim state penitentiary at Albany, New York, for two and one-half years with no pay. Did the Chief Executive agree? Of course he did. "Sentence approved. A. Lincoln Apl. 26, 1864."[5]

Private William B. Lucas had bizarre, even disgusting, tastes in stolen goods. The wards of Civil War hospitals were filled with cases of gangrene, festering wounds oozing the loathsome juices of men dying a hideous death. Lucas, a member of the 35th New York Infantry, stole enough towels, sheets, and blankets from the "soiled linen room" of a District of Columbia hospital "to fill a two-horse wagon." One might think that possessing these items would be punishment enough, but he was convicted of "theft" and given three months in the penitentiary and a dishonorable discharge.

Holt noted that "theft" is not one of the offenses listed in the Articles of War (Lucas should probably have been charged with "conduct prejudicial to good order and military discipline"), and concluded, "The sentence. . .was unauthorized and should not be carried into effect." Nicolay wrote, "Sentence disapproved for want of jurisdiction. May 20, 1863," and Lincoln signed.[6]

Unlike in the Lucas matter, a private of the 146th New York Infantry was properly charged with "conduct prejudicial," after stealing $40.00 from a comrade at Three Mile Station, Virginia. Since soldiers had no place to keep money safe, trust and honesty were essential in a regiment; stealing from a peer was strongly frowned upon and often produced a very heavy sentence. In Charles Balis' case, he was given five years in the penitentiary. General Romeyn Ayres thought this excessive and recommended prison to the end of Balis' enlistment. Lincoln agreed, and instructed Nicolay to write, "Recommendation of General Ayres approved. February 19, 1864." Lincoln signed.[7]

Private George W. Minnig of the 96th Pennsylvania, like Patrick Welch, was also foolish enough to steal from his own officers. In Minnig's case, he took $60.00 from the tent of his lieutenant. His conviction of "conduct prejudicial" netted him a year in the penitentiary, preceded by being drummed through the regiment with a "Thief" placard, followed by a dishonorable discharge. Again, Nicolay wrote, "Sentence approved, " and Lincoln signed. The day was February 10, 1864.[8]

"Cutpurse" is a term that has been used for centuries. Such thieves would open a purse or pocket with a razor and disappear before the victim noticed his (or her) money was gone. This ancient profession and skill was plied on the train from Alexandria to Warrenton (both in Virginia) by Private Alfred Smith of the 119th Pennsylvania Infantry. With the help of accomplices, who created a diversionary commotion, Smith cut open the pocket of an unsuspecting private and extracted $260.00 in cash—a huge amount in those days. Smith was clever, but not clever enough. He was caught, convicted of the fateful "conduct prejudicial," and sentenced to pay back the money, to have his head shaved, to wear a "Thief" placard, to be paraded through the regiment in this humiliating state, and then to be sent to serve five years in prison. And what did Lincoln think of cutpurses? "Sentence approved. A. Lincoln April 14, 1864." The Chief Executive had exactly one year to live.[9]

On the highway outside of Norfolk, Virginia, Private Michael Sullivan and an accomplice pointed a pistol at civilian Jesse Barry and took his gold watch. A few miles down the road, Sullivan accosted "a colored man," and beat him on the head until he gave up all his money—$4.00. Sullivan, this flower of the 11th Pennsylvania Cavalry, was given five years in the penitentiary with a 24-pound cannonball chained to his left ankle. At the end of this time, he would be presented with a certificate of dishonorable discharge and escorted to the gate. The President had no disagreement with this plan: "Sentence approved. A. Lincoln Feb. 15, 1864."[10] It is of interest that both victims, one white, the other "colored," testified. Earlier in the war, white defendants sometimes attempted to exclude testimony by non-Caucasians. But those days were over—at least until Reconstruction, when a Southern backlash ended the racial equality enforced by Union troops.

Private George Wilson of the 83rd Pennsylvania was no stranger to crime, at least judging by his modus operandi. One of his comrades was carrying $235.00 at Rappahannock Station, Virginia, probably the proceeds of an enlistment bonus. As usual, there was no convenient way to safeguard money, bank it, or send it home. (Adams Express was the best method for sending valuables, but one had to find an Adams office or representative.) Having identified his victim, Wilson decoyed the man into the woods on some pretext, where he and two accomplices separated the victim from his money by means of the usual threats and violence. Wilson was caught red-handed (or in this case, green-handed). Since he could not come up with a plausible defense, he pleaded guilty. A court-martial, which included Joshua Lawrence Chamberlain's brother Tom, found Wilson guilty and sentenced him to prison for the rest of his enlistment at no pay, followed with a dishonorable discharge. The April 14, 1864 review of cases contained several shameless robbers. By now, the President was probably tired of them. In any event, he once again wrote, "April 14, 1864. Sentence approved. A. Lincoln."[11]

The Great Lakes State contributed two men to this study. Privates Phillip Smith and Joshua Garrett, both of the 6th Michigan Infantry, were convicted together of having broken into the store of Rufus King, near Camp Hamilton, Virginia, and stealing a "large amount of goods." Garrett, age eighteen, pleaded for clemency on the basis that he had never been paid and was the sole support of his aged father. Smith's excuse was that his family was starving. Whatever the truth (or relevance) of these pleas, they were of no avail. Both men got three years of hard labor in prison, a sentence approved by General Robert Foster. Both men's records bear this note: "Sentence approved. A. Lincoln Feb. 15, 1864." Thievery did not sit well with this President.[12]

Private Sherman Dodge had a powerful conscience. On a July night in 1863, at Lake Springs, Missouri, this soldier of the 2nd Wisconsin Cavalry was on stable guard. A gray mare, "not of much value" and scheduled to be turned in as unserviceable, disappeared. Though Dodge was not a suspect, a month after the theft he confessed that he had taken the horse. His sentence of six months in the Missouri State Penitentiary was approved by General Schofield. Holt noted that "General Schofield, not being empowered to enforce the confinement, forwards the records for the order of the President." Lincoln wrote, "Sentence approved. Feb. 9, 1864," and Dodge went to prison for half a year for taking a nearly worthless horse.[13]

Dead drunk under a Memphis whorehouse—a dangerous place for anyone, including an unnamed cavalryman who had his pockets picked by Private William Phillips of the 8th Iowa. "On the street that the New Memphis Theater is on," Phillips also helped himself to a can of oysters, a plug of tobacco, and a canteen of whisky, all of which earned him five years in a military prison, at no pay, and a dishonorable discharge. However, the story was not finished. Phillips had friends, and they sent a long petition to Lincoln describing the culprit's many virtues and his firm resolve to act better in the future. Six months after the court martial, we see: "Pardon for unexecuted part of sentence. A. Lincoln Dec. 21, 1864."[14]

Private Harrison Thompson of the 14th Kansas Cavalry liked horses. Not only was one provided to him by the government, but he stole two more from civilians. This nifty little feat earned him three years in the penitentiary, a penalty confirmed by "Sentence approved. A. Lincoln April 21, 1864."[15]

A corporal of the 1st Missouri Cavalry was accused of having stolen a silver watch in New Madrid County, Missouri (site of the famous earthquake of 1811). His squad had visited a home, the watch was missing from the mantelpiece, and a "Private Seymour" testified that he had seen Thomas Keegan take the watch. The accused got a year in the penitentiary. General Schofield approved the sentence and sent the papers east, where they were reviewed four months later. Holt noted that the only witness was Seymour, whom two different officers said was a liar. Holt recommended that the sentence be disapproved, and so it was. "Findings and sentence disapproved. A. Lincoln April 26, 1864."[16]

Like Private Harrison Thompson, Private John Britton also had a thing for horseflesh. The scene of the latter's crime was Cape Girardeau, Missouri, where Britton saw fit to steal a horse. Not yet completely satisfied, he employed threats to exchange it for a better steed (a mare). There was no testimony in the case because Britton, a member of the 2nd Arkansas Cavalry (Union), pled guilty. His sentence was a harsh one: ten years at hard labor. General Clinton Fisk (teetotaler, abolitionist, and founder of Fisk University) recommended mitigation to a prison sentence until the end of the war. The President wrote: "Gen. Fisk's recommendation approved. A. Lincoln Feb. 9, 1864."[17]

Private Peter Shannon had devised a simple (if unoriginal) method of obtaining money: he hit a comrade over the head, and while the man lay unconscious, picked his pockets. Shannon was a member of Company C, 2nd Delaware Infantry, stationed then at Bolivar Heights, Virginia. When his victim recovered his wits, he identified Shannon as the assailant. The puzzling part of the story is that Shannon was tried by a military commission chaired by Brigadier General William French, and not by a court-martial. This unusual legal arrangement is not explained in the records, but two things are clear: the guilty party was given five years in the penitentiary, and he received a dishonorable discharge. Holt reviewed the case and simply remarked, "The sentence. . .is not regarded as too severe for the crime." The final note was even shorter: "Approved. A. Lincoln May 11, 1863."[18]

Peter Roos was drunk at Lynnville, Tennessee, and in this sorry condition broke into the sutler's store. The noise generated when Private Roos splintered the door attracted a guard, who found him combative and uncooperative. For this clumsy burglary Roos was given one year in prison wearing a ball and chain, followed by four more years in prison without the iron ball, all without pay and all followed with a dishonorable discharge.[19]

Roos' wife wrote to Lincoln, informing him that she had four children under the age of nine and no way to feed them or herself. Roos' old commander, Colonel Frederick J. Hurlburt of the 57th Illinois, wrote, asking for clemency. This was granted: "Pardon for unexecuted part of sentence. A. Lincoln Feb. 28, 1865." In less than two months, Lincoln would have a bullet in his brain, and Colonel Hurlburt would be found drowned in the Chicago River.

Before the introduction of the Uniform Code of Military Justice, justice was often quite non-uniform. The trial of Private John Hough of the 8th Missouri Militia was by military commission, although soldiers were supposed to be tried by court-martial. Hough's crime: stealing a horse from a nine-year-old boy. His punishment: death in front of a firing squad. Major General Samuel Curtis (Congressman and hero of the Battle of Pea Ridge) thought the sentence too severe and the use of a military commission irregular. He concluded, "A mitigation of the sentence is earnestly recommended." Holt agreed, and Lincoln wrote: "Sentence commuted to imprisonment in one of the military prisons for six months from this date. A. Lincoln May 11, 1863."[20]

For several decades, the U.S. army maintained a school for musicians at Fort Columbus, in New York Harbor. Their unit designation was simply "Music Boys." Potential tootlers and thumpers, as young as twelve years of age, were enlisted for a three-year hitch. Whatever their ages, they were held to adult justice. One of the graduates of this martial conservatory was Ambrose Hall. He was older than many of the Music Boys, being age nineteen when his mother Julia signed his enlistment papers. (Perhaps his height—sixty inches— made him seem younger.) Ambrose is brought to our attention because of his theft of $100.35 from a comrade. He pled guilty, and offered the rather limp explanation, "He got most of his money back." The court sent him to the District of Columbia Penitentiary for the rest of his enlistment, at no pay, which would be followed with a dishonorable discharge. Major General John Wool approved the sentence, as did Holt. Nicolay wrote, "Approved. May 20, 1863," and Lincoln signed. Hall's sentence would be a double whole rest in any musical score.[21]

The son of a Presbyterian deacon behaved outrageously at Duck River, Tennessee. Corporal Samuel Ewing of the 102nd Illinois, joined by other members of his regiment, ransacked a house, stealing whisky and $65.00 in Treasury notes. A court-martial reduced Ewing to the rank of private and sent him off to prison for three years. The reviewing general agreed, adding that the behavior of all the men involved was "disgraceful." The home folks did not agree. Lincoln was presented with a petition signed by hundreds of Ewing supporters, all asking for clemency. Two Congressmen asked Holt to investigate the matter. Fourteen months after the trial, the President wrote, "Pardon for unexecuted part of sentence. A. Lincoln Feb. 16, 1865."[22]

Sing Sing Prison in New York State is usually thought of in relationship to gangsters and murderers, but during the Civil War, with the shortage of prisons and a bumper crop of offenders, the Federal government placed many military prisoners in state facilities. Private John McKeone of the 8th U. S. Infantry was convicted of "conduct prejudicial" when he stole the musket of a corporal in his company and sold it. He also sold his own musket. For this, he was sent to Sing Sing for a year, after which he was to receive a dishonorable discharge. If he hoped Lincoln would look favorably on his actions, he was disappointed. Nicolay wrote "Sentence approved. February 10, 1864," and Lincoln signed.[23]

President Lincoln, on hundreds of documented occasions, looked after "his boys." He was concerned for their food, for their uniforms, for their weapons, for their pay. His visited hospitals, he shook hands, he attended days of reviews and parades, he granted interviews at the Executive Mansion, he appeared at charity fairs. For the first two years of the war, he literally worried himself sick trying to find a general for the Army of the Potomac, a leader who could do something more than just spill the blood of "his boys." When his tired young soldiers fell asleep at their lonely outposts, or went home without permission to see a dying child, he was willing to forgive, to remit, to give another chance.

But robbers and thieves were mostly just that—robbers and thieves. Their crimes were not related to saving the Union, and instead were usually a product of simple self-interest. For these offenders, it is not surprising that Lincoln endorsed the prescribed penalties in sixty-three percent (63%) of the cases, and was in agreement with Holt and with his generals in nearly every case. Table Twelve reproduced on the following page also reveals the political realities of the office of the President: where there was intense family pressure or Congressional demands, Lincoln yielded to their requests in every case.

Opinion Maker	Lincoln Agrees	Lincoln Disagrees	% Agreement
Trial Verdict	15	9	63
Authorizing Officer	3	0	100
Departmental Commander	6	1	86
Judge Advocate General	4	0	100
Interested Politicians	1	0	100
Friends, Family & Comrades	4	0	100

It was not until his death that Lincoln was "sainted." When in office he was, and needed to be, a politician. Without the support of Congress or of the voters at the next election, he was powerless. He had to balance dozens of factors. His stand on slavery was usually under criticism by either the abolitionists or the conservatives, or both. Congressmen wanted strict discipline in the army—except for their soldiers. Congress wanted honesty and fair prices from military contractors—except for those in their district. Lincoln wanted re-enlistment bonuses for veterans, which Congress denied at least once. Lincoln wanted a cook's and baker's school for the army, since most soldiers were sick from their own cooking; Congress wouldn't vote a nickel to train a cook.

Like every other President before and since, Lincoln had to "horse trade." If Lincoln won the support of a key legislator by not shooting a constituent, it seemed a small price to pay.

More Sleeping Sentinels

Our study began with the Sleeping Sentinel. It is now time to return to his drowsing comrades, who forsook the Fields of Mars for the comforting Arms of Morpheus.

Two Civil War traditions hold as follows: (1) You could be shot for sleeping on duty, and (2) William Tecumseh Sherman favored shooting miscreants. These are not merely myths or rumors, but reality. Consider, then, the case of Private Avery Sheridan of the 46th Ohio Infantry. Sheridan was found asleep by—Major General Sherman himself. Part of the case is routine: it was proved that Sheridan was on sentry duty, and that the army was near the enemy (at Corinth). As a result, Sheridan was found guilty of sleeping at his post and sentenced to be shot. The court-martial board recommended clemency and the case came first to Holt. He found nothing in the record to show that the Court had been sworn in the presence of the accused, which invalidated the proceedings. Hay wrote, "Report approved. July 18, 1863," and Lincoln signed.[1]

So far, nothing unusual—except that the trial papers contain a three-page essay by General Sherman himself, addressing the problem of sleeping sentinels:

"Headquarters, Fifth Division, Army of the Tennessee, Memphis. August 4, 1862. To: General L. [Lorenzo] Thomas, Adjutant General, Washington, D.C.

Sir: I have the honor herewith to enclose the original proceedings of a general court-martial held in my command and call attention to the case of Private Avery Sheridan of Company B, 46 Ohio Volunteers, on pages 19 and 23, convicted of sleeping on post and sentenced to be 'shot to death.' This case is submitted to the

President of the United States as required by the 65th Article of War, together with my orders in the case dated August 2nd instant. I also accompany these papers with a petition signed by all the members of the Court recommending the prisoner to mercy. I admit the appearance and manner of the youth appeal to all who see him. Still the circumstances of his sleeping when the whole army lay within sight of our enemy, the importance of the post, the factor which does not appear of record, that he could not have been fatigued, as he had not marched or worked in the trenches that day, and the necessity for an example in this too common an offense among volunteers, deter me from joining in the petition [for mercy].

I hope the President if he accedes to this petition for mercy may do it in such a manner as will not tend to diminish the importance attached by all military men to this particular offense. No body of men can be healthy and strong without natural sleep, and no man can sleep in the presence of an enemy without that sense of perfect security which can only be experienced when all know that the camp is guarded by vigilant sentinels. The Regular Soldier has this feeling of perfect safety, whilst the volunteer is ever-restless and uneasy because he knows that his comrades, like himself, are not ever-watchful. This simple fact accounts in part for the vast amount of sickness and debility among our volunteers and offers one reason why a superhuman effort should be made to correct the evil.

The known severity of the punishment has made me overlook many cases which come under my personal observation and I know that it is almost impossible to make volunteer officers report the cases which they discover, but it is now full time that we begin to consider ourselves soldiers engaged in Real War. I submit the case to the President. I am with great respect,

W. T. Sherman, Major General, Commanding."

Ohio boys seemed to have a gift for meeting the famous under adverse circumstances. Private Thompson Miller of the 10th Ohio was guarding Major General William Rosecrans' headquarters at Stevenson, Alabama, when he was found asleep in front of the headquarters. Miller, too, was sentenced to be shot, but the court recommended some mitigation because the sleeping sentry had been assigned to stand guard at these hours: 8:30 to 10:30 a.m., 2:30 to 4:30 p.m., 8:30 to 10:30 p.m., and 2:30 to 4:30 a.m. The court felt such a schedule might disrupt the normal sleep pattern. Rosecrans agreed with their views and recommended commutation to hard labor with a ball and chain to the end of his enlistment. In Washington, an unknown hand wrote, "Recommendation of General Rosecrans approved & ordered. Feb'y. 10, 1864." and Lincoln signed.[2]

That same day, another case involving the same Thompson Miller came to the President's attention. At Murfreesboro, Tennessee, there was a complex row involving a private family, an abused "colored boy," a colonel with a cocked pistol, and "female servants" with whom Miller was "misbehaving" in the kitchen. Somewhere in this donnybrook, Miller threatened the colonel with a revolver, which also earned him a trip to the firing squad. Again, Rosecrans recommended mitigation; Holt agreed. Nicolay's hand wrote words identical to those in Miller's other trial, and Lincoln signed. In a single month this Ohio private had twice escaped being shot.[3]

The 155th Ohio was the regiment of Private John Patterson, who passed out drunk on guard duty. He did not take kindly to being awakened in this state, and greeted his superiors with curses and blows. Patterson, too, was to be shot. The trial was held in July 1863, and the papers drifted through bureaucratic channels for seven months. In December 1863, Brig. Gen. Jacob D. Cox had an interesting basis for his recommendation of clemency: "In consideration of the fact that Private John Patterson had never seen any field service, and could therefore have but little appreciation of the duties of a soldier, I recommend that the sentence be mitigated." A rubber date-stamp reading January 4, 1864, marks the arrival of the papers in Holt's office. On February 15, Lincoln wrote: "Pardon for the remainder," and added his signature.[4]

At the trial of sleeping picket James Bishop, one officer said, 'He was so deep asleep, I had to touch him with my foot to awaken him." (It's likely that this was more like a kick in the ribs.) The young soldier, a private in the 17th Pennsylvania Cavalry, presented evidence that he had been on picket duty three consecutive days, and eight out of the previous ten days. The sentence—he was to be shot—was approved by General George Meade, who then recommended a commutation to prison at Dry Tortugas to the end of the war. Holt agreed with Meade; Lincoln did not. "Sentence remitted. July 9, 1864." Three months after his court martial, Bishop was back on duty.[5]

"I was sick with diarrhea and had severe pain," said Private William E. Guile, of the 8th New York Cavalry, when he was tried for sleeping on sentry duty. The court's decision? "To be shot to death." General Joseph Hooker approved the proceedings and sent the case on to the President. Holt quickly spotted the absence of the phrase "two-thirds of the Court concurring" (required on death sentences) and advised Lincoln that the sentence could not be enforced. Hay wrote, "Report approved. July 8, 1863," and Lincoln wrote his name. Guile was not shot.[6]

Private Rhodes' horse stood quietly by, nibbling on a haystack at 10:00 o'clock in the morning. Its rider, Franklin Rhodes of the 17th Pennsylvania Cavalry, assigned to vidette duty, lay stretched out on the grass nearby, sound asleep. This pastoral tableau, near Sperryville, Virginia, was interrupted by an officer who arrested Rhodes. At his trial, the defendant demonstrated that he had been on picket duty for fourteen consecutive days and also was sick. "Besides, I was not asleep, I was just resting." The court sentenced him to be shot, but urged clemency based upon "excessive labors." Again, Meade recommended commutation to prison at Dry Tortugas to the end of the war. Seven months after the trial, the case reached the President's desk. In his clear, distinctive hand, he wrote, "Sentence remitted. A. Lincoln July 9, 1864."[7]

The military prison at St. Louis was a dreadful place, and the only hope for escape lay in people like Private Adam Krachlanberger, of the 9th Wisconsin, who was sound asleep at his guard post at the prison. The court found him clearly in violation of the 46th Article of War and sentenced him to be "shot to death with musketry." General Schofield approved the sentence, recommended commutation, and passed the case on to Holt's office, where it was noted that the sentry post was "an important one." The Chief Executive's note, as usual, was brief: "Sentence remitted. A. Lincoln April 26, 1864."[8]

The men of the 20th Iowa marched all day in the heat and damp of late summer, finally reaching their campsite on Atchafayala Bayou, Louisiana, after dark. Private Alonzo Swartout, who had suffered severely from the heat, was posted as a guard over the horses, where he was found asleep near midnight. He was sentenced to be shot, but the members of the Court unanimously recommended mitigation because the soldier had "borne himself bravely in action." The next reviewer up the chain was a major general with the splendiferous name of Napoleon Tecumseh Jackson Dana, who recommended a fine of four months pay instead of death. Major General Nathaniel Banks agreed, and even Holt "believed that the sentence might be remitted without prejudice to the interest of the service." "Recom. of Gen. Dana approved & ordered. A. Lincoln April 14, 1864." It had been a long and exhausting day for Lincoln, who had reviewed a total of sixty-seven court-martial cases.[9]

Another Louisiana bayou, this one called LaFourche, was the site of Private John Jones' fateful nap. For many days this member of the 2nd Illinois Cavalry had been sent on scouting duty during the hours of sunlight, and put on picket at night, this time from 8:00 to 11:00 p.m., with a three-hour rest, and then back to his post from 1:00 a.m. to dawn. He never made it: at 5:00 a.m. he was sound asleep. The court's sentence was the firing squad, followed by a request for clemency because of "remarkably good" character. Generals Dana and Banks both approved the proceedings. Holt had no opinion. Nicolay wrote, "Sentence remitted. Feb'y 10, 1864," and Lincoln signed.[10]

Many people are surprised to learn that Arizona had been part of the Confederacy, if only briefly, with the capital located in a primitive adobe village called Tucson. When California troops arrived, the Southerners withdrew to Texas. Private Henry Lawson of the 1st California Cavalry was found asleep at his Tucson sentry post and sentenced to be shot. General James Carleton approved the sentence, then recommended pardon, believing "that discipline would not be injured thereby." The trial papers traveled up the Santa Fe trail by wagon, then, most likely, up the Ohio by steamboat. Seven months after the court-martial, the Chief Executive wrote, "Pardon. A. Lincoln July 18, 1863."[11] Elsewhere that same day, the 54th Massachusetts Colored Infantry made its suicidal charge upon Fort Wagner, South Carolina, a stoutly defended redoubt which was never taken by Union attackers.

Politics loomed large in the trial of Private William Blunt (also spelled Blount), of the 12th Missouri Cavalry. He was charged with sleeping on his post at LaGrange, Tennessee, and sentenced to nine months hard labor at the "death-trap," a disease-ridden Federal military prison near Alton, Illinois. Congressman Benjamin Loan wrote to Lincoln, "The officers there were conservatives, and young Blunt is a radical. The Court was constituted to convict." The soldier's father also wrote the President: "I recruited my son into my regiment. He had an inflamed leg and while still sick was put to guarding forage." The case concluded with this note: "Pardon, on condition of rejoining regiment & serving out term. A. Lincoln March 8, 1865."[12] That same day, the Confederate Senate approved the use of Negro troops, thus calling into question the fundamental reason for the existence of the Confederacy.

City Point, Virginia, a huge Union supply base, was crowded with steamboats bringing men and supplies for the Union siege of Richmond and Petersburg. On a September 1864 evening, around midnight, Private John McKeever of the 15th New York Engineers was serving on sentry duty. He was discovered sitting on the ground, his musket resting on his shoulder and his head on his hands. The Officer of the Guard seized the musket; McKeever clung to it and sprang to his feet. The officer said he was asleep; the sentry said he was not. Witnesses said that McKeever had served thirty-two months without any disciplinary action and was "a faithful and willing soldier," but the court sent him to Dry Tortugas to the end of his enlistment. On February 13, 1865, Holt wrote, "If the President should see fit to grant a pardon to this prisoner, it is necessary that it should be done today as the term of his sentence—and of his service—expire tomorrow." (Holt's suggestion was a gentle reminder to Lincoln: no pardon, no veteran's benefits.) That same day, we see the note, "Sentence remitted. A. Lincoln."[13]

The enemy was reported to be nearby at Beverly Ford, on Virginia's Rappahannock River, which made Albert Persons' sleeping on sentry duty especially serious. This private of the 94th New York was sentenced to be shot. Because so many executions had taken place recently, General John Robinson (Mexican War veteran and future lieutenant-governor of New York) recommended that it might be better for morale to demonstrate some clemency. He suggested instead hard labor in prison to the end of his enlistment. Meade agreed. "Recommendation of Gen. Robinson approved. A. Lincoln Nov. 7, 1863." Robinson's statement about the number of executions suggests there were death sentences which were kept from Presidential review.[14]

Private William von Gester had survived eight years in the Dutch army, but falling asleep in Georgetown, D.C., guarding Forrest Hall Prison, was almost the death of him. Witnesses described him as "the best man in his company," part of the 178th New York Infantry, and that he had served long hours as a cook the three days before he was posted as a sentinel. General John Martingale, Military Governor of the District of Columbia and future attorney general of New York State, recommended commutation to prison for the rest of von Gester's enlistment. Perhaps Lincoln was probably thinking that "the best man in the company" would be more use as a soldier than as a prisoner, as wrote, "Pardon, Feb. 15, 1864."[15]

Private A. B. Covert of the 126th New York was seen by the court as "not physically or mentally capable; he is not prompt, but does his duty—when he is well." (Which was not often.) Covert said he fell asleep at Union Mills, Virginia, because he had "a blister under [his] cartridge box." The court sentenced him to be shot, but recommended remission; so did Generals James Craig and Samuel Heintzelman. Nicolay wrote: "Sentence remitted, May 11th, 1863," and Lincoln signed.[16]

Andrew Shafer was to be "publicly shot," as a warning to other men not to fall asleep, as Shafer had, at Decherd, Tennessee. Witnesses said that this private of the 17th Indiana "had been on brigade guard every other 24 hours, on grand guard every third day, with the intervening hours on fatigue duty. He was exhausted." When the case came to Holt, he noticed that the judge advocate of the court-martial had not been properly sworn. In Nicolay's hand, we see: "Sentence disapproved for irregularity. May 20, 1863." In much darker ink is "A. Lincoln."[17]

Henry Wright of the 7th Vermont was a long way from home when he fell asleep at Fort Barrancas, Florida. He pleaded guilty and was to be shot. The court noted that he had been on guard or fatigue duty the preceding three days, had told the sergeant he was sick, and was put on night sentry duty anyway; they also noted his "extreme youth" (actual age not given). All this led them to recommend mitigation. This cut no ice with Wright's commander, Colonel William Holbrook, who had ordered the trial. He endorsed the firing squad—but not the mitigation. General Banks disagreed with Holbrook and approved clemency. Holt offered no opinion. "Sentence remitted. A. Lincoln Nov. 7, 1863."[18] It was Saturday. Outside of the President's office, along the Rappahannock River, men were killing each other at Kelly's Ford.

Sentinel John Hardesty of the 65th Ohio, waited and waited to be relieved from duty and finally fell asleep. Testimony showed that there was only one watch in his company, and it ran slow. Not only was his shift relief late, but it was also shown that Private Hardesty suffered from "a severe attack of cholera morbus." The same court-martial which sentenced him to die also recommended mitigation for these two reasons. Rosecrans suggested the loss of six months pay; Holt agreed. Nicolay took up his fine-tipped pen and wrote, "Sentence commuted to forfeiture of six months pay. June 16, 1863." as Lincoln signed his name to Hardesty's records, Robert E. Lee's army was crossing the Potomac River into Maryland and headed toward Gettysburg.[19]

Passed out drunk on sentry duty—that was Private Armand Jovanne of the 16th New York Cavalry. For his intemperance on an October night in 1863, he was sent to the harsh miseries of Dry Tortugas, guarded inside by rifles and outside by sharks. He was ordered to stay there for two years sporting a ball and chain "weighing not less than ten pounds." Jovanne was another man with friends willing to write letters, and they presented Lincoln with a dozen missives attesting to Jovanne's loyalty, efficiency, and splendid character. Holt reviewed the records and found "no reason to pardon him." This did not inhibit Lincoln from writing "Pardon. A. Lincoln March 17, 1865." Jovanne had eight months taken off his sentence; Lincoln would be murdered in twenty-eight days.[20]

At Falmouth, Virginia, in the late spring of 1863, Private Albert Smith of the 15th Massachusetts was found asleep while serving as a vidette (a sentinel on an advanced outpost). Smith told the court, "I was sick. I had a fainting spell." He was found guilty and sentenced to the usual death by firing squad. The court recommended mitigation because "some doubt exists as to his physical ability to perform the duty imposed upon him." Brigadier General John Gibbon noted, "The record shows a great neglect on the part of regimental and picket officers and I concur in the recommendation to mercy attached." Lincoln's signature follows Nicolay's note, "Sentence remitted. June 16, 1863."[21]

Mother love and insanity—two themes in the records of Private Harland Hubbard of the 1st Connecticut Artillery. He slept on sentry duty at Fort Richardson, Virginia, and in October 1863 was sentenced to a year at hard labor.[22] A petition addressed to the President and signed by fourteen leading citizens of Litchfield, Connecticut, including two medical doctors, asked for clemency for Hubbard. . .

now confined in Tortugas, Florida, for some offense said to have been committed by him against military rules. He is very young and of delicate constitution, nervous in temperament & doubtless less guilty than some who influenced him to his offensive conduct. Some years since, he was mentally deranged & in consequence kept for eight months in the Insane Retreat at Hartford [Connecticut]. We believe he ought to be released or restored to his position with his regiment.

The mother's letter to Lincoln, clearly written by a professional scribe, asked that the Judge Advocate General look into the case. "I know that your humane spirit will give him the benefit of the same." She went on to express her concern for young Harlan's "suffering of a life among men probably of far greater age and hardened nature than this youth of 19 years." Holt suggested that Hubbard's eleven months in confinement "may properly be accepted under the circumstances as an expiation for his offense." It is not a surprise to see, "Unexecuted part of sentence remitted. A. Lincoln July 8, 1864." The Chief Executive had other matters on his mind. In three days, Jubal Early would be in the suburbs of Washington, D.C., terrifying housewives and politicians.

Another mental case closes out our catalogue of sleepers on the brink of the precipice. Private Milton Armstrong, of the 68th Indiana, was asleep on picket duty at Nashville. At his court-martial, his captain told the court, "In spite of instruction, he had never comprehended the duties of a picket. I forgot to remove him from the picket roster." When Armstrong was found asleep, it was also noted that he was drunk. The court posed this interesting question in the record: "Is his imbecility Providential visitation or the result of dissipation?" Whatever the true answer, the members of the court agreed he should be shot to death. Holt, luckily for Armstrong, thought that there were grounds for mitigation. Into the cramped half-inch margin remaining at the bottom of the sheet of paper, the President squeezed this note, in his own hand. "Sentence commuted to imprisonment in some military prison for three months from this date. May 11, 1863. A. Lincoln."[23]

Lincoln's concern for the common soldier shows vividly in this analysis of sleeping sentinels. Not only does he demonstrate his reluctance to shoot soldiers, but he removed every sentence of death (see

Table Thirteen reproduced below). While he rarely wrote his reasons for any court-martial decision, he set forth his belief on the subject in conversations with petitioners, military men, and with his secretaries. Young men far away from home, he explained, usually sick and fatigued and accustomed to a farm routine of bed at dusk and arising at dawn, should be the objects of charity rather than treated as criminals. Certainly, he was aware of the validity of the commanders' concerns, such as those so aptly expressed by General Sherman. In the case of sleeping sentinels, however, the Lincoln reality and the Lincoln myth merge perfectly.

Opinion Maker	Lincoln Agrees	Lincoln Disagrees	% Agreement
Trial Verdict	0	23	0
Authorizing Officer	7	1	88
Departmental Commander	10	3	77
Judge Advocate General	8	1	89
Interested Politicians	1	0	100
Friends, Family & Comrades	2	0	100

Based upon 43,634 court-martial records, 1,922 men were tried for sleeping on duty. Of these, 78 received death sentences. So far as the record shows, Lincoln spared the life of every man who was found asleep on duty as a sentry, guard, picket, or sentinel.

Rapists and Miscellaneous Miscreants

The President especially disliked crimes of meanness and cruelty, and tended to withhold his clemency in such cases. Lincoln, who ran an Executive Mansion without a breath of sexual scandal, seemed likely to be doubly repulsed by the crime of rape, which combines both cruelty and sexuality. Our criteria for selection in this study (a note by Lincoln, and an absence from Basler's index) have identified six rapists. What will Lincoln do with these cases?

Private James Robinson of the 8th Missouri State Militia Cavalry was stationed near Lebanon, Missouri. He and another soldier left camp at night, pistols in hand, and broke into the homes of "utterly defense-less" citizens, including a household composed of a widow and her small children. In the words of Joseph Holt, "They robbed with the remorselessness of professional highwaymen." From the widow, they took not only her rings, but even the stockings that warmed her legs. Then they threw her onto the floor and tried "to violate her person." Robinson was given three years in prison and a dishonorable discharge. Once again, the citizenry sprang into action. A long petition, signed by dozens of Robinson's home town neighbors, begged for his release. His colonel forwarded the petition, adding that Robinson's pre-war character was excellent, and that Robinson had suffered enough.

Holt brushed aside these entreaties as though they were pesky flies: "These suggestions of citizens, kind-hearted but wholly uninstructed as to the facts of the case, cannot. . .justify any mitigation. The robbery committed by him and his comrade. . .was in every way atrocious. . .the sentence pronounced is one of extreme mildness, and it is earnestly recommended that it be not disturbed." The President agreed. "Sentence approved. A. Lincoln Jan. 25, 1865."[1]

Another Missouri private was William T. Cox of Company I, 8th Missouri Cavalry. He was not only a rapist, but a horse thief. In Greene County, Missouri, he stole a horse, a bridle, and a sidesaddle. Miss Josephine Rose begged him not to take her sidesaddle, but he did. Worse, he raped Mrs. Nancy Rose, as her small children and her ten-year-old Negro servant girl watched. She told the trial board: "He pushed me down on the bed and did what he pleased with me. I got away from him twice, but he threw me down. I did not give up to him at all; he overcame me by main strength. He ran his saber through my dress and threatened to kill me if I did not yield to his desires."

The military commission which tried him found him guilty and sentenced him to be shot. The record was first reviewed by then-Brigadier General Francis Herron (who, at age 25, was the youngest major general in the Civil War). Herron expressed some concern: "The deft. was tried by only three of the original commission." This legal technicality did not trouble Major General Samuel Curtis, who approved the proceedings, and sent them on to the President. Holt had little sympathy for Cox: "This is a case of robbery and rape, committed upon a defenseless woman by the accused, aided by an accomplice. The ruffians were armed & the perpetration of the crime was accompanied with threats of death or the burning of the home of the victim, if any resistance was offered. The sentence should be carried into execution." In large, bold letters, the President agreed: "Sentence approved. A. Lincoln May 20, 1863." William Cox was about to be ushered into the next world.[2]

Near Lebanon, Kentucky, Joseph Blair was away on business, leaving his wife and her sister, Sally McKune (or McKeene) alone. Private Stephen Stilwell, of the 37th Kentucky Infantry, entered the house and ordered Mrs. Blair to go to a distant neighbor's home and inquire about some allegedly stolen government horses. She protested. "Leave the house," he insisted in rather strong language, "or I'll blow your God damned brains out." She left. According to Mrs. McKune, Stilwell "forced me, he uncovered me, he exposed himself and then he did as he pleased." The court-martial board gave Stilwell fifteen years in the Kentucky State Penitentiary. Holt noted that he had "forcibly dragged Mrs.

McKune. . .into a retired room and by force and against her will and consent, had carnal knowledge of, and connexion with, her body." ("Connexion" was the favored spelling in these trials.) Holt saw no reason for clemency; nor did the President. "Sentence approved. A. Lincoln April 14, 1864."[3]

The 8th U. S. Infantry was stationed at Rectortown, Virginia, when one of its privates, William Elliott, attempted "to commit the crime of rape upon the body of a colored woman named Kate Brooks. This on the premises of her master, R. M. Johnson." According to one witness, "His fly was open, his person [Victorian euphemism for genitals] exposed. He was on top of her, she crying 'Oh, please, Master, don't hurt me!'" Holt commented on the matter, writing that it was "a brutal attempt at rape on a gray-haired Negro woman between 60 and 70 years of age. Guilt was complete." In a note now lost or stolen, Lincoln approved the sentence: William Elliott was to spend the rest of his life in New York's Sing Sing Prison.

Two years later, a pair of letters came to the Executive Mansion. The first, a letter by a Mr. H. Herringshaw, asked for Elliott's release. The other missive came from Elliott himself. In it, he called attention to his age (twenty) and to his loyal service. Further, he stated that he never committed the crime, but was framed by an old man whose liquor jug he had broken. Whatever factor moved the President, we see in the record this badly smeared note, entirely in the President's hand: "Partly on account of the youth of this boy, partly that he served faithfully and creditably in the field after his conviction, and partly that he has already been severely punished, he is now pardoned for the unexecuted part of his sentence. A. Lincoln Nov. 7, 1864." Perhaps Lincoln thought that a vision of forty more years in that grim prison might have a maturing effect on the young man; whatever the reason, he chose to give Elliott another chance.[4]

A Pennsylvania saddler met his match at McMinnville, Tennessee. Jacob Leonhart, who repaired the horse gear for the 26th Pennsylvania Artillery Battery, was an uninvited guest in the kitchen of a "Mrs. Young," who later told the court, "He had my old black woman, Sally, down on the floor and was on top of her, trying to violate her person, so I hit him with an ax handle." She apparently did not hit him hard enough, as he got up and punched Mrs. Young with sufficient force to knock her to the floor.

In his defense, Leonhart produced his captain, who testified that this was the only instance of misbehavior since Leonhart joined the regiment. The court sentenced him to hard labor for the rest of his enlistment, with a 12-pound ball and chain. General Rosecrans approved the sentence. Holt pointed to a technical flaw in the charges, by which only the charge of drunkenness was allowed to stand. Leonhart was saved by the obfuscation of legal logic and the President, restricted by this opinion, wrote: "Term of confinement reduced to six months. A. Lincoln April 21, 1864."[5] Lincoln reviewed 72 court-martial cases that day; one can only imagine the mental fatigue such a caseload—combined with everything else—inflicted upon him.

The 109th New York Infantry was stationed at Laurel, Maryland, long enough to get to know the neighbors well. Too well in the case of Private William H. Cole. In late 1863, Cole was tried for the rape of Mrs. Alvisa Brown, wife of Nicholas Brown. The private was convicted and sent to Albany State Prison for ten years. In March 1864, Lincoln received a parcel of papers regarding Cole. Three of his comrades—Ixes Brink, Silas Tripp and Ezra Bills—swore that the Brown household (father, mother and grown daughter, Ellen) was more barroom–brothel than a normal home. "We depose. . .that Alvisa and Ellen are lewd women and that. . .Nicholas Brown is cognizant of the fact and that they keep a bawdy house." Ezra Bills swore that he had seen a man in bed with Ellen with the full concurrence of her mother.

These petitions were carried to the President by Congressman Giles W. Hotchkiss, who paused in the foyer long enough to write this note on Executive Mansion letterhead: "July 9, 1864. I specially request the President to pardon William H. Cole of the 109th Regt. of N.Y. Vols.—now in the Penitentiary at Albany on charge of rape." On the same piece of paper is, "Pardon, according to above request. A. Lincoln July 9, 1864."[6] Lincoln was no amateur politician. If the Congressman came to him later, asking the President to tighten discipline in the army, the President had only to remind him of this favor.[7]

A Miscellany of Miscreants

The following fifteen cases do not fit neatly into the categories already described. As such, they constitute a true miscellany while illustrating such varied topics as fraud, forgery, drunkenness, tuberculosis, medical records, onanism, and dangerous horseplay.

In an era before modern personnel record-keeping, the management of a huge army was often inefficient, and there are thousands of examples where the left hand of the government did not know what the right hand was doing. A case in point might be Private Joseph Stone of the 17th Illinois, who was convicted of "misbehavior before the enemy"—usually meaning cowardice or fleeing during a battle. He was sentenced to be shot. The testimony showed that he was under fire with his regiment near Vicksburg, was wounded, and went to the hospital. Stone presented a certificate, signed by a surgeon at a Union hospital in Memphis, discharging him from the hospital, and an order from General James Veatch detailing him to special duty at the Memphis Commissary Department, where he was set to work making barrels. Since his time away from the regiment was accounted for, it was unclear why he was to be shot. General Stephen Hurlbut recommended some clemency, and on this basis, General Ulysses S. Grant suspended the execution and sent the case to the President, via Holt, with a recommendation of prison to the end of Stone's enlistment, followed by a dishonorable discharge. Holt added, "There is a possibility that the prisoner was wounded, as he claimed, and the recommendation is therefore concurred in." What is clear here, is that the government had no idea whether Stone had been wounded or not, did not seem to have a method of finding out, and did not seem to care. "Recom. of Gen. Grant approved & ordered. Aug. 17, 1864 A. Lincoln."[8]

Private John Robinson of the 17th U. S. Infantry was "stupid drunk" near Culpeper, Virginia, when he shot his own sergeant in the chest for no particular reason. Fortunately for the victim, the wound was serious but not fatal. There was little testimony, since nothing seems to have led up to the shooting, and Robinson claimed to have no memory of the entire day. He was sentenced to three years in prison. Holt had no comment. Lincoln wrote, "Imprisonment reduced to one year," perhaps thinking that after a year of drying out his brain, Robinson might be good for something. "Feb. 15, 1864."[9] It was a Monday, and Meridian, Mississippi was still burning.

In Howard County, Missouri, on the north bank of the Missouri River, the bitter Civil War continued unabated. A company of 6th Missouri Militia Cavalry was out looking for bushwhackers, and arrested a "Mr. Champion." He refused to go as ordered. The lieutenant ordered Private William Brown to bring the prisoner, who again refused to budge. Brown was not pleased by Champion's recalcitrance. Taking matters into his own hands, the private leveled his gun and shot the alleged bushwhacker, wounding him twice. For this act Brown was charged with assault with intent to kill and sentenced to a year in prison. Schofield noted that the witnesses against Brown were all Rebel sympathizers, and that while Brown was "culpable" for losing his temper, he had been greatly provoked by the suspect. Holt agreed with Schofield that the charges were "not sufficiently sustained." One word finished the dispute. "Pardon." The President signed his name on February 9, 1864.[10] That same day Lincoln had his picture taken, the one which now appears on the $5.00 bill.

William Hill was a "general service" soldier (they did administrative work at permanent installations), stationed at the District of Columbia, who was caught selling forged discharges. This 20-year-old former farmer seems to have been a rather amateur criminal, as he was caught soon after he began his forgeries. He pleaded guilty. At his September 1863 trial, he was sentenced to eighteen months at hard labor and a dishonorable discharge. After he had been in prison a few months, his wife wrote to Lincoln that her husband was desperately sick, asking that he and his family be spared the disgrace of his dying in prison. Lincoln made inquiries. The doctor (whose signature is illegible) at the State Penitentiary, Albany, New York, wrote, on Christmas Eve 1863: "William Hill. . .is in a decline and in my opinion cannot survive but a few months in prison." The Prison Clerk, Louis Pilsbury, added, "William Hill has the consumption [pulmonary tuberculosis]. He is now in the hospital of the prison, confined to his bed, and can probably live but a few months at most." A scrap of paper in the record bears this note: "Let this man be pardoned. A. Lincoln Jan. 7, 1864." It seems everyone was correct; Hill was dead by May.[11]

One of Hill's co-conspirators, Francis Sullivan, also a "general service" man, was convicted of the same charge and received the same sentence as did Hill. In May 1864, he wrote to Lincoln, enclosing a petition signed by many friends asking for a pardon. He reminded Lincoln that he had earlier pardoned Hill for the same crime, but omitted mentioning that the basis of Hill's pardon was a terminal illness. On June 24, 1864, Lincoln wrote, "Please allow the bearer to bring the record of this case to me." (Can one imagine showing up at the White House today, with a petition, and asking to see the President? The likely result would be a trip to jail, or to St. Elizabeth's Mental Hospital.) The President reviewed these papers and could find no compelling reason to release this non-terminal supplicant. "Application denied. A. Lincoln July 16, 1864."[12]

The next case is a mystery story. John Brady of the 151st New York was drunk on duty in Baltimore in February of 1864, and was sentenced to six months of hard labor wearing a ball and chain. Worse, he was to forego $10.00 each month of his $13.00 pay. Since he had not been paid at all in thirteen months, this left his wife and child worse than poor. The record contains a heart-rending three-page letter from Mrs. Brady to her husband. He had recently sent her $5.00, for which she was most grateful, but since she had already borrowed $1.00 from a friend, and had been living off her family, which humiliated her, this still left her only $4.00, too little to set up a new household and feed herself and their child. She wrote to her husband, "i do not care if i have to go to the poor house for just as well be tear [there?] as to be the wase i am asking a dollar of Miekel. . . ." The possibility of mitigation was presented to the President. His written decision is in the hands of some "collector," since the entire Lincoln notation has been neatly scissored out, by an unknown but despicable person, leaving only a hole in the page.[13]

The Invalid Corps was the predecessor of the Veterans Reserve Corps. Men assigned to these units were too impaired for field service, yet too well to discharge. Bernard Monahan (also spelled Monahon) of the 14th Battalion of the Invalid Corps had the twin traits of his forebears: extraordinary bravery in battle and berserk behavior when intoxicated. When he was last drunk on duty, the Captain of the Guard found it necessary to "hit him with a musket to calm him for handcuffing." As so often occurs, when such a man is being calmed, he is free with his opinions, and in this case called the captain and the captain's subordinates "sons of bitches," and offered to "break every bone" in their bodies. The end result was a sentence of three years at hard labor. After he went off to prison, there were a number of petitions on his behalf, noting that he was the sole support of his 80-year-old mother. The Massachusetts State Agent wrote to Lincoln, asking clemency. Eleven months after the guilty verdict, we see this note: "Pardon for unexecuted part of sentence. A. Lincoln Jan. 23, 1865."[14]

Private Joseph Armstrong didn't want to be one of the 24,645 casualties at the Battle of Stone's River. On December 31, 1862, he ran away from the 15th U. S. Infantry and did not return until January 8, 1863. At his court-martial eighteen days after his return, he was found guilty of cowardice and sentenced to be shot. General Rosecrans—perhaps in a good mood given his near-brush with catastrophic defeat—recommended commutation of the sentence, and the President added, "Recommendation of Gen. Rosecrans approved. A. Lincoln. Nov. 7, 1863."[15]

According to the charges filed against him, Corporal John M. Boyer of the 91st Pennsylvania left his unit during the fight at Mine Run, Virginia, and shot himself in the hand. His version of events differed, in that he claimed he had fallen and his gun had gone off. His captain spoke well of his behavior at the battles of Fredericksburg, Chancellorsville and Gettysburg. Boyer was reduced to the rank of private and ordered to forfeit $10.00 a month for the rest of his enlistment (77% of his pay). After the court-martial, many people wrote on his behalf. Five months after his conviction, we see: "Judge Advocate General please examine and report on this case. A. Lincoln Sep. 12, 1864." Further notes by the President are not apparent in this file.[16]

The 13th Massachusetts was at Waterloo, Virginia when Corporal Albert Brooks was absent without leave for four months. Part of the problem was that the army did not know where its people were. At his trial, Brooks presented copies of the orders sending him home on permanent recruiting duty. It is true that he was absent part of the time from that duty, as he was tending his sick wife, but the rest of the time was properly accounted for. He was sentenced to lose four months pay and to add four months to his enlistment. Brooks requested some mitigation of this penalty. On July 14, 1864, the President penned a brief note to Edwin Stanton, Secretary of War, asking for information in this case. After examining the file that came to him, the President wrote, "Disability removed. A. Lincoln Aug. 17, 1864."[17]

Private James O'Rourke of New York's 149th Regiment of Volunteer Infantry was an enterprising, if unethical, soldier. Somehow he obtained thirty blank furlough forms, which he sold for $5.00 each. Whether the $150.00 he grossed was worth the five years of hard labor he received, only he could answer, although at one cent per day, the cost-benefit ratio seemed unfavorable. O'Rourke wrote to Lincoln, citing "my aged father and mother," and Lincoln wrote to Holt, "Judge Advocate General please procure record and report on this case. A. Lincoln March 2, 1865." It seems likely that the lack of further notes by Lincoln is best explained by his assassination. Andrew Johnson, the new President, remitted O'Rourke's sentence.[18]

In November 1862, two men of the 112th Pennsylvania had their own private war—against a citizen of the District of Columbia. Joseph Carson and James Harris were offended by "Mr. Fenwick's" barking dogs. Carson hit Fenwick with an ice hook; Fenwick hit Carson with a shovel. Carson and Harris retreated, only to return with muskets, with which they perforated Fenwick's house until arrested. Both men were convicted of being absent without leave and of assault with intent to kill, and sentenced to two years in prison. For reasons apparent only to the highly trained legal mind, this was not a military case, according to Holt. Nicolay wrote, "Sentence in this case disapproved and the prisoners directed to the civil authorities. May 11, 1863." Lincoln signed.[19]

It seems that you cannot be convicted of insulting an officer if you did not know he was an officer. Private Martin Troy of the 34th New York was raising a fuss at a private home in Rectortown, Virginia, smashing furniture, threatening the family, and stealing things that took his fancy. A man appeared and ordered him to cease this disturbance. Troy suggested that the man perform a number of anatomically impossible acts, and made a series of speculations regarding the man's ancestry. Troy was convicted of several crimes, including disrespect to an officer, and sentenced to be shot. Holt was of the opinion that Troy had not seen the "marks of rank" and was therefore innocent of the intent of disrespecting an officer. Nicolay wrote, "Sentence commuted to imprisonment for three months and disgraceful discharge. June 16, 1863." Lincoln signed.[20]

Like many legal cases, the one involving Robert Noble was more complicated than it seemed at first blush. He was a private in Company K, 12th Indiana Infantry, and was charged with shooting at John Wilkinson and William Kitts, both of his own company, "with intent to kill." Noble was sentenced to five years in prison and a dishonorable discharge. However, a letter from Captain Joseph Draper, Noble's company commander painted a different picture:

> Robert Noble had always proved himself a brave and true soldier. At Dam No. 4, Maryland, at night, he crossed the Potomac River and assisted me to capture a large amount of Reb property. On the morning of the third of December, Noble was detailed to assist to capture a band of Rebel guerrillas and lay all day in cover of woods in a winter storm in Virginia. At night, the command returned to the Potomac River and 18 of his comrades passed over the river in a small boat; being cold and chilly, they started for camp, leaving Noble and the command on the Virginia shore. Some of the others pointed their guns across the Potomac—300 yards wide—and, all jestingly, threatened to shoot. Noble's gun went off, and the ball passed near two of his best friends, soldiers he had no difficulty with before or since. Said Noble has already been in confinement four months and 20 days and has returned to duty without a sentence. This regiment's time of serving has expired and it is the voice of the regiment to release him and to restore him to his rights.

The President agreed with Captain Draper. "Let the pardon be granted. A. Lincoln May 17, 1862."[21]

In the "miscellaneous" category, no one seems more miscellaneous than Camillus Nathans of Company F, 90th Pennsylvania Infantry. In March 1862, when he enlisted, he was age 23 and stood 68 inches tall. Six months after he joined the army, he deserted, at Washington D.C., and was arrested in December 1862 in Philadelphia. (Other records show him deserting in early September at Sharpsburg, Maryland, and being absent most of 1863.) He disappeared for nearly a year, only to surface again as a patient in Washington, D.C.'s Armory Square Hospital. There, on November 3, 1864, Surgeon D. W. Bliss wrote: "I have carefully examined Private Camillus Mathews, Company F, 90th Regt. . .Pa V and find he has general debility and dementia sequella of nocturnal emissions, and I believe he is the subject of self-abuse. . .he is entirely incompetent to do military duty." The same day, Bliss' letter was forwarded to "His Excellency the President" by Joseph K. Barnes, Surgeon General of the U.S. Army, with a cover note referring to "Dementia, the result of Self Abuse." (The messengers in the capital must have been busy, since also on the same day, there are several memos, clarifying the private's correct name.) The next note is by His Excellency himself. "The name is Camillus L. Nathans. Let him be discharged. A. Lincoln Nov. 3, 1864." When Nathans died in 1870 of "mania a potu" (a fatal delirium from prolonged alcoholism), his mother applied for a pension; her claim was rejected. Why the highest levels of government were in involved in this case of the "solitary vice" remains a mystery. Yet again, though, we see Lincoln doing something for somebody.[22] The case of Camillus Nathans closes this assembly of men whose lives, in one way or another, were touched by Lincoln.

Opinion Maker	Lincoln Agrees	Lincoln Disagrees	% Agreement
Trial Verdict	5	1	83
Authorizing Officer	NA	NA	NA
Departmental Commander	2	0	100
Judge Advocate General	5	0	100
Interested Politicians	1	0	100
Friends, Family & Comrades	2	1	66

With the cases of rape, Lincoln thought that the court-martial verdict was correct in five of the six cases (see Table Fourteen above). The

President was clearly much less forgiving of rapists than of sleeping sentinels. In one case of rape, Lincoln yielded to a Congressman, who entered the Executive Mansion and spoke on behalf of his constituent, but in nearly every case the President's displeasure was evident and his clemency rare and grudgingly given. The mixture of sexuality and cruelty found in most cases of rape was a bad combination for any man hoping for forgiveness by Abraham Lincoln.

Opinion Maker	Lincoln Agrees	Lincoln Disagrees	% Agreement
Trial Verdict	1	11	8
Authorizing Officer	1	0	100
Departmental Commander	3	0	100
Judge Advocate General	5	0	100
Interested Politicians	1	0	100
Friends, Family & Comrades	3	1	75

In the "miscellaneous" cases, reproduced in Table Fifteen above, it is hard to make a generality or to identify trends, largely because of a lack of common themes. However, it is worth noting than in ninety-two percent (92%) of these cases, Lincoln was willing to extend some degree of clemency. In brief, he extended the same degree of forgiveness as found in most of his decisions regarding soldiers who had deserted.

16

The Statistics of Compassion

Lincoln has been, and still, is recalled in manifold guises. He was, and is, many things to many people. While he lived, he was the object of verbal blasts and degrading caricatures—not only in the Southern press, but in hostile Northern publications across the spectrum from the Peace Democrats to the wild-eyed radical Republicans. Several periodicals in Great Britain excoriated him unmercifully during his Presidency.[1]

His own General-in-Chief, and sometime Commander of the Army of the Potomac, George B. McClellan, was condescending to the President, brazenly condescending. McClellan snubbed Lincoln and kept him waiting, intentionally, on several occasions. In the presence of his own military staff, McClellan often referred to the President as a "baboon" and "an old stick." McClellan seems not to have noticed that he was violating the Fifth Article of War and should, himself, have been court-martialed.

As with all Presidents, Lincoln never came close to pleasing everyone. The Abolitionists denounced him for moving too slowly on the question of emancipation, while the Democrats and the Copperheads (and of course the Confederate press) reviled him for moving too quickly. At Ford's Theater, all that changed.

Within hours of his death, Lincoln was given many of the attributes of a saint. The funeral train, which carried his body from the nation's capitol to Springfield, Illinois, was viewed by many hundreds of thousands of mourners. In the cities where he lay in state, men and women waited in line for hours, shuffling in tears and anguish past his catafalque. In the vast spaces between cities, along lonely rural railroad tracks, mourners waited day and night for a momentary glimpse of the slow-moving black-draped train carrying the martyred President out of America—and into history.

Around that remarkable man has grown a great Himalaya of myth, legend, and folk tale, built upon the actual realities of his life and embellished by countless embroideries upon the canvas of known facts.

Lincoln and the Generals

The officers who commanded armies and departments were mostly major generals, the highest rank obtainable through much of the war. Most of the court-martials reviewed here contain an opinion rendered by the responsible departmental commander. Taking the average of all types of crimes (as shown on the next page), we see that the President and his departmental commanders were in agreement eighty-four percent (84%) of the time. There is a tradition that Lincoln was carelessly generous with clemency and in disagreement with the military establishment on the subject of discipline. Our findings show little basis in reality for such tradition, and in fact quite the opposite is true. Much of Lincoln's clemency consisted of endorsing the recommendations of the several levels of reviewers as the case moved upwards towards the Presidential office.

The final step between the generals and the President was the review and opinion generated in the office of Joseph Holt, Lincoln's Judge Advocate General. The table on page 260 shows the levels of agreement between Holt and Lincoln for eleven categories of offense. An average of these agreements yields eighty-four percent (84%)—exactly the same level of concordance found with the military commanders. To a remarkable degree, Lincoln, his chief legal adviser, and his generals, agreed upon the recipients of the President's clemency decisions.

Lincoln and the Soldiers

A recent study of Lincoln and his "boys," based upon many thousands of soldier's diaries and letters, demonstrates that even at the lowest point of Union fortunes, when morale was at a dangerous ebb, and even while McClellan was the hero of the hour, a majority of Union soldiers

President Abraham Lincoln's Agreement (in percent) with Court-Martial Verdicts	
Sleeping Sentries	0%
Deserters, 1863-1865	5%
Miscellaneous	8%
Violence to Officers	8%
Deserters, 1861-1862	23%
Lieutenants, Surgeons	24%
Missouri Civilians	26%
Miscellaneous Bushwhackers	36%
Spies	40%
Generals, Colonels, Majors & Captains	41%
Murderers	50%
Robbers & Thieves	63%
Rapists	83%
Confederate Recruiters	100%

SLEEPING SENTRIES: Men convicted of sleeping on sentry duty.

DESERTERS, 1863-1865: Convicted deserters in the final two years of the war.

MISCELLANEOUS: The non-rapists described in Chapter 15.

VIOLENCE TO OFFICERS: Men convicted of mutiny and related crimes.

DESERTERS, 1861-1862: Convicted deserters in the first two years of the war.

LIEUTENANTS, SURGEONS: Convicted men of these ranks

MISSOURI CIVILIANS: Convicted men described in Chapter 11.

BUSHWHACKERS: men convicted of guerrilla activity, summarized in Chap. 12.

SPIES: Convicted persons from Chapter 10.

GENERALS, COLONELS, MAJORS AND CAPTAINS: Chapter 3.

MURDERERS: Convicted killers from Chapter 9.

ROBBERS AND THIEVES: Convicted men from Chapter 13.

RAPISTS: Soldiers and civilians convicted of rape from Chapter 15.

CONFEDERATE RECRUITERS: Recruiters captured in Union territory.

perceived Lincoln as personally concerned about their welfare and felt that his interest in them was genuine and unwavering.[2]

President Abraham Lincoln's Agreement (in percent) with Opinions of Judge Advocate Generals Joseph Holt	
Missouri Civilians (Chapter 11)	63%
Confederate Spies (Chapter 10)	65%
Murderers	69%
Deserters, 1861-1862	75%
Mutiny & Violence to Officers	88%
Court-Martialed Lieutenants	88%
Sleeping Sentries	89%
Deserters, 1863-1865	90%
Bushwhackers (Chapter 12)	100%
Robbers and Thieves	100%
Rapists	100%

Certainly there was the inevitable bitching and griping, customs as old as armies themselves. But even in the darkest days of lost campaigns and botched battles, these complaints were only wavelets, bits of spume and froth flying along the troubled surface of the deep water of that bond between Lincoln and his soldiers; the union of his aims and their aims, an implacable current, as relentless in its motion as the turning of the earth. If the moral harmonics of that current could be made audible, could be transmuted into words, two phrases might express those forces: "Let Every Man Have His Chance," and "The Union Forever."

These underlying concepts were never absent; they were like the pianist's left hand, which sustains a theme carried by the bass notes while the right hand renders the bright trills and arpeggios which fly upward, catching the ear with melody.

For the soldiers, the long-term goal—the preservation of the Union—was the left hand; unceasing, ever present, while the right hand and its more memorable, more melodic music, was brought into being by moments of personal contact; when Lincoln, who did his best to be visible to the soldiers, met an individual man; a handshake at a railroad station, a friendly word in a hospital corridor, a listening ear on the lawn of the Executive Mansion, a willingness to provide an autograph, a direct and riveting glance on a field where fifty thousand men were drawn up for review.

When these same men were bent with age, their beards long and white, they regaled their audiences with that moment, perhaps embellished and magnified through many tellings, but always with a central kernel of truth: he shook hands with me; he touched my arm; he looked into my eyes and spoke to me. Me.

If these long-recalled encounters, these brief moments of positive contact, were momentous, consider the overwhelming impact when the President sat down to decide whether that man would live or die. Die, not just of old age, or of the time and chance of the battlefield, but die an announced, premeditated, intentional death; to be publicly and deliberately killed, killed at a time and place posted in orders; to be shot under the gaze of his comrades, to be shot standing in front of his own coffin, to be shot standing next to the hole in the ground where he would spend eternity. What could be more meaningful than the President's decision regarding such a moment?

Thus, these cases of court-martial review and Presidential decision contain the ultimate distillation of the relationship between Lincoln and the soldier: Lincoln looking at the papers, which stood as the condemned man's proxy, and weighing all the factors, both inside that room and out, which would shape his decision. Those hundreds of moments of truth presented earlier in this study can be compressed into a single sheet of paper, a single column of numbers—in this case, the first table presented here. And a moment's glance will show vividly that, in Lincoln's mind, not all crimes were equal.

Consider first, the sleeping sentinels. In this study, Lincoln reprieved all of them. Every one. Whether they were returned to their regiment or went on to prison was not the issue. The real issue was then, as always, to die or not to die, and under Lincoln's hand, no sleeper died.

With the soldiers who deserted, we see not just a number, but a transformation. In the first two years of the war, Lincoln approved twenty-three percent (23%) of the sentences imposed upon the deserters. Yet, in the trials occurring during the last two years of the war, these figures dropped to less than a quarter of what they had been earlier in the war. In these latter two years, as the war built to its crescendo, its final fury, Lincoln reprieved, in one way or another, not seventy-seven percent (77%) of the deserters but ninety-five percent (95%) of those desertion cases which came before him. His inclination to soften, to remit, to mitigate, to extend clemency, was monumental.

Lincoln's views on ultimate justice are suggested in yet another area: discipline for officers when contrasted with discipline for enlisted men. In armies, there is an imbalance between the rules governing enlisted men and those for officers. R.H.I.P.—rank hath its privileges. Hundreds of Civil War Union soldiers were shot by firing squads. If a Union officer stood before a firing squad, we have not seen the record. (A few were condemned, but seemed escape their fate.) Officers could resign, soldiers could not. Officers were paid better. Some officers, like Colonel John Turchin, brought their wives on campaign, something soldiers could not do. Infantry officers rode, while the soldiers went on foot. Indeed, rank hath its privileges.

Lincoln, egalitarian to the core, saw the deep iniquity in this chasm between officers and men, an iniquity more galling in a volunteer army, and was visibly more severe on officers than on privates. Regard, for example, the figures for officers of high rank. Lincoln endorsed the sentences rendered against forty-one percent (41%) of them, while for crimes committed by lower-ranking officers, such as lieutenants, the figure is only twenty-four percent (24%). In the cases where enlisted men insulted or attacked their officers, Lincoln agreed with only eight percent (8%) of the sentences—a compelling difference! In brief, the higher the rank, the less the chance that Lincoln would extend clemency. If Lincoln had a bias, it was one against rank.

The crimes which resembled ordinary civilian felonies, such as murder, theft, and rape, were reprieved at a much lower rate than "military" crimes, such as sleeping on sentry duty. A soldier boy might fall asleep through fatigue; a drunken private might dye the night air blue with oaths; a desperate man might desert to see his dying child or feed his starving wife. But no such motives or excuses could be attributed to the thief or to the rapist. Their motive was to do evil, and Lincoln saw little reason to extend his mercy to men who chose evil.

The final and most dramatic findings in this study were Lincoln's decisions regarding men who were commissioned by the Confederate States to come north, into Union territory, to recruit men to fight that Union. Here we see no trace of Lincoln's legendary compassion. He reprieved not a single one. He offered no reason, but the numbers speak for themselves. One can only conclude that he regarded an enemy recruiter as more offensive, and less worthy of compassion, than a rapist, a thief, or a murderer.

This, then, is the ultimate distillate of Lincoln and the Soldier: Lincoln's Compassion. Lincoln looked for a chance to spare the nonviolent offender. He did not like crimes of meanness or cruelty, nor did he look kindly upon crimes against women, and, most vividly of all, he did not tolerate men who came into the Union seeking candidates for the job of killing Union men. But in nearly every other category, the legend of his compassion is not legend at all, but truth.

This study has shown the actual numbers by which Lincoln's compassion can be measured. These numbers reflect the underlying theme of his life—Every man should have his chance. Lincoln's urge to remit was very real, but it was selective, not universal. Through these numbers, we can further comprehend the moral and political values which guided Lincoln through our nation's most terrible calamity.

17

Lincoln at the Millennium

The millennium fast approaches. The periodicals and the pundits, who have labored the past few generations to select the Man of the Year (more rarely, a woman), the Man of the Decade, and the Man of the Half Century are even now at work on the Man of the Millennium.

How does one select the single individual who has had the greatest significance in human affairs in the past ten centuries? Textbooks tend to mark events by wars: the War of the Roses, the Hundred Years' War, the Taiping Rebellion, the War of 1812. Will a great military leader fit the bill for the Man of the Millennium? How about Genghis Khan? Or William the Conqueror? Or perhaps Suleiman the Magnificent or Napoleon Bonaparte? Would an influential political leader be a better choice? Winston Churchill or Mao Ze-dong or Franklin D. Roosevelt or Sun Yat-Sen? In a parallel category, political leaders of surpassing and destructive evil, Joseph Stalin or Adolph Hitler, come readily to mind. Perhaps, however, this list should be limited to persons who do good.

There have been many changes in technology since the year 1000. A scientist or inventor should certainly be in the running. There are the Wright brothers, Albert Einstein, Watson and Crick, Louis Pasteur, Isaac Newton, Charles Darwin, Galileo, Copernicus—it is difficult to know where to stop. The flaw with nominations from the fields of science and technology are that each new invention tends to obscure the importance of the previous one. The inventor of the stirrup is long forgotten, and in the distant future, so will be the inventors of the Internet.

An equally important group to consider would be the great spiritual leaders, men and women who changed or influenced the beliefs of others. Martin Luther comes to mind, as does Mother Teresa and Albert Schweitzer. If the criteria included religious innovations, we could consider Henry the Eighth, Mary Baker Eddy, or Joseph Smith.

These preliminary attempts to select a Man (or Person) of the Millennium fall short, because they have no guiding principle, no established criteria by which to narrow the search. Each candidate named is an important person—but important by what standards? The author suggests two benchmarks by which the search might be narrowed and clarified, two criteria by which a final candidate might be selected. These twin pillars are Endurance and Universality.

Consider the first factor, Endurance. Many influential leaders and their creations have been remarkably transient. Lenin and Stalin created the Soviet Union, now in the trash heap of history, lying next to Hitler's Thousand-Year Reich. Queen Victoria presided over the British Empire, which now consists of Gibraltar. Tito fused nests of hatred into a workable nation called Yugoslavia, which dissolved when he died.

Endurance is a quality of innate stability, which makes it survive the changes always brought by the passage of the years. Unlike the periodic crazes that sweep populations, such as the South Seas Bubble, the Tulip Crazes, the Dancing Madness, the plague-inspired pogroms, the Children's Crusade, the European war fever of 1914, and the cultists who chant and beg in airports, the Man of the Millennium must embody qualities and principles which are as valid in one century as the next, and will have an appeal which will persist down the long corridors of time. Thus, Endurance is the first of the two pillars which must support any candidate for this nomination.

Consider the second pillar, Universality. Candidates from the field of religion pose an immediate problem. A leader that inspires one group many be anathema to another. One man's prophet may be another man's infidel. A similar problem affects politicians. A man who founds a system of government or economics which is repugnant to large numbers, even if embraced by others, cannot achieve Universality.

What is needed to qualify in this dimension of Universality is to be a person whose teachings—and example—reach the widest audience; whose appeal strikes chords in the heart of Everyman, and creates a spark of warm recognition in the breast of the sweating miner in South

Africa, the shopkeeper in Glasgow, the taxi driver in Singapore, the sunburned wheat farmer in Minnesota. The Universal must be an attribute which is rejected only by the despot and the thief.

The person who best meets these twin criteria—Endurance and Universality—is, in my opinion, Abraham Lincoln. The basis for this assertion rests on the concept of a single unifying principle, one which encompasses and joins Endurance and Universality.

Physicists seek a General Theory, one which will explain and include forces as diverse as gravity and the mysterious adhesions inside the atomic nucleus. I suggest that there is in Lincoln one fundamental and unifying principle which can be shown—not by the criteria of abstract historiographic formulations, or by the Freudian speculations of "psychohistorians," but by concrete, specific acts by Lincoln himself during the course of his career. This quality, this essence, can be expressed in ordinary words.

There is no shortage of studies of Abraham Lincoln. Indeed, there is a plethora. *Lincoln and the Generals. Lincoln and the Indians. Lincoln and Tariffs. Lincoln and his Ancestors. Lincoln and the Railroads. Lincoln and Religion.* But it seems that each subject is only a secondary manifestation of a unifying principle; each is only a planet around the great sun, the helios of Lincoln's central and fundamental belief. And that steady, unwavering principle, visible throughout the entire span of his public life, is the right of every man to rise.

And in all the thousands of books about the Sixteenth President, two works stand out, two seminal writings which demonstrate and confirm this unifying principle: Gabor S. Boritt's *Lincoln and the Economics of the American Dream*, and Garry Wills' *Lincoln at Gettysburg*.[1]

Professor Boritt demonstrates that as far back as 1837, in the earliest days of Lincoln's political life, the wish to create an environment in which every man could make the most of himself dominated Lincoln's legislative program. In Illinois, back then, there was little except neighborhood commerce. Without railroads or canals or all-weather roads, a farmer had little market for his products. A manufacturer had no way to send his goods to the farmer or to the farmer's village. The term in use in the 1840s, the political label for roads and bridges and tracks and canals and locks, was "internal improvements," a wonderful term, a pair of evocative words. Poetry is filled with such words, words which suggest multiple levels of meaning and call up emotional states, words which have harmonics and reverberations, words which echo, rather than just fade away. Internal improvement is more than railroads. Education is internal improvement, as is insight, comprehension, understanding, love, loyalty, and heightened awareness. Receiving the grace of The Divine is an internal improvement. The acquired virtues of thrift, planning, industry, and foresight are all "internal improvements." The self-made man has made internal improvements, as has the man who has turned from sin, the man who has abandoned a life of crime, the man who accepts that he may be in error.

Lincoln had no time for the sentimental hogwash about the romance of the family farm in the wilderness. He had been there; he knew the brute, hard labor needed, the mental isolation, the lack of intellectual stimulation. He knew that "internal improvements" such as railroads, would inevitably bring internal improvements in the mind, would help men and women be more in touch with the greater economy and the wider culture. He also knew, as he lectured his spendthrift, feckless relatives, that the possibility of rising in life can only be offered, it cannot be forced on a man. It has to be grasped; the lazy and the self-pitying will not rise, but they should always have their chance.

Through good economic times and bad, even when such notions were unpopular, Lincoln championed railroads, bridges, and central banks, because he saw them as sources of potential prosperity for all, that each man might have an expanded opportunity to rise. In 1840, he championed a national bank, politically unpopular then, as necessary for the benefit of "the many." Unthinkable as it is today, until the Civil War this nation had no national currency. Lincoln saw clearly the value of a dollar bill which had the same worth and reliability from Maine to Texas, from California to Florida; he believed that a national currency was essential for the benefit of all.

In youth, Lincoln's ideal was Henry Clay, orator, statesman, and originator of the term "self-made man." Not only was Clay a political moderate and a supporter of social order, but, in Lincoln's view, Clay stood for the elevation of all people everywhere.

Lincoln's guiding light in economic theory was Francis Wayland, who believed that any involuntary exchange between capital and labor was "robbery," and that "every man be allowed to gain all that he can." In terms of our unifying theme, this was, once again, the right of every man to rise.

An open society, with equality of opportunity, was Lincoln's goal, and he saw an essential role for the government in the development of this concept. He felt that there should be more government, not less; that government's role was to do those things not possible for the individual to do. He supported labor unions and the right to strike, and viewed charities and orphanages as legitimate responsibilities of government.

His views on race, of enormous importance in and of themselves, can be shown to be secondary extensions of his central belief that working men, and their right to rise, were the foundations of the nation—his nation. In 1863, deeply disturbed by the New York draft riots in which white working men murdered black working men, Lincoln said, "The strongest bond of human sympathy, outside of the family relation, should be one uniting all working people, of all nations, and tongues and kindreds."

A further example of Lincoln's principle of the right of every man to rise was in his selection of military leaders. Many men were given their chance to succeed: McClellan, Burnside, Hooker, Pope. They all failed. In the end, Grant and Sherman were given the lead, not because of a cozy personal bond with the President, but because they succeeded at the task for which they were employed. (By contrast, there is some evidence that the brilliant Confederate general, Patrick R. Cleburne, was passed over for corps command because of his open dislike of slavery.) Every man has the right to rise—and the opportunity to fail. Utter pragmatism and utter fairness were always central in Lincoln's system of belief.

Lincoln, Slavery, and the Civil War

Nearly 140 years have passed since the Civil War. In the New England States and along the Pacific Coast, that conflict is, for most people, a settled issue, a healed wound. Not so in the South. Just across the Potomac River, within sight of the White House, there is Jefferson

Davis Highway, Robert E. Lee Highway, and Stonewall Jackson High School. On the interstate to Richmond, a large highway marker directs the driver to the Stonewall Jackson Shrine. In Vicksburg, Mississippi, the museum director tells his visitors, "I've never liked Mr. Lincoln, and I never will." In April 1998, the president of Virginia's Heritage Preservation Association told the press that on Southern plantations, "Master and slave loved and cared for each other and had a genuine family concern."

These issues and their interpretations form the earliest memories of many men and women; language and beliefs imprinted so early in life may never be subject to reconsideration, indeed, may be beyond ordinary discourse.

The issue becomes further clouded by the twin subjects of courage and bravery. To question the issues which men fought for may quickly be misinterpreted as questioning the integrity of those who fought. In the perhaps vain hope that they may be kept as separate issues, it should be said at the outset that few armies in history have fought so long, so bravely, and so skillfully, as those of the Confederacy. The central point, however, in understanding the Civil War is not courage, but issues. Beliefs about the causes, the origins, of the war have undergone a remarkable transformation since 1865.

In the century following Lee's surrender at Appomattox, it became fashionable in some circles to trace the origins of the conflict to sectional rivalry, or to state's rights, or to economic factors, or to an invasion by the North, or to a failure to recognize Southern interpretation of the Constitution. An edifice called the Lost Cause loomed over the South, as does the Eiffel Tower over Paris. In the final analysis, each of these explanations were attempts to deny the centrality of slavery.

The success of this shifting of focus has rested upon the utter ignorance of most persons graduating from our public schools. A few points might be in order to clarify this matter before considering Lincoln's central principle as it related to the issue of human bondage.

In 1820, the entrance of Maine into the Union as a state free of slavery threatened the political power in Congress of the slave states. This first threat to the Union was "solved" by the admission to the Union of Maine as a free state, Missouri as a slave state, and a prohibition on further extension of slavery north of 36 degrees, 30 minutes, a line nearly parallel with the northern boundaries of North Carolina, Tennessee, and Arkansas. This package of agreements was called the Missouri Compromise.

The next crisis centered on Texas. Immigrants from the north overthrew the Mexican government of Texas in 1836 and introduced slavery, which had been declared illegal in Mexico. For nine years, the anti-slavery forces in Congress defeated Texas' request to join the Union, and it remained the Republic of Texas until its annexation by the United States in 1845. This act directly precipitated the Mexican War, and the loser ceded California and New Mexico to the United States. Now, a fresh struggle for the extension of slavery erupted, with New Mexico and California as the targets. War between the North and South was averted, once again, by a new balance of slave and free states: The Compromise of 1850. California was admitted as a free state, the slave trade was abolished in the District of Columbia, slave-catchers in the North were granted additional rights, and New Mexico and Utah were each to decide their status as slave states by "popular sovereignty," a concept urged by politician and orator Stephen Douglas. Under this doctrine, the inhabitants of each state would vote whether or not to legalize slavery in their own state.

By now, immigrants were flooding into the areas now known as Kansas and Nebraska. As these areas were north of 36 degrees, 30 minutes, the slave states violently objected to their admission as new territories, since they would be closed to slavery. Another desperate compromise was reached by Congress, in 1854, with the Kansas-Nebraska Act. The anti-slavery clause of the Missouri Compromise was abolished and the two new territories were also to decide their slave status by "popular sovereignty." This had the expected result: Pro-slavery and anti-slavery forces rushed settlers into Kansas where, under various labels—such as bushwhacker and jayhawker—they set to murdering one another.

Three years later, the United States Supreme Court in the Dred Scott decision added fuel to the fire by declaring that Congress had no right to exclude slavery from any territory, and that "Negroes were so far inferior that they had no rights which the white man was bound to respect."

The anti-slavery factions were thrown into a frenzy by the political implications of the first part of the decision and into a rage by the moral ramifications of the second. The feelings of free blacks in the North can be imagined. As might be expected, the slave states were overjoyed by this remarkable judicial decision.

Certainly, the forty years of slavery-driven internal crises just described were bad enough, but the slavery issue also directly clouded our diplomatic relations with Haiti, Spain, Brazil and Mexico, not to mention the disgust and repugnance felt by civilized nations, such as France and England, which had long ago abolished slavery. And yet more mischief was set in motion by slavery. The Seminole Wars were fought to prevent the swamps of Florida from being a refuge for escaped slaves; slavery can only exist within closed borders. The vast and totally illegal displacements of Indian tribes from their traditional lands in Georgia and the Carolinas, to the wind-swept miseries of the plains of Oklahoma, were done to make room for plantations, worked by slaves. (It seems only fair to note here that New England skippers had their share in the ocean slave trade, that racism was and is prevalent in the North, that many Union soldiers denounced emancipation, and that the abolitionists had no clear plan for dealing with millions of liberated slaves.)

In addition to the rewriting of history, which attempts to make slavery less important, there is another revision popularized by various "heritage" groups: the assertion that "we just wanted to be left alone with our peculiar institution, and our own unique way of life." Yet the Civil War was far more than just intrusive Yankees marching into the South. The advocates of slavery had labored long and hard, militarily and politically, to extend slavery throughout the United States and into Mexico. The Sibley invasion of New Mexico and Arizona had as its explicit goal the extension of the Confederacy (and slavery) into New Mexico, Arizona, Colorado, California, and two of the northern states of Mexico. One of the objectives of the Confederacy was to impress slavery upon the country from the Atlantic to the Pacific, from the tropics to Canada.

Slavery, in the early 1800s, was spoken of almost apologetically by Southern leaders. By the 1850s, it was widely praised, not as merely economically useful, but as a positive benefit to both slave and master.

Pastors proclaimed from the pulpit that slavery had brought Christianity to the benighted Africans, and that their servitude was based upon Scripture. A common editorial view was that expressed in the Louisville (Kentucky) *Courier-Extra* on August 3, 1861: "The present editor of this paper. . .has never doubted that slavery is a great moral, social and political blessing. . .he has belonged to that school of politics that teaches. . .the divinity of slavery."

The Mississippi secession convention declared that "a blow at slavery is a blow at our commerce and our civilization." Jefferson Davis told the Confederate Congress, "the labor of African slaves was and is indispensable" to the Southern economy. Alexander Hamilton Stephens, vice-president of the Confederate States of America, put the matter even more clearly: "Our new government's foundations are laid, its cornerstone rests, upon the great truth that the Negro is not equal to the white man, that slavery—subordination to the superior race—is his natural and normal condition. The proper status of the negro. . .was the immediate cause of the late rupture and present revolution [the Civil War]."[2] What words could be clearer? What sentiments could more opposite to the principle that every man should have the right to rise? Lincoln and the Confederacy—absolute opposites. As different as night and day, as up and down.

It is hard to escape the conclusion that slavery was the central issue in the United States during Lincoln's lifetime, and that it was directly contrary to his belief that every man had the right to rise. He expressed the relationships of slavery to this central theme at many times and at many places, but perhaps never so perfectly as in his Second Inaugural Address: "It may seem strange that any men should dare to ask a just God's assistance in wringing their bread from the sweat of other man's faces; but let us judge not that we be not judged."

The first phrase of that sentence states clearly that any class of men who are denied the possibility of rising—ever—are certainly excluded from the central tenet of the American dream: the right to receive the fruits of their own labor, and the opportunity to make the best of themselves. The second phrase, which speaks of "judgment," brings us to one of the central themes of Professor Wills and his extraordinary study of the Gettysburg Address. He calls our attention not only to what is in the

Gettysburg Address, but what is not.[3] There is no mention of the Constitution; or of the Confederacy; or of the blue and the gray; or of slavery.

Four score and seven—87 years—brought the listener back to 1776 and the Declaration of Independence, which says in unmistakable terms, that all men are created equal. Four score and seven years ago, our fathers brought forth. . .a new nation. Not just an assembly of states, but a nation. With but a few phrases, Lincoln established (certainly to his own satisfaction and probably to that of most Americans today) the Declaration of Independence as the founding document of our country. The nation, in Lincoln's view, came into being with the Declaration of Independence, not with the Constitution. He saw the Constitution, a document which came much later, as a work in progress, one which would need modification with the changing times and, indeed, such has been the case. And he noticed that the Constitution did not prohibit slavery. The founding fathers never used the "S" word, but referred to slaves as "persons held to service." The reasons for these evasive words, in Lincoln's view, was a sense of shame about slavery, an evil condition which needed to be sugar-coated, glossed over in a euphemism.

Elsewhere, Lincoln had addressed with derision the efforts of the framers of the Constitution as they struggled with the problems of "life, liberty and the pursuit of happiness" (for white people), in order to secure the cooperation of the slave states. He compared the inclusion of slavery in the Constitution to a disease. "The thing is hid away, in the Constitution, just as an afflicted man hides away a wen or a cancer, which he dares not cut out at once, lest he bleed to death; with the promise, nevertheless, that the cutting may begin at the end of a given time."

Thus, in the first section of the Gettysburg Address, Lincoln proposed the Declaration of Independence as the controlling document, with the Constitution as an evolving creation, to be modified as changing times demanded. Then he addressed the "brave men, living and dead, who struggled here. . ." Not just Union men, but all the soldiers who struggled at Gettysburg, stressing again that the United States had continued to be whole; viewing inhabitants of the so-called Confederacy as still citizens of the United States of America, erring at the moment, certainly, but as worthy and brave and as American as those who wore the blue. Lincoln's words specifically avoided creating an "us" and a "them." In the battle monuments erected by the ancient leaders of Assyria, the winner disparaged the losers, portrayed himself as heroic, and the defeated as weak, incompetent, and afraid. At Gettysburg, in Lincoln's words and in his mind, there were no superior men and inferior men—only brave men, brave Americans. Americans all. Every man there.

In the final, monumental paragraph, he addressed the issue of a new dedication, a dedication to "a new birth of freedom." And while he did not say who was to receive this rebirth, it certainly included the former slaves. But not just the slaves. In his writings before the war, Lincoln had many times identified how white working men, North and South, also suffered from slavery, that they were forced into competition with unpaid labor. Lincoln always saw labor as at least equal to capital, espoused the causes of working men on many occasions, white and black working men, and did his best to call to their attention the mutual interests of all working men. This new birth of freedom was to be for any person who chose to better himself.

What is entirely missed in the Lost Cause interpretations of the war is that Lincoln's views offered salvation and redemption not just to the slaves, but to their masters, men unwittingly corrupted and debased by the institution they fought so hard and so bravely to preserve.

And, finally, of course, there is in the Gettysburg Address "of the people, by the people and for the people." Not just white people, not just Union people, but the American people—all of them. Every one of them. In his words, perhaps so familiar now that we do not truly hear them, he issued a call to North and South, a call to create from the ashes of the Civil War a nation where every person would have the right to rise, that the effort and dedication of any man would bring rewards. It should matter not who your parents were or what the color of your skin might be, but all were entitled to an honest wage for honest work, and always, the right to rise.

Lincoln's Gettysburg Address did not mention tactics, strategy, artillery, generals, blood, slavery, or a host of other specifics. Others would do that, and at another place and time, so would Lincoln. Instead, the Gettysburg Address is a statement of principle, a hope for an infinite future, a refinement of concepts, a luminous abstraction that soars above the specific and sordid details of the field of mangled bodies. His words and his concepts lift up like an eagle, above the commonplace, closer to Heaven than to Earth, calling attention to eternal verities, to the finest possibilities of the human spirit, for all men. All men. All women. Everyone. Everywhere. And for all time.

Far below that soaring eagle, whose gaze was fixed at a distant horizon of aspiration and possibility and idealism, were men still deaf to his message of hope.[4] Captain Hilton Graves, commanding the *CSS Morgan*, wrote home around the time of Gettysburg, "Every species of property is selling now at a very high price—Negro men for $1500.00 to $2,000.00, fancy girls [i.e., human sex toys] and women with one or two children at about the same." Days before the fight at Gettysburg, Colonel Henry Burgwyn of the 26th North Carolina urged his father to put every available dollar into slaves: "I would buy boys and girls from 15 to 20 years old and take care to have a majority of girls. The increase in the number of Negroes by this means would repay the difference in the amount of available labor."

Even the defeat at Gettysburg did not deter General James Long-street's capable artillerist, Colonel E. Porter Alexander, who instructed his wife in late July to buy a wet nurse for their twins, "For Carline and her baby would be a fine speculation at $2,000.00."

The eagle, soaring upward, sees out beyond the hills of Pennsylvania, sees distant lands, sees future nations, sees the possibilities of mankind reconciled. Far below, scratching in the earth for the bugs and seeds of mundane, momentary commercial advantage, are those who cannot even see the eagle. "Buy Negroes. . .a fine speculation."

Even the impending collapse of the Confederacy did not deflect its authorities from their prior views. The *Richmond Daily Examiner* of March 15, 1865, published just twenty-four days before the final collapse of the Confederacy and Lee's surrender, and certainly at a time that any man with eyes to see knew that the end was near, announced that "Richard, a slave, for associating and cohabiting with Delia Mack, a white woman," was to receive "one hundred and seventeen lashes, to be well laid on at the whipping post."

This defiance of the locomotive of history, this last grasp at a chance for cruelty, demeaned the South. It was a cruelty of petulance, the last sullen shrug of a naughty boy before being hauled down the corridor to the principal, pulling the remaining wing off a fly. But "Richard" was not a fly, but a man, and that many lashes could be not just painful and humiliating and mutilating, but fatal. This whipping, perhaps the last of the war, was neither noble nor brave—but is worth remembering.

It would seem that Lincoln's words of unity, reconciliation, forgiveness, and opportunity were not to fall on fertile ground.

The Central Idea & the Court-Martials

Lincoln's willingness to pardon or remit has been ascribed to a variety of causes: political expediency, lack of will, excess sentimentality. He said himself of one day's decisions that he simply wished to avoid the "butchering business." But another factor seems to have played a large role: his central concept that every man had the right to rise, to better himself, to have another chance. So often it appears that the President was fully aware of the seriousness of the crime and the justice of the punishment, but entertained the hope of the criminal's redemption, that the reprieved man might have a change of heart, begin a new life, perhaps, one might even say, be born again. The President professed no formal religious affiliation, but are not forgiveness and redemption at the heart of Christianity? Lincoln seemed almost always willing to give a man another opportunity, which is another facet of his central principle: every man is entitled to the opportunity to rise, and its corollary, every man should have his chance. Every man. Every woman. Everyone. Everywhere.

Lincoln at the Millenium

Lincoln's concept of the right to rise was an idea, not a material object. Men can be killed, and objects can be broken, but ideas, if they are good, are hard to destroy. In every country today, however imperfectly formed and however ill-received, the right to rise demonstrates its Endurance and its Universality.

The lonely Chinese youth, confronting a tank in Tiananmen Square, wanted his right to rise. So did the Freedom Riders in the 1960s in the American South. So do the protesters today in the streets of Jakarta, and the brave patriots confronting the gangsters and old Communists of St. Petersburg. The impulse to be free, to benefit from one's own labor, does not just endure, it grows. It is not just in America, it is in Mexico, Brazil, Bosnia. Everywhere. It permeates the consciousness of the world.

The findings described in this study, the new information about Lincoln's decisions in the court-martials, were taken up by the newspapers in Japan and Great Britain and by Voice of America broadcast to French-speaking Central Africa. The Americans who fought fascism in Spain in 1937 are remembered as the Lincoln Brigade. It would seem that the world still cares about Abraham Lincoln.

In America, where we have become complacent about freedom and more concerned for our rights than for our responsibilities, even Lincoln's birthday has disappeared, merged into a vague, generic President's Day, which allows more children and their parents to go skiing. But elsewhere, Lincoln's name is still almost magical. In lands where the struggle to be free is still opposed and often punished, Lincoln is more honored than in his own home. He is honored because of that central principle that every man should have the chance to rise.

His beliefs and his principles are demonstrably universal. Time has shown their endurance. If any man is a candidate for the Man of the Millennium, it is Abraham Lincoln.

NOTES

Introduction

1. General Order No. 6, September 4, 1861, and General Order No. 8, September 8, 1861, National Archives Building, Washington, DC.

2. Roy K. Basler, *The Collected Works of Abraham Lincoln* (Brunswick, 1953), Vol. IV, p. 202.

3. Carl Sandburg, *Abraham Lincoln: The War Years* (New York, 1939), p. 529.

Sandburg was a poet, not a historian. His gripping narrative is rarely buttressed with citations of primary sources.

4. National Archives Record Group 153, Records of the Judge Advocate General's Office (Army), entry 15, Court-martial Case File, file OO209, National Archives Building, Washington, DC, cited as RG 153, OO209. Hereafter, court-martials will be cited as RG 153, followed by the folder number.

Chapter 1: What We Know About Lincoln

1. RG 153, LL1075

2. RG 153, MM1182

3. John G. Nicolay and John M. Hay, *Complete Works of Abraham Lincoln*, 12 vols. (New York, 1905).

4. Gilbert Tracy, *Uncollected Letters of Abraham Lincoln* and *Lincoln Letters at Brown University* (Providence, 1917 and 1927).

5. Paul M. Angle, *New Letters and Papers of Abraham Lincoln*, (Boston, 1930).

6. Mark E. Neely, Jr., *The Abraham Lincoln Encyclopedia* (New York, 1982).

7. Roy P. Basler (Editor), *The Collected Works of Abraham Lincoln* (New Brunswick, 1955).

8. Carl Sandburg, op. cit., p. 521. Once again, Sandburg's touching story is hard to verify.

9. David C. Mearns, *The Lincoln Papers* (Garden City, 1948).

10. Robert V. Bruce, *Lincoln and the Tools of War* (Urbana, 1989).

11. Mark E. Neely, Jr., *The Fate of Liberty – Abraham Lincoln and Civil Liberties* (New York, 1991).

12. Harold Holzer, *Dear Mr. Lincoln* (Reading, 1993).

13. Michael Burlingame, *The Inner World of Abraham Lincoln* (Urbana, 1994).

14. David H. Donald, *Abraham Lincoln* (New York, 1995).

15. Michael Burlingame, *An Oral History of Abraham Lincoln – John G. Nicolay's Interviews and Essays* (Carbondale, 1996).

16. It should be noted that Basler hints at the material presented here. As an example, in Volume VIII, page 549, under "August 9," he mentions "ten routine endorsements," and gives a folder number. Since a folder can contain up to fifty trials, and Basler gives no names in this compilation, it is our opinion that such persons can reasonably be considered "uncatalogued."

Chapter 2: The Court-martial Path

1. Anonymous, *Revised Regulations for the Army of the United States – 1861* (Philadelphia, 1862)

2. Mark E. Neeley, Jr., *Encyclopedia* op. cit., p. 61.

3. Lloyd A. Dunlap, "White House Routine Under Lincoln," in Ralph G. Newman (Editor), *Lincoln for the Ages* (Garden City, 1960).

4. Neely, op. cit., p. 291.

5. Neely, op. cit., p. 220.

6. Michael Burlingame, *Oral History,* p. 68.

Chapter 3: Generals, Colonels, Majors & Captains

1. RG 153, MM1367.

2. RG 153, MM682.

3. RG 153, MM118.

4. RG 153, MM262.

5. RG 153, MM1347, folder 2.

6. RG 153, II706.

7. RG 153, MM1352.

8. RG 153, MM1053.

9. RG 153, LL75.

10. RG 153, MM144.

11. RG 153, MM376

12. RG 153, LL12.

13. RG 153, MM999.

14. RG 153, KK205.
15. RG 153, MM651.
16. RG 153, LL1635.
17. RG 153, MM198.
18. RG 153, KK371.
19. RG 153, MM1208.
20. RG 153, LL2253.
21. RG 153, MM 782.
22. RG 153, MM918.
23. RG 153, MM921.
24. RG 153, MM403.
25. RG 153, II705.
26. RG 153, MM112.
27. RG 153, KK376.
28. RG 153, MM807.
29. RG 153, MM1387.
30. RG 153, MM1014.
31. RG 153, LL2161.
32. RG 153, MM1460.
33. RG 153, KK506.
34. RG 153, LL877, folders 1 and 2.
35. RG 153, MM87.
36. RG 153, MM421.
37. RG 153, MM143.
38. RG 153, MM234.
39. RG 153, MM645.
40. RG 153, MM881.
41. RG 153, MM667.
42. RG 153, LL1738, LL1744 and MM1390.
43. RG 153, MM1213.
44. RG 153, MM1002.
45. RG 153, MM1319.
46. RG 153, MM396.
47. RG 153, MM397.
48. RG 153, MM398.
49. RG 153, MM268.
50. RG 153, LL204.
51. RG 153, MM278.
52. RG 153, MM571.
53. RG 153, MM165.
54. RG 153, MM890.
55. RG 153, MM831.

56. RG 153, MM1214.
57. RG 153, LL1366 and LL1363.

Chapter 4: Lieutenants, Chaplains & Surgeons

1. RG 153, MM919.
2. RG 153, MM186.
3. RG 153, MM117.
4. RG 153, MM113.
5. RG 153, MM402.
6. RG 153, KK506, KK507.
7. RG 153, MM1205.
8. RG 153, MM744.
9. RG 153, LL847, LL852, MM920.
10. RG 153, LL847, LL852, MM920.
11. RG 153, MM159.
12. RG 153, LL852, MM794.
13. RG 153, MM187.
14. RG 153, MM1296.
15. RG 153, MM1130.
16. RG 153, LL1812.
17. RG 153, MM1025.
18. RG 153, MM988.
19. RG 153, MM1026.
20. RG 153, MM668.
21. RG 153, MM1131.
22. RG 153, MM162.
23. RG 153, MM810.
24. RG 153, MM104.
25. RG 153, MM669.
26. RG 153, MM904.
27. RG 153, MM407.
28. RG 153, LL75.
29. RG 153, MM1237.
30. RG 153, MM450.
31. RG 153, MM111, MM156.
32. RG 153, MM957.
33. RG 153, MM192.
34. RG 153, MM833.
35. RG 153, MM874, MM901.
36. RG 153, MM1054.

37. RG 153, MM766, MM1042.

38. RG 153, MM492.

39. RG 153, MM1062.

40. RG 153, MM307.

41. RG 153, MM765.

42. RG 153, MM267.

43. RG 153, MM219.

44. RG 153, MM878, MM1317.

45. RG 153, MM760.

46. RG 153, LL75.

47. RG 153, MM269.

48. RG 153, MM646.

49. RG 153, MM146.

50. RG 153, MM662.

51. RG 153, MM982.

52. RG 153, LL866.

53. RG 153, MM1086.

54. RG 153, MM1035.

55. RG 153, KK535.

56. RG 153, MM364.

57. RG 153, LL204.

58. RG 153, MM280.

59. RG 153, KK680.

60. RG 153, MM222, folder 2.

61. RG 153, MM494.

62. RG 153, MM864.

63. RG 153, MM111.

64. RG 153, MM1133.

65. RG 153, MM759.

66. RG 153, MM70.

67. RG 153, KK280.

68. RG 153, MM1307.

69. RG 153, MM1232.

70. RG 153, II528.

71. RG 153, KK248.

72. RG 153, MM1293.

73. RG 153, MM1137, MM1176.

74. RG 153, MM167.

Chapter 5: Deserters 1861-1862

1. Neely, *The Fate of Liberty*, p. 128.
2. Ella Lonn, *Desertion During the Civil War* (New York, 1928) pp. 21-37.
3. RG 153, MM271.
4. RG 153, MM298.
5. RG 153, LL4.
6. RG 153, MM533.
7. RG 153, MM541.
8. RG 153, MM555.
9. RG 153, MM254.
10. RG 153, MM239.
11. RG 153, MM531.
12. RG 153, MM570.
13. RG 153, MM562.
14. RG 153, MM99.
15. RG 153, MM777.

Chapter 6: Deserters January 1863 through March 1863

1. RG 153, KK716, folders 1 and 2.
2. RG 153, LL428.
3. RG 153, MM123.
4. RG 153, MM123.
5. RG 153, MM535.
6. RG 153, MM365.
7. RG 153, MM164.
8. RG 153, MM563.
9. RG 153, MM265.
10. RG 153, MM552.
11. RG 153, MM561.
12. RG 153, MM561.
13. RG 153, MM561.
14. RG 153, MM552.
15. RG 153, MM561.
16. RG 153, MM561.
17. RG 153, MM552.
18. RG 153, MM561.
19. RG 153, MM123.
20. RG 153, MM107.
21. RG 153, MM569.

22. RG 153, MM566.

23.RG 153, MM549.

24. RG 153, MM564.

25. RG 153, MM560.

26. RG 153, MM551.

27. RG 153, LL 296.

28. RG 153, KK662.

29. RG 153, KK662.

30. RG 153, MM537.

31. RG 153, MM548.

32. RG 153, MM374.

33. RG 153, MM246.

34. RG 153, MM247.

35. RG 153, MM527.

36. RG 153, MM240.

37. RG 153, MM529.

38. RG 153, MM244.

39. RG 153, MM528.

40. RG 153, MM532.

41. RG 153, MM530.

42. RG 153, MM534.

43. RG 153, MM995.

44. RG 153, MM802.

45. RG 153, MM572; RG 153, MM573.

46. RG 153, MM572.

47. RG 153, MM552.

48. RG 153, MM572; RG 153, MM538.

49. RG 153, MM572.

50. RG 153, MM573.

51. RG 153, MM573.

52. RG 153, MM572.

53. RG 153, MM573.

54. RG 153, MM550.

55. RG 153, MM547.

56. RG 153, MM539; RG 153, MM565.

57. RG 153, MM242; RG 153, MM249.

58. RG 153, MM255.

59. RG 153, MM245; RG 153, MM236.

60. RG 153, MM237.

61. RG 153, MM252.

62. RG 153, MM251.

63. RG 153, MM248.

64. RG 153, MM114.
65. RG 153, MM116.
66. RG 153, MM250.
67. RG153, MM559.
68. RG 153, MM96.
69. RG 153, LL218.
70. RG 153, MM420.
71. RG 153, MM238
72. RG 153, MM526.
73. RG 153, MM253.
74. RG 153, MM554.
75. RG 153, MM525; RG 153, MM568.
76. RG 153, MM536.
77. RG 153, MM102.
78. RG 153, MM102.
79. RG 153, MM102.
80. RG 153, MM132.
81. RG 153, MM347.
82. RG 153, MM243.
83. RG 153, MM300.
84. RG 153, MM331.

Chapter 7: Deserters April 1863 through April 1865

1. RG 153, LL422.
2. RG 153, LL545.
3. RG 153, MM230.
4. RG 153, MM791.
5. RG 153, MM775.
6. RG 153, LL529.
7. RG 153, MM235.
8. RG 153, MM231.
9. RG 153, MM545. All seven men are in one folder.
10. RG 153, MM284.
11. RG 153, MM721.
12. RG 153, MM797.
13. RG 153, MM229.
14. RG 153, MM191.
15. RG 153, LL551.
16. RG 153, MM972.
17. RG 153, LL589, folder 2.

18. RG 153, MM803.

19. RG 153, MM761.

20. RG 153, MM1019.

21. RG 153, MM843.

22. RG 153, MM832.

23. RG 153, MM769.

24. RG 153, MM818.

25. RG 153, MM837. Both men are in the same folder.

26. RG 153, MM1009.

27. RG 153, LL832.

28. RG 153, MM997.

29. RG 153, MM841.

30. RG 153, MM726.

31. RG 153, MM1168.

32. RG 153, MM1174.

33. RG 153, MM939.

34. RG 153, MM970; RG 153, MM969.

35. RG 153, MM973.

36. RG 153, MM1173.

37. RG 153, MM1151.

38. RG 153, MM1152.

39. RG 153, MM1043.

40. RG 153, MM1010.

41. RG 153, MM1132.

42. RG 153, MM1203.

43. RG 153, MM1215.

44. RG 153, LL1037.

45. RG 153, LL1024.

46. RG 153, MM1215.

47. RG 153, MM949.

48. RG 153, MM1222.

49. RG 153, LL1417.

50. RG 153, LL1584, folder 2.

51. RG 153, LL1508, folder 2.

52. RG 153, LL1524.

53. RG 153, MM1359.

54. RG 153, LL2709.

55. RG 153, LL1844.

56. RG 153, LL1763.

57. RG 153, LL1932.

58. RG 153, LL1809.

59. RG 153, MM1689.

60. RG 153, LL2411.
61. RG 153, LL2626.
62. RG 153, LL2744, folder 1.
63. RG 153, LL2575.
64. RG 153, LL2682, folder 1.
65. RG 153, LL2832.
66. Shelby Foote, *The Civil War: A Narrative*, vol. 3 (New York, 1974), p. 771.
67. RG 153, LL2832.
68. RG 153, LL2910, LL2911.
69. RG 153, MM241.
70. RG 153, LL2832.
71. RG 153, LL2977.

Chapter 8: Mutiny and Violence to Officers

1. RG 153, MM65.
2. RG 153, MM90.
3. RG 153, KK559, KK539.
4. RG 153, MM105.
5. RG 153, MM142.
6. RG 153, MM103.
7. RG 153, MM145.
8. RG 153, MM166.
9. RG 153, KK288.
10. RG 153, KK290.
11. RG 153, MM163.
12. RG 153, MM188.
13. RG 153, MM189.
14. RG 153, MM777.
15. RG 153, MM373.
16. RG 153, MM334.
17. RG 153, MM672.
18. RG 153, MM301.
19. RG 153, MM303
20. RG 153, MM1067.
21. RG 153, MM302.
22. RG 153, LL322.
23. RG 153, MM971.
24. RG 153, LL422, folder 1.
25. RG 153, MM489.
26. RG 153, MM91.

27. RG 153, MM659.
28. RG 153, MM983.
29. RG 153, MM233.
30. RG 153, MM1137.
31. RG 153, MM998.
32. RG 153, MM856.
33. RG 153, MM663.
34. RG 153, MM573.
35. RG 153, MM68.
36. RG 153, MM1076.
37. RG 153, MM1083.
38. RG 153, MM822.
39. RG 153, LL2670.
40. RG 153, LL1523.
41. RG 153, LL2679, folder 1.
42. RG 153, LL2679, folder 1.
43. RG 153, LL1265, LL1266.
44. RG 153, MM1442.
45. RG 153, MM1447.
46. RG 153, MM1324.
47. RG 153, LL2044.
48. RG 153, LL3219, folder 1.
49. RG 153, LL2059.
50. RG 153, MM1479.
51. William C. Davis, *Lincoln's Men* (New York, 1999), p. 173.

Chapter 9: Murderers

1. RG 153, II822.
2. RG 153, LL254.
3. RG 153, KK435.
4. RG 153, LL2.
5. RG 153, MM323.
6. RG 153, MM762.
7. RG 153, MM825.
8. RG 153, MM952.
9. RG 153, MM1395.
10. RG 153, MM954.
11. RG 153, MM394.
12. RG 153, MM1138.
13. RG 153, LL2255.

14. RG 153, MM1331.
15. RG 153, MM1440.
16. RG 153, LL1489.

Chapter 10: Confederate Recruiters, Spies & Soldiers

1. RG 153, MM77.
2. RG 153, MM1003.
3. RG 153, MM1005, MM1016.
4. RG 153, MM77.
5. RG 153, MM917.
6. RG 153, MM990.
7. RG 153, MM128.
8. RG 153, MM1031.
9. RG 153, MM680.
10. RG 153, MM1092.
11. RG 153, MM993.
12. RG 153, MM1058.
13. RG 153, MM672.
14. RG 153, MM1006.
15. RG 153, MM944.
16. RG 153, MM1008.
17. RG 153, MM943.
18. RG 153, MM1109.
19. RG 153, MM1016.
20. RG 153, MM978.
21. RG 153, MM681.
22. RG 153, MM1029.
23. RG 153, MM1340.
24. RG 153, MM1298.
25. RG 153, MM1024.
26. RG 153, MM1136.
27. RG 153, MM1254.
28. RG 153, MM1384.
29. RG 153, MM1386.
30. RG 153, MM1149.
31. RG 153, MM1030.
32. RG 153, MM161.
33. RG 153, MM556.
34. RG 153, MM1128.
35. RG 153, MM962.
36. RG 153, MM1148.

37. RG 153, MM1013.

38. RG 153, LL713.

39. RG 153, MM1408.

40. RG 153, MM946.

41. RG 153, MM1057.

42. RG 153, MM100.

43. RG 153, MM1457.

44. RG 153, MM1142.

45. RG 153, MM149; RG 153, MM147; RG 153, MM148.

46. RG 153, MM1332.

Chapter 11: Missouri Spies & Bushwhackers

1. RG 153, LL1756, LL1791, MM1289.

2. RG 153, MM1309.

3. RG 153, MM1302.

4. RG 153, MM1017; RG 153, MM1012.

5. RG 153, MM1381.

6. RG 153, MM632.

7. RG 153, MM517.

8. RG 153, MM136.

9. RG 153, MM1020.

10. RG 153, MM1258.

11. RG 153, MM125.

12. RG 153, MM1000.

13. RG 153, MM671.

14. RG 153, MM353.

15. RG 153, MM127.

16. RG 153, MM1303.

17. RG 153, MM1300.

18. RG 153, MM749.

19. RG 153, MM996.

20. RG 153, MM1185.

21. RG 153, MM137.

22. RG 153, MM1032.

23. RG 153, MM1184.

24. RG 153, MM1021.

25. RG 153, MM1185.

26. RG 153, MM155.

27. RG 153, LL2944.

28. RG 153, MM518.

Chapter 12: A Potpourri of Military Commissions

1. RG 153, LL2067, folders 1, 2, and 3.
2. RG 153, KK520.
3. RG 153, MM1072.
4. RG 153, LL2953.
5. RG 153, LL2699.
6. RG 153, MM1028.
7. RG 153, MM1038.
8. RG 153, MM158.
9. RG 153, MM1406.
10. RG 153, MM1407.
11. RG 153, MM94.
12. RG 153, MM557.
13. RG 153, MM1329.
14. RG 153, MM751.
15. RG 153, MM1431.
16. RG 153, MM1204, MM1206.
17. RG 153, MM1270.
18. RG 153, MM1192.

Chapter 13: Thieves & Robbers

1. RG 153, LL2872.
2. RG 153, MM834.
3. RG 153, MM1261.
4. RG 153, MM1267.
5. RG 153, MM1289.
6. RG 153, MM160.
7. RG 153, MM1198.
8. RG 153, MM924.
9. RG 153, MM923.
10. RG 153, MM1065.
11. RG 153, MM1322.
12. RG 153, MM941.
13. RG 153, MM937.
14. RG 153, LL2586.
15. RG 153, MM1357.
16. RG 153, MM1301.
17. RG 153, MM930.
18. RG 153, MM115.

19. RG 153, LL1554, folder 2.
20. RG 153, MM126.
21. RG 153, MM139.
22. RG 153, LL1527.
23. RG 153, MM951.

Chapter 14: More Sleeping Sentinels

1. RG 153, MM567.
2. RG 153, MM991.
3. RG 153, MM219.
4. RG 153, MM1234.
5. RG 153, MM1428.
6. RG 153, MM520.
7. RG 153, MM1239, MM1424.
8. RG 153, MM852.
9. RG 153, MM1227.
10. RG 153, MM1228.
11. RG 153, MM276.
12. RG 153, LL3186.
13. RG 153, LL2508.
14. RG 153, MM947.
15. RG 153, MM735.
16. RG 153, MM97.
17. RG 153, MM163.
18. RG 153, MM793.
19. RG 153, MM232.
20. RG 153, LL1296, folder 2.
21. RG 153, MM228.
22. RG 153, LL2050.
23. RG 153, MM98.

Chapter 15: Rapists & Miscellaneous Miscreants

1. RG 153, MM1444.
2. RG 153, MM138.
3. RG 153, MM940.
4. RG 153, MM150.
5. RG 153, MM766.
6. RG 153, NN751.
7. William C. Davis, *Lincoln's Men*, p. 181.

8. RG 153, MM992.

9. RG 153, MM1197.

10. RG 153, MM860.

11. RG 153, MM846.

12. RG 153, MM844.

13. RG 153, MM335.

14. RG 153, LL1500, LL1501.

15. RG 153, MM123.

16. RG 153, LL2156.

17. RG 153, LL1557.

18. RG 153, LL1825, LL1827.

19. RG 153, MM95.

20. RG 153, MM216.

21. RG 153, II751.

22. Record Group 94, Entry 409, File Ppr-793 (EB) 1864, National Archives, Washington, DC, courtesy of Michael P. Musick.

Chapter 16: The Statistics of Compassion

1. Rufus R. Wilson, *Lincoln in Caricature* (New York, 1953).

2. William C. Davis, *Lincoln's Men*.

Chapter 17: Lincoln at the Millenium

1. Gabor S. Boritt, *Lincoln and the Economics of the American Dream* (Urbana, 1978).

2. Gary W. Gallagher, "Dollars & Cents, Black & White," *Civil War*, February 1999, p. 8.

3. Gary Wills, *Lincoln at Gettysburg* (New York, 1992).

4. James M. McPherson, *For Cause and Comrade: Why Men Fought the Civil War* (New York, 1997), p. 108.

Bibliography

Almost all of the information contained in this book is taken from thousands of pages of original transcripts of the Union Army general court-martials during the Civil War. The additional bibliographic refererences below assisted in rounding out the tale.

MANUSCRIPTS

Record Group 153, National Archives, Washington, DC. Original transcripts of the Union Army general court-martials during the Civil War.

BOOKS

Boritt, Gabor S. *Lincoln and the Economics of the American Dream*. Urbana: The Uni versity of Illinois Press, 1978.

Davis, William C. *Lincoln's Men*. New York: The Free Press, 1999.

Foote, Shelby *The Civil War: A Narrative*. New York, Random House, 1974.

Long, E. B. *The Civil War Day by Day*. New York, Da Capo Press, 1971.

Lonn, Ella *Desertion During the Civil War*. New York, Century, 1928.

McPherson, James M. *For Cause and Comrades: Why Men Fought the Civil War*. New York, Oxford University Press, 1997.

Wills, Gary *Lincoln at Gettysburg*. New York, Simon & Shuster, 1992.

Wilson, Rufus R. *Lincoln in Caricature*. New York, Horizon Press, 1953.

ARTICLES

Gallagher, Gary W. "Dollars & Cents, Black & White," *Civil War*, February 1999.

INDEX

Abear, Lewis, 99

Abercrombie, Brig. Gen. John, 50, 60

Abingdon, Confederate District of, 185

Acker, First Lt. John, 63

Adams Express, 229

Adams, Henry, 106

Adams, Martin, 209

Advena, Joseph, 132

Albany NY, 227

Albany State Prison NY, 39, 248, 250

Albertson, David, 105

Albertson, Martin, 99

Albright, Mr., 194

Alcatraz Island CA, 169

Aldie VA, 32

Alexander, Col. E. Porter, 276

Alexandria VA, 89, 92, 101, 103, 119, 228

Algiers LA, 36

Allegheny County Prison PA, 222

Alton Prison IL, 154

Amnesty proclamations, 88, 91, 92, 96, 97, 98, 99, 100, 101, 102, 103, 105, 108, 110, 116, 117, 119, 159, 200

Anderson, James, 209

Andrew County MO, 204

Andrews, Daniel, 115

Andrews, William, 192

Angell, William, 103

Annapolis, MD, 124, 131

Antietam, MD, 71, 91, 97, 99, 102, 103, 105, 106, 108, 118, 122, 139

Appomattox VA, 270

Aquia Creek, VA, 98, 107

Armstrong, Pvt. Joseph, 252

Armstrong, Pvt. Milton, 243

Army of the Potomac, 35, 72

Aroostook War, 93

Arthur, Capt. Charles, 35

Articles of War, 10, 144, 227. Article 1, 85; Article 4, 108; Article 5, 258; Article 6, 144; Article 7, 144; Article 8, 144; Article 9, 144, 149, 159, 165; Article 15, 45; Article 20, 85; Article 39, 77; Article 45, 45, 71; Article 46, 238; Article 64, 10; Article 65, 10, 235; Article 75, 10; Article 89, 31, 38

Ashland, KY, 110

Atchafayala Bayou, LA, 238

Atlanta, GA, 117

Auburn, VA, 35

Aughenbaugh, William, 129

Axtell, Maj. Nathan G., 82

Ayres, Brig. Gen Romeyn, 26, 61, 165, 228

Ayres, Lemuel, 196, 197

Babbett, Robert, 93

Babbitt, Pvt. Robert, 151

Baker, John, 101

Balis, Charles, 228

Baltimore MD, 37, 221, 251

Bamberge, William, 189

Bank's Ford, VA, 91

Banks, Maj. Gen. Nathaniel, 28, 36, 37, 58, 60, 66, 67, 68, 74, 80, 102, 127, 176, 239, 241

Bans, Pvt. Andrew, 122
Barber, First Lt. Thomas, 63
Bardstown, KY, 64, 124
Barker, Second Lt. James, 72
Barry County, MO, 205
Barry, Jesse, 228
Bartee, Andrew, 194
Barth, Pvt. Jacob, 122, 123
Bartman, Robert, 124, 125
Basler, Roy P. *Collected Works of
    Abraham Lincoln*, 3, 19, 20,
    186, 201, 225, 245
Bates, Edward, 13
Batesville, AR, 165
Baton Rouge, LA, 67
Battery Wagner, SC, 56
Bealton Station, VA, 165
Bean, George, 106
Beard, Capt., 206
Beatty, Edgar, 97
Beaufort SC, 41, 153
Beaver Creek KS, 72
Behan, Capt. John H., 43,44
Bell, Maj. William, 158
Belle Plain Landing VA, 109
Benham, Lt., 74
Benning, Pvt. Charles, 165
Benson, Cpl. James, 127
Bent, Pvt. George, 92
Bentonville, NC, 136
Bergemeyer, Henry, 127
Berrian, Patrick, 123, 124
Berry, Capt. Milton, 46
Berry, Gen. Hiram, 103, 106, 107
Betts, Samuel, 200
Beverly Ford, VA, 67, 240
Big Pine Railroad Bridge, MO,
    127
Big Springs TN, 68
Bills, Ezra, 248
Birch Coolie MN, 170

Birney, Brig. Gen. David, 51, 101
Bishop, James, 237
Black, Alexander, 195
Black Hawk War, 166
Black River, MS, 179
Bladensburg, MD, 92
Blair, Francis P., 136
Blair, Francis Preston, Sr., 139
Blair, Joseph, 246
Blanchard, Frederick, 116
Bledsoe County TN, 192
Bliss, Surgeon D.W., 255
Blunt, Pvt. William (also Blount),
    239
Boirs, Charles H. (also Boyce and
    Boyers), 125, 126
Bolivar Heights, VA, 72, 231
Boone County, MO, 207
Booth, John Wilkes, 70, 115, 136,
    158
Borden, First Lt. John H., 56
Boreman, Arthur I., 166
Boston, MA, 105
Bowen, Dr. Ardius, 157
Bowling Green, KY, 162
Bowling Green, OH, 62
Boyd, Pvt. John, 120
Boyd, Pvt. Thomas, 227
Boyer, Cpl. John M., 252
Boylan, Pvt. Thomas, 152
Boyle, Brig. Gen Jeremiah, 79
Boyle, William T., 152
Brabbon, Anthony, 109
Brackenridge, Thomas, 220
Bradley, Pvt. Sterling, 164
Brady, John, 251
Braffit, Sgt. Charles, 145, 146
Bragg, Gen. Braxton, 89, 124, 126
Bragg, Second Lt. William F., 71, 72
Brandingham, Pvt. Edward, 174
Brandy Station, VA, 110

Brannan, Brig, Gen. John, 41, 57
Brant, William, 103
Brawner, Second Lt. Joseph H.,
   73, 74
Breitenbach, Capt. John R., 49
Brentwood, TN, 78
Brewster, Capt. John A., 47
Briggs, Second Lt. William J., 71
Brink, Ixes, 248
Bristley, Frederick, 128
Britton, Pvt. John, 231
Brockett, Pvt. Justus, 119
Brockway, Lt. C.B., 161
Brook Station, VA, 106
Brookhaven, MS, 110
Brooks, Cpl. Albert, 252
Brooks, Kate, 247
Brown, Mrs. Alvisa, 248
Brown, Gen. Egbert, 46, 206,
   207, 209
Brown, Ellen, 248
Brown, Nicholas, 248
Brown, Col. Philip, 117, 118
Brown, W.G., 136
Brown, Pvt. William, 250
Brown, Pvt. William H., 105
Brundridge, Charles, 110
Bryant, Thomas, 189
Buchanan, President John, 12
Buel, Sylvester, 91
Bull Run, VA, 24, 71 ,92, 104,
   124
Burgwyn, Col. Henry, 276
Burnell, James, 124
Burnside, Maj. Gen. Ambrose,
   31, 35, 63, 64, 91, 97, 110,
   115, 120, 121, 129, 155, 185,
   269
Butler, Maj. Gen. Benjamin, 34,
   132, 134, 152, 162, 199
Butler, John, 170

Butler, Lt. LaFayette, 79
Butler, Luther, 130, 131
Butler, Pvt. Bradford, 117, 118
Butterfield, Brig. Gen. Daniel, 147
Buzzell, Dr. A. J., 43

Cabin Creek, Indian Territory, 137
Cahawba, 60
Cahill, Lt. Edward, 166
Caldwell, Capt. F.M, 50
Caldwell, George, 204
Caldwell, Thomas, 206, 207
Calhoun, MO, 39
Camp Berry, ME, 129
Camp Big Springs, MS, 117
Camp Cook Dakota Territory, 157
Camp Hamilton, VA, 170, 229
Camp Parole, MD, 225
Camp Piatt, WV, 135
Camp Relief DC, 148
Camp Rufus King, 107
Camp, William, 128, 129
Campbell, Charles, 106
Campbell, Pvt. John, 176
Campbell, Robert, 130
Campbell County KY, 185
Canby, Brig. Gen Edward, 62, 126,
   128
Canby, Charles, 177
Cape Girardeau, MO, 231
Capron, Henry, 132
Carleton, Brig. Gen. James, 90, 93,
   239
Carnes, Henry C., 150
Carney, Richard, 194
Carney, Wright, 194
Carpenter, Pvt. George, 117, 118
Carrigan, Pvt. John, 169
Carrion Crow Bayou LA, 80
Carson, Joseph, 253
Carthage, TN, 69

Casey, George, 189
Cass County, MO, 204
Castleberry, George W., 104
Castor River, MO, 110
Catlettsburg, KY, 110, 129
Cavada, Lt. Col. Frederick F., 31
Cedar Mountain, VA, 35
Central City, CO, 96
Chain Bridge, VA, v
Chalk Bluff, AR, 175
Chalmers, Capt. George B., 50, 51
Chamberlain, Joshua Lawrence, 43
Chamberlain, T. D., 129
Chamberlain, Thomas, 229
Chambersberg, PA, 111
Champion, Mr., 250
Chancellor, Pvt. James, 166
Chancellorsville, VA, 25, 123, 252
Chantilly, VA, 66
Chaplin Hills, KY, 49
Chapman, William, 99
Charles Osgood, 226
Charleston, SC, 98, 111, 115, 121
Chase, John A., 159
Chase, Salmon P, 56, 162
Chattanooga, TN, 62, 81, 82, 130
Chatten, John, 165, 166
Cheek, Capt. Christopher, 48
Christie, Richard C., 82
Cincinnati, OH, 122, 162
City Point, VA, 240
Clark, Second Lt. James, 71
Clarksville, TN, 63, 193, 194
Clawson, First Lt. Phineas, 66
Clear Creek, MS, 163
Cleary, Lance Cpl. John, 109
Cleburne, Gen. Patrick, 269
Clifford, Charles, 187

Clifford, George E., 129
Clifton, Pvt. Thomas, 90
Clinton, Capt., 62
Clokey, Emma, 227
Cobb, William, 128
Cockrill, Nathaniel, 177
Coffee County, TN, 196
Cole, Joseph, 110
Cole, Lt. John P., 78
Cole, Pvt. William H., 248
Coleman, Mr., 186
Colerick, Second Lt. William, 70
Collins, Cornelius, 172
Columbia, SC, 190
Columbus, KY, 146
Conant, Capt. Cardinal, 42, 43
Conant, Pvt. Daniel, 225
Concord, NH, 129
Confederate Troops: Arkansas, 3d Infantry, 199; Black Horse Cavalry, 91; Bolin's Band of Bush whackers, 203; Braxton Bragg's Army, 192; Burbridge's Regiment, 190; Colonel Clark's Command, 197; Colonel Green's Regiment, 188; Colonel Mitchell's Regiment of Guerillas, 189; Dunbar's Horse, 197; Green's Regiment, 208; Hughes Band, 199; Jackman's Independent Partisan Regiment, 185; Kentucky 5th Infantry, 115; Kitchen's band of horse thieves, 204; Louisiana Crescent City Regiment, 199; Major Livingston's Company, 191; Missouri, 2d Cavalry, 190; Missouri, 3d Cavalry, 188; Missouri, 5th Infantry, 220; Missouri, Captain Powell's Company, 191; Missouri Infantry, Stein's Regiment, 188; North Carolina 26th, 276;

Pickett's Regiment, 189; Porter's Command, 207; Tennessee 20th Infantry, 192; Thornton's band of horse thieves, 210; Virginia, 4th Cavalry, 91; Wick's Band of Outlaws, 191
Conklin, Second Lt. Alfred, 69
Conner, Pvt. Gilbert W., 165
Connolly, Henry, 126, 127
Conzet, Second Lt. Charles, 110
Cook, John F., 208
Cook, Lt. Col. Henry A., 29
Cooper, Pvt. Richard, 180
Corbin, Sgt. William, 185
Corcoran, Col. Michael, 23, 24, 25, 27
Corinth, MS, 62, 104, 145, 154, 190, 199, 235
Cothran, Capt. George W., 37, 38
Cotter, Capt. Owen, 37
Couch, Maj. Gen Darius, 56, 60, 61, 75, 180
Court martials of officers, 10, 20, 23-84
Covert, Pvt. A.B., 241
Covington, KY, 160
Cox, Brig. Gen. Jacob D., 237
Cox, Pvt. William T., 245
Cozad, Lt. David, 162
Crab Orchard KY, 63
Craig, Brig. Gen James, 219, 241
Creardon, Pvt. John, 159
Crim, Smith, 205
Crittenden County, AR, 214
Crittenden, L.E., ix
Crokers, Mr., 201
Crossman, First Lt. George, 62
Crystal Springs, MS, 93
Culpeper, VA, 69, 174 , 223, 249
Cumberland Gap, WV, 115
Cumberland, MD, 116

Cumberland River TN, 198
Cunningham, John, 106
Currier, Edward, 106
Currituck County, NC, 216
Curry, Lt., 198
Curtin, Andrew, 111, 121, 141
Curtis, Lt. Henry R., 79
Curtis, Maj. Gen. Samuel, 77, 207, 232, 246
Cushman, First L.. Richard, 66
Custer, Gen. George A., 136, 141

D'Utassy, Col. Frederick G., 27, 28
Dade County, MO, 206
Daly, Hon. M., 157
Dana, Maj. Gen. Napoleon Tecum seh Jackson, 66, 238, 239
Daniels, Lloyd, 188
Danville, KY, 129
Davidson, Gen. John, 76, 175
Davis, Pvt. Charles, 164
Davis, Jefferson, 70, 75, 123, 135, 139, 154, 269, 273
Davis, John, 197
Davis, Pvt. John, 90
Dawes, Congressman Henry L., 39
Dawson, James B., 222
de la Croix, Louis (also Louis Robert, Dennis Robert, Louis Leon), 95, 96
Decherd TN, 45, 149, 241
Deck Bridge, MO, 187
Deep Run, VA, 110
Deming, Henry, 137
Dent County, MO, 32
Dessyn, Ludwig, 158
Detroit, MI, 166
Dever, Capt. John, 198
Dewitt County, IL, 179
Dickson County, TN, 198
Dilks, James, 107

Dillard's Farm, NC, 152
District of Columbia Peniten
    tiary, 232
Dix, Maj. Gen. John, 62, 77, 79,
    91, 115, 128, 129, 130, 131,
    153, 170, 172
Dixon County, TN, 194
Dodge, Gen. Grenville, 122
Dodge, Pvt. Sherman, 230
Dodge, William, 117
Dodson, James, 196, 197
Dolan, James, 147
Doneho, John, 99
Dormody, Pvt. William, 170,
    171, 172
Dorris, John, 108
Doss, First Lt. T.F., 4
Dougherty, Gabriel, 24
Drake, William, 116
Draper, Capt. Joseph, 254
Drummer, Hospital Steward
    Charles A., 169
Dry Tortugas, 4, 39, 87, 88, 96,
    121, 125, 132, 148, 155, 237,
    238, 240, 242, 243
Dubois, Henry, 101
Duck River, TN, 232
Dudley, Capt. T.R., 0, 41
Duffy, Michael, 153
Dugan, Pierre, 221
Dunklin County, MO, 203, 204
Dunn, Henry, 9
Dunn, Pvt Joseph, 163
Dunning, Theodore, 0
Durnin, William, 107

Early, Lt. Gen. Jubal, 62, 164,
    243
Eberhardt, Capt. Conrad, 51
Eddy, First Lt. Adelbert, 60
Egan, Capt. William P., 48

Egan, Lt. Michael J., 77
El Paso, TX, 90
Elizabethtown, KY, 45, 124
Elk Run, VA, 35
Eller, John, 205
Elliott, Pvt. William, 138
Elliott, Pvt. William, 247
Emancipation Proclamation, 23, 68,
    214
Englehart, Joseph, 207
Entler, Mr., 201
Erskine, Lt. Albert, 77
Estep, Henry, 115
Etherly, Alfred, 196
Evans, John, 150
Evans, Mathew, 150
Ewing, Cpl. Samuel, 232, 233

Fagan, Reuben, 107
Fair Oaks, VA, 106, 130
Fairfax County Court House, VA, 66
Fairfax Station, VA, 100
Fairmont, WV, 110
Falls Church, VA, 82
Falmouth, VA, 38, 56, 67, 75, 82, 92,
    97, 99, 102, 103, 105, 106, 110,
    226, 242
Faribault, David, 170
Farmington, MO, 178, 189
Fasha, Capt. Edward, 45
Fayetteville, VA, 116
Federal Troops: U.S. 2d. Cavalry, 74;
    3d Cavalry, 40; 6th Cavalry, 174;
    4th Infantry, 98, 99; 6th, 99, 169;
    7th, 99; 8th, 125, 126 127, 128,
    233, 247; 10th, 62; 11th, 105, 115,
    139, 159; 12th, 99, 153; 14th, 61,
    76, 77, 99, 106, 140, 165; 15th,
    96, 97, 100, 252; 17th, 106, 147,
    249; 18th, 146; U.S. Colored
    Troops, 40, 155, 156; U.S. En-

gineers, 106; U.S. Volunteers, 39, 81;Veterans Reserve Corps (also Invalid Corps), 138; Veterans Reserve Corps 2d, 133; Veteran Reserve Corps 14th, 137, 251
Fenwick, Mr., 253
Ferguson, First Lt. Septimo, 57
Ferrill, James, 106
Figgy, Christian, 205
Finlan, Patrick, 148, 149
Finley, Martin, 149, 150
Finnerty, John, 127
Fisher, John, 98
Fisk, Gen.Clinton, 21
Fitters, Pvt. Ellis, 91
Fitzgerald, Pvt., 179
Fitzgibbons, Pvt. Michael, 15, 105
Fitzpatrick, Barney, 107
Flake, Christopher, 109
Fletcher, Thomas, 179
Flippin, Pvt. John, 177
Florida, 119
Floyd, Jackson, 116
Flynn, Cpl. William, 147
Focht, James, 97
Folly Island, SC, 68
Ford, Pvt. John, 179
Ford's Theater, 122, 188, 258
Fornshall, Moses, 208, 209
Forrest Hall Prison, 240
Forrest, Maj. Gen. Nathan Bedford, 156, 159
Fort Anderson, NC, 131
Fort Barancas, FL, 241
Fort Columbus, NY, 109, 125, 128, 232
Fort Craig, NM, 90
Fort Delaware, DE, 96, 225
Fort Ethan Allen, VA, 60

Fort Fisher, NC, 134, 162
Fort Hamilton, NY, 62, 79, 153
Fort Hindman, AR, 73
Fort Jefferson, FL, 96
Fort Kearney, NB, 219
Fort Leavenworth, KS, 120
Fort Lyon, VA, 79, 116
Fort McHenry, MD, 213
Fort Mifflin, PA, 180
Fort Monroe, VA, 131
Fort New Ulm, MN, 170
Fort Pickering, TN, 65
Fort Pillow, TN, 78, 156
Fort Richardson, VA, 242
Fort Runyan, VA, 66
Fort Snelling, MN, 43
Fort Stanton, NM, 151
Fort Stevens, DC, 120
Fort Sumter, SC, 121
Fort Thayer, DC, 111, 120, 121
Fort Wagner, SC, 239
Fort Ward, VA, 101
Fort Yorktown, VA, 172
Foster, Asst. Adj. Gen. C.W., 79
Foster, Maj. Gen. John, 47, 119,
Foster, Gen. Robert, 229
Fox, Pvt. James, 117, 118
Fraim, Pvt. Logan, 111
Fraly, James, 193
Franklin County, PA, 112
Franklin, Maj. Gen. William B., 80, 91, 147
Franklin, TN, 117, 125, 187
Franklin, TX, 90
Frantz, Pvt. Carl, 144
Frederick, MD, 98, 160, 164
Fredericksburg, VA, 31, 35, 55, 97, 99, 102, 103, 105, 106, 107, 108, 117, 123, 252
Free, James, 108
Fremont, John C., 2

French, Maj. Gen. William, 223, 231

Frog Bayou, AR, 100

Fulton County, KY, 219

Gaines' Mill, VA, 102

Gainesville, VA, 107

Gallatin, TN, 192

Gamble, Gov. Hamilton, 30

Gannon, Lt. William J., 80

Ganson, Capt. John, 46

Garey, St. Jacob, 75

Garibaldi Guards, 27

Garrett, Pvt. Joshua, 229

Garside, Sgt. John, 159

General Hunter, 40

General Order 38, 185

General Order 76, 39

Georgetown, DC, 240

Getty, Brig. Gen George, 119

Gettysburg Address, 273-276

Gettysburg, PA, 35, 72, 109, 123, 130, 131, 139, 242, 252, 276

Gianini, Lt.Charles, 75

Gibbon, Brig. Gen. John, 26, 49, 117, 242

Gibbons, Pvt. John, 163

Gibson, Col., 50

Giles, Mr., 186

Gillis, Pvt. Francis, 105

Gillmore, Brig. Gen. Quincy, 57, 93, 144, 155

Gilmer, Maj. Joseph, 32

Glasgow, KY, 72

Gleghorn, James, 103

Glore, Capt. John (also, Glove, John), 47, 48

Gloucester Point, VA, 176

Glover, John J. (Jake), 214, 215

Gooch, Bugler John, 163

Good, Col., 60

Goodsell, Capt. Joseph, 36

Gordon, First Lt. John A, 55

Graeff, Capt. Jacob, 50

Graham, Col. Samuel, 136

Grand Gulf, MS, 110

Granger, Gen. Gordon, 93

Grant, Maj. Gen. Ulysses S., 40, 43, 60, 63, 65, 72, 74, 75, 88, 104, 122, 124, 154, 179, 196, 219, 223, 249, 269

Grantsyn, Capt. William S. (also Gruntsynn), 36

Granville, Mr., 214

Gratiot Street Prison, St. Louis MO, 173

Graves, Capt. Hilton, 276

Gray, Pvt. Thomas, 175

Green, Pvt. Richard, 155

Greene County, MO, 246

Greiner, August, 107

Grice, Second Lt. Joseph B., 66

Grierson, Col. Benjamin, 67

Griffin, Gen. Charles, 131

Griffith, Parris, 150

Griffith, Thomas, 150

Griswold, Pvt. Albert, 137

Guice, Thomas, 103

Guile, Pvt. William, 237, 238

Gurley's Tank, AL, 199

Hall, Ambrose, 232

Hall, Pvt. Benjamin, 137

Hall, Lt. .Col. James, 144

Hall, Richard M., 213

Hall, Sgt. Thomas, 169

Halleck, Henry W., 26

Hambrick, Bradford, 216, 217

Hamlin, Richard, 92

Hammond, Surgeon General William, 10

Hancock, Gen. Winfield, 26, 98

Hanover Switch MD, 135
Harbecker, Louis, 99
Harbronck, Romanzo, 109
Hard Labor Prison VA, 134
Hardesty, John, 241, 242
Hardy, First Lt. George, 65
Harlen, MO, 46
Harpers Ferry, VA, 27, 72, 133,
    156, 201
Harris, Charles H., 199
Harris, Pvt. Charles H., 139
Harris, Ephraim, 190
Harris, James, 253
Harrison, Edward, ,110
Hartsville, MO, 191
Hartwood Church, VA, 117
Harwood, A.A., 178
Hascall, Gen. Milo, 129
Haupt, Gen. Herman, 117
Hawkins, Pvt.Wesley, 91
Hawks, Dr. I.M., 41
Hay, John M., 2, 14, 15, 16, 18,
    42, 45, 49, 68, 71, 74, 118,
    119, 125, 136, 152, 153, 159,
    190, 205, 221, 235, 238
Hayes, Maj. Charles, 145, 146
Hayes, First Lt. H.N., 65
Hayford, Charles W., 106
Hays, William, 120, 127, 128
Heath, Charles, 100
Heckman, Gen. Charles, 60
Heintzelman, Maj. Gen. Samuel,
    32, 50, 55, 60, 70, 78, 79, 116,
    119, 241
Hembree, Richard, 116
Henderson, KY, 79
Henreri, Pvt. John, 144
Herbage, William, 102
Herbert, Capt. J.K., 34
Herrick, Aaron, 136
Herringshaw, H., 247

Herron. Brig. Gen. Francis, 246
Hessey, Franklin, 154
Heusel, Pvt. James, 154
Hicks, Lt. Col. John W., 57
Highsmith, Henry, 210, 211
Hill, William, 250
Hilton Head, SC, 57, 144
Hiner, George, 92, 93
Hitchcock, Maj. Gen. Ethan, 28
Hoblitzel, Capt. William, 47, 48
Hoboken, NJ, 124
Hodges, James W., 186
Hodson, Pvt. Gideon, 173, 174
Hoey, Second Lt. James W., 67
Hoffman, First Lt. Edward G, 58, 59
Hoffman, Pvt. John, 119
Holbrook, Col. William, 241
Holland, George, 177
Holland, J.P., 210, 211
Holmes, Gideon, 101
Holmes, John, 195
Holt, Joseph, 6, 8, 12, 13, 17, 18, 21,
    22, 23, 28, 30, 32, 33, 34, 36, 37,
    38, 39, 40, 41, 42, 43, 45, 46, 47,
    49, 50, 51, 55, 56, 57, 60, 61, 62,
    63, 64, 65, 66, 67, 68, 69, 70, 71,
    72, 73, 74, 75, 76, 77, 78, 79, 81,
    82, 90, 91, 92, 93, 96, 98, 100,
    104, 105, 106, 107, 108, 112, 115,
    116, 119, 120, 121, 122, 123, 124,
    125, 127, 128, 129, 130, 132, 135,
    145, 146, 147, 148, 149, 150, 151,
    152, 153, 154, 155, 156, 158, 160,
    162, 163, 164,165, 166, 169, 170,
    172, 173, 174, 175, 177, 178, 179,
    180, 187, 188, 189, 190, 191, 193,
    194, 195, 196, 197, 198, 199, 200,
    201, 202, 203, 204, 205, 206, 207
    208, 209, 211, 214, 215, 219, 220,
    221, 222, 223, 227, 230, 231,
    232, 233, 235, 237, 239, 240,

241, 242, 243, 245, 246, 247, 249, 250, 253, 258, 260
Holton, James, 190
Homer, Lt., 65
Honey Springs, Indian Territory, 151
Hood, Lt. Gen. John Bell, 117, 134, 187
Hook, Mr., 219
Hooker, Maj. Gen. Joseph, 2, 26, 31, 38, 43, 49, 56, 67, 70, 75, 91, 92, 97, 99, 100, 101, 102, 103, 104, 105, 106, 107, 108, 109, 110, 111, 112, 117, 118, 140, 147, 151, 155, 159, 173, 200, 238, 269
Hope, James, 138, 139
Horn, Albert, 31
Hotchkiss, Giles, 248
Hough, Pvt. John, 232
Houston, Sam, 157
Howard County, MO, 250
Howard, Gen. O.O., 118, 123
Howland, Capt. John W., 39
Hoy, Pvt. John, 151, 152
Hubbard, Pvt. Harland, 242
Hudson, Mr., 201
Huffnagle, Pvt. James, 139
Hughes, Maj., 111
Hughes, Moses, 176
Hunter, Maj. Gen. David, 145
Huntsville, MO, 32
Hurlburt, Col. Frederick J., 231, 232
Hurlbut, Maj. Gen. Stephen, 151, 177, 249
Huston, Lt., 76
Hyatt, First Lt. Effingham T., 62, 63

Imperial, 60

Ingersoll, Col. Robert G., 163
Iott, John, 106
Iron Brigade, 61, 109
Ironton, MO, 163
Iuka, MS, 104
Ives, Rev. S.P., 173

Jackman, Col. S.D., 185
Jackson, Gov. Claiborne, 30
Jackson, Judge, 197
Jackson, Capt. Robert, 38
Jackson, Shadrack, 36
Jackson, Lt. Gen. Thomas J. "Stonewall", 26, 107, 109, 217, 270
James, Dr. Aaron J., 198
Janvier, Francis de Haes, viii
Jayhawkers, 210
Jillson, Pvt. Martin, 105
Johns, Samuel, 220
Johnson, Andrew, 179, 207, 253
Johnson, Pvt. George W., 176, 177
Johnson, James, 209
Johnson, James F., 193
Johnson, Dr. John D., 81, 82
Johnson, R.M., 247
Johnson, Quartermaster Sgt. William C., 156, 157
Johnson's Island OH, 63, 155, 185
Jones, Capt. Edward P., 35
Jones, Pvt. John, 239
Jones, Second Lt. John A., 72
Jovanne, Pvt. Armand, 242

Kaim, Pvt. John, 99
Keefe, Pvt. James, 146, 147
Keegan, Thomas, 230
Kellison, Pvt. William, 105
Kelly, Brig. Gen. Benjamin, 73, 116, 156
Kelly, Daniel, 134
Kelly, Pvt. Frank, 146

Kelly, Lt. Henry K., 78, 79
Kelly, John, 226
Kelly's Ford, VA, 110, 117, 241
Kemp, Simon, 221
Kent's Landing, AR, 40
Kerr, Pvt. Hugh, 140
Kestison, John, 122
Key West, FL, 37, 60, 77, 87,
    121
Keyes, Gen. Erasmus, 172
Kight, Simeon, 216, 219
Killeen, Pvt. John, 151
Kimball, Lt. Col. Edward A., 25
King, Lt. Edward, 1
King, Rufus, 229
Kirby, James R., 186
Kirby, Muse, 191
Kirby, William, 219
Kirkwood, Samuel J., 154
Kitts, William, 254
Knights of the Golden Circle,
    111, 186
Knittle, Second Lt. August, 67
Knowles, Seth, 105
Knox County TN, 23
Krachlanberger, Pvt. Adam, 238

L.M. Kennett, 161
La Grange, TN, 110
LaFourche Bayou, LA, 239
LaGrange, TN, 239
Lake, Ellis, 134
Lake, Henry, 134, 135
Lake, John, 134
Lake, Joseph, 134
Lake, Rachel, 134
Lake Providence, LA, 150
Lake Springs, MO, 230
Lamb, David, 214
Lamine Bridge, MO, 46
Lancaster, Pvt. St.Clair, 93

Lanier, Joseph, 204
Larbe, Mr., 179
Las Vegas, NM, 93
Laster, Pvt. Jasper, 178
Laurel, MD, 248
LaVergne, TN, 192
Lawrence County, AR, 220
Lawrence County, MO, 189
Lawson, Pvt. Henry, 239
Lawson's Station, MO, 127
Laypole, Andrew   (also Isadore
    Leopole, Andrew Layopole), 200
Leach, Second Lt. Ephraim, 69
Learned, Henry, 91, 92
Lebanon, KY, 246
Lebanon, MO, 245
Leddy, Joseph, 220
Lee, Gen. Robert E., 72, 109, 135,
    150, 242, 270
Lee, Maj, John F., 80
Lee's Mill, VA, vi
Leeson, Pvt. John, 118, 120
Leonhart, Jacob, 247, 248
Letz, Frederick, 170
Leufrene, Louise, 214
Levee Steam Press LA, 58
Lewis, Second Lt. Charles, 74, 75
Lexington, KY, 92
Libby Prison, VA, 90
Lincoln, President Abraham, agree-
    ment with generals, 258; Confed-
    erate spies, recruiters, bushwhack-
    ers and guerrillas, analyzed, 201-
    202, 260; deserters, analyzed, 86-
    90, 93-94, 112-114, 141-142, 260-
    262; military commissions, ana-
    lyzed, 201-202,260; murders, ana
    lyzed, 180-181, 260; mutiny
    cases, analyzed, 166-168, 260; of
    fenses of officers, analyzed,
    52-53, 83, 260, 262; rape and

other crimes, analyzed, 255-
256, 260; slavery, 269-277;
sleeping on duty, analyzed,
233-234, 226; thieves, ana-
lyzed, 233-234, 260
Lincoln, Mary Todd, 5, 18, 46,
47
Lincoln, Robert Todd, 4, 46, 47,
178
Lincoln, Tad, 46
Linton, Thomas, 133
Linville, Marion, 104
Little Bighorn, MT, 141
Little Round Top, PA (Gettys
burg), 43
Livingston, William J., 209
Loan, Benjamin, 239
Lockport, NY, 178
Lohmann, Second Lt. Edward,
70
Long, Alonzo, 129
Long Bridge, DC, 174
Longstreet, Gen.James, 276
Lonn, Ella, 88, 89
Louisville, KY, 63, 98
Loveland, John H., 139
Lucas, Pvt. William, 227
Lyle, Daniel, 205
Lynn, Sgt. Robert, 121
Lynnville, TN, 231
Lyons, British Ambassador Lord,
38, 213

Mabrey, George W., 23
Mack, Delia, 276
Mackey, First Lt. Charles W., 55
Mahoney, William, 136
Malvern Hill, VA, 75, 130
Manassas, VA, 100
Manaydier, John, 199
Manchester, MO, 190

Marigold, Frank, 216
Marmaduke, Brig. Gen. John S., 208
Marshall, Brig. Gen. Humphrey, 185
Martial law, 219
Martin, David, 192, 193
Martin, John P., 106
Martingale, Gen. John, 241
Martinsburg, WV, 164
Maryland Heights, VA, 133
Mason, Second Lt. Robert, 157
Mast, Capt. Charles, 173
Mathews, D.W., 150
Matlack, Cpl. Thomas, 102
Matthews,Charles, 176
May, James, 197
McCartney, Mr., 219
McCarty, John, 107
McClellan, Maj. Gen. George B., v,
ix, 38, 63, 75, 85, 258, 269
McClelland, Lt. Col. James, 64
McCloy, Pvt. Bernard, 1
McClurg, J.W., 179
McClusky, Pvt. Michael. 105
McCool, Second Lt. James, 71
McDaniels, William, 206
McFann, Jackson, 110
McGarvey, Cpl. Michael, 98
McGaw, Sgt. Henry, 102
McGee, Pvt. James, 174
McGee, Patterson, 46
McGinnis, William, 207
McGraw, T.G., 186
McKeever, Pvt. John, 240
McKeone, Pvt. John, 233
McKinley, Second Lt, John, 67
McKinney, Pvt. John, 105
McKnight, Capt. George F., 223
McKune, Sally (also McKeene), 246,
247
McLaughlin, Lt. William E., 79
McMahon, Capt. Bernard J., 33

McMahon, Pvt. Timothy, 138
McManus, Capt., 33
McManus, David, 103
McMinnville TN, 159, 247
McMoran, Pvt. James, 227
McNiel, Rees, 206
McPherson, Edward, 111, 112
McPherson, Maj. Gen. James,
     164
Meade, Maj. Gen. George, 29,
     30, 35, 36, 51, 61, 64, 67, 69,
     71, 72, 117, 118, 122, 124,
     125, 131, 147, 160, 161, 165,
     174, 226, 237, 238, 240
Meek, James, 206
Mehan, Pvt. John, 105
Memphis, TN, 71, 74, 124, 161,
     164, 214, 249
Mendham, Charles, 180
Mendocino City, CA, 169
Meredith, Brig. Gen. Solomon,
     61
Meridian, MS, 250
Mesilla, NM, 153
Mexican War, 29, 33, 75, 93,
     100, 126, 240, 270
Miles, Brig. Gen. Nelson, 40
Military commissions, 183, 184,
     185, 189, 193-202, 213-224,
     231, 232, 246
Mill Springs, KY, 23
Millar, Capt. William, 46
Miller, Pvt. Alexander, 163
Miller, George, 102
Miller, First Lt. James A., 64
Miller, Mathew A., 195
Miller, Pvt. Michael, 117, 118
Miller, Pvt. Thompson, 236, 237
Miller, Maj. William H., 32, 33
Mine Run, VA, 252
Miner's Hill, VA, 43

Minnesota Sioux uprising, 170
Minnig, Pvt. George W., 228
Missionary Ridge, TN, 130
Missouri State Penitentiary, 230
Mitchell, Dr. George H., 80
Mitchell, Pvt. John, 161
Mobile Bay, AL, 40
Monahan, Bernard (also Monahon),
     251
Montgomery County, TN, 194
Moore, Henry, 97
Moore, Samuel, 104
Moore's House, MD, 93
Morgan, Senator Edwin D., 36
Morgan, Gen. John Hunt, 45, 192
Morgan, Col. Joseph, 37
Morgan's Bend, LA, 66
Morganza, LA, 35
Morris, William, 219
Morrison, Pvt. John, 96
Morton, Capt. George C., 149
Morton, First Lt. Thomas, 56
Mott, Capt. Judd, 43
Moul, Henry, 221, 222
Mount Washington, KY, 186
Mountain Run, VA, 51
Mud March, 97, 102, 103, 105, 106,
     108
Mulholland, Lt. Eleazer, 58, 60
Mulvany, Pvt. John, 153
Murdoch, James Edward, viii
Murfreesboro, TN, 23, 62, 64, 100,
     189, 237
Murphy, Lawson J, 194
Murphy, Patrick, 122
Murphy, Patrick, 217
Murphy, Samuel, 105
Murray, Pvt. John, 226
Musgrave, Francis, 189
Musgrave, Mrs. Columba, 189
Music Boys, 128, 232

Myers, Robert, 124

Nashville, TN, 47, 110, 243
Nassau River, FL, 116
Nathans, Camillus, 254, 255
Neill, Edward D., 18
Nelson, Cornelius, 36
Nesler, Pvt. Simon, 117, 118
New Albany, IN, 111
New Baltimore, VA, 40
New Berne, NC, 178
New, Dr. George W., 80, 81
New Haven, CT, 226
New Madrid County, MO, 203, 230
New Orleans, LA, 58, 93, 101, 199
New Orleans & Jackson Railroad, 93
New River Bridge, VA, 165
New York, NY, 62, 69
Newell, Lt. Nathaniel, 157
Newport, KY, 128
Newport News, VA, 101
Newton, Maj. Gen. John, 75, 103, 124
Nicholasville, KY, 121
Nichols, Capt. C.H,41, 42
Nicolay, John G, 2, 14, 15, 16, 18, 22, 36, 38, 46, 55, 56, 57, 63, 64, 67, 69, 72, 73, 78, 79, 80, 81, 93, 97, 98, 99, 100, 101, 102, 103, 104, 105, 108, 109, 110, 117, 118, 125, 129, 130, 146, 147, 148, 149, 151, 158, 159, 169, 174, 189, 195, 196, 205, 206, 207, 209, 210, 220, 227, 228, 232, 233, 237, 239, 241, 242, 253, 254
Nicols, John, 207, 208
Nihne, Daniel, 115

Noble, Capt., 192
Noble, Robert, 253
Nodaway County, MO, 206
Norfolk, VA, 220, 228
North Mountain, VA, 133
Norvell, First Lt. Hugh, 64
Norvell, Francis, 206

O'Brien, Pvt. John, 153
O'Connor, Pvt. Cornelius, 163
O'Connor, Pvt. Richard, 175, 176
O'Malley, First Lt. George W., 56
O'Neil, First Lt. John, 57
O'Rourke, Pvt. James, 253
Offenses: abandoning a post, 50; absent without leave, 35, 43, 46, 49, 55, 56, 58, 60, 61, 64, 65, 66, 69, 70, 71, 72, 73, 77, 78, 81, 82, 148, 153, 159, 252, 253; advising soldier to desert, 27, 110; allowing a prisoner to escape, 69; allowing men to put down their guns on duty, 66; allowing prisoners to enter saloons and drink, 63, 78; arson, 39, 204, 220; assault, 81; assault with intent to kill, 250, 253; assaulting an officer, 20, 62, 144-168, 249; attempted hanging, 216, 219; being a bad and dangerous man, 205; being a guerrilla, 183, 192, 193, 196, 197, 199, 204, 106, 108, 208, 209, 210, 216; being too kind to a soldier, 38; blowing up a railroad, 200; breach of arrest, 57, 70, 71; burglary, 220; bushwhacking, 192-198, 203-212, 250; carousing, 29; carrying mail for the Confederacy, 183-202, 221; causing sedition, 145; certifying men present who

Offenses (continued)
were absent, 37; changing payroll, 27; conduct prejudicial to good order and military discipline, 36, 40, 58, 62, 67, 68,145, 161, 227, 228, 233; conduct unbecoming an officer, 10, 32, 33, 34, 36, 47, 50, 58, 64, 74, 78, 145; cowardice, 32, 35, 49, 252; cursing, 163; derailing a train, 209; desertion, 1, 20, 21, 73, 85-142, 221, 254, 262, 262; disloyal language, 23; disloyalty, 58; disobeying orders, 31, 38, 43, 51, 56, 69, 75, 82; disrespect of an officer, 253; drinking hospital liquor, 81; drunkenness, 1, 25, 29, 32, 35, 39, 40, 45, 47, 50, 51, 57, 60, 62, 63, 64, 66, 67, 68, 70, 71, 72, 76, 78, 79, 80, 101-102, 108, 128, 129, 130, 145, 146, 147, 148, 151, 153, 154, 155, 157, 158, 159, 161, 163, 165, 166, 169, 172, 173, 226, 230, 231, 237, 242, 243, 248, 249, 251, 252; eating enlisted men's food, 51; embezzlement, 33, 39, 40; evading duty, 63; extortion, 27; failure to appear as Officer of the Day, 35; failure to arrest deserters, 39; failure to file reports, 76, 77; failure to report for duty, 61; failure to visit pickets, 82; forgery, 221, 222; fraud, 43; gambling, 66, 69, 75; giving password to unauthorized person, 79; hiring a private as regimental surgeon, 37; inciting murder, 144; inciting mutiny, 47, 65; indecent behavior, 68; insolence, 57, 58; insubordination, 30, 145; keeping a mistress, 28; keeping false accounts, 37; keeping money paid to nonexistent soldiers, 49; kidnaping, 74, 196; leaving sick and wounded without care, 80; losing control of men, 76; lurking, 188; lying, 61, 69; making a false return, 36; making a false muster, 43, 49, 145; making false vouchers, 40; misbehavior before the enemy, 26, 31, 55, 73, 75, 249; murder, 20, 23, 33, 74, 122, 169-181, 192 193, 194, 195, 201, 204, 205, 206, 207, 209, 221; murder, accessory to, 214; murder, attempted, 163, 196; mutiny, 30, 48, 63, 140, 145; neglect of duty, 26, 223; obtaining money by false pretenses, 194; opening camp to liquor-peddlers and prostitutes, 28; playing cards with enlisted men, 70; plundering, 204; rape, 209, 214, 245-248, 255, 256; rape, attempted, 56; receiving bribes, 42; receiving kickbacks, 27; recruiting for the Confederacy, 183-202; refusing to bear arms, 159, 160; refusing to drill one's company, 58; refusing to obey orders, 30; refusing to parade a regiment, 24; releasing prisoners, 72; removing ball and chain from prisoners, 37; returning slaves to their owner, 46; robbery, 177, 188, 192, 193, 194, 195, 205, 208, 209, 219, 220, 226, 227, 229, 230, 231, 245, 246; rudeness to president, 60; running a blockade, 213; self-

Offenses (continued)
  abuse, 255; selling blank fur
  lough forms, 253; selling com-
  misions, 27; selling forged discharges, 250, 251; selling government property, 27, 65; selling hospital liquor, 80; shooting self in hand, 252; shooting
  with intent to kill, 254; signing
  travel passes for money, 42;
  sleeping on duty, v-ix, 20, 30,
  46, 235-244, 261; smuggling,
  195, 216, 220; socializing with
  enlisted men, 79; spying for
  the Confederacy, 183-212,
  220, 221; submitting false
  vouchers, 27; surrender to the
  enemy, 45; swearing, 43, 70,
  71, 72, 78; theft, 20, 27, 32,
  33, 37, 43, 60, 66, 70, 109,
  117, 120, 130, 132, 133, 135,
  148, 165, 191, 192, 196, 197,
  203, 204, 205, 206, 207, 209,
  210, 223, 225, 226, 227, 228,
  229, 230, 231, 232, 233, 246;
  threatening an officer, 146;
  trading with the enemy, 213;
  treason, 86, 152, 200, 220,
  221; using coarse language,
  64; using forged leave papers,
  35; using threatening lan-uage,
  144; using vile and inde-cent
  language, 28; violating
  oath of allegiance, 188, 189,
  191, 192, 194, 196, 208, 211,
  219, 220; violence against a
  superior officer, 160
Ogle, Henry, 204
Old Capitol Prison, DC, 148, 149
Oliver, James, 200
Osborn, Second Lt. John W., 74

Oswego, NY, 82, 126
Overland Campaign, 41
Owen, Capt. Christopher C., 39

Page County VA, 221
Page, Pvt.William, 174
Palmer, Gen. Innis N., 178
Palmyra, MO, 209
Paris, Pvt. Jacob, 206
Park Barracks, NY, 126
Parrish, A.P., 177
Patton, Thomas, 102
Pattterson, Pvt. John, 237
Pea Ridge, AR, 186, 189, 190, 232
Peacock, Elijah, 110
Pearson, Second Lt. Joseph, 68
Peck, Maj. Gen. John, 55, 152
Pender, William, 106
Pensacola, FL, 28
Perkins, Henry W., 106
Perryville, KY, 62, 116
Persons, Pvt. Albert, 240
Petersburg, VA, 138
Pettis County, MO, 207
Philadelphia PA, 254
Philips, Henry, 133
Philips, James A., 131
Phillips, Pvt. William, 230
Pierce, James H., 223
Pilant, Jesse, 195
Pilot Knob, MO, 155, 176, 178
Pilsbury, Louis, 250
Pilzer, Pvt. Conrad, 144
Pinckney Island, SC, 43
Pittsburg, MO, 39
Pittsburgh, PA, 222
Platte County, MO, 206
Pleasanton, Gen. Alfred, 90
Point of Rocks, MD, 165
Polk, Gen. Leonidas, 75
Pollock, Pres, 194

Polson, William, 120
Pope, Gen., 269
Port Hudson, LA, 28, 58, 74,
    137, 156, 161
Porter, First Lt. Robert H., 61
Porter, Maj. Gen. Fitz John, 10
Portland, OR, 122
Post, Peter, 102
Potomac Creek, VA, 56, 99, 103,
    105, 159
Potomac River, 254
Potosi, MO, 189
Pottsville, PA, 137, 180
Powell, James A., 191
Powers, Dr. Robert H., 172
Prairie Grove, AR, 188, 189
Pratt's Point, VA, 104
Price, Dr. M.F., 160
Price, Sterling, 163
Prince, Col. Edward, 71
Pryor, Edward, 106
Pugh, Mrs. Susan, 195
Pulaski County, MO, 189
Putnam, Pvt. Daniel, 159, 160

Quinan, Surgeon Pascal, 169
Quincy Township, PA, 111
Quinlan, Pvt. John, 105

Raccoon Ford, VA, 159
Randolph, Capt. Robert, 91
Randolph Forges, TN, 177
Rankin, A.N., 111, 112
Rappahannock River, VA, 97,
    200, 240, 241
Rappahannock Station, VA, 51,
    64, 24, 229
Raymond, MS, 60
Reading, PA, 76
Rectortown, VA, 247, 253
Red River, LA, 89

Redman, George, 214
Reno, Col. Marcus, 141
Revere, Brig. Gen. Joseph W., 25,
    26, 27
Revere, Col. Paul, 123
Reynolds, Gen. John, 80, 110, 159
Reynolds, Gen. Joseph, 45
Reynolds, Capt. Joshua, 51
Rhodes, Pvt. Franklin, 238
Rice, Pvt. John, 227
Richmond, VA, 38, 90, 131, 152,
    193, 270
Ricketts, Brig. Gen. James, 91
Rider, James, 200
Riker's Island, NY, 226
Rio Hondo, NM, 98
Ripley, OH, 162
Rittig, Gottleib, 91
Robbins, Pvt. John, 105
Roberts, William, 209
Robertson County, TN, 195, 196
Robinson, Pvt. James, 245
Robinson, Brig. Gen. John, 92, 240
Robinson, Pvt. John, 249
Rochester, James K., 72, 73
Rocket, 60
Rocky Mountain Expedition, 93
Rodgers, Joseph, 104
Roescher, Charles, 49, 50
Rolla, MO, 32
Rollins, Pvt. Paris, 119
Rome, TN, 69
Rookey, Edward, 131, 132
Roos, Peter, 231
Root, Capt. James N., 38
Rose, Josephine, 246
Rose, Mrs. Nancy, 246
Rosecrans, Maj. Gen William,
    39, 45, 46, 48, 64, 65, 69, 70,
    72, 73, 76, 77, 78, 79, 96 97,
    98, 100, 110, 112, 116, 117,

124, 125, 146, 159, 192, 193, 198, 236, 237, 242, 248, 252
Round Pond Massacre, 204
Round Valley, CA, 32
Rouse's Mills, KY, 186
Rousseau, Gen. Lovell, 70
Roys, Capt. Charles H., 34, 35
Rush, Richard, 100
Russell, John, 106
Ryan, John, 196

Sackett, Lt. Col. William, 30, 31
Sailor, John W., 221
Saint Meurice, 36
Salem, TN, 157
Salem, VA, 56
Saline County, MO, 206, 208
Salisbury, NC, 104
Sandberg, Carl, 3
Sanders, Col. William, 47
Sanders, Thomas F., 187
Sangamon County, IL, 161
Savage, Col. James, 178
Savage Station, 130, 139
Saxon, 155
Saxton, Brig. Gen Rufus, 41, 57, 153, 154
Schalowsky, Peter, 117,118
Schenck, Maj. Gen. Robert C., 37, 93, 108
Schoepf, Brig. Gen. Albin, 96
Schofield Barracks, MO, 78
Schofield, Maj. Gen. John, 23, 30, 33, 76, 78, 127, 156, 158, 179, 187, 188, 189, 190, 191, 197, 204, 205, 206, 207, 208, 230, 238, 250
Schrader, Lt. Alex, 78
Schramm. Pvt. Adolph, 144, 145
Schuyler County, MO, 205
Schwaggers, Sgt., 174

Scott, Dred, 270
Scott, John, 221
Scott, Pvt. William, v-x, 19, 85
Scott, Gen. Winfield, 29
Sears, Pvt. Josiah, 148
Sedgwick, Gen. John, 97
Seinn, Christopher, 129
Sembling, Pvt. August, 174
Semple, First Lt. James, 62
Serrell, Col. Edward W., 145
Seven Pines VA, 75
Seward, William, 96
Seymour, Governor, 60
Seymour, Pvt., 230
Shafer, Andrew, 241
Shannon, Pvt. Peter, 231
Sharpsburg, MD, 91, 147, 254
Shattuck, Mr., 223
Shaw, Calvin, 162
Shaw, Col. Robert Gould, 56
Shaw, Pvt. Edward, 154
Shaw, Pvt. Hugh, 149
Sheehy, Pvt. Michael, 136
Shenandoah, 163
Shenandoah Valley VA, 110, 149
Shenk, Maj. Rudolph W., 32
Shepard, First Lt. John T., 60
Sheperdsville, KY, 47
Shepherdstown, MD, 201
Sheppard's Ford, MD, 147
Sheridan, Gen. Philip, 110
Sheridan, Pvt. Avery, 235
Sherman, Maj. Gen William T., 62, 71, 74, 140, 190, 215, 235, 236, 244, 269
Sherman, Senator John, 62
Shevlin, Ormsby, 101
Shiloh, TN, 62
Ship Island, MS, 42, 68, 199
Shore, Pvt. John (also Schorr, Shorr), 155

Shrigley, Noah, 150
Sidelinger, Manuel, 92
Sigler, David F., 188
Simpson, Benjamin, 191
Simpson. R.B., 222
Sims, George P., 200
Sing Sing Prison, NY, 28, 233, 247
Singleton, Benjamin, 188
Sipes, Henry, 209
Sir John's Run, VA, 199
Sirwell, Col.William, 82
Sisk, Timothy, 194
Skaggs, John, 207
Skull Creek, SC, 42, 43
Slaven, Michael, 172
Slingluff, Samuel, 97
Smart, Capt. John, 78
Smith, Lt. Col. Abel, 58
Smith, Pvt. Albert, 242
Smith, Pvt. Alfred, 228
Smith, Pvt. Bill, 96
Smith, Second Lt. Charles H., 69, 70
Smith, Lt. Charles N., 77, 78
Smith, Edmund, 178
Smith, Fernando, 106
Smith, First Lt. Frank B., 57, 58
Smith, J.G., 221
Smith, James, 203
Smith, Pvt. Martin, 164
Smith, Matthew H., 130
Smith, Pvt. Philip, 229
Smith, Col. Richard, 71
Smith, Simeon, 133, 134
Smith, Brig. Gen. William F., ix
Smyth, Capt. Edward D., 37
Snyder, Pvt. George, 159
Snyder's Mill, 110
Somersville, TN, 154
South Mountain, MD, 91

Sparta, TN, 193
Spears, Brig. Gen. James G., 23, 24, 27
Spence, Alexander, 220
Spence, First Lt. Belden, 160
Spencer, TN, 192
Sperryville, VA, 238
Spicer, Henry, 135, 136
Spinner, Francis E., ix
Spinner, General, vi-ix
Spooner, First Lt. Hallett, 65
Springfield, IL, 258
Springfield, MO, 187, 210
Squibb, Pvt. Andrew, 140
St. Helena Island, SC, 145
St. John, John R., 178
St. John's Island, SC, 93
St. John's River, FL, 40
St. Joseph, MO , 173, 204
St. Louis, MO, 93, 188, 189, 211, 238
St. Simeon's Sound, GA, 155
St.Clair, Pvt. Stewart, 140
Stacey, Lt. M.H., 153
Stackhorn, Pvt. Henry, 157, 158
Stafford County, VA, 101
Stafford Court House, VA, 70, 117
Stahr, Uriah, 99
Standley, Francis, 165
Stanton, Edwin, 17, 28, 95, 96, 109, 117, 179, 253
Starkey, Capt. James, 43, 45
Stedman, Edmund, 13
Steele, John, 162
Steele, Maj. Gen. Frederick, 220
Stephens, Alexander Hamilton, 273
Stephens, James, 103
Stephens, Lt.Col. John W., 30
Stetter, Pvt. George, 158
Stevens, Lucien, 162

Stevenson, AL, 40, 236

Steward, Joseph, 99

Stewart County, TN, 195, 197

Stewart, Second Lt. William S., 73

Stilwell, Pvt. Stephen, 246

Stoddard, William O., 17, 18

Stoker, James A., 210

Stokes, Hezekiah, 170, 171

Stone, Capt. David C., 48, 49

Stone, Pvt. Joseph, 249

Stone's River, TN, 48, 64, 96, 110, 252

Storm, John N., 150

Strang, Aaron, 121

Strang, Jacob, 120, 121

Striblen, Lt. William, 164

Strong, Brig. William K., 45

Stuart, John T., 161

Stuart, Maj. Gen. J.E.B., 92, 104

Suffolk, VA, 55

Sullivan, Eugene, 123

Sullivan, Francis, 251

Sullivan, Pvt. John, 147

Sullivan, Pvt. Michael, 228

Sullivan County, MO, 205

Summer, Gen. Edward, 71

Summers, Ephraim, 196

Swain, Col James B., 149

Swan, Lanford, 101

Swartout, Pvt. Alonzo, 238

Sykes, Maj, Gen. George, 99, 100, 159

Tarbell, Lt. Col. Jonathan, 28

Taylor, Col., Alfred W., 29

Taylor, William, 99

Taylor's Ridge, GA, 160

Telford, Capt. Joseph G., 40

Temple, ME, 226

Tennallytown, MD, 118

Terry, Brig. Gen. Alfred, 43, 144

Texas War for Independence, 157

Thibodeaux, LA, 214

Thomas, Gen. Lorenzo, 146, 235

Thomas, Maj. Gen. George, 40, 41, 68, 81, 82, 158, 177, 193, 196, 197

Thompson, Pvt. Christian, 156

Thompson, Pvt. Harrison, 230

Thompson, Pvt. John A., 118

Thompson, Capt. R.W., 40

Three Mile Station, VA, 228

Tiernay, Pvt. Rayran (also Kayran Turnay), 156

Todd, Maj. Stephen, 120

Tom Reeve's Missouri outlaws, 209

Tompkins, Moses, 108

Toon-nan-na-kin-ya-chatka, 170

Torrence, Milford, 133

Treat, Amos, 107

Trinity River, CA, 115

Tripp, Silas, 248

Triune, TN, 46

Troy, Pvt. Martin, 253

Tucson, AZ, 152, 239

Turchin, Col. John, 262

Tuscumbia, AL, 104, 148

Tybee Island, GA, 144

Tyndale, Gen. Hector, 122

Underhill, Lt. Edward H., 60, 61

Uniform Code of Military Justice, 232

Union Mills, VA, 50, 241

Union Regiments and Units: Arkansas, 2d Cavalry, 231; California, 1st Cavalry, 239; 2d Cavalry, 90; 1st Infantry, 152, 153; 2d, 122; 6th, 122; Colorado, 1st Cavalry, 96, 173; Connecticut 1st Artillery, 242; 6th Infantry, 41,

Union Regiments (continued)
226; 15th, 119;17th, 65; Corps
d'Afrique, 7th, 74; Delaware,
2d, 65, 231; 3d, 135; 4th, 176;
District of Columbia, 2d 174;
Illinois 2d Cavalry, 239; 3d
Cavalry, 161; 5th Cavalry,
163; 7th Cavalry, 71, 148;
11th Cavalry, 122, 163; 13th
Cavalry, 77; 2d Artillery, 177;
11th Infantry, 150; 17th, 249;
20th, 179; 24th, 70; 25th, 64;
57th, 231; 81st, 124; 82d, 122;
91st, 45; 98th, 45; 102d, 232;
109th, 155; 122d, 104, 127;
123d, 110; 131st, 65; Indiana
8th Artillery, 110; 5th Infantry,
116; 7th, 64, 80, 104; 12th,
254; 14th, 111; 16th, 176;
17th, 241; 20th, 104; 58th,
149; 63rd, 47; 65th, 79; 68th,
243; 73d, 47, 64; 88th, 76;
Iowa 7th Infantry, 154; 8th,
230; 20th, 238; 23d, 76; 25th,
76; Kansas 14th Cavalry, 230;
8th Infantry, 120; Kentucky,
3d Cavalry, 63; 5th Cavalry,
47, 48; 7th Cavalry, 154; 9th
Cavalry, 121; 10th Cavalry,
63; 1st Artillery, 48; 8th Infantry, 198; 10th, 124; 14th, 115;
23d., 48,72; 26th, 120, 130;
27th, 124; 37th, 246; 52d, 130;
Louisiana 9th Infantry (Afri
can), 164; Maine 1st Cavalry,
130; 1st Artillery, 129; 4th In
fantry, 92; 16th, 159; 17th,
225; Maryland, 1st Artillery,
103; 1st Infantry, 138; 7th, 93,
133; 9th, 73; Massachusetts 2d

Cavalry, 115; 12th Light Artillery,
137; 2d Infantry, 91, 92; 11th, 92;
12th, 103; 13th, 252; 14th, 33;
14th (Heavy), 66; 15th, 242;
16th, 123; 20th, 117, 123; 24th,
71; 28th, 226; 31st, 42; 32d, 103;
34th, 116; 34th, 156; 45th, 79;
54th (Colored), 239; 82d, 75;
Michigan, 1st Cavalry, 70; 1st In
fantry (Colored), 166; 6th, 229;
9th, 70; 12th, 122; 14th, 78, 117;
16th, 43; 24th, 109; 27th, 147;
Minnesota, 1st Mounted Rangers,
43; 1st Infantry, 72; 2d, 72; Mis
souri, 1st Cavalry, 230; 3d State
Militia Cavalry, 163, 178; 6th Mi
litia Cavalry, 250; 8th Cavalry,
246; 8th Militia Cavalry, 39; 8th
State Militia Cavalry, 245; 11th
Cavalry, 30, 133; 12th Cavalry,
239; 2d Light Artillery, 156; 1st
State Militia, 78, 127, 158; 5th
Enrolled Militia, 46; 8th, 73; 8th
Militia, 232; 23d Infantry, 46;
25th Enrolled Militia, 173; 35th,
62; Enrolled Militia, 186, 207;
Merrill's Horse, 175; Nebraska,
1st Cavalry, 165; 2d Cavalry, 156;
1st Infantry, 188;New Hampshire,
2d Infantry, 100; 3d, 42, 43; 6th,
160; New Jersey, 1st Infantry,
124; 3d, 102, 118; 5th, 102, 103;
7th, 103; 10th, 180; 13th, 118;
New Mexico, 1st Infantry, 3, 151;
New York, 5th Cavalry, 35,
66, 149; 8th Cavalry, 237; 9th
Cavalry, 30; 11th Cavalry
(Scott's 900), 101, 148; 12th
Cavalry, 178; 16th Cavalry,
242; 1st Light Artillery, 37;
1st Artillery, 60; 4th Artillery,

Union Regiments (continued)
60; 7th Artillery, 227; 9th Artillery, 151; 12th Light Artillery, 223; 2d Heavy Artillery, 95, 96; 5th Heavy Artillery, 37,136; 9th Heavy Artillery, 227; 14th Heavy Artillery, 79; 1st Infantry, 101; 2d, 106; 3d, 91; 4th, 29; 9th, 25; 18th, 101; 21st, 106; 24th, 38,155, 159; 30th, 82; 34th, 253; 35th, 107; 36th, 38; 37th, 91; 41st, 132; 42d, 153; 44th, 131; 45th, 117; 50th, 107; 55th, 75; 66th, 1; 71st, 67; 73d, 107; 90th, 37, 77; 91st, 28; 92d, 131; 94th, 240; 98th, 58; 105th, 91, 147; 106th, 133; 109th, 248; 117th, 34,102; 121st, 101; 125th, 35; 126th, 241; 137th, 100,101; 140th, 1, 36; 142d, 82; 144th, 78; 146th, 228; 147th, 138; 149th (Volunteer), 253; 150th, 108; 151st, 251; 157th, 117; 162d, 36; 165th, 58, 101; 170th, 77; 174th, 67; 176th, 36; 178th, 240; 15th Engineers, 240; 50th Engineers, 101; Volunteer Engineers, 144; 1st Mounted Rifles, 152; 20th State Militia 107, 172; 69th Militia, 23; Independent Battery, 68; Ohio, 5th Cavalry, 145; 9th Cavalry, 128; 1st Light Artillery, 157; 2d Heavy Artillery, 162; 1st Infantry, 192; 9th, 46; 10th, 236; 11th, 68, 69; 12th, 116; 13th, 125; 24th, 63; 44th, 93, 129; 46th, 235; 65th, 241; 99th, 159;

117th, 110, 129; 155th, 237; Pennsylvania, 1st Cavalry, 51; 8th Cavalry, 136; 10th Cavalry, 55; 11th Cavalry, 228; 12th Cavalry, 140; 13th Cavalry, 158; 17th Cavalry, 237; 18th Cavalry, 32; 1st Light Artillery, 160, 170; 2d Artillery, 111,120; 26th Artillery, 247; 51st Infantry, 97; 55th, 57; 63d, 50; 71st, 33, 71; 72d, 29, 130, 140; 75th, 71; 76th, 57; 78th, 82; 79th, 98; 81st, 56; 83d, 56, 229; 85th, 55; 88th, 80, 81; 90th, 92, 124, 254; 91st, 252; 96th, 151, 228; 99th, 109; 106th, 49; 107th, 134; 112th, 49, 148, 253; 114th, 31; 115th, 56; 119th, 228; 135th, 32; 140th, 98; 154th, 10; 157th, 50; 9th Reserve Corps, 51; Lafayette Cavalry, 57; Potomac, 1st Home Brigade, 165; Rhode Island, 3d Artillery, 153; 2d Infantry, 103; 4th, 134; 7th, 132; South Carolina, 1st (African Descent), 155; Tennessee, 1st Infantry, 23; 3d Eastern, 64; Vermont, 3d Infantry, v, vi; 5th, 69; 7th, 41; West Virginia, 4th Cavalry, 5; 7th Cavalry, 165; 5th Infantry, 116; 9th, 104; 12th, 164; 16th, 43, 119; Wisconsin, 2d Cavalry, 32, 230; 6th Infantry, 109; 8th, 146; 9th, 238; 20th, 66
United States,60
Utz, John, 210, 211

Vallandigham, Clement L., 85
van Sickle, David, 96
Van Buren, MO, 76
Van Cleve, Gen. Horatio, 125
Van Zandt, Col. Jacob, 28
Vance, Lt. W. Henry, 58

Vaughn, James, 125
Veatch, Gen. James, 249
Verdier, James E., 111, 112
Vicksburg, MS, 43, 49, 60, 73,
    163, 216, 249, 270
Victoria, MS, 158
Vincent, Asst. Adj. Gen. Thomas,
    79
Vittenhof, William, 211
Vogdes, General Israel, 68
von Gester, Pvt. William, 240,
    214
Wade, Capt. William, 45
Waggoner, Pvt. William, 117,
    118
Walker, Capt., 76
Wallace, Gen. Lew, 3
Wallace, Gen. William H.L., 3
Wallenus, Second Lt. Francosi,
    68
Walsh, James, 135
Walters, First Lt. John L., 63, 64
Wanbeck, Andrew, 109
Warren, Gen. Gouverner K., 161
Warrenton, VA, 104, 107, 228
Washburn, Henry, 162
Washburn, Maj. Andrew, 33
Washington County, MO, 188
Washington, DC, 66, 69, 78, 106,
    109, 111, 119, 120, 137, 138,
    140, 148, 221, 227, 243, 250,
    253, 254
Washington, John, 177
Waterloo Creek, VA, 134
Waterloo, VA, 252
Waterman, 60
Watkins, Capt. W.G., 185
Watkins, Charles, 105
Watson, John, 124
Watson, William, 103
Waverly, MO, 206

Webb, Gen. Alexander, 71
Webb, John, 203
Weir, Lt. James W., 76, 77
Welch, Pvt. Partick, 226, 228
Weldon, Pvt. James, 148
Welles, Gideon, 38
Wells. Capt. Asa, 48
Welsh, Robert L., 199,200
Wentworth, George, 117
Whaley, Hon.K.V., 136
Whippey, Mrs., 56
Whistler, Col. Joseph, 96
White Cloud, 208
White, Col. Richard, 57
White, John S., vi, ix
White Oak Church, VA, 102, 103
White Oak Run, VA, 110
White, William H., 223
Whiting, Capt. H.G., 162
Whitmore, Sgt.John, 163
Whitset, Mrs., 33
Whitted, Lt. Newton W., 76
Wiggins, Capt. Samuel, 70
Wilbur, Capt. John, 42, 43
Wilcox, William, 150
Wild Cat Mountain, KY, 23
Wilderness, VA, 110
Wildman, Lt. William, 76
Wilkinson, John, 254
Willcox, AZ, 47
Willcox, Gen. Orlando, 47
Williams, Pvt. Charles, 160
Williams, Franklin S., 197
Williams, James, 204
Williams, Col.John, 173
Williams, John, 161
Williams, Second Lt, John D., 70
Williamson, Capt. Emanuel, 47
Williamsport, PA, 134
Wilmington, NC, 138
Wilmott, Henry, 128

Wilsey, John, 101
Wilson, Benjamin, 124
Wilson, Pvt. George, 229
Wilson, Pvt. John, 144
Wilson, John W., 204
Wilson, Nathan, 205
Wilson's Creek, MO, 190
Winchester, VA, 40, 57
Windmill Point, VA, 151, 172
Wiseburn, Second Lt. George D.,
    67, 68
Wolf, Pvt., 120
Wolf, Pvt. Joseph, 160, 161
Wood, Fernando, 109
Wood, Col. W.D., 30
Wood, William P., 149
Wood Lake, MN, 170
Woods, Sgt, Arthur, 178
Woodstock, FL, 158
Wool, Maj. Gen. John, 98, 232
Worlds, Silas, 192
Wright City, MO, 207
Wright County, MO, 32
Wright, Frederick, 109
Wright, Brig. Gen. George, 122,
    169
Wright, Henry, 241
Wright, First Lt. Henry, 64
Wright, Maj. Gen. Horatio, 93,
    125, 147
Wright, John, 196

Yates, Alfred, 188
Yates, Richard, 161
Yazoo City, MS, 116
Yazoo River, MS, 73
Yorktown, VA, 100, 130, 170
Young, Mrs., 247
Young's Point, LA, 73

Zerphy, Jacob, 9

X 2002

OCT   1999